CRITICAL SURVEY

OF

LONG FICTION

Russian Novelists

Editor

Carl Rollyson

Baruch College, City University of New York

SALEM PRESS

Ipswich, Massachusetts • Hackensack, New Jersey

978-1-4298-3697-5

CONTENTS

CONTRIBUTORS

Jean-Pierre Barricelli
Original Contributor

Mitzi M. Brunsdale
Original Contributor

Suzan K. Burks
Original Contributor

Julian W. Connolly
University of Virginia

J. Madison Davis
Original Contributor

Margot K. Frank
Original Contributor

Peter B. Heller
Manhattan College

Joe W. Jackson, Jr.
Original Contributor

D. Barton Johnson
Original Contributor

Lothar Kahn
Original Contributor

Irma M. Kashuba
Original Contributor

Steven G. Kellman
University of Texas at San Antonio

Leigh Husband Kimmel
Indianapolis, Indiana

Rebecca Kuzins
Pasadena, California

Charles E. May
California State University, Long Beach

Laurence W. Mazzeno
Alvernia College

George Mihaychuk
Original Contributor

Robert M. Otten
Original Contributor

Allene Phy-Olsen
Austin Peay State University

Philippe Radley
Original Contributor

Sven H. Rossel
Original Contributor

Victor Terras
Original Contributor

Christine D. Tomei
Columbia University

Janet G. Tucker
Original Contributor

RUSSIAN LONG FICTION

The eighteenth century is generally considered the beginning of modern Russian literature for several reasons. The most important is that a clear break occurred with the age of faith, as Serge Zenkovsky calls it in the introduction to his anthology, *Medieval Russia's Epics, Chronicles, and Tales* (1974). The acceptance of Christianity in 988-989 C.E. by Vladimir the Great (who ruled Kievan Rus from 980 to 1015) from culturally superior Byzantium established the authority of the Orthodox Church and enabled it to determine the nature of literature, such as it was, for several centuries. Written by clergy and monks in Old Church Slavonic, a language elaborated for the Slavs in the ninth century by Saints Cyril and Methodius, the literature ("writings" would perhaps be a better term) consisted of the Bible, liturgical texts, Church books, sermons, saints' lives, chronicles and annals, military tales, and some translated literature. The latter included popular works of a secular nature, such as the historical heroic romances *Aleksandriya* (c. twelfth century; the story of Alexander the Great) and *Troyanskoe deyanie* (c. eleventh century; Trojan deeds), which, however, often contained religious motifs. Didactic stories offering instruction in the form of a fable or homily, such as "Varlaam i Yosafat" (c. thirteenth century; Barlaam and Yosaphat), a Christian version of the story of Buddha, were also common. It is important to note that the great classical Greek and Roman heritage was not transmitted to Rus: The Byzantines regarded the Russians as culturally inferior, unworthy of this heritage, while the Orthodox Church considered such writings pagan literature.

The destruction of Kievan Rus by the Mongols from 1238 to 1240 was followed by more than 150 years of Tatar domination (the Tatar Yoke, as it is called), which ended with the rise of Muscovy as the new center of power. Religious literature continued to dominate throughout the fifteenth and sixteenth centuries, although secular themes, realistic details, and the vernacular gradually became more widespread. This is particularly evident in the gradual changes in the canonical form of the saint's life, which by the seventeenth century was supplanted by secular biography, autobiography, and first-person confession. A good example of this is "Povest o Yulianii Lazarevskoy" (c. 1620; the life of Juliania Lazarevsky), which, although written in the traditional form of a saint's life, is, in fact, a secular biography in conception.

There was also a gradual shift from Church Slavonic, a language that virtually none but clergy spoke, toward the vernacular, a shift that was closely linked to the rise of secular literature. Consequently, an account of a Tver merchant's journey to India, "Khozhdeniye za tri morya Afanasiya Nikitina 1466-1472 gg" (c. 1475; "The Travels of Athanasius Nikitin"), describing its exotic animals, lush landscapes, and strange customs, is written in a language almost entirely free of Church Slavonicisms. The vernacular was also dispersed by numerous stories satirizing corruption, irreligious practices among the clergy and monks, and a host of other common abuses, as seventeenth century literature moved to a closer portrayal of everyday life.

MODERN RUSSIAN LITERATURE

The passage from the age of faith into modern Rus sian literature is strikingly illustrated by the story "Povest o Frole Skobeyeve" (late seventeenth century; "Frol Skobeev, the Rogue," 1963). The story introduced a new type for Russian literature, the rogue, the social outsider who managed through his scheming to rise in station. Sharply satiric in its portrayal of the relationships between the rich and the poor, the story also contains erotic scenes and realistic details of Moscow life. Written in the vernacular, it is devoid of any religious features and is an excellent example of native Russian literature of the Petrine period (1682-1725).

In addition to the secularization of literature, there are other reasons for considering the eighteenth century as the beginning of modern Russian literature. The efforts of Peter the Great (1682-1725) to westernize Russia increased contacts with Western Europe and freed Russia from its relative isolation. This led to a large influx of foreign literature, which served as a model for Russian authors and stimulated their own literary efforts; it also prepared the ground for the acceptance of French classicism—which was, however, modified by native Russian traditions.

French classicism exerted its greatest influence on Russian poetry, which was the dominant genre of the eighteenth century. Prose, which was not regarded as on an equal footing with serious art such as poetry or drama, had to struggle for recognition and legitimacy, and rose to prominence only in the last quarter of the century, after the demise of classicism in the early 1770's. In keeping with the distinction made by classicism between high and low genres, Russian prose fiction of the eighteenth century tended primarily toward the low genres—the picaresque, the satire, the adventure story, and the romance—rather than the high genres—the tragedy or the *Staatsroman*, the novel concerned with how the ideal state should be governed. The latter was influenced by the Enlightenment belief in reason and centered on the discussion of the correct way a monarch was to rule his or her subjects; it was considered, therefore, to have a serious purpose. The former, the lower genres, were considered mere amusement and diversion. These popular forms were, however, much more widely read, and as a result, they furthered the penetration of the vernacular into literature.

The eighteenth century also saw the first conscious efforts made to fix the standard of the Russian literary language, which to that time consisted of an incongruous mixture of Church Slavonic, the vernacular, chancellery terms, and foreign borrowings. Under the influence of classicism, Mikhail Lomonosov (1711-1765), a prominent poet and scholar, established the doctrine of three styles—high, middle, and low—which were distinguished by the relative abundance of Church Slavonicisms. The high style, with its predominance of archaisms and Church Slavonicisms, was deemed appropriate for heroic poems, odes, and prose orations on important matters; the middle style, for epistles in verse, satires, eclogues, theatrical productions, and elegies; and the low style, for comedies, songs, humorous epigrams, and prose letters to friends. As one can see, prose fiction was not an art form recognized by Lomonosov, although he accepted the satiric novel as a tool for edification. In the ongoing debate concerning the novel, the principle of usefulness was, in fact, often invoked by its defenders, who pointed out that the novel conformed to Horace's doctrine of *dulce et utile* and therefore deserved to be recognized. The expectation that literature should serve as a force for social change, a notion upheld throughout the nineteenth century as well, was fostered by the Russian satiric tradition and the hostile reaction of the nativists to the flood of popular French literature entering Russia.

Translations of European novels, primarily French but later German and English, played a crucial role in the development of Russian prose fiction of the eighteenth century. They provided models for Russian authors and were themselves very popular. Handmade copies of novels circulated extensively among the aristocracy—which, by and large, spoke French, as did nearly every educated Russian of the eighteenth century. The French novels generally provided entertaining reading, especially the popular adventure novel, which described travels to strange countries, exotic landscapes, fantastic encounters, and amorous adventures. Consisting of loosely connected episodes, the popular novels emphasized melodramatic action rather than character development. They first appeared in large numbers in the early 1760's; only one novel was published in Russian between 1725 and 1741, and that was a translation of Paul de Tallemant's *Voyage à l'isle d'amour* (1663; Russian translation, 1730).

The influence of French literature is evident in the works of Russia's first novelist, Fyodor Emin (c. 1735-1770). He wrote six original novels between 1763 and 1769, intertwining melodramatic plots characteristic of the adventure novel with verbose digressions on politics, society, geography, and love. He made extensive use of clichés in his portrayal of character and wrote in a pathetic-emotional style, but he was also among the first to voice sympathy with the plight of the peasants. His first novel, *Nepostoyannaya fortuna ili pokhozhdenie Miramonda* (1763; fortune inconstant, or the voyage of Miramond), is a typical adventure novel in which the hero travels through Europe and offers a commentary on geography, political systems, the relationship between rich and poor, and so on. Similar topics appear in his *Priklyucheniya Femistokla* (1763; the adventures of Themistocles), which is set in the Athenian age and consists of conversations between a father and son about politics and society—in particular, the way an enlightened monarch should govern. In this regard, Emin was influenced by François Fénelon's popular novel *Les Aventures de Télémaque* (1699; *The Adventures of Telemach*, 1720; Russian translation, 1766), the translation of which went through eight editions in Russia by 1800, and by his wish to flatter Catherine the Great (r. 1762-1796), who fancied herself an enlightened monarch. Emin's most noted work is his four-volume novel *Pisma Ernesta i Dovravry* (1766; the letters of Ernest and Dovravra), the first Russian epistolary novel. Influenced by *Julie: Ou, La Nouvelle Héloïse* (1761; *Eloise: Or, A Series of Original Letters*, 1761; better known as *The New Héloïse*), by Jean-Jacques Rousseau (1712-1778)—but without its social conflict—it is the story of the unhappy love of the socially equal but poor nobleman Ernest for the wealthy Dovravra. Its weaknesses are its style, too clumsy and awkward for depicting the fine sentiments of the two lovers; its overly melodramatic and emotional tone; and its numerous digressions. It was through these digressions, however, that Emin expressed his criticism of the aristocracy, corruption, and political inequality, and his sympathy for the plight of the peasants. The novel also foreshadowed the rise of a later literary movement, sentimentalism, by some twenty years.

PICARESQUE LITERATURE

Along with the adventure novel, another popular genre of the eighteenth century was the picaresque. Although the picaro had appeared in earlier works of Russian literature, the popularity of the genre was primarily the result of the translations of the works of Alain-René Lesage (1668-1747). The Russian translation of Lesage's *Histoire de Gil Blas de Santillane* (1715-1735; *The History of Gil Blas of Santillane*, 1716, 1735; better known as *Gil Blas*, 1749, 1962), for example, went through eight editions from 1754 to 1800, while Lesage's *Le Diable boiteux* (1707; *The Devil upon Two Sticks*, 1708, 1726) went through five editions from 1763 to 1800, quite an achievement when one considers that in eighteenth century Russia, only twenty works of belletristic prose went through more than four editions. The popularity of the picaresque novels prompted Russian authors to try their hand at the genre.

Although itself not a picaresque novel, *Peresmeshnik: Ili, Slavyanskie skazki* (1766; the mocker , or Slavic tales), by Mikhail Dmitrievich Chulkov (c. 1743-1792), combined elements of the picaresque with those of the fairy tale and knightly romance. Influenced by Giovanni Boccaccio's *Decameron: O, Prencipe Galetto* (1349-1351; *The Decameron*, 1620) and *The Arabian Nights' Entertainments* (fifteenth century; Russian translation, 1763), Chulkov's novel consists of separate stories told by three narrators, and, in comparison to other works of fiction of its time, it stands out for its native Russian character. His second work, *Prigozhaia povarikha: Ili, Pokhozhdenie razvratnoy zhenschiny* (1770; *The Comely Cook: Or, The Adventures of a Depraved Woman*, 1962), was the first Russian work to present a picara: It is the story of a young widow's trials and amorous adventures told in the form of a confession and limited to her naïve perspective. There is, however, very little that is genuinely Russian—the characters' names are foreign, the places and events are typical of the genre rather than specifically Russian, and virtually no Russian customs or traits are mentioned.

The most frequently published work influenced by the picaresque (as well as by the Russian satiric tradition) was "O Vanke Kaine, slavnom vore i moshennike kratkaya povest" (1775; a short tale about the famous thief and swindler Vanka Kain). The story of a real Moscow thief and police informer, it went through three versions and sixteen editions, thus surpassing all other single works of belletristic prose published in the eighteenth century. Strongly influenced by the Russian folktale, it describes real Russian types and the actual setting of Moscow; it contains few foreign words and many folk sayings and expressions, and even includes thieves' jargon, with translations provided in the footnotes by the unknown author, who maintains the first-person narration and the satiric intent characteristic of the genre. In 1779, it was reworked by Matvey Komarov (eight of the sixteen editions are of his version), who included witnesses' statements, police reports, and folk songs about Kain. He also added a moralistic, sentimental tone and stressed the value of education in turning evil into good, points uncharacteristic of the picaresque.

Works containing picaros or tricksters continued to appear throughout the century and maintained their popularity until the early 1830's, but by the 1780's a gradual shift in literary taste had occurred. Once again, translations of European works—Rousseau's *Émile* (1762; Russian translation, 1779), Johann Wolfgang von Goethe's *Die Leiden des jungen Werthers* (1774; Russian translation, 1781), Oliver Goldsmith's *The Vicar of Wakefield* (1766; Russian translation, 1787), Samuel Richardson's *Pamela: Or, Virtue Rewarded* (1740-1741; Russian translation, 1787), and the idylls of Thomas Gray, Edward Young, and Goethe—played a crucial role in shaping the movement called sentimentalism. Sentimentalism (also referred to as pre-Romanticism) asserted the primacy of the individual and the emotions (instead of reason) as the source of moral virtue and developed the cult of friendship and sensibility. It emphasized the virtues of the countryside as opposed to the corrupt city and the honest simplicity of the peasant as opposed to the worldly veneer of the aristocrat.

The transition to sentimentalism can be seen in the works of the minor writer Nikolay Emin (died 1814), son of Fyodor Emin. His *Roza* (1786; Rosa) and *Igra sudby* (1789; the play of fate) combine the classicist conflict of duty versus feelings with the melodramatic plot of the adventure novel and attempt, unsuccessfully, to incorporate the new sensibility in describing fine emotions. The influence of foreign works can also be seen in the absence of real Russian characters. The same is true of another minor writer, Pavel Lvov (1770-1825), in his novel *Rossiyskaya Pamela: Ili, Istoriya dobrodetelnoy poselyanki* (1789; the Russian Pamela, or the history of a virtuous peasant girl). Influenced by the idyll and the adventure novel as well as by Richardson's *Pamela*, it, too, contained very few Russian elements.

SENTIMENTALISM

Critics of the time were quick to point out that few of the numerous stories written in the sentimental vein described Russian reality and characters. Striving for grace and pleasantness (*priyatnost*) in literature, sentimentalist writers offered idyllic images of Russia and its society that occasionally ended in absurdity, especially in the portrayal of peasants, who were often shown speaking in the high style and occasionally even singing songs from French operas. The influence of the French rococo, with its emphasis on playfulness and lightness, was also evident in the predilection for short fiction of various types, designated by a number of sometimes overlapping terms: *skazka, rasskaz, romanets, novost* (from the French *nouvelle*), or *povest* (which could refer to a short story but more often designated a long tale, a novella, or a short novel). The absence of clearly defined generic features merely reflected the nascent stage of Russian prose fiction.

One of the leading writers of the sentimental *povest* was Nikolai Mikhailovich Karamzin (1766-1826). Among his most important contributions was the development of a smooth, readable literary style, achieved by forgoing the heavy syntax of Lomonosov's German model and approximating the lightness and elegance of French. This Karamzin accomplished by shortening the syntactic period, avoiding Slavonicisms, and establishing a middle style of educated speech. Although criticized by Admiral Aleksandr Semyonovich Shishkov (1754-1841) and the conservatives (*Arkhaisty*) for his rejection of native Slavonic words and his introduction of Gallicisms, Karamzin's reform shaped the language in which the poetry of Russia's golden age was written and established an elegance that was imitated but unsurpassed in the eighteenth century. His most famous tale was "Bednaya Liza" (1792; "Poor Liza," 1803), with its theme of seduced innocence. Contemporaries praised his artistic rendition of the two lovers, the weak nobleman Erast and the poor country girl Liza, and their emotional and psychological portrayal. The story's great success was also a result of the absence of exaggeration, the careful use of detail, and the native Russian elements, such as the character types and the setting (Moscow and its environs). The story's immense popularity led to numerous literary imitations and even to pilgrimages to the pond near Simonov Monastery, where, in the story, Liza drowned herself. Karamzin also wrote one of the first Russian gothic tales, "Ostrov Borngolm" (1793; "The Island of Bornholm," 1821). A gloomy, Romantic atmosphere is evoked by features typical of the genre—a subterranean dungeon, vaults, a gothic castle, nocturnal settings, storms, fogs, and the suggestion of a terrible sin (incest) that has doomed the hero.

In addition to his stories, Karamzin left a fragment of a novel (thirteen chapters were published), *Rytsar nashego vremeni* (1803-1804; a knight of our time), in which he focused not on plot or incident but on the psychological portrait of his hero, the young boy Leon. Influenced by Rousseau's *Les Confessions de J.-J. Rousseau* (1782, 1789; *The Confessions of J.-J. Rousseau*, 1783, 1790; Russian translation, 1797), which also deals with childhood, and by Laurence Sterne's *Tristram Shandy* (1759-1767; partial Russian translation, 1791-1792), with its whimsical play with narration, the fragment remains an interesting if incomplete document. Another of Karamzin's contributions to long fiction was his popular travelogue *Pis'ma russkogo puteshestvennika* (1797; *Letters of a Russian Traveler, 1789-1790*, 1957). The epistolary form enabled him to combine personal expression and commentary with factual description of his journey through Europe. The later entries, however, resembled essays, as Karamzin shifted his attention from his surroundings to general philosophical topics. The success of Karamzin's work was a result of his moderate use of facts and statistics, the absence of pronounced sermonizing, and his elegant literary style.

THE TRAVELOGUE

The travelogue was the most popular genre at the end of the eighteenth century and the start of the nineteenth century. One of the first Russian authors in this genre was Denis Fonvizin (1745-1792), with his "Pisma iz vtorogo i tretego puteshestvij po Evrope" (written 1777-1778, 1784-1785, and published in his complete works of 1959; letters from the second and third journeys abroad). Addressed to his sister and his friend, Count Peter Panin, these letters were written in colloquial Russian and were not necessarily intended as a finished literary work. The patriotic Fonvizin wished, however, to point out that social and economic conditions were not better in France than in Russia. By exposing sham, corruption, hypocrisy, and immorality in European countries, Fonvizin wished to show that human vices and frailties were universal and that Russian imitation of European culture was, therefore, pointless.

Because of its political significance, the best-known Russian work in this genre is *Puteshestvie iz Peterburga v Moskvu* (1790; *A Journey from St. Petersburg to Moscow,* 1958), by Aleksandr Radishchev (1749-1802). Without undertaking an actual journey, Radishchev utilized the form of the travelogue to launch an attack against Catherine II and the Russian nobility, arguing for a constitutional monarchy and the abolition of serfdom. In spite of the illusion of a real journey, there is little description of the countryside or local customs. Instead, Radishchev discusses law, the individual's rights in relation to the state, new concepts of morality, and a variety of other subjects. Often relying on allegory to convey his didactic message, Radishchev wrote in a ponderous, uneven style incorporating Church Slavonic syntax, Latinisms, archaisms, and grammatical forms of his own creation in order to approximate the elevated high style established by Lomonosov. While the work has its faults , Radishchev was admired (and is today) for his courageous protest, for which he was sentenced to death for sedition, a sentence commuted by Catherine II to ten years' exile in Siberia.

Censorship was a problem facing literature throughout the eighteenth century (and it continues to be a problem in modern times). During Catherine II's reign, the struggle between the autocracy and literature was graphically played out in the satiric journals. Publishing her own rather harmless satiric journal, *Vsyakaya vsyachina* (1769; all kinds of things), Catherine encouraged others to follow suit, and several leading literary figures did so, only to have the censors close the journals for their hostile attitudes toward the government: Nikolai Ivanovich Novikov (1744-1818) published *Truten* (1769-1770; the drone); Chulkov published *I to i se* (1769; this and that); and Emin published *Adskaya pochta* (1769-1774; hell's post). In addition to the political significance of the satiric journals, which were sharply critical of the autocracy, the nobility, and serfdom, they sustained native Russian traditions by presenting Russian reality and characters, folk sayings, and customs, serving as a counterbalance to the influx of European literature. They were closely watched and were frequently shut down by the censors, particularly following the Pugachov Rebellion (1772-1774), after which not a single satiric journal appeared until the end of the 1780's.

Censorship was again vigorously enforced by Catherine as news and reports of the French Revolution (1789) became known in Russia; her fear of radical ideas and political unrest led to Radishchev's arrest in 1790. It also led to Novikov's arrest in 1792 and the burning of twenty thousand books published by him, as well as the burning of Karamzin's translation of William Shakespeare's *Julius Caesar* (pr. c. 1599-1600) as seditious. As a means of increasing government control over litera ture, Catherine closed down all private publishing houses in 1796, the last year of her reign. Matters did not improve under Paul I (r. 1796-1801), who well understood the potential political danger inherent in literature. This point was also grasped by many of the leading political and social thinkers of the nineteenth century, who wished to make literature a tool for edification and social criticism, an issue that remained hotly debated throughout the nineteenth century.

THE NINETEENTH CENTURY

The first three decades of the nineteenth century are appropriately referred to as Russia's golden age of poetry, an age that was dominated by Russia's greatest poet, Alexander Pushkin (1799-1837). Unable to rival the achievements of poetry, prose fiction continued to struggle for acceptance as a serious art form. Many of the issues facing prose fiction in the eighteenth century remained unresolved by the relatively minor authors who wrote in the popular prose genres of the previous century. Minor contributions to the travelogue, which continued to enjoy popular success, were made by Vasily Zhukovsky (1783-1852), with *Puteshestvie po Saksonskoy Shveytsarii* (1821; journey to Saxon Switzerland); Konstantin Batyushkov (1787-1855), with "Puteshestvie v Zamok Sirey" (1814; journey to the Chateau Sirey), an essay describing his visit to Voltaire's château at the conclusion of the Napoleonic War; and Aleksandr Aleksandrovich Bestuzhev (1797-1837), with *Poezdka v Revel* (1821; journey to Revel).

Translations of picaresque novels also enjoyed continued success, as evidenced by the four editions of *Gil Blas* and the two editions of *The Devil upon Two Sticks* that appeared between 1800 and 1821. The influence of Lesage is seen in *Rossiiskii Zhilblaz: Ili, Pokhozhdeniia kniazia Gavrily Simonovich Chistiakova* (1814; complete version, 1938; the Russian Gil Blas, or the adven tures of Prince Gavrilo Simonovich Chistakov), by Vasilii Trofimovich Narezhny (1780-1825), the last three parts of which were forbidden by the censor. The novel was immensely popular for its Russian character and spawned numerous imitations. One of the most famous of these was *Ivan Vyzhigin: Ili, Russkiy Zhil Blas* (1825; *Ivan Vyzhigin, or the Russian Gil Blas*), by Faddei Bulgarin (1789-1859), excerpts of which appeared in the journal *Severny arxiv* (the northern archive). In the final version, it was called *Ivan Vyzhigin, nravstvenno-satiricheskiy roman* (1829; *Ivan Vejeeghen: Or, Life in Russia*, 1831); the novel went through three editions by 1830 and was translated into French, German, Polish, English, Swedish, and Spanish. Its popularity resulted from Bulgarin's successful adaptation of the picaresque novel to Russian conditions. Modifying the traditional worldview of the picaro, Bulgarin focused on descriptions of the Russian countryside, villages, and customs, and on the life of the middle class. In this respect, Bulgarin shrewdly assessed the literary tastes of the newly established average reader, who was primarily interested in entertaining books about Russian life.

The major task of forming a readership, shaping public opinion, and introducing Russian authors and European literary and philosophical movements to the public was carried out by the journals and newspapers. As in the eighteenth century, their significance extended to the political arena as well. Often advocating a particular literary tendency, they were carefully scrutinized by the censors, and many were suppressed—*Moskovskiy Telegraf* (1825-1834), *Literaturnaya gazeta* (1830-1831), *Evropeets* (1832), and the monthly *Teleskop* (1830-1836), to name but a few. Survival depended less on the literary qualities of the publications than on coming to terms with the authorities and successfully catering to the public, a point not lost on publishers and editors scrambling to increase circulation.

Fueled by the defeat of the French in the Napoleonic War (1814), new demands were being placed on prose fiction—namely, that it represent Russian reality. The current genres were considered inadequate: The travelogue, while interesting, focused on foreign countries and had no specific form; the picaresque form, in spite of adapting to Russian conditions, lacked the dignity appropriate for high art; and the sentimental novel of manners, although presenting scenes from everyday life, was unable to express the new sense of national pride.

THE HISTORICAL NOVEL

In the 1820's, the Russian sense of national pride found expression in the historical novel, which combined everyday reality (*byt*) with the heroic fate of the nation. Elements of the historical novel could already be found in Bestuzhev's early works, *Zamok Neygauzen* (1824; the castle of Neuhausen) and *Revelskiy turnir* (1825; the tournament at Revel), which were influenced by Sir Walter Scott's Waverley novels. It was not until 1829, however, that the historical novel proper made its presence felt with the appearance of the popular *Iurii Miloslavskii: Ili, Russkie v 1612 godu* (1829; Yuriy Miloslavskiy, or the Russians in the year 1612), by Mikhail Nikolaevich Zagoskin (1789-1852), which he followed with *Roslavlev: Ili, Russkie v 1812 godu* (1831; Roslavlev, or the Russians in the year 1812). So successful was the historical novel that it soon outpaced all other genres of prose fiction of the time; numerous authors, among them the popular Ivan Lazhechnikov (1792-1869) and even the great writers Pushkin and Nikolai Gogol (1809-1852), turned to this Romantic genre. Its success was, however, short-lived, and by the mid-1830's it had lost its appeal to a public demanding that fiction reflect contemporary life.

The late development of the historical novel is indicative of the delayed influence of Romanticism on Russian literature. Reacting against classicism, with its distinct genres, rules, and emphasis on clarity, Romanticism sought to fuse disparate elements into new forms by combining reality with fantasy and the rational with the irrational. It introduced the folk and folklore as subjects worthy of attention; it championed the individual's sincerity and passion over society's hypocrisy and constraints. In Russia, the influence of Romanticism was spread through the works of Scott, Lord Byron, the English and German balladeers, and the German Romantics, particularly Goethe, Friedrich Schiller, Ludwig Tieck, and E. T. A. Hoffmann. The full development of Russian Romantic long fiction was slowed by peculiarly Russian conditions. First, the novel was still in its early stages of development, and therefore there were no models of successful novels; second, the readership demanded a Russian national literature representing Russian reality; and third, by the time the Romantic influence affected Russian prose, Western European literature was already turning to realism. Nevertheless, a limited impact of Romanticism can be seen among both major and minor writers and both short and long fiction in nineteenth century Russia.

In addition to the historical novel, the influence of Romanticism on prose is evident in the current theme of the alienated hero in conflict with his surroundings, a conflict already expressed in Russian poetry of the 1820's, particularly in Pushkin's southern poems and in the poetry of Mikhail Lermontov (1814-1841). Several popular writers of the Russian novel of the 1830's incorporated this theme into their works. Nikolai Polevoy (1796-1846), in his *Mechty i Zhizn* (1834; dreams and life), presented the theme as a conflict between the alienated artist-genius and his society, a popular interpretation. Bestuzhev treated it in his *Frigat Nadezhda'* (1833; the frigate *Hope*) as a conflict between the hero's code (being true to himself) and society's code, but in his *Mulla-Nur* (1836), it received a new twist: The mountain tribesman Mulla-Nur overcomes his alienation and returns to society. Similar themes and variations thereof were widespread in the literature of the 1830's as prose fiction supplanted poetry as the dominant form.

In spite of the steady rise of prose fiction, several major problems remained. The language of prose fiction still had to be elaborated, for neither the rhetorical bookish style nor the measured precision of poetry was appropriate for depicting everyday reality. Writers also faced the problem of defining the form of the novel, their readership, and themselves as writers of Russian literature. In the 1830's, the novel was still an eclectic genre characterized by narrative digressions, fragmentation, lyric pathos, and episodic plots. There were as yet no brilliant successes that could have served as models for the large form. A transitional step appeared in the guise of the story cycle, a form that provided the justification for unifying separate stories into a larger whole. Fairly common in the 1830's, this form also appeared among the major precursors of Russian realism—Pushkin, Gogol, and Lermontov.

THE STORY CYCLE

Pushkin's first attempt at prose fiction resulted in a fragment of a planned historical novel, *Arap Petra velikogo* (1828-1841; *Peter the Great's Negro*, 1896). Although he made several attempts at long fiction, he had only limited success, leaving several prose fragments and only one completed novella, *Kapitanskaya dochka* (1836; *The Captain's Daughter*, 1846), a historical romance about the Pugachov Rebellion, influenced by Scott. Pushkin's most famous work, the long narrative poem *Evgeny Onegin* (1825-1832, 1833; *Eugene Onegin*, 1881), subtitled *A Novel in Verse*, is of interest because of its subsequent influence on long fiction. The work is remarkable for its fine portraiture, its factual description of Moscow and Saint Petersburg, and its details of everyday life (it has been called an encyclopedia of Russian life), all of which produced an accurate description of the period and milieu and served to individuate the characters. In prose, Pushkin was more successful with short forms; in 1831 he published *Povesti Belkina* (*Russian Romance*, 1875; better known as *The Tales of Belkin*, 1947), a collection of five stories parodying current genres and styles.

Pushkin's lack of success with long fiction and his turning to the story cycle, a form then in vogue, are indicative of the ongoing efforts to master the large form. Although he reformed and shaped the language of poetry, he did not choose to take up this issue in regard to prose. His prose language, influenced by the constraint, precision, and simplicity of his poetry, gave the impression of artificiality and was not well suited to bridging the gap between the normal spoken language and the bookish style. This step in the development of prose language was successfully carried out by his younger contemporary, Nikolai Gogol.

Gogol's importance for Russian prose rests on several notable achievements. He was able to develop a middle prose style that raised the spoken idiom to an acceptable literary standard, which he achieved by blending Russian and Ukrainian, a language (to many Russians a dialect) in which the stylistic distinction between the literary language and the spoken language was not as pronounced as in Russian. This fusion arose quite naturally out of his cycle of stories about the Ukraine: *Vechera na khutore bliz Dikanki* (1831, 1832; *Evenings on a Farm near Dikanka*, 1926) and *Mirgorod* (1835; English translation, 1928). The latter collection included Gogol's historical romance *Taras Bulba* (expanded 1842 ; English translation, 1886), an exaggerated heroic account of the Polish-Cossack conflict. The stories were well received by the reading public, which perceived Ukraine, with its bountiful landscape, colorful peasants, and former Cossacks, as exotic and foreign yet still within the Russian sphere. In spite of presenting an abundance of realistic details of everyday life, Gogol did not fall into ethnographic realism. Contemporaries were misled by the details and considered him a realist, often overlooking the comic devices and the presence of the mysterious and supernatural—the latter influenced by the German Romantics Tieck and Hoffmann.

Stories about Ukraine, often referred to as Little Russia (Malorossiya), had appeared earlier, in the works of the minor Romantic writers Aleksey Perovsky (the pseudonym of Antoni Pogorelsky, 1787-1836) and Evgeny Grebenka (1812-1848), and for a time rivaled the exotic Caucasus as a literary subject. Gogol's treatment of the subject spurred interest in folklore and in the folk (*narod*), as well as demands for their portrayal in works about Russian life. Not surprisingly, Russia turned to Gogol after Pushkin's death in 1837, expecting him to create the national literature, and was not disappointed by his two fine novels *Myortvye dushi* (1842, 1855; *Dead Souls*, 1887) and *Taras Bulba* the latter an expanded version of a short story published in 1835. Influenced by Henry Fielding, Sterne, Lesage, and Narezhny, Gogol's novel is full of stylistic devices—non sequiturs, hyperboles, illogicalities, obfuscation, and lyric digressions. Contemporaries, however, attracted by the wealth of accurate details from Russian life, the Russian types, and the passages concerning Russia's destiny, proclaimed Gogol a realist. Only a fragment remains of part 2 of the novel, the bulk of which Gogol burned in 1852 under the influence of the mystical religious orientation that dominated the last decade of his life. Gogol's influence on Russian literature has been immense; many of his characters have served as prototypes, and many of his stylistic devices have been imitated by later writers. He developed the theme of the abused little man (usually a government clerk) and of Saint Petersburg (the artificial city created by the will of Peter the Great), themes introduced by Pushkin in his poem *Medniy vsadnik* (1837; *The Bronze Horseman*, 1899). Gogol's Petersburg tales brought forth a host of stories about poor clerks and prompted Fyodor Dostoevski (1821-1881) to offer his own interpretation of those two themes. Gogol's influence extends into the twentieth century, when he was rediscovered and reinterpreted by the Symbolists, and is still vital today. ·

Gogol's contemporary Mikhail Lermontov was, like Pushkin, a poet who later turned to prose, and his prose work was of great importance to the development of the Russian novel. Lermontov's first two attempts at prose produced the fragment *Vadim* (written 1832-1834 but not serialized until 1873; published in book form, 1935-1937; English translation, 1984) and the unsuccessful novel *Knyaginya Ligovskaya* (written 1836-1837; published in book form 1935-1937; *Princess Ligovskaya*, 1965). His third attempt was the remarkably successful novel *Geroy nashego vremeni* (1839, serial; 1840, book; *A Hero of Our Time*, 1854). Influenced by Benjamin Constant's *Adolphe* (1816; Russian translation, 1831) and the Byronic tradition of the alienated hero who despises society for its hypocrisy and corruption, the novel is set in the Caucasus—an exotic region popular in the literature of the time, as evidenced by Bestuzhev's popular tale *Ammalat bek* (1832; English translation, 1843). Using the travelogue and diary forms, Lermontov's book consists of five stories set within a frame narrative. Although he avoided many of the shortcomings typical of the novel in the 1830's, he was unable to show character developing over time and had to rely on the form of the story cycle to illustrate different aspects of his hero's character. The static portrayal of the hero does not, however, detract from the novel's significant achievements—Lermontov's ability to create atmosphere and his excellent psychological study of the hero, the ironic, analytical Pechorin.

REALISM

The psychological study of the individual was a significant step in the development of realism, as was the focus on details of everyday life. The latter point was the hallmark of the natural school (*naturalnaya shkola*) that appeared in the 1840's. Paying careful attention to details, they presented the unpleasant, harsh side of reality commonly found among the poor and the peasants. This aspect was dealt with by the minor writer Dmitri Grigorovich (1822-1899) in his two novels, *Derevnya* (1846; the village) and *Anton Goremyka* (1847), in which he attempts to describe peasant and village life from the peasant's point of view. The striving for verisimilitude and accurate detail was also apparent in the physiological sketch (*fisiologichesky ocherk*) popularized by the writers of the natural school. Influenced by the French *feuilleton*, the sketches describe social types and milieus, city quarters, and nature in minute detail.

The demand for verisimilitude was not, however, the only expectation placed upon literature in the 1840's. The influential literary critic Vissarion Belinsky (1811-1848) also insisted that literature should be inspired by socially significant ideas, and similar views were to be heard throughout the nineteenth century. First attracted to the German Idealists Friedrich Schelling (1775-1854), Johann Gottlieb Fichte (1762-1814), and Georg Wilhelm Friedrich Hegel (1770-1831), Belinsky later adopted a materialistic position that judged literature not in aesthetic terms but in terms of its utilitarian social function. Oriented toward Europe, Belinsky and the Westernizers were sharply attacked by the Slavophiles, who stressed the superiority of native Russian traditions, institutions, and laws and championed the Russian soul. For both parties, the question concerned Russia's relationship to Europe, an issue frequently found in the novels of Russia's great realists, Ivan Turgenev (1818-1883), Dostoevski, and Leo Tolstoy (1828-1910).

The late 1840's witnessed the development of a remarkable range of novelistic talents. While the novel *Dvoynaya zhizn* (1848; *A Double Life*, 1978), by Karolina Pavlova (1807-1893), reflects the passing of the Romantic era by contrasting a young society woman's stifling daytime experiences with the rich dream world that opens up to her at night, other works display the pronounced shift toward realism urged by Belinsky. For example, Dostoevski's first novel, *Bednye lyudi* (1846; *Poor Folk*, 1887), was enthusiastically reviewed by Belinsky himself and was soon followed by *Dvoynik* (1846; *The Double*, 1917) and "Gospodin Prokharchin" (1846; "Mr. Prokharchin," 1918). Polemicizing with but not parodying Gogol in these three works, Dostoevski gave his own interpretation to the themes of the little man and St. Petersburg. The stories also reflected the influence of the natural school, as evidenced by his focus on ugliness, poverty, and the dull, dirty milieu of the city. The Petersburg theme surfaced in a very different guise, as a dreamer's city, in his "Khozyayka" (1847; "The Landlady," 1917) and "Belye nochi" (1848; "White Nights," 1918), the latter published in the year in which Dostoevski was arrested for being a member of the Petrashevsky Circle, a group that discussed socialist ideas and criticized existing conditions in Russia. His four years of penal service in Siberia and subsequent military service interrupted his literary activity; he did not return to St. Petersburg until 1859.

From 1850 to 1880, Russian literature was dominated by three writers—Turgenev, Dostoevski, and Tolstoy—whose works defined the form of the novel as well as the broad literary movement called realism. Their focus on details of everyday life, on the surroundings, on the social milieu, on individuals and their psychology, and their narrative technique of staging scenes rather than commenting through narrative intrusion, became the hallmarks by which realism was defined.

Although the 1850's were dominated by Turgenev, several writers made significant contributions to the novel in this period, among them Tolstoy, who published his first major work, a nonautobiographical trilogy about a young boy growing up: *Detstvo* (1852; *Childhood*, 1862), *Otrochestvo* (1854; *Boyhood*, 1886), and *Yunost'* (1857; *Youth*, 1886). Influenced by Sterne, Charles Dickens, Rousseau, and Rodolphe Töpfler, Tolstoy utilized a child's own peculiar angle of perception to present familiar objects and experiences in a new and unusual manner—an example of the device, frequent in Tolstoy's works, which the Russian Formalist critic Viktor Shklovsky calls *ostranenie* ("making strange," or "defamiliarization"). A similar subject was treated by Sergey Aksakov (1791-1859) in his trilogy of family generations and a young boy's development: *Semeynaya khronika* (1856; *Chronicles of a Russian Family*, 1924), *Vospominaniya* (1856; *A Russian Schoolboy*, 1917), and the best-known volume, *Detskiye gody Bagrova-vnuka* (1858; *Years of Childhood*, 1916). The last of these, an example of an *Entwicklungsroman*, is a captivating study of a child's psychology as he begins to understand the conflicts and tension among members of his own family; it is also remarkable as a realistic narrative of ordinary life.

Another author known for a realistic narrative of ordinary life was Ivan Goncharov (1812-1891), whose first novel, *Obyknovennaya istoriya* (1847; *A Common Story*, 1890), was hailed by Belinsky as an example of realistic fiction second only to Dostoevski's *Poor Folk*. His novel *Oblomov* (1859; English translation, 1915) is best known for its phlegmatic eponymous hero, whose philosophy of resignation and inactivity aroused the ire of many activists—including the radical socialist critic Nikolay Dobrolyubov (1836-1861), who wrote an arti cle, "Chto takoye Oblomovshchina?" (1859-1860; "What Is Oblomovism?" 1903), in which he denounced the gentry for being an obstacle to progress.

These relatively minor achievements of the 1850's were overshadowed by Turgenev's success, which was readily acknowledged by critics and the public. Turgene v began his literary career writing poetry, but by the late 1840's, he had turned to writing the stories that he later incorporated into his collection *Zapiski okhotnika* (1852 ; *Russian Life in the Interior*, 1855; better known as *A Sportsman's Sketches*, 1932), which made him an overnight success. The volume was noted for its lyric mood and atmosphere evoked by the detailed nature descriptions and for its sympathetic portrayal of the serfs. In addition to this volume, Turgenev wrote many stories, several plays, and six novels. In the novels, plot is secondary to character, which is skillfully revealed through polished dialogue and social milieu. Turgenev's novels are generally structured around a romance between a morally superior woman and a weak, irresolute man, a theme made famous by Pushkin in *Eugene Onegin*, and at the same time, around a current political issue. Although he was a civil-minded liberal Westernizer, Turgenev avoided becoming tendentious in his depiction of the ideological struggle between the generations (between the fathers and the sons). He supported the cause of the young radicals but failed to portray a positive Russian political activist. Stung by the radicals' criticism of his portrayal of Bazarov, the nihilistic hero of *Ottsy i deti* (1862; *Fathers and Sons*, 1867), Turgenev decided to remain abroad and settled in France for most of the remainder of his life. In his last two novels, *Dym* (1867; *Smoke*, 1868) and *Nov* (1877; *Virgin Soil*, 1877), he gave vent to his bitterness toward Russia, but although it was clear that he had lost touch with Russian life, he remained a popular writer. Pushkin's influence is evident in Turgenev's poetic prose, masterfully shaped for expressing nuance, atmosphere, and character. Turgenev was the first Russian author to achieve fame in Western Europe, particularly in France, where he died in 1883.

While Turgenev was a member of the nobility and a Westernizer, Dostoevski was a *raznochinets* (educated plebeian). His experience in prison, which he chronicled in his novel *Zapiski iz myortvogo doma* (1861-1862; *Buried Alive: Or, Ten Years of Penal Servitude in Siberia*, 1881; also known as *The House of the Dead*, 1915), produced a profound change in his personal and political views. Arrested for his socialist and Western views, Dostoevski returned from exile having rejected them along with Rousseauism, utopianism, rationalism, and Schillerian Romanticism and having embraced Christ, a belief in Russia and its elect status, and the human need for freedom. He was the first in world literature to find a literary medium for the metaphysical novel, which he combined with the crime story, a combination found in varying degrees in all five of his major novels but particularly evident in his famous *Prestupleniye i nakazaniye* (1866; *Crime and Punishment*, 1886).

Plumbing the depths of his characters' souls, Dostoevski presents the dialectic struggle of good and evil. His characters are shown testing the strength of their rational position against their emotions. Salvation for the proud, the guilty (murders are committed in four of the major novels), and the "supermen" (those who assume that they are beyond good and evil) can be achieved, according to Dostoevski, only through suffering and humility, which will lead to faith in Christ, an issue masterfully illustrated in his *Bratya Karamazovy* (1879-1880; *The Brothers Karamazov*, 1912). Dostoevski also assigned to God a crucial role in Russia's salvation and messianic mission. In perhaps his best novel, *Besy* (1871-1872; *The Possessed*, 1913; also known as *The Devils*), he attacked the atheistic ideological offspring of the liberals of the 1840's (the novel included a vicious satire of Turgenev). *The Possessed* is an excellent example of polyphony, in which each character's voice is given equal weight in the frequent metaphysical arguments. Aspiring to a "higher realism," Dostoevski sought to penetrate to the essence of his characters, avoiding narrative intrusion, and this remains one of his major achievements.

The literary activity of Leo Tolstoy, one of the greatest figures in world literature, falls into two distinct periods, divided by his spiritual crisis in 1879, after which Tolstoy the moral philosopher took precedence over Tolstoy the artist. In his early long fiction, written in the 1850's—the childhood trilogy, the Sevastopol stories, *Kazaki* (1863; *The Cossacks*,

1872), and *Semeynoye schast'ye* (1859; *Family Happiness*, 1888)—he introduced many of the themes he developed further in his two great novels, *Voyna i mir* (1865-1869; *War and Peace*, 1886) and *Anna Karenina* (1875-1877; English translation, 1886): the morality of killing, the enigmatic question of death and the meaning of life, and the question of how one should live, to mention but a few. In his pursuit of truth, he debunked many popular myths concerning war, patriotism, and romantic heroism, particularly in *War and Peace*. In form, *War and Peace* resembles a classic epic, charting the collective experience of the Russian nation during the Napoleonic era; at the same time, it is a modern novel in which the individual searches for meaning and his or her relation to the collective, to society. While Tolstoy's heroes often serve as subjective centers, their individual perceptions revealed through the devices of estrangement (*ostranenie*) and interior monologue, the objectivity of outside reality is not challenged. Tolstoy's interest in the development of character and society over time (and in the question of causation) led him to focus on the individual's changing relationship to family and society. Through this self-reflection within a social setting, an influence of sentimentalism, his characters learn the obligations of responsibility and responsiveness.

This theme also appears in Tolstoy's *Anna Karenina*, a novel about upper-class society of the 1870's. Structured around two contrasting love relationships, the novel focuses on the moral and personal dilemma of transgressing society's ethical code for the sake of love. Through the introduction of stream of consciousness, Tolstoy gives an excellent rendition of the heroine's psychological and emotional turmoil, adding a consummate truth to an already memorable portrait of an individual human being.

Carefully differentiating even minor characters by specific details or traits, even in his large works, Tolstoy was not content with remaining only an observer; he felt the need to guide the reader to the truth by means of direct appeals, narrative intrusions, and digressions. Tolstoy's tendency to instruct, a characteristic feature of his fiction, and his personal search for faith and the meaning of life led to a spiritual crisis that culminated in his work *Ispoved'* (1884; *A Confession*, 1885). Thereafter, his long fiction took on an increasingly moralizing tone, attacking the state, the church, and society as he turned literature into a vehicle for his views. He still produced several great works, such as the novellas *Smert' Ivana Il'icha* (1886; *The Death of Ivan Ilyich*, 1887) and *Khadzi-Murat* (1911; *Hadji Murad*, 1911), but in the last two decades of his life his fame rested not on his fiction but on his moral teachings.

The thirty years from 1850 to 1880 were also a period of activity among socialist critics whose articles and novels were of literary and political significance. Among them was the influential critic Aleksandr Herzen (1812-1870), the author of the *povest Kto vinovat?* (1847; *Who Is to Blame?*, 1978) and publisher of the enormously influential weekly *Kolokol* (1857-1867), which was frequently smuggled into Russia, where it had a wide readership. He advocated a positivist, national socialism and was close to the Slavophiles. Much more radical were N. G. Chernyshevsky (1828-1889), who wrote the famous and tendentious radical novel *Chto delat?* (1863; *What Is to Be Done?*, 1886) and who was arrested in 1862 and later exiled to Siberia, and Dobrolyubov, who was the most influential critic after Belinsky. They both advocated a scientific rationalism as a means to achieve progress, and they professed great faith in the Russian peas ant, whose emancipation from serfdom (granted in 1861) they ardently championed. Dobrolyubov also served as the literary critic of the successful journal *Sovremennik* (1836-1866) and had a great impact on succeeding generations.

In addition to the great realists, numerous writers of varying caliber also appeared, among them Aleksey Pisemsky (1820-1881). His novels were known for their unadorned, unidealized view of humankind and for their portrayal of Russian characters not of noble birth, whose dialect Pisemsky expertly rendered. Another notable writer of this period was Mikhail Saltykov-Shchedrin (1826-1889), acclaimed for his many satiric novels, some excessively topical and written in Aesopian language. His crowning achievement, which established his place among the realists, was *Gospoda Golovlyovy* (1872-1876; *The Golovlyov Family*, 1955), a gloomy depiction of the materialistic provincial gentry. Other civic or plebeian writers include Nikolay Pomyalovskiy (1835-1863), Gleb Uspenskiy (1843-1902), and Ivan Kushchevsky (1847-1876). Populist novels celebrating the virtues of the peasants also appeared, generally written by minor authors, such as Nikolay Zlatovratsky (1845-1911) and Pavel Zasodimsky (1843-1912).

A writer of considerable talent was Nikolai Leskov (1831-1895), known for his excellent rendition of speech, which he often expressed through *skaz*, a narrative form in which the narrator's presence is marked by his or her individualized language and tone. Leskov, who excelled in short fiction, was contemptuously treated by the critics for his portrayal of the radicals and for his works on ecclesiastical life, which he sympathetically described in his popular novel *Soboriane* (1872; *The Cathedral Folk*, 1924).

THE 1880's AND 1890's

The early 1880's are generally taken as a watershed in the history of the Russian novel. Two of the great realists had passed from the scene, Dostoevski in 1881 and Turgenev in 1883, and Tolstoy, after his crisis, produced no major novels. There was also a change in the political climate following the assassination of Alexander II (r. 1855-1881), an event that ended the period of political reforms and introduced the repressive measures of Alexander III (r. 1881-1894). In the prose fiction of the 1880's and 1890's, there was a movement away from long fiction, from the globalism (the philosophical questions of existence and the thorough representation of everyday life) of the nineteenth century novel, toward shorter forms with a narrower field of vision.

Several minor but popular writers of this period continued, however, to make use of the novel. One such writer was Aleksandr Ertel (1855-1908), known for his popular novel *Gardeniny, ikh dvornya, priverzhentsy i vragi* (1888; the Gardenins, their retainers, their friends, and their enemies), the second edition of which was prefaced by Tolstoy himself.

The novel presents a vast panorama of contemporary life on a provincial gentry estate in southern Russia. Another popular author of the time was Vladimir Korolenko (1853-1921), known for his romantic though rather shallow *povesti* with nature descriptions reminiscent of Turgenev, whose works enjoyed a revival at that time. Also popular was N. Garin (the pseudonym of Nikolay Georgievich Mikhaylovskiy, 1852-1906), whose trilogy about a young boy's education was immensely successful.

In addition to the short form of prose, poetry flourished once again, dominated by the Symbolists, who heralded in Russia's silver age of poetry. The Russian Symbolists, influenced by their French counterparts, spoke of a higher reality existing beneath the surface of everyday life. Defending the aesthetic value of literature, one of the leading Symbolist critics, Dmitry Sergeyevich Merezhkovsky (1865-1941), who also wrote a trilogy of novels in the 1890's, blamed the social tendentiousness of the civic critics for the decline of Russian literature. This new critical position, which denied the basic tenets of the nineteenth century, is indicative of the social crisis experienced by the intelligentsia and the writers. It forced a reevaluation of their relationship to literature and society, as well as a reconsideration of the role of literature itself. These issues, raised at the close of the nineteenth century, became even more pertinent in the twentieth century.

THE EARLY TWENTIETH CENTURY

Russian literature of the twentieth century began like the literature of the nineteenth century, with the dominance of poetry and under the influence of Western European writers, among them Henrik Ibsen (1828-1906), August Strindberg (1849-1912), the French Symbolist poets, and the German philosopher Friedrich Nietzsche (1844-1900). There was, however, a distinct break with the commonality of issues and viewpoints characteristic of the nineteenth century. Instead of consensus, division prevailed among schools of poetry, whose positions were provocatively stated in literary manifestos, an entirely new phenomenon in Russian literature.

The Symbolists, the leading school of poetry in the first decade of the twentieth century, also produced several interesting novels. They believed that the visible world is symbolic of a higher reality behind it and that the poet, as a superior being (a Romantic conception of the artist), is able to articulate this truth, which can only be alluded to, through art. Their writing is, therefore, intentionally vague and ambiguous. They question the identity of objects and only hint at the essence hidden beneath the surface. These traits are clearly evident in *Melkiy bes* (1907; *The Little Demon*, 1916; also known as *The Petty Demon*, 1962), written by Fyodor Sologub (the pseudonym of Fyodor Terternikov, 1863-1927), a work strongly influenced by Gogol, whom the Symbolists reinterpreted. Similar qualities inform the works of another Symbolist novelist, Valery Bryosov (1873-1924), whose best-known novel was *Ognenny angel* (1908; *The Fiery Angel*, 1930). Both were surpassed by Andrey Bely (the pseudonym of Boris Bugayev, 1880-1934), a Symbolist poet and a disciple of Rudolph Steiner's Anthroposophy. Although best known for his poetry, Bely wrote several novels, the most remarkable of which was *Petersburg* (serial 1913-1914, book 1916, revised 1922; *St. Petersburg*, 1959; better known as *Petersburg*), considered by the renowned novelist and critic Vladimir Nabokov (1899-1977) to be one of the best novels of the twentieth century. Revised several times, it offers a philosophical and metaphysical interpretation of Russian history in terms of two opposing forces—Western rationalism and a destructive Asiatic-Tatar element of irrationalism. Complex in style and structure, and full of literary allusions, it continues the great tradition of the Petersburg theme, portraying the city's malevolent atmosphere and artificial existence.

There were few identifiable schools of prose fiction prior to the Russian Revolution (1917); one small group of writers, however, did appear. Centered on the journal *Znanie*, from which it took its name, this group was led by the internationally renowned Maxim Gorky (the pen name of Aleksey Maksimovich Peshkov, 1868-1936). The group consisted of Aleksandr Kuprin (1870-1938), known for his realistic novels of military life and his compassionate novel about prostitutes, *Yama* (1909-1915; *Yama: The Pit*, 1929); the minor writer Mikhail Artsybashev (1878-1927), whose popularity rested on his sensational novel *Sanin* (1907; *Sanine*, 1917), with its violence, erotic scenes, and empty metaphysical discussions; Leonid Andreyev (1871-1919), an extremely popular writer of stories focusing on the pathos of the soul; and Ivan Bunin (1870-1953). Bunin was a direct descendant of the nineteenth century realist tradition, as is evident from his short novel *Derevnya* (1910; *The Village*, 1923) and its companion piece *Sukhodol* (1912; *Dry Valley*, 1935). After the Russian Revolution, he emigrated to Paris, where he continued to write on Russian subjects. In 1933, he was awarded the Nobel Prize in Literature, the first Russian to receive the award.

The most significant member of the *Znanie* group, which soon dissolved, was Gorky, who in the Soviet Union became the center of a personality cult, although he himself was critical of the revolution and suspicious of the masses. Having developed from an early Nietzschean Romanticism, Gorky turned from the principle that literature should beautify life to the depiction of current political issues. His novel *Mat* (1906; *Mother*, 1906), based on the events of a May Day demonstration in Sormovo in 1902, gave the first comprehensive portrait of the Russian revolutionary movement. Influenced by Tolstoy, whom he knew personally, Gorky wrote an autobiographical trilogy depicting the hard life of the lower classes in the provinces, of which the first volume, *Detstvo* (1913; *My Childhood*, 1915), is the best. Living in Italy for many years because of poor health, Gorky did not return to Russia for good until the early 1930's. Up to the time of his death, a suspicious affair, he worked on his four-volume "novel-chronicle" *Zhizn Klima Samgina* (1927-1936; *The Life of Klim Samgin*, 1930-1938). It has something of the scope of Tolstoy's *War and Peace*, offering a vast panorama of historical events and social change seen through the eyes of a developing intellectual. Often rhetorical, uneven, and heavy-handed in his fiction, Gorky the publicist outweighed Gorky the artist. While serving as a bridge between the two centuries, he continued the nineteenth century tradition of the Russian writer acting as a public figure. He had an immense influence on the progress of literature and the arts in the Soviet Union and has been called the father of Soviet literature.

THE BOLSHEVIK REVOLUTION

The most decisive event in twentieth century Russian history was the revolution that brought the Bolsheviks to power. It had a profound impact on all spheres of life, including literature. Control over literature was only gradually asserted, however, and as a result, the 1920's were years of relative artistic freedom. Although a radical break with the past political system had occurred, that was not so with regard to culture; the nineteenth century literary tradition continued to exist alongside modernist experiments. Intellectuals, writers of the intelligentsia, often derogatorily referred to as "fellow travelers," had not yet been displaced by the proletarian writers who swarmed to the metropolis to establish the new literature, to reflect the new morality.

The issue facing the writers of the 1920's was how the novel should depict the new reality. World War I, the revolution, and the bitter Russian Civil War (1918-1921) had shattered the belief in the wholeness of the world, in the collective experience so frequently reflected in the nineteenth century novel. In the West, this experience led to the sense of alienation, epitomized by the lost generation. While the same was true for some Russians, in particular for the intellectuals and those who emigrated, the strong sense of an ending was countered by a firm belief that a new and better time was at hand. The sense of fragmentation did indeed lead to a reassessment of the individual's relationship to society, to the new collective, but the 1920's were still a period of optimism. These issues surfaced in various forms in the prose fiction of nearly every literary school or movement of the time, which made the 1920's a variegated and productive literary period.

The intellectual exuberance of the early 1920's is particularly evident in the works of the Formalist critic Viktor Shklovsky (1893-1984). The Formalists—whose influence on modern criticism, both direct and via French structuralism, has been enormous—emphasized the internal dynamics of literary works, the devices by which they are "made." (Thus, in a characteristic passage, Shklovsky boasts, "I know how Don Quixote is made.") Shklovsky's *Sentimental'noye puteshestviye: Vospominaniya, 1917-1922* (1923; *A Sentimental Journey: Memoirs, 1917-1922*, 1970), *Zoo: Ili, Pis'ma ne o lyubvi* (1923; *Zoo: Or, Letters Not About Love*, 1971), and *Tret'ya fabrika* (1926; *Third Factory*, 1977) combine a sophisticated awareness of literary forms with a strikingly original tone; part novel, part memoir, part literary criticism, these works are marked by the spirit of artistic freedom for which Shklovsky and others were to be attacked in the late 1920's.

Shklovsky's language, fresh and colloquial yet able to accommodate technical literary terms, reflects in part the influence of Aleksey Remizov (1877-1957). Remizov, who emigrated from Soviet Russia to Berlin in 1921, settling in 1923 in Paris, where he remained for the rest of his life, sought to invigorate the Russian literary language with a return to its native resources. In his novels, which resist translation, Remizov forged a style at once racy and ornate, drawing heavily on colloquial speech, proverbs, and folktales, mixing many different levels of diction and different genres within a single work.

One loosely organized group of nonproletarian writers active in the 1920's was the Serapion Brotherhood. Vaguely influenced by E. T. A. Hoffmann but also by Shklovsky and the Formalists, they combined reality and social criticism with fantasy and action plots. Not unsympathetic to the revolution, they resisted pressure to write works praising the new society and focused instead on the individual consciousness in an alienated world. An excellent illustration of this theme appears in *Zavist'* (1927; *Envy*, 1936), a novel that made Yury Olesha (1899-1960) an overnight success. The historical background of the 1920's is present in the novel but on a reduced scale, and reality becomes subject to the laws of fantasy. Olesha creates this fantasy through his method of "magic photography," whereby he transforms reality into images of an alternative world for his superfluous, imaginative little man, estranged from the materialistic, pedestrian new world he envies.

The theme of alienation is also expressed by Konstantin Fedin (1892-1977) in his novel *Goroda i gody* (1924; *Cities and Years*, 1962). Using the technique of montage to convey the fragmentation of reality, Fedin traces the demise of a superfluous man, an intellectual, not able to fully accept the revolution and the new regime. His second novel of the 1920's, *Bratya* (1928; brothers), also portrays a sensitive intellectual out of step with the times.

One of the most interesting novels to appear in the 1920's was *My* (corrupt text published 1927, reissued 1952; *We*, 1924), written in 1920-1921 by Yevgeny Zamyatin (1884-1937), a member of the Serapion Brotherhood. The novel was first published in English and was not published in the Soviet Union for several decades because it is an antiutopian novel. Combining two genres, the diary and the utopian novel, it denies the possibility of utopian happiness and, by implication, the possibility of a future communist paradise. Zamyatin's novel appeared before the rise to power of Joseph Stalin (1879-1953) and is not, therefore, merely a satire on totalitarianism; it is also a novel about communication and language. The conflict between the individual and the state is expressed through the hero's discovery of many languages—the languages of love, poetry, and the past—that create a threatening polyphony that the authorities suppress in the name of collective happiness. After the publication of *We*, Zamyatin served as head of the Leningrad section of the Union of Writers until 1929, when the Stalinist crackdown on literature began. He was fortunate to be allowed to emigrate in 1931.

Utopias and the future were topics widely discussed in the 1920's. Another novel that raises similar questions is *Chevengur* (1972, written 1928-1930; English translation, 1978), an idiosyncratic novel with an unusual history of publication. Written by the unorthodox Andrey Platonov (1899-1951), the novel is constructed as a pilgrimage through the steppe, as a search for utopian solutions. Full of literary allusions to Dostoevski, Novalis (1772-1801), and Miguel de Cervantes' *Don Quixote de la Mancha* (1605, 1615), it ironically focuses on the inherent contradiction of the revolution as a dynamic, ongoing force and utopia as a static state of collective happiness.

A critical appraisal of the revolution also appears in *Goly god* (1922; *The Naked Year*, 1928), written by an influential writer of the 1920's, Boris Pilnyak, also a member of the Serapion Brotherhood. Influenced by Andrey Bely's prose style, the novel is composed of episodes and fragments that intentionally disrupt and obscure the chronology and logical sequence of events to convey the disruptive force of the revolution itself. The revolution is represented as an elemental deed of blind biological forces and organized, machinelike movement . Pilnyak wrote several other novels, and his style and manner were widely imitated during the 1920's.

In contrast to the critical attitude of many intellectuals, the proletarian writers widely acclaimed the revolution, glorifying its heroes and achievements. Forming their own groups, such as Proletcult, Pereval, and the Smithy, they were quite conservative as writers and continued the literary traditions of the nineteenth century. Their novels are simple and straightforward rather than experimental and convey a social message that usually takes precedence over artistic and technical considerations. Their heroes are portrayed as individual representatives of the collective, for which they make personal sacrifices in combat or on the industrial front. The relationship of the individual to the collective created problems that became the center of considerable debate in the 1920's and that remained an unresolved issue in Soviet literature.

Among the works glorifying the revolution and the revolutionary hero was the novel *Chapayev* (1923; English translation, 1935), by Dmitri Furmanov (1891-1926). Basing the novel on events from Vasily Chapayev's life, Furmanov subordinated this charismatic figure (an actual leader of Red partisans) to the historical context and produced a kind of documentary, not a photographic realism, but a "literature of fact" (*literatura fakta*), a literary phenomenon of the 1920's. Not as well known, Furmanov's second novel, *Myatezh* (1925; the uprising), was also about the partisan movement in the southeastern steppe.

In the enthusiasm for glorifying the revolution, many early works of the proletarian writers portrayed the revolution as a historical movement and overemphasized the role of the collective. A case in point is the popular epic *Zhelezny potok* (1924; *The Iron Flood*, 1935), by Aleksandr Serafimovich (the pen name of Aleksandr Popov, 1863-1949). The novel describes the transformation of an anarchic mass into an organized fighting force that overcomes the Whites. Although ideologically sound, the novel was criticized for its abstractness, its undistinguished characters, and the absence of an individuated revolutionary hero.

The novel that successfully struck a balance between portraying the hero as an individual yet representative of the collective, as resolute and disciplined but with human weaknesses, was the popularly acclaimed *Razgrom* (1927; *The Nineteen*, 1929), by Aleksandr Fadeyev (1901-1956). Fadeyev adequately presented the Marxist notion of historical processes (the revolution) finding expression through concrete individuals. The novel was later praised as a paragon of Socialist Realism, and Fadeyev was proclaimed the "Red Leo Tolstoy." Tolstoy's influence on Fadeyev and the proletarian writers in general was pronounced: Attempting to establish the legitimacy of the new literature, the proletarian writers turned to the classic author of Russian realism, Tolstoy, with whose concept and portrayal of reality they could identify.

Tolstoy's influence is particularly apparent in *Tikhii Don* (1928-1940; partial translation *And Quiet Flows the Don*, 1934; also known as *The Don Flows Home to the Sea*, 1940; complete translation *The Silent Don*, 1942; also known as *And Quiet Flows the Don*, 1967), an extremely popular novel in four volumes that has often been compared to *War and Peace*. Written by Mikhail Sholokhov (1905-1984), the novel focused on the turbulent and brutal events among the Don Cossacks from World War I to the end of the civil war. Controversy arose concerning both authorship (charges of plagiarism were made, revived in the 1970's by Aleksandr Solzhenitsyn) and the portrayal of the reflective hero, who questions the legitimacy of the revolution and thus suggests the possibility of a third way, the existence of which is denied by communism. Avoiding simplistic oppositions and taking a critical attitude toward the communists, Sholokhov achieved a complexity and verisimilitude that was immediately acknowledged by readers and critics alike.

Few works written by the proletarian writers went so far as to suggest the possibility of a third way between communism and capitalism. Even when presenting the shortcomings of the revolution or the defeat of the communist forces, such setbacks were presented as temporary, as heroic sacrifices necessary to achieve the goals of the revolution. Such a position is taken by Yury Libedinsky (1898-1959) in his novel *Nedelya* (1922; *A Week*, 1923), in which a small detachment of communists is sacrificed for the general good. Libedinsky also wrote two novels on a subject current in the 1920's—the reappearance of bourgeois influences during the period of the New Economic Policy (NEP), a particularly disturbing phenomenon for orthodox communists and one sharply attacked in the novel *Shokolad* (1922; *Chocolate*, 1932), by Aleksandr Tarasov-Rodionov (1885-1938).

Anecdotes, stories, and novels satirizing the return of philistinism, the ineptness of the bureaucracy, and the mundane concerns of everyday life during the NEP were a welcome relief from the steady stream of novels about the revolution. Particularly popular were the satiric novels of Ilya Ilf (1897-1937) and Evgeni Petrov (1903- 1942), such as their *Dvenadtsat stuliev* (1928; *The Twelve Chairs*, 1961) and *Zolotoy telyonok* (1931; *The Little Golden Calf*, 1932). Another author of interest was Ilya Ehrenburg (1891-1967), who had been allowed to travel to the West and later wrote several works critical of Western culture and the capitalist economic system. Some of the first Russian science fiction also appeared during the NEP. One writer of Wellsian fantasies was Aleksey Tolstoy (1883-1945), who is better known for his unfinished historical novel *Pyotr Pervy* (1929-1945; *Peter the First*, 1959). Although of aristocratic background, he was a willing apologist for the Stalin regime.

The conditions under which literature developed during the NEP did not continue for long. In 1928, the First Five-Year Plan was adopted, and the Communist Party decided that literature was to be harnessed to the needs of the state. By 1932, all autonomous literary organizations were disbanded by a party directive, and all writers were exhorted to follow the precepts of Socialist Realism. Socialist Realism remained an intentionally vague term, to be defined as the authorities wished; novelists were to avoid psychological realism focusing on the individual and objective realism revealing negative aspects of Soviet life, concentrating instead on the positive, inspiring aspects of Soviet life. In 1934, the First Congress of Soviet Writers was held, and the Union of Writers was launched; membership was virtually obligatory. During the 1930's, many writers were forced to publicly admit their errors and "heresies"; arrests were frequent, and many writers and poets perished in the charged atmosphere of the infamous Stalinist purges from 1936 to 1938. Those who survived were forced to be silent or accept a role as an instrument of education and propaganda within the Soviet apparatus.

The novels of the 1930's primarily focused on the subject of industrialization, a topic that had already replaced revolutionary romanticism in the 1920's. The model for the writers of the 1930's was *Tsement* (1925; *Cement*, 1929), by Fyodor Gladkov (1883-1958), which downplayed the hero's family tragedy and emphasized his constructive role in rebuilding a local factory. Virtually all the major writers responded with novels on the theme of industrialization: Sholokhov wrote about collectivization, as did Fyodor Panferov (1896-1960); Pilnyak wrote about the construction of a great dam and hydroelectric station; Valentin Katayev (1897-1986) wrote about the construction of a huge metallurgical plant in the Ural Mountains in *Vremya vperyod!* (1932; *Time Forward!*, 1933); Ehrenburg also contributed to the subject, as did many others.

The 1930's also saw the appearance of autobiographical educational novels such as *Kak zakalialas' stal'* (1932-1934; *The Making of a Hero*, 1937; also known as *How the Steel Was Tempered*, 1952), by Nikolai Alekseevich Ostrovsky (1904-1936), and *Pedagogicheskaya poema* (1935; *The Road to Life*, 1954), by Anton Makarenko (1888-1939). Such novels depicted the development of exemplary communists in the face of great obstacles and the process of disciplining the dynamic forces of the revolution. They were clearly intended to inspire the reader with appreciation for the sacrifices made and to provide the proper ideological orientation.

The literature of the 1940's was concerned with the patriotic efforts of the Red Army, the party, and the *narod* (the folk) in the defense of the motherland, a theme that remained a staple of popular Soviet literature. Again, writers responded to social demand and produced novels of varying quality. Among the more inter esting are Gladkov's *Klyatva* (1944; the vow), Fadeyev's *Molodaya gvardiya* (1946; *The Young Guard*, 1958), and *V okopakh Stalingrada* (1946; *Front-Line Stalingrad*, 1962), by Viktor Nekrasov (1911-1987). In spite of the emphasis on the role of the collective in the war effort, several works "rediscovered" the individual. One such novel was *Sputniki* (1946; *The Train*, 1948), by Vera Panova (1905-1973). In her presentation of the members of a medical team during World War II, she focused on their personal lives and portrayed the collective as a group of individuals with a common goal: a new conception of the collective. The 1940's were also saturated with memoirs relating to the war experience.

THE POST-STALIN NOVEL

A significant change in Soviet literature occurred after the death of Stalin in 1953. Commonly referred to as the "thaw," after the title of Ehrenburg's novel *Ottepel* (1954, 1956; *The Thaw*, 1955; also known as *A Change of Season*, 1962), it led to the revival of the novel genre and reasserted the individual's role within the collective. Mild criticism of the system, evident in *Vremena goda* (1953; *The Span of the Year*, 1956), by Panova, and *Russkii les* (1953; *The Russian Forest*, 1966), by Leonid Maksimovich Leonov (1899-1988), was not, however, a departure from the tradition of the Russian novel (as one can see from the novels of the nineteenth century), but it was an attempt to break away from the dogmatic treatment of political and social issues. Such works were indicative of the paradoxical relationship between literature and politics. The demand by authorities that literature reflect the goals and needs of the state allowed a realistic (convincing) portrayal of characters in conflict, but it introduced contradictions and ambiguities that obscured the simplistic Communist Party point of view. At such moments of crisis, as in 1954, the party periodically stepped in to reassert its control over literature.

It is not surprising, therefore, that the famous poetic novel of Boris Pasternak (1890-1960), *Doktor Zhivago* (1957; *Doctor Zhivago*, 1958), which was announced in the journal *Znamya* as forthcoming, was rejected when submitted in 1956 and had to be published abroad. Concerned with symbolic truth, Pasternak gave a metonymic representation of the revolution and the civil war, as witnessed by the passive but receptive poet Yuri Zhivago. The novel provides a remarkable portrait of an individual in the nineteenth century tradition and opens a critical dialogue with the past.

This dialogue was continued by the publication of the rediscovered works of Mikhail Bulgakov (1891-1940), written some thirty years earlier. Among his novels satirizing Soviet life and deflating Soviet institutions was his masterpiece *Master i Margarita* (written 1940; censored version 1966-1967; uncensored version 1973; *The Master and Margarita*, 1967). A modern treatment of the Faust theme with a fantastic, dreamlike atmosphere, it is a metaphysical inquiry into the evil of Stalin and the cult of personality; it is also a novel about the creative process, about the writing of a novel about Christ and Pilate. The appearance of the novel created a sensation in Russia, and in the context of Soviet literature, it was indeed a magnificent achievement.

Another author whose works were rediscovered was Platonov. His *Chevengur* (mentioned earlier) and his novel *Kotlovan* (1968; *The Foundation Pit*, 1973, 1975) were not originally published in the Soviet Union, though samizdat (underground) copies of both circulated widely . Full of symbolic images and folklore and written in a peculiar style, *The Foundation Pit* is a dark, ironic satire of early Soviet industrialization and education.

A work that focused on a relatively unexplored side of the Soviet past was *Odin den' Ivana Denisovicha* (1962; *One Day in the Life of Ivan Denisovich*, 1963), by Aleksandr Solzhenitsyn (1918-2008). Its appearance was made possible by a change in the political climate following a speech by Nikita Khrushchev at the Twentieth Congress of the Communist Party in 1956, in which he acknowledged Stalin's "mistakes" (that is, his crimes). The next year, Vladimir Dmitrievich Dudintsev (1918-1998) published his novel *Ne khlebom yedinym* (1957; *Not by Bread Alone*, 1957), in which he defended the individual's rights against the vulgar careerists wielding power. Dudintsev was sharply attacked by the Communist Party, which quickly moved to curb the liberal tendencies appearing after Khrushchev's speech. Three years later, however, controls were eased again, and with Khrushchev's personal intervention, Solzhenitsyn's novel was published.

One Day in the Life of Ivan Denisovich is a stunning indictment of the labor camps of the Stalin era. Describing life in reduced situations, a characteristic of nearly all of his fiction, Solzhenitsyn illustrates the struggle of the *zeks* (prisoners) to survive with dignity. He portrays the harshness of the prison but points out that, paradoxically, freedom is possible only within the camp. Introducing a wide range of characters in his novels *V kruge pervom* (1968; *The First Circle*, 1968) and *Rakovy korpus* (1968; *Cancer Ward*, 1968), Solzhenitsyn skillfully renders their speech and creates a polyphony of views that constitute a complete picture of Soviet society. Solzhenitsyn's position as a moral conscience and a voice for those not able to speak out is well in evidence in his monumental *Arkhipelag GULag, 1918-1956: Opyt khudozhestvennogo issledovaniya* (1973-1975; *The Gulag Archipelago, 1918-1956: An Experiment in Literary Investigation*, 1974-1978), which exposed the magnitude of the evil of Stalin's camps. It is a historical document shaped by an artist into a powerful and profound epic.

Of the many works written about the camps and the purges, most are a mixture of history, biography, confession, and memoir, emphasizing the factual nature of the content, its truth value. Many courageous people did leave accounts: Varlam Shalamov (1907-1981), who wrote of his experiences in Kolyma; Evgenia Ginzburg (c. 1906-1977), who wrote of her arrest in the purges; and Anatoly Marchenko (1938-1986), who was arrested several times for his defiance of the state, are but a few.

Three major waves of emigration from Russia occurred in the twentieth century: after the revolution, after World War II, and during the 1960's and 1970's. A number of Russian novelists found themselves cut off from their homeland and confronted with a new reality, a new freedom that affected their creativity in various ways. Among the more prominent Russian writers outside the Soviet Union were Bunin, Merezhkovsky, Remizov, Zamyatin, the minor novelists Boris Zaitsev (1881-1972) and Ivan Shmelyov (1873-1950), both of whom wrote about the émigré experience, and Mark Aldanov—the pen name of Mark Landau (1886-1957), a prolific and serious writer of novels on Russian history. One of the most accomplished writers to have emigrated was Vladimir Nabokov, who, before turning to English, wrote eight novels in Russian, only two of which are not about émigrés. An exquisite craftsman influenced by Gogol and Bely as well as by Marcel Proust (1871-1922), Franz Kafka (1883-1924), and the German expressionists, Nabokov enjoyed great success with his English-language novels such as *Lolita* (1955) and *Ada or Ardor: A Family Chronicle* (1969). Several other émigré writers of note are Andrei

Sinyavsky (1925-1997), who often wrote under the pen name Abram Tertz, the author of surreal novels and tales in the tradition of Gogol, as well as of brilliant, idiosyncratic critical studies; Vassily Aksyonov (born 1932), a prolific and original novelist; Vladimir Voinovich (born 1932), best known for his satiric Chonkin trilogy; and Vladimir Maximov (1932-1995), whose novels exhibit a pronounced hostility both to communism and to Western liberalism—views similar to those of Solzhenitsyn, who was himself forced into exile and only allowed to return to Russia in the mid-1990's. Two other émigrés who created distinctive works of fiction are Sergei Dovlatov (1941-1990) and Sasha Sokolov (born 1945), whose novel *Shkola dlia durakov* (1976; *A School for Fools*, 1977) offers a unique vision of the lyric freedom found in mental illness.

Many of the émigré writers had published in the Soviet Union before arriving in the West. Aksyonov and Voinovich both represented the young generation, critical of the stale abstractions, political slogans, and dullness of Soviet life. Others had to rely on samizdat to circulate their work; among these was Venedikt Erofeev (1938-1990), whose novel *Moskva-Petushki* (1973; *Moscow to the End of the Line*, 1980), about alcoholism as an escape from the banality of Soviet life, had no chance of being officially published. While not officially sanctioned, the literature of protest was tolerated to a certain degree, the limits of which fluctuated with the political climate. When necessary, the authorities simply reasserted their control.

A significant trend in Soviet literature appeared in the late 1950's. Writers of the same generation as the writers of protest turned to village and rural themes. Surprisingly, the nineteenth century did not produce a single significant work about peasant life, while in the twentieth century, the Marxists have found little more in the peasant than an obstacle to progress, to socialism. The village writers were the first to show a reverence for peasants, describe their traditions, present their uneven struggle with the bureaucracy, and portray them as individual human beings. Many of the novels on peasant life espouse such conservative and traditional Russian values as love of nature and pride in one's work. They are critical of collectivization, often seeing it as the reason for the poor state of Russian agriculture, and of the treatment that the peasants have received at the hands of government officials. These themes can be found throughout the works of some of the leading village writers: Fyodor Abramov (1920-1983), Vasily Belov (born 1932), Valentin Rasputin (born 1937), and the popular and talented Vasily Shukshin (1929-1974).

THE LATE TWENTIETH CENTURY AND BEYOND

Also widespread in the 1960's and the 1970's were novels dealing with urban themes. They focused on problems in the workplace, the harried life of women in Soviet urban society, careerism, and the mundane concerns of everyday life. Novels returning to the subject of the revolution and World War II also continued to appear, focusing primarily on the individual's private experience. The major writers on such themes include Yury Trifonov (1925-1981), I. Grekova (the pseudonym of Elena Ventzel, born 1907), Yury Kazakov

(1927-1982), Andrei Bitov (born 1937), Vasily Bykov (1924-2003), and Viktoria Tokareva (born 1937).

The elevation of Mikhail Gorbachev to the post of general secretary of the Communist Party in 1985 opened a new era for Russia's writers. Eager to reform the stagnant economy, Gorbachev encouraged a new openness (glasnost) in Soviet society. During the last few years of the Soviet Union, from the mid-1980's to 1991, many works that had hitherto been prohibited from publication were allowed to appear in print for the first time. The year 1988, for example, saw the first Soviet publication of Pasternak's *Doctor Zhivago*, Zamyatin's *We*, several works by Nabokov, and the controversial novel by Vasily Grossman (1905-1964), *Zhizn i sudba* (finished in 1960, published in the West in 1980; *Life and Fate*, 1985). Many of the newly published works, including Grossman's novel and the novel *Deti Arbata* (wr. 1966, pb. 1987; *Children of the Arbat*, 1988), by Anatoly Rybakov (1911-1998), countered official views of Soviet society and politics, and they generated considerable debate among the reading public. Yet while much attention was focused on works previously unavailable for general consumption, other developments in literature also triggered excited discussion. New writers appeared in print, along with some older writers whose work had not been readily accessible. Among the most celebrated of the "new" writers are Lyudmila Petrushevskaya (born 1938), Vladimir Makanin (born 1937), Yevgeny Popov (born 1946), Vyacheslav Pyetsukh (born 1946), and Viktor Erofeev (born 1947), all of whom depict the seamier side of Soviet life. Their writing ranges from the farcical to the grotesque. Although they often prefer shorter genres, they also have produced longer works of haunting intensity, such as Petrushevskaya's *Vremya noch* (1992; *The Time: Night*, 1994), which challenges the myth of the "nurturing mother" in Russia.

Women, including the familiar Lyudmila Petrushevskaya, achieved a new literary prominence at the end of the twentieth century and the beginning of the twenty-first century. Tatyana Tolstaya (born 1951) is best known for her short fiction, but her dystopian novel *Kys* (2001; *The Slynx,* 2003) has been widely read internationally. Lyudmila Ulitskaya (born 1943) has been both a critical and a popular success, beginning with her first novella, *Sonechka* (1992; *Sonechka, and Other Stories*, 1998). Her later works include *Kazus Kukotskogo* (2000; Kukot sky's case), which won the Russian Booker Prize, and her American debut, *Veselye pokhorony* (1998; *The Funeral Party*, 1999). Aleksandra Marinina (born 1957; pen name of Marina Anatol'evna Alekseeva) is a best-selling writer of detective novels, a genre that has become increasingly popular in Russia.

The swirling currents of change came to a head in 1991, when the failed coup attempt by a group of hard-line Communists led to the final dissolution of the Soviet Union. This breakdown of traditional state authority had major consequences in the literary sphere as well. Writers and publishers could no longer count on hefty state subsidies to support their work; publishing houses had to adapt to the pressures of a free market economy. For a year or two, Russian intellectuals fretted about a crisis in literature. In their rush to make a profit, publishers began to turn out an enormous quantity of pulp fiction, from detective stories to erotic thrillers. Demand for "serious" literature diminished considerably. Without official constraints on what could appear in print, literature was deprived of its traditional role as the prophetic voice or moral conscience of the nation. Within a few years, however, the sense of crisis died down, and Russian literature saw a new flowering of individual talents. The creation of the Russian Booker Prize in 1992 helped provide a focus for the literati, and signs of renewed growth soon became evident. In addition to the original publication of long-suppressed or buried works, such as the memoir-novel *Vremenà* (1994; *How It All Began*, 1998), written by the Bolshevik Nikolay Ivanovich Bukharin in prison in 1937-1938 before his execution at Stalin's behest, fresh writers appeared in print. Many of the authors who came to prominence in the 1990's were distinguished by their innovative approach to fiction writing, and several seemed to reflect a particularly Russian brand of European postmodernism. Among the most interesting of these writers are Vladimir Georgievich Sorokin (born 1955) and Victor Pelevin (born 1962). Their work, including Pelevin's *Zhizn'nasekomykh* (1994; *The Life of Insects*, 1996), raise existential questions through extraordinary forms of pastiche and parody. With the arrival of this new generation of writers, the prospects for the future development of Russian literature once again looked bright.

George Mihaychuk
Updated by Julian W. Connolly

BIBLIOGRAPHY

Barker, Adele Marie, and Jehanne M. Gheith, eds. *A History of Women's Writing in Russia*. New York: Cambridge University Press, 2002. Collection of essays presents topics in chronological order, beginning with the images of women in medieval Russian literature and continuing through the years of perestroika.

Brown, Deming. *The Last Years of Soviet Russian Literature*. New York: Cambridge University Press, 1993. Examines currents in Russian literature that surfaced in the Soviet Union between 1975 and 1991. Designed to follow the author's earlier book, *Soviet Russian Literature Since Stalin* (1978).

Cornwell, Neil. *The Routledge Companion to Russian Literature*. New York: Routledge, 2001. Extremely useful reference work contains introductory essays to major topics in Russian literature, biographical essays, and articles on numerous individual works.

Emerson, Caryl. *The Cambridge Introduction to Russian Literature*. New York: Cambridge University Press, 2008. Excellent chronological literary history provides analysis of the major works, writers, and themes. Includes a glossary, pronunciation guide, and bibliography of primary and secondary sources.

Freeborn, Richard. *The Rise of the Russian Novel*. New York: Cambridge University Press, 1973. Stimulating study examines some of the most famous works of nineteenth century Russian literature, including *Eugene Onegin*, *Dead Souls*, *A Hero of Our Time*, *Crime and Punishment*, and *War and Peace*.

Jones, Malcom V., and Robin Feuer Miller, eds. *The Cambridge Companion to the Classic Russian Novel*. New York: Cambridge University Press, 1998. Fourteen essays by prominent scholars cover a wide range of subjects reflected in the Russian novel, from politics and religion to psychology and gender.

Kelly, Catriona. *A History of Russian Women's Writing, 1820-1992*. New York: Oxford University Press, 1994. Comprehensive study of the evolution of wom en's writing in Russia combines sociohistorical analysis with close readings of individual works.

_____. *Russian Literature: A Very Short Introduction*. New York: Cambridge University Press, 2001. Explores the role of literature in Russian culture, using one of Russia's most influential writers, Alexander Pushkin, to illustrate the major ideas.

Ledkovsky, Marina, Charlotte Rosenthal, and Mary Zirin , eds. *Dictionary of Russian Women Writers*. Westport, Conn.: Greenwood Press, 1994. Contains a wealth of information on a broad range of literary figures.

Moser, Charles A., ed. *The Cambridge History of Russian Literature*. New York: Cambridge University Press, 1989. Collection of essays by noted scholars traces the evolution of Russian literature from the medieval period to 1980.

Shneidman, N. N. *Russian Literature, 1995-2002: On the Threshold of the New Millennium*. Toronto, Ont.: University of Toronto Press, 2004. Analyzes Russian literature after the breakup of the Soviet Union, considering how the economy and the market have shaped literary production.

VASSILY AKSYONOV

Born: Kazan, Russia, Soviet Union (now in Russia); August 20, 1932
Died: Moscow, Russia; July 6, 2009
Also known as: Vassily Pavlovich Aksyonov

PRINCIPAL LONG FICTION

Kollegi, 1960 (*Colleagues*, 1962)
Zvezdnyi bilet, 1961 (*A Starry Ticket*, 1962; also known as *A Ticket to the Stars*)
Apelsiny iz Marokko, 1963 (*Oranges from Morocco*, 1979)
Pora, moi drug, pora, 1965 (*It's Time, My Friend, It's Time*, 1969)
Zatovarennaya bochkotara, 1968 (*Surplussed Barrelware*, 1985)
Stalnaya ptitsa, 1977 (novella; *The Steel Bird*, 1979)
Poiski zhanra, 1978
Zolotaya nasha Zhelezka, 1979 (*Our Golden Ironburg*, 1986)
Ozhog, 1980 (*The Burn*, 1984)
Ostrov Krym, 1981 (*The Island of Crimea*, 1983)
Bumazhnyi peizazh, 1983
Skazhi izyum, 1985 (*Say Cheese!*, 1989)
Moskovskaia saga: Trilogiia, 1993-1994 (includes *Pokolenie zimy, Voina i tiurma*
    [*Generations of Winter*, 1994], and *Tiurma i mir* [*The Winter's Hero*, 1996])
Novyi sladostnyi stil, 1997 (*The New Sweet Style*, 1999)
Kesarevo svechenie, 2001
Volteryantsy i Volteryanki, 2004
Redkiezemli, 2007

OTHER LITERARY FORMS

Vassily Aksyonov (uhk-SYUH-nuhv) was primarily a novelist, but he also worked in many other genres. As a young Soviet writer, he produced short stories in the 1960's that were enormously popular among Russian readers. He was also the author of numerous Russian film scripts and several plays, of which the best is *Tsaplya* (pb. 1979; *The Heron*, 1987). Children's books and a fictionalized biography, *Lyubov k elektrichestvu* (1971; love for electricity), are also found in his oeuvre. His travel writings, especially *Kruglye sutki: Non-stop* (1976; around the clock nonstop), a collage account of a visit to the United States, are a remarkable blend of fantasy and reportage. A steady stream of diverse journalism also came from his pen, particularly after his emigration to the United States.

ACHIEVEMENTS

Vassily Aksyonov holds a unique position in modern Russian literature. From the early 1930's until the death of dictator Joseph Stalin in 1953, Soviet literature stagnated under the official aesthetic doctrine of Socialist Realism. Aksyonov, as a controversial leader of the "young prose" movement in the post-Stalin period, revitalized Russian prose by introducing fresh themes, characters, and living speech into his work. He was an idol of and spokesman for the new generation of young Soviet technocrats, who dreamed of a Western-oriented humanist socialism. As the dream dimmed, Aksyonov was forced to turn to "writing for the drawer," knowing his work could not be published in the Soviet Union. These new works, increasingly surrealistic, detailed the disillusion of the young intelligentsia. Published in the West only after Aksyonov's emigration, they confirm his reputation as the preeminent chronicler of his generation as well as its most innovative literary stylist.

BIOGRAPHY

Vassily Pavlovich Aksyonov was born in Kazan, Russia, on August 20, 1932. His parents, both committed Communists, were falsely arrested as "enemies of the people" in 1937. The future writer rejoined his freed mother and stepfather, a Catholic doctor-prisoner, in Siberia at age seventeen. Because "it's easier for doctors in the camps," it was decided that Aksyonov would attend medical school in Leningrad, from which he graduated in 1956, the year in which Premier Nikita S. Khrushchev denounced the crimes of Stalin. Taking advantage of the cultural "thaw," the young practitioner began writing. After his successful first novel, *Colleagues*, was published in 1960, Aksyonov turned to full-time writing. The early "optimistic" period of his career came to an end on March 8, 1963, when Khrushchev himself publicly demanded recantation of his work. Publication became increasingly difficult, especially after the Soviet invasion of Czechoslovakia in 1968, but Aksyonov was permitted to accept a one-term Regents' Lectureship at the University of California at Los Angeles in 1975.

In the late 1970's, Aksyonov and a number of colleagues boldly undertook to publish an uncensored literary anthology to be called *Metropol*. Those involved were subjected to reprisals, and Aksyonov was, in effect, forced to emigrate in 1980. In the United States, Aksyonov published several works written earlier and taught at various universities. He was also a fellow at the prestigious Woodrow Wilson International Center. As a resident of Washington, D.C., Aksyonov continued to write novels, including *Say Cheese!*, a fictionalized version of the *Metropol* affair. An energetic publicist, Aksyonov occupied a leading position in émigré cultural affairs. In 2004, Aksyonov and his wife, Maya, moved back to Russia, taking an apartment in Moscow. They retained a second home in Biarritz, France, however, and Aksyonov made it clear that if the Russian federal government should begin heroizing Stalin once again, he would disown his own country. Aksyonov died in Moscow on July 6, 2009.

ANALYSIS

The major theme in Vassily Aksyonov's fiction is the nature and fate of the Soviet Union and the role of Aksyonov's generation in trying to reshape the nation after the death of

Stalin. His works chronicle these years first from the optimistic perspective of a generation on the rise, confident that a new day has dawned, then from the perspective of growing doubt, and finally in a mood of despair.

A TICKET TO THE STARS

A Ticket to the Stars is a landmark book that became the rallying point for the new generation. The young people it portrays and those whom it inspired when it appeared took the name "star boys" as their banner. Conservatives of the older generation used the name as a term of condemnation. The story begins in the early summer in Moscow, circa 1960. Three friends who have just finished high school are hanging out in the courtyard of their apartment building. The neighbors look askance at their clothes and the music blaring from their tape recorder. All three are from professional families, and all are headed for college and careers in accord with the expectations of society and the wishes of their families. Dimka Denisov, the ringleader, confides to his older brother Victor that he and his friends have decided to kick over the traces, defy their parents, and head for the Baltic seacoast for the summer, and perhaps longer.

Victor, who narrates parts of the story, is twenty-eight, a doctoral candidate in space medicine. A model son, a scholarship student, he looks with affection but mild alarm at his aimless younger brother and his friends. Victor's goal in life is represented by the night view from his bedroom window, from which he can see a small rectangle of sky dotted by stars. The sight reminds him of a tram ticket punched with star-shaped holes.

The teenagers pass their summer on the beach. Among their haunts is a restaurant bar with a star-painted ceiling. As their money disappears, they join an Estonian collective fishing enterprise. The young Muscovites at first find their companions crude and the work difficult, but at length they begin to take pride in the endeavor. Victor, now on the verge of a brilliant career, comes to visit Dimka, who is still wary of a "programmed" future. Suddenly called back to Moscow, Victor is killed in a plane crash. After the funeral, Dimka lies on Victor's bed and sees for the first time "the starry ticket." It is now his ticket to the stars, but where will it take him?

At the time *A Ticket to the Stars* was published, Soviet readers, unlike their Western counterparts, were not accustomed to sympathetic accounts of youthful alienation. Even though the story has a reassuring ending, readers were shocked by the novel's racy language and its young heroes' flippant attitude toward authority.

THE STEEL BIRD

The Steel Bird, written in 1965 but not published until 1977, marks a crucial turning point in Aksyonov's writing both stylistically and thematically. His earlier novels are stylistically within the limits of realism, and their themes are more social than political. The young heroes, whose rebellion is against cant and excessive conformity, ultimately affirm the values of a socialist society. *The Steel Bird* is a political allegory in a modernist stylistic framework. In the spring of 1948, an odious creature named Popenkov (who subsequently proves to be part human and part mechanical bird) presents himself at a large, decaying Moscow apartment building and begs a corner in the entry-hall elevator. As the years pass, the creature expands his domain and enlists the residents in an illegal fake antique tapestry business. Eventually the tenants, a diverse cross section of Soviet society, are reduced to entering the building through a cramped back door.

The 1960's arrive. Soviet life has changed for the better. The residents of the older generation are retired, and their children are making their mark as leaders of a cultural revolution. The apartment building, weakened by age and Popenkov's constant remodeling, is on the verge of collapse. The Steel Bird nevertheless decides that for the convenience of his nocturnal flights the elevator should be extended through the roof. Seeing their home in danger, the residents finally rise. A coalition of worker-tenants and the young cultural leaders confront the Steel Bird on the roof, but as the residents drive off his minions, the building starts to crack. The building collapses, but all the residents are saved and moved to a splendid new building, while the Steel Bird remains perched atop the old elevator shaft. Months later, as bulldozers start to clear the rubble, Popenkov slowly flies off. The spirit of Stalinism departs, but it may return at any time.

The story, told by means of third-person narrative, eyewitness accounts, official reports, interludes of poetry, and authorial asides, is punctuated by the Stalinist house manager's cornet improvisations, thus echoing the story's themes. The Steel Bird increasingly lapses into using an autistic bird language.

THE BURN

The Burn, written in the post-Czech invasion years (1969-1975), presents a far bleaker stage in the evolution of Aksyonov's views. The events of *The Burn*—a long, complex, often hallucinatory novel—are perceived through the alcoholic haze that is the response of the intelligentsia to the demise of their hopes for a new Russia. The novel features five more or less interchangeable heroes—or rather antiheroes—all members of Aksyonov's generation, all liberals, all superstars in their professions. Kunitser is a physicist; Sabler, a jazz saxophonist; Khvastishchev, a sculptor; Malkolmov, a physician; and Pantelei, a writer whose past resembles that of author Aksyonov. Although the men have certain almost identical and seemingly concurrent experiences, they lead independent existences. The narrative focus alternates among them, and on occasion they change identities. Most remarkably, they share flashbacks to a single, common childhood, when they were Tolya von Steinbock.

The heroes have retreated before a renascent (but much milder) Stalinism, withdrawing into their creative work, sex, and alcohol. On the evening of the first day portrayed in the novel, they individually encounter an old friend, Patrick Thunderjet, a visiting Anglo-American who is obviously their Western counterpart. The day's drinking expands into a binge that takes the collective hero, a friend, and Thunderjet through a set of bizarre experiences ending in the Crimea, where they are ultimately arrested and confined to the drunk tank. The collective hero, too valuable an asset to Soviet society to be abandoned, is sent to a detoxification hospital. Released, the protagonists undertake a sober life, each engaged in a major creative endeavor. Soviet society, however, is too corrupt for their survival. Each has a professional colleague, a close friend from the heady days of the early 1960's. The old friends, who have compromised with the authorities, betray the trust of the heroes, who again succumb to drink. Now merged into a single nameless "I," the protagonist descends into alcoholic hallucinations, ultimately leaping to his death while fantasizing a lunar space flight.

The main story line of *The Burn* describes the smashed hopes of a generation. There is also a story behind the story. The five heroes share a childhood very much like Aksyonov's. Tolya von Steinbock joins his mother in Siberia when she is released from a ten-year sentence toward the end of Stalin's reign. He wants nothing more than to be a model Soviet youth and is vaguely embarrassed by his ex-prisoner mother and stepfather, a doctor and Catholic lay priest of German origin. Among a group of new women prisoners, he sees a girl of Polish-English origin named Alisa and dreams of a daring rescue. As he daydreams, another young man, a former prisoner, offers modest aid to the girl. Tolya becomes friends with the young man, Sanya Gurchenko, who is a friend of his stepfather. Their courage and idealism greatly impress him. Tolya's mother is soon rearrested, as is Sanya. They are interrogated, Sanya brutally, by two political police officers. Sanya eventually escapes to the West, where he becomes a Catholic priest and, years later, briefly encounters the hero.

These events of twenty years before lie deeply buried in the minds of the successful heroes, who do not wish to confront either their impotent past or their compromised present. The past, however, is very much with them. Wherever they go, they encounter two figures, cloakroom attendants, drunk-tank aides, and the like, vaguely reminiscent of the former police officials. They also yearn for a beautiful, promiscuous woman who moves in corrupt, elite Moscow circles and seems to resemble the Polish-English Alisa. The heroes, however, remain incapable either of vengeance or of rescuing their ideal. Unlike Sanya, who actively resisted evil, they have tacitly compromised with the system.

It is Sanya, the priest, who offers Aksyonov's solution with his philosophy of "the third mode." Its basic postulate is that all human beings, atheists and believers alike, seek God. There are always two models: an idea and its antithesis. One must seek a third, qualitatively different model through which one may strive to see the face of God. Humankind comes close to it only in moments of free, irrational creativity, the "burn" of the book's title. The higher emotions, such as compassion for one's neighbor, charity, and the urge for justice, are rationally and biologically inexplicable, fantastic. Christianity, precisely because it is concerned with these emotions, is sublime. Christianity is likened to a breakthrough into space, an image that corresponds to the hero's final, hallucinatory suicide flight. *The Burn*, Aksyonov's most important novel, is a diagnosis and indictment of his generation.

THE ISLAND OF CRIMEA

The Island of Crimea, written between 1977 and 1979, continues some of the themes of *The Burn*, but with a different emphasis. Although more traditional in style, *The Island of Crimea* is based on two fantastic premises. The Crimea, in reality a peninsula in the Black Sea, is, in the novel, an independent island-country. Historically, the Red Army defeated the White Armies during the Russian Civil War, and the Whites were driven into overseas exile. Fictionally, the Whites have successfully defended the island of Crimea and established a capitalistic Western political democracy that, in the late 1970's, is a fabulously wealthy, technological supercivilization.

Andrei Luchnikov, a jet-set member of one of the country's most prominent White émigré families, is the editor of an influential liberal newspaper. Luchnikov's political program, which reflects his generation's nostalgia for Mother Russia, calls for the voluntary reunification of the Crimea with Russia. Although realizing that the Soviet Union is, by the standards of the Crimea, politically and economically primitive, he believes that the historical motherland is moving forward and that both countries would profit from a symbiotic union. Eventually, the island's voters approve the reunification. The Soviet government, unable to comprehend the idea, responds with a massive military invasion in which most of Luchnikov's family dies, Luchnikov goes mad, and his son flees into exile. The novel, which reads like a James Bond thriller, is, in some sense, a very black comedy.

The Island of Crimea sums up Aksyonov's twenty-year meditation on the nature, history, and fate of his native country. From *A Ticket to the Stars* to *The Island of Crimea*, Aksyonov charted the evolution of the Russian intelligentsia: from the optimism of the early 1960's through the cynicism and despair of the late 1960's and early 1970's, to dissidence and emigration. It is the saga of a generation.

GENERATIONS OF WINTER

In his 1985 novel *Say Cheese!*, a largely autobiographical novel in which Aksyonov reflects on his emigration to the United States, he permits free rein to his satirical side, poking playful fun at the foibles of Soviet society. However, Aksyonov would soon prove himself capable of very serious historical writing as well as satiric comedy. In 1993, only two years after the Soviet Union's collapse and replacement by a new, democratic Russian Federation, he published *Generations of Winter*, a generational saga of a family living in the Soviet Union under Stalin, intended to be a masterpiece on the level of Leo Tolstoy's *Voyna i mir* (1865-1869; *War and Peace*, 1886).

In the beginning of *Generations of Winter*, the big family headed by renowned surgeon Boris Nikitich Gradov is enjoying the prosperous last few years of the New Economic Policy, the program of limited small-business capitalism that was permitted by Soviet leader Vladimir Ilich Lenin as a means of rebuilding prosperity after the catastrophe of the Russian Civil War. Boris is roped into the medical conspiracy that results in the death of military leader Mikhail Vasilievich Frunze, and as a result the family becomes entangled in a sequence of major events during the Great Purges and World War II. In several cases, sons or grandsons redeem the memories of their forebears through acts of courage in situations that parallel earlier acts of cowardice. For instance, whereas the patriarch Boris Gradov acted in cowardice and became complicit in the death of Frunze, his grandson, also named Boris, protects a Jewish colleague who was falsely implicated in the Doctors' Plot, the infamous attacks on high-ranking Jewish physicians that many historians believe to have been intended as the beginning of a new round of purges on the level of the 1930's Great Terror, which was stopped only by Stalin's sudden death. Similarly, as Boris's son Kiril is haunted by pangs of conscience for having helped to suppress the Krondstadt rebellion, his son, also named Kiril, refuses to betray a group of Polish soldiers in World War II to whom he had promised safe passage. Although it may not be strictly realistic that so many members of a single family keep encountering high-ranking individuals at key turning points in history, this conceit permits Aksyonov to comment on these events more pungently than would be possible if he always kept the great actors of Soviet history strictly at arms' length, in the tradition of Sir Walter Scott's historical novels.

THE NEW SWEET STYLE

In 1997, Aksyonov published *The New Sweet Style*, the story of Aleksandr Iakovlevich Korbakh, a Russian émigré who rises from pushing drugs on the streets of Los Angeles to being a respected professor in Washington, D.C. Although there are certain autobiographical elements in this novel, Aksyonov plays fast and free with his character to create the literary effects he wants. In no way should any particular scene in the novel be seen as a confession of the author's personal history, although it is clear that Aksyonov's own experiences informed many of the scenes.

KESAREVO SVECHENIE

With the new millennium, Aksyonov returned to work that borders on science fiction. In *Kesarevo svechenie* he portrays a future in which his heroes wrest numerous wonderful inventions from the vaults of a greedy oil company that had hidden them away to protect its own profits. These inventions had been bought from their inventors and sequestered because they promise the generation of limitless clean, green power. Releasing them to the world brings the protagonists only a moral victory, however—not material rewards. In the final scenes, set sometime in the middle of the new century, they have become very old but are still too poor to afford a fully robotic home or lifesaving medical treatments; they have withered into miserable and ridiculous elders, tormented by their own frailties. They finally have clones made of themselves, and only when they themselves die do the clones finally attain the radiance of the original characters.

In a sense, Aksyonov himself came full circle as a writer in this work, returning to his original satirical roots, but for new reasons. In the old, repressive Soviet Union, satirical works set in fantastical worlds could often slip subtly political messages past the censors. In the post-Soviet world, where there are no longer official government censors, humor becomes a way to handle ideas that would be dismissed as mere conspiracy theory if they were presented as straight narrative. By taking the reader on a wild and delightful romp through an imaginary future, Aksyonov can slip a few heavy ideas past the reader's own internal censor.

D. Barton Johnson
Updated by Leigh Husband Kimmel

OTHER MAJOR WORKS

SHORT FICTION: *Katapulta*, 1964; *Na polputi k lune*, 1965; *Zhal, chto vas ne bylo s nami*, 1969; *The Steel Bird, and Other Stories*, 1979; *Pravo na ostrov*, 1983; *The Destruction of Pompeii, and Other Stories*, 1991; *Negativ polozhitel'nogo geroia*, 1996.

PLAYS: *Potselui, Orkestr, Ryba, Kolbasa . . .* , pb. 1964; *Vsegda v prodazhe*, pr. 1965; *Chetyre temperamenta*, pb. 1967 (*The Four Temperaments*, 1987); *Aristofaniana s lyagushkami*, pb. 1967-1968; *Vash ubiytsa*, pb. 1977 (*Your Murderer*, 1999); *Tsaplya*, pb. 1979 (*The Heron*, 1987); *Aristofaniana s lyagushkami: Sobranie pes*, 1981 (includes *Potselui, Orkestr, Ryba, Kolbasa . . .* , *Vsegda v prodazhe, Chetyre temperamenta, Aristofaniana s lyagushkami*, and *Tsaplya*).

NONFICTION: *Lyubov k elektrichestvu*, 1971 (biography); *Kruglye sutki: Non-stop*, 1976; *V poiskakh grustnogo bebi*, 1987 (*In Search of Melancholy Baby*, 1987).

EDITED TEXT: *Metropol: Literaturnyi almanakh*, 1979 (*Metropol: Literary Almanac*, 1982).

MISCELLANEOUS: *Quest for an Island*, 1987 (plays and short stories); *Sobranie sochinenii*, 1994- (works; 5 volumes).

BIBLIOGRAPHY

Dalgard, Per. *Function of the Grotesque in Vasilij Aksenov*. Translated by Robert Porter. Århus, Denmark: Arkona, 1982. Discusses how Aksyonov portrays commonplace things and events as grotesque or ridiculous, often as a method of social criticism.

Kustanovich, Konstantin. *The Artist and the Tyrant: Vassily Aksenov's Works in the Brezhnev Era*. Columbus, Ohio: Slavica, 1992. In-depth study examines how Aksyonov uses satirical and fantastical motifs to criticize the failings and evils of the Soviet regime. Includes analysis that compares motifs found in Aksyonov's plays with those in his prose works.

Lowe, David. "E. Ginzburg's *Krutoj marsrut* and V. Aksenov's *Ozog:* The Magadan Connection." *Slavic and East European Journal* 27 (Summer, 1983). Examines the biographical connections between Aksyonov's *The Burn* and his mother's account of her exile.

Matich, Olga. "Vasilii Aksyonov and the Literature of Convergence: *Ostrov Krym* as Self-

Criticism." *Slavic Review* 47, no. 4 (1988). Provides in-depth discussion of *The Island of Crimea*.

Mozejko, Edward, Boris Briker, and Peter Dalgård, eds. *Vasily Pavlovich Aksenov: A Writer in Quest of Himself.* Columbus, Ohio: Slavica, 1986. Collection of essays addresses various aspects of Aksyonov's writing, including his novels.

Proffer, Ellendea. "The Prague Winter: Two Novels by Aksyonov." In *The Third Wave: Russian Literature in Emigration*, edited by Olga Matich and Michael Heim. Ann Arbor, Mich.: Ardis, 1984. Essay focusing on *The Burn* and *The Island of Crimea* is part of a collection devoted to the works of Russian authors.

Simmons, Cynthia. *Their Fathers' Voice: Vassily Aksyonov, Venedikt Erofeev, Eduard Lemonov, and Sasha Sokolov.* New York: Peter Lang, 1994. Compares and contrasts the works of three leading writers of the post-Stalin generation.

SHOLOM ALEICHEM

Born: Pereyaslav, Russia (now Pereyaslav-Khmelnitsky, Ukraine); March 2, 1859
Died: New York, New York; May 13, 1916
Also known as: Sholom Naumovich Rabinowitz

Principal long fiction

Natasha, 1884
Sender Blank und zayn Gezindl, 1888
Yosele Solovey, 1890 (*The Nightingale,* 1985)
Stempenyu, 1899 (English translation, 1913)
Blondzne Shtern, 1912 (*Wandering Star,* 1952)
Marienbad, 1917 (English translation, 1982)
In Shturm, 1918 (*In the Storm,* 1984)
Blutiger Shpas, 1923 (*The Bloody Hoax,* 1991)

Other literary forms

Sholom Aleichem (ah-LAY-kehm) is best known for his short narratives, impressionistic sketches, and literary slices of life. The stories surrounding two of his characters—Tevye, the milkman, and Menahem-Mendl, the unsuccessful jack-of-all-trades—are frequently brought together in collections that form episodic but coherent wholes. The adventures of a third character, Mottel, the cantor's son, are sometimes published as young adult fiction, though divisions of Aleichem's audience according to age distinctions are artificial. Aleichem's stories have been published throughout Europe, in Israel, and in the United States. At least eight separate compilations are now available in English.

Some of Aleichem's writings, descriptions, or reactions to events and people are difficult to classify and are sometimes labeled simply "miscellany." Even his autobiography—*Fun'm yarid,* 1916 (*The Great Fair: Scenes from My Childhood,* 1955)—contains as much fantasy as fact. Although he had planned the book for many years, it was left incomplete at his death and covers only his youth.

Achievements

Sholom Aleichem is regarded as one of the founders of Yiddish literature and is perhaps the most beloved writer in that language. While his longer fiction adds little to the development of the novel, even these works demonstrate the strengths for which he is loved throughout the Jewish world. Although, like most educated East European Jews of his time, he began by writing in Hebrew, the language of sacred learning and of scholarship, he soon discovered that Yiddish was the proper vehicle for relating the exploits of people like those he had known in his youth. The wisdom, the humor, and even the foolishness of these folk could be fully captured only as they actually spoke. In his hands, this despised "jargon" became a vivid, lively, literary instrument. Fluent in the Russian language, and a correspondent with Leo Tolstoy and Anton Chekhov, Aleichem brought to Yiddish fiction the compassion for the insulted and injured that was such a dominant note in classic Russian fiction.

By the end of the twentieth century, Yiddish was spoken only in small pockets of the United States, East Europe, and Israel, and was spoken chiefly by older people. The Yiddish newspapers had almost disappeared, and the theater was preserved only as a relic. Though much of the humor was lost in translation, Aleichem's writing survived and reached large Gentile as well as Jewish audiences in English, Russian, Hebrew. and other languages. Aleichem's fictional characters were introduced to even wider audiences with the popularity of his Broadway musical *Fiddler on the Roof* (pr. 1964), adapted from his Tevye tales, and an operatic adaptation of the novel *The Nightingale* (music by Noam Elkies and libretto by Jeremy Dauber), which was performed at Harvard University in 1999.

Aleichem's central value, though, is his preservation in fiction of a milieu that has vanished, of a people dispersed through pogroms, immigration, revolution, assimilation, and the Holocaust. His books are populated by rabbis, cantors, religious teachers, and kheder students, and yet his books have social and political dimensions. The society of the shtetl (a small Jewish townlet) is already changing in these writings. Revolutionaries who identify themselves as Russians more than as Jews and seek to rid their lives of czars, bishops, and rabbinical tyrants alike begin to appear in his novels. Other characters dream of wealth in America, while Zionists preach a return to the land of their spiritual ancestors.

Along with a large continuing readership, Aleichem has received many posthumous honors, including, in his name, statues in Russia's Kiev and Moscow and a street in New York City. His likeness is also on postage stamps in East Europe and Israel. His home in Kiev is now a place of literary pilgrimage.

BIOGRAPHY

Sholom Aleichem was born Sholom Naumovich Rabinowitz in 1859 in Pereyaslav, Russia (now in Ukraine), to a family of means, although family fortunes fluctuated during his childhood as they did throughout his entire life. His family moved to Voronkov, a small town nearby, which would be the model for his fictional town of Kasrilevke. Even though he received a traditional Jewish religious education, his father was aware of his talents and made sure they were supplemented by training at a Russian secondary school.

Sholom was thirteen years old when his beloved mother died. According to Jewish custom, it was not long before he had a stepmother; in this case, she could have stepped from the tales of the Brothers Grimm. However, she inspired his first published Yiddish work, a dictionary of humorous curses commonly uttered by stepmothers.

Because of the precarious financial situation of his family, young Sholom accepted a position as a government rabbi, an elected but despised functionary who mediated between the czarist government and the Jewish community. Later he was able to find more congenial employment as tutor to Olga Loyeff, daughter of a wealthy Jewish family. Falling in love and fearing her father's disapproval, Aleichem and Loyeff eloped. Their marriage lasted until his death.

Around 1883, Sholom wrote a humorous sketch that appeared in a Yiddish paper under the pseudonym Sholom Aleichem, a Hebrew greeting meaning "Peace unto you." He used the pseudonym initially as an apology for not writing in Hebrew, but he would come to use this pen name exclusively, just as he would continue to write in Yiddish. As business concerns and stock-market speculation took him to cities such as Kiev, Odessa, Paris, and Vienna, his writing continued, with brief narratives, character sketches, extended anecdotes, and even poems. Also a skilled reader, he was soon in demand as a performer, reading his own stories.

As times became ever more difficult in the Pale of Settlement (the area of the czarist empire in which Jews were permitted to live), immigration to the United States became an attractive possibility. In 1905, a devastating pogrom in which many Jews perished convinced Aleichem to relocate his family to the United States, where he was widely read and the Yiddish theater promised a decent livelihood.

It was in his later years that Aleichem aspired to be a playwright. His ear for the rhythms of speech of many different personalities, along with his imaginative portrayal of different character types, would seem to have fitted his work for the stage. However, he had limited success in the American Yiddish theater.

Even as his sales mounted on two continents, Aleichem, who was not an especially skilled businessman, received limited royalties and often was compelled to earn his living with lectures and readings. Never fully at home in the United States, he died in New York City in 1916. Enormous crowds attended his funeral, acknowledging him as a folk hero. His plays met with some acclaim after his death.

ANALYSIS

Sholom Aleichem excelled in character development. The personalities of his protagonists unfold through their thoughts, desires, dreams, worries, and hopes; their interactions with others; and, most of all, through their speech. Their language—a lively, colloquial Yiddish—is rhythmic and rustically poetic. They curse one another, express affection, identify with animals, misquote Scripture, and misuse Talmudic lore, though, even in their innocent, or calculated, mangling of Scripture and tradition, they often reveal a higher folk wisdom.

Because Aleichem was basically a writer of short impressionistic sketches, it is difficult to diagram a clear plot in his narratives. He was largely indifferent to the literary architecture required of longer works. His novels, often picaresque, are therefore disjointed and episodic. He may introduce a character, leave him or her for several chapters, take up another character, and only later return to the first. The natural environment is rarely or only briefly described, yet the little towns and bustling cities through which his characters move come alive as they struggle to survive in whatever setting God has placed them.

The most famous Aleichem characters struggle with poverty, dream of what it would be like to be rich, and ultimately accept their plight. They are not, however, above arguing with the Deity. There is frequently a nearly magical, even mystical element in some of Aleichem's writing, which may reflect the influence of his grandfather, a Hasidic Jew and Kabbalistic mystic.

Preferring the epistolary narrative form or the monologue, Aleichem allows his protagonists to speak for themselves. Sometimes they address their unseen listener respectfully, but the author appears rarely to interfere with them. This encourages the reader to laugh with rather than at the characters so compassionately presented. In his novels, Aleichem appears to be telling rather than writing a story.

It has been customary to refer to Aleichem as the Jewish Mark Twain. There is a story, almost certainly apocryphal, of his meeting with the American humorist: When introduced, Twain is modestly rumored to have said "I understand that I am the American Sholom Aleichem." Certainly, in their use of first-person narrative, often in dialect, to individualize their fictional creations and bring out the humor of situations, the two are similar. They are alike in their kindly satire, as they comment on the foibles of society. However, Aleichem, as several critics have suggested, might more appropriately be compared to Charles Dickens, who displays, as does Aleichem, a stoic quality of writing and a "laughter through tears" humor.

IN THE STORM

An early short novel presented as if it were a two-act play, *In the Storm* is a story of three different families who live together at one address in Russia in 1905. In the background are revolution, pogroms, and riots. The characters try to cope through assimilation, religion, and rebellion against tradition. Jews of three different social classes further represent different economic orders. One family is headed by a prosperous businessman who bullies his way through the Jewish community; another father is a struggling druggist, trying to assimilate. The third head of household is a shoemaker, very conscious of his poverty. Although there is little sustained action, the novel is a fine mirror of its time and place.

STEMPENYU

Stempenyu, the novel's title character, is a fiddler, with the soul of an artist. He has made an unfortunate marriage to Friedl, a shrew. He meets the gentle Rachel, and the two fall in love. She, too, is unhappily married, to a rich young man who ignores her in his enthusiasm for Talmudic study. Stempenyu and Rachel meet only a few times, once significantly against a monastery wall, and their love is never consummated. Rachel's virtue is, in fact, rewarded, when her husband is exhorted by his mother that his family is as important as his religion. While the chief interest of the novel is its examination of Jewish life in the Pale of Settlement, with its arranged marriages, the narrative also enables Aleichem to express his rejection of sentimental romances and the adulterous tradition of "love in the Western world." In Jewish life, readers are reminded, love comes in marriage, not before or apart from it.

WANDERING STAR

Aleichem's final attempt at sustained fiction allowed him to express his opinion of actors, the Yiddish stage, and theatrical promoters. This novel is strung together by a thin love story about two youths who escape their oppressive homes to become wandering performers. The main interest of *Wandering Star*, however, resides in descriptions of the magic of theater, reflections on the differences between sacred and secular music, and a lively review of the history of Yiddish theater. Aleichem focuses on the theater's origins in Romania to its degeneration in New York City at the hands of impresarios more interested in money than in Jewish folk art.

THE BLOODY HOAX

The Bloody Hoax is a novel based on a real event, known as the Beiliss affair, in which a Ukrainian Jew was accused of a ritual murder in 1911. In Aleichem's recasting of events, two friends, one Jewish and the other Gentile, decide to exchange places in order to expand their experience of life. The Gentile boy initially encounters problems through his inability to speak Yiddish, but his trouble really begins with the surfacing of "the blood libel," an unfounded but pervasive accusation made against Jews in times of persecution. He is accused of using Gentile blood to make Passover bread. Despite its serious subject, the novel is marketed as a comedy, and it is especially notable in its treatment of Russian Jewish intellectuals and the Zionist movement at the beginning of the twentieth century.

Allene Phy-Olsen

OTHER MAJOR WORKS

SHORT FICTION: *Tevye der Milkhiger*, 1894-1914 (*Tevye's Daughters*, 1949; also known as *Tevye the Dairyman*); *Menakhem-Mendl*, 1895 (*The Adventures of Menachem-Mendl*, 1969); *Der farkishnefter Shnayder*, 1900 (*The Bewitched Tailor*, 1960); *Mottel, Peyse dem Khazns*, 1907-1916 (*The Adventures of Mottel, the Cantor's Son*, 1953); *Jewish Children*, 1920; *The Old Country*, 1946; *Inside Kasrilevke*, 1948; *Selected Stories of Sholom Aleichem*, 1956; *Stories and Satires*, 1959; *Old Country Tales*, 1966; *Some Laughter, Some Tears*, 1968; *Holiday Tales of Sholem Aleichem*, 1979; *The Best of Sholom Aleichem*, 1979 (Irving Howe and Ruth R. Wisse, editors); *Tevye the Dairyman and the Railroad Stories*, 1987; *The Further Adventures of Menachem-Mendl*, 2001.

PLAYS: *A Doktor*, pr. 1887 (*She Must Marry a Doctor*, 1916); *Yakenhoz*, pr. 1894; *Mazel Tov*, pr. 1904; *Tsuzeyt un Tsushpreyt*, pr. 1905; *Die Goldgreber*, pr. 1907; *Samuel*

Pasternak, pr. 1907; *Stempenyu*, pr. 1907; *Agenten*, pb. 1908; *Az Got Vil, Shist a Bezem*, pb. 1908; *Konig Pic*, pb. 1910; *Shver Tsu Zein a Yid*, pb. 1914; *Dos Groyse Gevins*, pb. 1915 (*The Jackpot*, 1989); *Menshen*, pb. 1919; *Der Get*, pr. 1924; *The World of Sholom Aleichem*, 1953; *Fiddler on the Roof*, pr. 1964.

NONFICTION: *Fun'm yarid*, 1916 (*The Great Fair: Scenes from My Childhood*, 1955); *Briefe von Scholem Aleichem und Menachem Mendl*, 1921.

BIBLIOGRAPHY
Butwin, Joseph, and Frances Butwin. *Sholom Aleichem*. Boston: Twayne, 1977. A general review of the life and work of Aleichem, with insightful descriptions of all major writings and critical reactions to them. Part of Twayne's World Authors series.

Halberstam-Rubin, Anna. *Sholom Aleichem: The Writer as Social Historian*. New York: Peter Lang, 1989. A scholarly consideration of Aleichem's reconstruction of his native East European Jewish community written as a background study for the Broadway production of *Fiddler on the Roof*.

Howe, Irving. *World of Our Fathers: The Journey of the East European Jews to America and the Life They Found and Made*. New York: Simon & Schuster, 1976. A thorough examination of East European Jewish immigrants in the United States, the role of Yiddish in their lives, and their love of the Yiddish theater and Yiddish writers. This is the world Aleichem entered in his later years.

Liptzin, Solomon. *A History of Yiddish Literature*. New ed. Middle Village, N.Y.: Jonathan David, 1985. A thorough survey of the entire sweep of Yiddish literature and Aleichem's dominant place within it. Especially helpful are the discussions of characteristic Yiddish humor and the problems of translation. Equally pertinent is the examination of the rise and ultimate decline of Yiddish as a language of literature, theater, and cultural exchange.

Samuel, Maurice. *The World of Sholom Aleichem*. New York: Random House, 1973. A readable reconstruction of the world about which Aleichem wrote, the towns and villages of the Jewish Pale of Settlement. Illustrations are taken from the writings of Aleichem, in a demonstration of the ways in which fiction can imaginatively recapture an actual time and place now vanished.

Silverman, Erica, and Mordicai Gerstein. *Sholom's Treasure: How Sholom Aleichem Became a Writer*. New York: Farrar, Straus and Giroux, 2005. An illustrated biography aimed at younger readers. Covers events of the author's early life, including his problems with a difficult stepmother and his fascination with Jewish folklore.

Waife-Goldberg, Marie. *My Father, Sholom Aleichem*. New York: Schocken Books, 1971. A loving, carefully prepared biography of the author by his youngest daughter. Waife-Goldberg discusses the reception of Aleichem's works, the fluctuations in his career, and his sometimes-precarious financial situation even after he became famous as a writer.

SHOLEM ASCH

Born: Kutno, Poland, Russian Empire (now in Poland); November 1, 1880
Died: London, England; July 10, 1957
Also known as: Szulim Asz; Shalom Ash

PRINCIPAL LONG FICTION

Dos Shtetl, 1905 (*The Little Town*, 1907)
Amerike, 1911 (*America*, 1918)
Motke Ganev, 1916 (*Mottke the Thief*, 1917)
Onkl Mozes, 1918 (*Uncle Moses*, 1920)
Kiddush Hashem, 1920 (English translation, 1926)
Toyt Urteyl, 1926 (*Judge Not*, 1938)
Khayim Lederers Tsurikkumen, 1927 (*Chaim Lederer's Return*, 1938)
Farn Mabul, 1927-1932 (*Three Cities*, 1933)
Der Tilim Yid, 1934 (*Salvation*, 1934)
Three Novels, 1938 (includes *Uncle Moses, Judge Not*, and *Chaim Lederer's Return*)
The Nazarene, 1939
The Apostle, 1943
Ist River, 1946 (*East River*, 1946)
Mary, 1949
Moses, 1951
Der Novi, 1955 (*The Prophet*, 1955)

OTHER LITERARY FORMS

Although Sholem Asch (ahsh) is remembered chiefly as a novelist, much of his early work consists of dramas. When *Der Got fun Nekome* (pr. 1907; *The God of Vengeance*, 1918) was performed on Yiddish stages in Russia and Poland, Max Reinhardt, who understood Yiddish, decided to produce it at the Deutsche Theater. This was the first time that a Yiddish work had appeared in the international literature. This play, in which a brothel owner purchases a Torah to place in his daughter's room, hoping it will protect her from the impurities in the apartment below, was widely condemned as sacrilegious. Many other dramas followed, including adaptations of such novels as *Mottke the Thief*, which enjoyed considerable success on Yiddish stages.

Asch also published *From Many Countries: The Collected Stories of Sholem Asch* (1958) and other collections of short fiction, as well as an autobiographical essay, *What I Believe* (1941), in which he reacted to criticism levied against him by the Jewish community.

Sholem Asch
(Library of Congress)

ACHIEVEMENTS

Until 1950, Sholem Asch was indisputably the best-known, most translated, most successful Yiddish writer. More than anyone before him, he managed to inject the Yiddish word into world culture, making the world aware of a major literature that had been unjustly ignored. This broader world sometimes seemed more kindly disposed to him than the segment of his Jewish readers who objected to his delineation of the seamier aspects of Jewish life in some works and to his sympathetic treatment of Christianity in others. The bulk of his Jewish readers remained faithful and recognized in him a lover of the poor and weak, a God-seeker, a gentle soul keenly aware that humans did not live by bread alone.

In spite of his high regard for Christianity, Asch remained faithful to Jewish life and tradition, acutely aware of the anti-Semitism all around him. While his characters accept this intolerance as a fact of life, Asch himself could not always assume the same stance. He returned a medal awarded to him by the Polish government when he realized that the policies of that government permitted a heightened anti-Jewish feeling.

A student of the revered I. L. Peretz, whose influence he acknowledged as late as 1951, Asch went beyond the teachings of this master and dealt with topics that Yiddish literature had theretofore avoided. His work marks an abandonment of the rational ways that the Jewish enlightenment had made obligatory for Jewish writers. Like Isaac Bashevis Singer, who replaced him as _the_ Yiddish writer on the world stage, Asch was attracted to folkloristic and irrational elements. Because of the diversity of his oeuvre, critics have found it difficult to classify Asch. There is the Romantic who idealized the life of simple

Jews and insisted on the primacy of tradition and faith in faith; there is the naturalist who brilliantly depicted the milieus of thieves, jugglers, and prostitutes; there is the didactic moralist who strove to teach the meaning of the good life. There is even a hint of the publicist who fought Hitlerite anti-Semitism by underscoring the basic nobility of Jewish existence and demonstrating the common bonds uniting Judaism and Christianity. This very multiplicity suggests Asch's enduring appeal.

BIOGRAPHY

The tenth child of a pious and prosperous Hasid, Sholem Asch underwent an early formal education in Hebrew language and literature, especially the Bible. His progress indicated sufficient promise for his father to entertain hopes for him in a rabbinic career. As a teenager, Asch came upon his first secular book and became "enlightened." He found employment as a scribe, writing letters for the illiterate, which likely gave him unique insights into the human psyche. At the same time, he was teaching himself German, Russian, and Polish and reading whatever books by major writers became available to him.

At the age of sixteen, Asch visited Peretz, whose stories he had admired, and requested that the master comment on his own efforts, which he was then writing in Hebrew. Peretz liked what he read but urged the youngster to change to Yiddish. Asch's first story, "Moshele," appeared in *Der Jud* in late 1900. A collection of Hebrew stories published in 1902 was followed in 1903 by another in Yiddish. (His writing then, as later, was colored by the dark and dingy places in which he had lived and the hunger he had suffered and which he was never to forget.) Asch married Mathilda Shapiro, the daughter of a teacher and minor poet. In 1904, he serialized his "poem in prose" *The Little Town* in *Der Freint*; in 1905, it was published as a book that quickly established him at the forefront of Yiddish writers.

Asch visited Palestine in 1907 and the United States in 1909. He was awed by biblical sites in Palestine and the evidence of Jewish and Christian events. In America, the landscapes impressed him, but he was repelled by the sweatshops, the tenements, and the quality of the life he observed.

In the ten years preceding World War I, Asch completed ten plays. He lived mostly in France but was forced to leave upon the outbreak of the conflict. In addition to *Mottke the Thief*, his wartime writing, emanating mostly from New York City, included *Uncle Moses*, a novel of immigrants in their initial years in New York.

After the war, Asch revisited Eastern Europe as the representative of a Jewish relief agency. He was horrified by the slaughter of Jews at the hands of Cossacks and White Russians. What he saw reminded him of a seventeenth century Ukrainian slaughterer of Jews whose soldier-peasants terrorized the countryside. The result was the first of his historical novels, *Kiddush Hashem* (sanctification of the name).

In the words of Sol Liptzin, Asch in the postwar years continued "glorifying Jewish deeds of brotherly love and quiet heroism." Before Adolf Hitler rose to power, Asch believed that contrasting such quiet deeds of Jews with the crude Hitlerite reliance on force would be his way of fighting the Nazi menace. *Salvation*, written in 1932, was the most spiritual novel he wrote, and he was embittered by its poor reception.

Asch's spiritual orientation, accompanied by the desire to strengthen the Jewish position, led to novels on Jesus (*The Nazarene*), Paul (*The Apostle*), and Mary (*Mary*). These works alienated his Jewish readers, who feared a case of apostasy at a time when Hitler was decimating European Jewry. *The Nazarene* was published in English before a Yiddish publisher would touch it. The controversy continued for nearly a decade. The resilience of European Jews and the establishment of a Jewish state tore Asch out of his isolation and prompted him to turn to *Moses*, which he had begun long before and had laid aside in favor of his Christian novels.

In 1954, having lived in the United States and France, Asch settled permanently in Israel, where he wrote *The Prophet* (1955). As the chronicler of a world that had disappeared, Asch became again an object of admiration—a condition that his insatiable ego demanded. In 1957, he suffered a mild stroke. While in London for an operation, he died before surgery could be performed.

ANALYSIS

Nearly all of Sholem Asch's works are related, in a broad sense, to some religious concern. His many themes are clearly intertwined: the simple, traditional life of the Jew; saintliness in the quest for God and service to humans; the ugliness of poverty but the distinct possibility of meaningful beauty even in poverty; the emptiness of a purely material existence; the Jewish roots of Christianity and the need to close the gap between the two faiths. In fact, faith in both its meanings—trust in God and different institutionalized ways of reaching Him—is a thread running through all of Asch's works, but especially his later works.

THE LITTLE TOWN

Even in his first major work, *The Little Town*, Asch had romanticized the inwardness of Jewish life in the shtetl, a different approach from the ridicule usually heaped upon the backward enclaves in literature. Asch perceived nobility and charm in the poverty-ridden, filth-infested shtetl.

Similarly, Asch dealt with spiritual and sacrificial heroism before dealing with it directly in *Kiddush Hashem*. Living far out in the Padolian steppe, a Jewish innkeeper, Mendel, dreams of the day when other Jews will join him in the town and enable him to build a synagogue and lead a Jewish existence. Mendel eventually overcomes the threats of the local priest, and a small but flourishing Jewish community comes into being. Mendel and the congregation are dangerously sandwiched between the machinations of the Catholic priest and the Greek Orthodox priest. The former is intent on humbling the latter. What better means of debasing his rival than to force him to go to the Jew Mendel to obtain the key to his own church? In his frustration, the Orthodox priest threatens Mendel: Sooner or later "the little brothers" will come to liberate the peasants from the Polish lords and the filthy Jews.

The little brothers eventually come, under the leadership of Bogdan Chmelnitzky, and lay waste not only to Mendel's but also to every Jewish community far and wide. Mendel's attachment to his synagogue is such that he refuses to leave, but the rabbi reminds him that the synagogue is only stone, while a human life is a human life. Mendel's Jews flee, joining the stream of refugees; they put up a heroic fight with virtually no weapons. They are finally conquered through the betrayal of the Polish lords, who are only too willing to sacrifice their Jewish allies in the mistaken belief that they can thereby save themselves.

Through Mendel and his family, which includes a learned son and his beautiful wife, Asch depicts the simplicity and piety of Jewish life and the Jews' willingness to live and die for "the sanctification of the name." Jews are offered a chance to save their lives by bowing before the Cross, but they will bow only before their one and only God. All resist the easy way out, sacrificially preferring to suffer cruelty, death, and martyrdom. Although the body may be destroyed, the will and spirit are indestructible. Asch only implies that the Jews' imperishable faith in God has ensured their survival in the past and will ensure it in the future.

Charles Madison has stated that "Asch's compassionate brooding gives the tragic tale the poignant quality of imaginative truth." This critic has also distinguished between two forms of martyrdom—Mendel's, which is not a pure martyrdom in that it is wholly passive, and his daughter-in-law's, which is active: She persuades the Cossack captor who loves her that he should shoot her, on the pretense that no bullet can hurt her.

KIDDUSH HASHEM

Kiddush Hashem is perhaps Asch's only novel in which religious motifs and Jewish historical destiny, especially the Jews' suffering for their survival as a group, fuse successfully. The structure of the novel, on the other hand, is awkward, which prevents it from becoming the masterpiece it might have been.

MOTTKE THE THIEF

If *The Little Town* and *Kiddush Hashem* are, to use Liptzin's words, in a Sabbath mood, *Mottke the Thief* is decidedly workaday. Asch abandons the idealized Jews of earlier works to offer such sad human specimens as Blind Layb and Red Slatke, Mottke's parents. Layb is a vicious, irresponsible father whose only guidance to his child is the lash, which he uses freely and cruelly. Not only is Jewish life imperfect in *Mottke the Thief*, in spite of some obedience to forms and tradition, but it also exists on the lowest levels of humanity. Asch shows an exceptional virtuosity in this novel. The first half combines picaresque with gargantuan, larger-than-life features; the second half is Zolaesque in its depressing naturalism. The abused Mottke, first open enough to seek affection even from a curious dog, is transformed into a callous pimp and murderer, a development that calls for considerable skill, which Asch demonstrates in good measure.

Asch's earlier work might have given rise to the impression that there was something do-goodish in the writer, that his feet were not firmly planted on the ground. With the creation of Mottke, this impression was swept aside. From the moment Mottke joins a group of vaudevillians, uses and abuses them, seduces or is seduced by Mary, the rope dancer, and competes with the treacherous Kanarik, he becomes a character apart from any that Asch had previously created. The erstwhile thief's descent into total depravity continues. With Mary's help, he kills Kanarik, assumes Kanarik's identity, and acquires his own small staff of prostitutes. Yet the Mottke who had once enjoyed something of a Jewish upbringing, however atypical, is not wholly dead. He is fatally attracted to a decent girl, and his love generates decent impulses that have long been submerged. The desire for chastity, piety, and living in the love of and reverence for God, however, has been resurrected too late. Perhaps Mottke's conversion, which comes to naught, is not the most persuasive part of the book; in any case, Mottke is betrayed by the sweet girl he loves. Yet even in the novel's variety of depressing settings, Asch still emerges as a man with a profound faith in faith.

SALVATION

Salvation, a story of the saintly Jekhiel and his quest for God and ways of serving humanity, is more in the mainstream of Asch's fiction than is *Mottke the Thief*. It is probably the most purely "spiritual" of Asch's novels—a term he himself used to describe it—and he attributed its relative failure with the reading public to the refusal of the modern world to address spiritual questions.

Jekhiel's father was a Hasid who left his wife and younger son to join his rabbi in study. Jekhiel was a deep disappointment to him, for, unlike Jekhiel's older brother, Jekhiel has failed to grasp the subtleties of the Talmud. Jekhiel, oppressed by a sense of failure, helps his mother eke out a bare living in the marketplace. She dies, and the youngster serves as tutor to an innkeeper's children, to whom he teaches the elements of the Hebrew language. Jekhiel is heartened one day by a wise stranger, who tells him that knowing the Psalms, with their simple yet warm teachings, is every bit as important in the sight of God as the subtle shadings of talmudic disputation. Soon Jekhiel is known as the Psalm-Jew (which was, indeed, the original Yiddish title of the novel).

In this first half of *Salvation*, Asch poses several questions, to which his answers are clear. He is not enamored of the father, who puts study—however strong an ethic in Jewish tradition—ahead of his familial obligations; Asch does not place learning the Talmud above simpler aspects of the Jewish obligation to ponder the ways of God. A cold, rational approach to religion attracts him less than a warmer, human, perhaps less rational mode.

Jekhiel, without wishing it, develops a following of his own, becoming the rabbi of the Psalms, simple and humble. He is also known for miracles, for which, however, he claims no credit. On one occasion, Jekhiel, under great pressure, commits God to giving a child to a hitherto barren woman. A girl is born. When Jekhiel's wife dies shortly thereafter, the pious rabbi sees it as a sign from Heaven. He leaves home and, in the manner of ascetic saints of all faiths, roams the countryside in rags. He is finally recognized and forced to return.

The years pass, and the girl whose birth he had promised has grown to maturity and fallen in love with a strapping young Polish soldier. They plan to marry. In preparation for her conversion to Catholicism, she enters a convent. There is consternation in the girl's family. Torn by conflicting pressures, the girl jumps to her death. Jekhiel, who had fought the conversion, is troubled for the second time: Has he overstepped proper bounds again? Was not human life and the search for God more precious than the particular way of reaching Him: the Jewish or the Christian?

Asch's implied tolerance of intermarriage again brought him into conflict with his Jewish readers. *Salvation* paved the way for a work that would nearly lead to a rupture with these readers: the story of Jesus of Nazareth, whose emphases within Judaism were not that different from those of Jekhiel the Psalm-Jew.

THE NAZARENE

The problem of Christian anti-Semitism is omnipresent in the oeuvre of Sholem Asch. Considering the author's vision of Jesus, an extension of his characterization of Jekhiel, it is not surprising that Asch often felt bitter about the crimes against Jews committed in the name of the saintly Nazarene. Throughout *The Nazarene*, Asch has his Rabbi Jeshua repeat that he has not come to destroy the Law but to fulfill it. Jeshua observes all but one or two of the ritual commandments, but it is his failure to observe those that his wealthy detractors use against him. Asch's Jesus is learned in the Torah; the character appears to be depicted in the tradition of the great teacher Hillel; he has infinite wisdom and compassion. If, in spite of its strengths, *The Nazarene* fails to satisfy completely, that failure must be attributed to the nature of the subject.

Jeshua as a man, as a self-revealed Messiah, and as a Son of Man (interpreted to mean the Son of God) is a difficult fusion to achieve. Asch is as successful as any novelist who has ever attempted it or, for that matter, biographers and interpreters. There are times, however, when Jeshua, ever mysterious—now very human, now very enigmatic, even furtive—suggests ever so slightly the religious charlatan. Yet this was far from Asch's intent and has not been the impression of all readers.

Jeshua's teachings are within the frame of Jewish tradition, but as he himself says, the fulfillment of that tradition requires new interpretations and emphases. The occasional impressions of hucksterism are held only by the more cynical modern reader, reacting to Jesus' refusal to answer questions directly, to speak in parables only, to select carefully his moments of healing and revealing, to satisfy the doubts of the most searching and spiritually avid of his disciples and admirers. Rabbi Jeshua has a talent for the grand gesture and for the attention-getting phrase or figure of speech, but this image is not one created by Asch; it is, rather, inherent in the subject matter, which he derives entirely from New Testament sources. There are few famous sayings of Jesus that are not quoted, and the endless quotations, although necessary, at times slow the pace of the narrative.

Asch underscores the innovations of the teachings of Jesus: compassion for the poor, the sick, the neglected; the emphasis on the spirit, not the forms, of observance; the primacy of faith; a piety that adds to fervor of the divine humility and an all-encompassing pity; and an involvement in the affairs of humans. Jesus attacks privilege, be it hereditary or earned. The task of involving oneself in the suffering of others must be never-ending; it must lead to the more fortunate assisting those who are suffering. Rabbi Jeshua's leniency toward the sinner, reassurance of the untutored and ignorant, and forbearance vis-à-vis those who have disappointed him all contribute to making him an innovative teacher and preacher. In the end, Jeshua dies, like so many of Asch's noble characters, for the sanctification of the name.

Asch was attracted to the story of Jesus on an early trip to Palestine, but he did not turn to writing it until decades later, when the need for closer Jewish-Christian ties seemed to him highly desirable. The device he finally employed for telling it was ingenious: A half-demented anti-Semitic Polish scholar, imagining that he was Pontius Pilate's right-hand man, relates the first third of the novel. Judas Ischariot, Jesus' most learned disciple, whom Asch rehabilitates in the novel, tells the next third in the form of a diary. The final third, recounted by a Jewish disciple of Nicodemus, a rabbi sympathetic to Jeshua, reports on the political and religious evasions within the Sanhedrin and Pilate's desire to rid himself of the troublemaking revolutionary.

Again, Asch displays his mastery of painting different milieus. The messianic craving among lowly and wealthy Jews, the Roman cynicism toward this strangest of peoples, the Jews, the doings in the Temple, the political rivalries between priests and scholars, the evocation of historical figures, the atmosphere of Jesus' preaching and reception in Galilee—all come alive in Asch's prose. If Rabbi Jeshua is only partly convincing, it is because his dual status as man and Messiah may well elude even the most skillful of writers.

EAST RIVER

Set on New York's East Side, another radically different milieu, *East River* is hardly one of Asch's better novels. The writing, even the syntax, appears a bit sloppy, and the work bears the marks of haste. The novel does, however, pull together many of Asch's most typical themes and interests: the poor sorely tried, and not by poverty alone; one son given to learning, the other to practical pursuits; traditional Jewish religious learning transformed into secular equivalents; anti-Semitism and the need for Jewish-Christian dialogue; the spirit of a religion versus its mere forms. Intermarriage, which unleashed a minor religious war between contending religious leaders in *Salvation*, is treated here with sympathy and understanding.

To be sure, Moshe Wolf, symbol of the old life, cannot reconcile himself to his wealthy son's intermarriage, but neither can he accept—in spite of, or because of, his own poverty—this son's exploitation of Jewish and Christian workers. Wolf, a near saint, accepts with love and understanding the burdens imposed on him by God: his beloved older son's crippling polio, this son's failure to use his dazzling intelligence to study Scripture, applying it instead to secular ideas, which often frighten the traditional Jew in him. Wolf's wife, Deborah, thoroughly Americanized, has more understanding for the tycoon son than for the "cripple." For her, the former has succeeded; the latter, with his superfluous learning, is useless.

The Catholic girl who originally loved the cripple but then married the tycoon is treated sympathetically and is ultimately accepted by Wolf as a God-loving, God-seeking human being. Mary breaks with her pathologically anti-Semitic failure of a father and leads her husband back to the ways of decency and righteousness. Mary's relationships with her father and husband are not credible and detract seriously from any power the novel might have. Yet for whatever it is worth, Mary convinces her husband not to live only for himself or even his immediate family, but to enlist himself in the war against poverty, injustice, and cruelty. The old lesson is repeated here in less subtle form: Humans do not live by bread, or money, alone.

Asch's daring in tackling milieus that cannot have been close to him is admirable: a grocery store, Tammany Hall, sweatshops, synagogue politics, Jewish-Irish relations, the garment industry. It is interesting to speculate what this book would have been like at the height of Asch's literary power. A courageous failure, it testifies to the profoundly ecumenical spirit of his fiction.

Lothar Kahn

OTHER MAJOR WORKS

SHORT FICTION: *From Many Countries: The Collected Stories of Sholem Asch*, 1958.
PLAYS: *Tsurikgekumen*, pr. 1904; *Der Got fun Nekome*, pr. 1907 (*The God of Vengeance*, 1918).
NONFICTION: *What I Believe*, 1941; *One Destiny: An Epistle to the Christians*, 1945.

BIBLIOGRAPHY

Brodwin, Stanley. "History and Martyrological Tragedy: The Jewish Experience in Sholem Asch and Andre Schwarz." *Twentieth Century Literature* 40 (1994): 72-91. An excellent comparative analysis of Asch's novel *Kiddush Hashem* and Andre Schwarz-Bart's *Le Dernier des justes*. The novels focus on the biblical injunction of *Kiddish hashem*, in which both the Jewish individual and the Jewish community are called upon to sanctify the name of God by suffering martyrdom.
Fischthal, Hannah Berliner. "Christianity as a Consistent Area of Investigation of Sholem Asch's Works Prior to *The Nazarene*." *Yiddish* 9 (1994): 58-76. Focuses on how Asch

treated Christianity in the works he wrote prior to *The Nazarene*, his controversial 1939 novel based on the life of Jesus Christ.

Lieberman, Herman. *The Christianity of Sholem Asch*. New York: Philosophical Library, 1953. Lieberman, a columnist for the Yiddish-language newspaper *Forward*, provides a scathing denunciation of *The Nazarene*, claiming that Asch's novel about the life of Jesus "may lure away ignorant Jewish children into worshipping foreign gods."

Norich, Anita. *Discovering Exile: Yiddish and Jewish American Culture During the Holocaust*. Stanford, Calif.: Stanford University Press, 2007. Studies the writings of Asch and other Jewish authors who published works in both Yiddish and English during the Holocaust to demonstrate how the Yiddish- and English-speaking worlds of the 1930's and 1940's drew upon each other for inspiration.

Siegel, Ben. *The Controversial Sholem Asch: An Introduction to His Fiction*. Bowling Green, Ohio: Bowling Green State University Press, 1976. Often cited as the best introduction to Asch's life and work, this book is especially good for its examination of the controversy that followed the publication of *The Nazarene*. Includes a chronology, bibliography, and detailed index.

Slochower, Harry. "Franz Werfel and Sholem Asch: The Yearning for Status." In *No Voice Is Wholly Lost: Writers and Thinkers in War and Peace*. New York: Creative Age Press, 1945. This essay is another good comparative analysis to be read in conjunction with that of Stanley Brodwin.

Stahl, Nanette, ed. *Sholem Asch Reconsidered*. New Haven, Conn.: Beinecke Rare Book and Manuscript Library, Yale University, 2004. Reprints lectures delivered at a conference held at Yale in 2000, in which Yiddish literary critics reevaluated Asch's work. Includes a discussion of his christological novels, plays, and American fiction, as well as his novels dealing with the radical change and dislocation experienced by European Jews at the beginning of the twentieth century. Also includes an overview of Asch's life by his great-grandson, David Mazower.

Steinberg, Theodore. L. "Sholem Asch's *Three Cities*." In *Twentieth-Century Epic Novels*. Newark: University of Delaware Press, 2005. Steinberg analyzes *Three Cities* and four novels by other authors to demonstrate how the novels' themes and contents, especially their heroic elements, qualify them as modern epics.

MIKHAIL BULGAKOV

Born: Kiev, Ukraine, Russian Empire; May 15, 1891
Died: Moscow, Russia, Soviet Union (now in Russia); March 10, 1940
Also known as: Mikhail Afanasyevich Bulgakov

<small>PRINCIPAL LONG FICTION</small>

Belaya gvardiya, 1927, 1929 (2 volumes; *The White Guard*, 1971)
Teatralny roman, 1965 (*Black Snow: A Theatrical Novel*, 1967)
Master i Margarita, 1966-1967 (uncensored version, 1973; *The Master and Margarita*, 1967)
Sobache serdtse, 1968 (novella; wr. 1925; reliable text, 1969; *The Heart of a Dog*, 1968)

<small>OTHER LITERARY FORMS</small>

Mikhail Bulgakov (bewl-GAH-kuhf) wrote some thirty-six plays, of which eleven were published and eight performed during his lifetime. His writings for theater and film include adaptations from Miguel de Cervantes, Molière, Charles Dickens, Nikolai Gogol, and Leo Tolstoy. Only one of the opera libretti Bulgakov composed for the Bolshoi Theater, *Rachel* (wr. 1938, pr. 1947), based on a story by Guy de Maupassant, was ever produced. Among his more notable plays made available in English during the 1960's and 1970's are *Adam i Eva* (pb. 1971; *Adam and Eve*, 1971), *Dni Turbinykh* (pr. 1926; *Days of the Turbins*, 1934), *Beg* (pr. 1957; *Flight*, 1969), *Zoykina kvartira* (pr. 1926; *Zoya's Apartment*, 1970), *Ivan Vasilievich* (pb. 1965; English translation, 1974), and *Posledniye dni (Pushkin)* (pr. 1943; *The Last Days*, 1976). Bulgakov also wrote numerous short stories, many of them collected in the volumes titled *Diavoliada* (1925; *Diaboliad, and Other Stories*, 1972), *Zapiski iunogo vracha* (1963; *A Country Doctor's Notebook*, 1975), and *Traktat o zhilishche* (1926; *A Treatise on Housing,* 1972). He also published miscellaneous journalism. Bulgakov's close identification with the life of Molière produced one of his most interesting plays, *Kabala svyatosh* (pr. 1936; *A Cabal of Hypocrites*, 1972; also known as *Molière*), as well as a novelistic biography, *Zhizn gospodina de Molyera* (1962; *The Life of Monsieur de Molière*, 1970).

<small>ACHIEVEMENTS</small>

Some twenty-five years after his death, Mikhail Bulgakov began to receive increasing recognition—both in the Soviet Union and abroad—as a major figure in modern Russian literature. *The Master and Margarita* is a complex, ambitious masterpiece that has won an intensely loyal readership and much critical scrutiny since its first serialized publication in 1966-1967. This novel's posthumous success in turn began to direct attention to Bulgakov's other neglected works.

The hazards of cultural life under Soviet leader Joseph Stalin frustrated Bulgakov's aspirations in prose fiction, where he did his finest work, and channeled him into the theater, where, though productive, he was probably temperamentally out of place. Bulgakov's narratives combine acute, if perforce oblique, social analysis with a strain of playful fantasy. Beyond the deprivation, hypocrisy, and cruelty of contemporary Soviet life, his Horatian satires suggest a transcendent spiritual force. In *The Master and Margarita* and *The White Guard*, it is tender devotion to a beautiful, mysterious woman that represents the apocalyptic possibility of overcoming an oppressive present existence. *Black Snow* offers the advice that "you have to love your characters. If you don't, I don't advise anybody to try writing; the result is bound to be unfortunate." This sentimental belief in the liberating power of love—of characters for one another, of author for reader—is tempered by terminal melancholia. In the imperfect world portrayed by Bulgakov, those in power are never graced with imagination, though they must be humored, but it is the power of imagination and of humor that lifts the reader beyond the tyranny of the quotidian.

There is at least an allusion to Faust in almost all of Bulgakov's books, where the quest for an elusive truth becomes an explicit and central theme. Bulgakov's work frequently foregrounds itself, calling attention to its own formal inventions in the service of a sense of values against which the elaborate structures of society and art seem petty and transient indeed.

BIOGRAPHY

Mikhail Afanasyevich Bulgakov, the eldest of seven children, was born in Kiev on May 15, 1891, into a family that was both devout and intellectual. His father, who died when Mikhail was sixteen, was a professor of divinity at the Kiev Theological Academy. Bulgakov developed an early interest in music and the theater, but he pursued a medical degree at Kiev University. In 1913, he married Tatyana Nikolaevna Lappa, and in 1916 he graduated with distinction as a doctor. He subsequently served as a military doctor in remote village hospitals, settings that were to provide the material for the stories in *A Country Doctor's Notebook*. The isolation depressed him, and he attempted to obtain his release, only succeeding in 1918 after the Bolshevik Revolution.

Bulgakov returned to Kiev to establish a private practice in venereology and dermatology. During this time, the tense atmosphere of which is re-created in *The White Guard*, Kiev was a battleground for the Germans, the Ukrainian nationalists, the Bolsheviks, and the Whites. In November, 1919, Bulgakov fled south to the Caucasian town of Vladikavkaz. While he was confined to bed with typhus, Vladikavkaz was captured by the Bolsheviks. He abandoned the practice of medicine and began devoting himself entirely to writing.

In 1921, Bulgakov moved to Moscow, where, amid general hardship, he attempted to support himself and his wife through a variety of literary and journalistic jobs. In 1924, he divorced Tatyana and married Lyubov Yevgenievna Belozerskaya. Soon thereafter, with the publication of satiric stories later collected in *Diavoliada*, Bulgakov began achieving some recognition and was able to abandon the newspaper work he detested. The publication, in 1925, of parts of *The White Guard*, based on his experiences in Kiev during the civil war, dramatically changed his life in ways recounted in the autobiographical novel *Black Snow*. Bulgakov's work came to the attention of the producers of the Moscow Art Theater, and he was asked to adapt *The White Guard* for the stage. The result, after considerable revision, was *Days of the Turbins*, which opened in October, 1926, to intense, polarized reaction. Bulgakov was harshly attacked for portraying the opponents of Bolshevism too sympathetically, but the play proved enormously popular. During its lengthy run, Stalin himself saw it fifteen times.

A sudden celebrity, Bulgakov continued writing plays, but by the end of the decade, as Soviet cultural and political life became severely repressive, his works were banned, and his financial position deteriorated. Near despair, he sent letters in 1930 to Soviet officials complaining of the campaign of vilification against him and his inability to get his work accepted. Stalin's personal intercession resulted in Bulgakov's appointment as a producer at the Moscow Art Theater. His subsequent years in the theater were productive but frustrating, in part because of friction with the flamboyant director Konstantin Stanislavsky, whose production of *A Cabal of Hypocrites* in 1936 led Bulgakov to resign in disgust from the Moscow Art Theater. For the remainder of his life, he was employed by the Bolshoi Theater as librettist and consultant.

In 1929, Bulgakov had begun a clandestine love affair with Elena Sergeyevna Shilovskaya, wife of the chief of staff of the Moscow Military District. In 1932, after both succeeded in obtaining divorces, they were married, and Bulgakov adopted Elena's five-year-old son, Sergey. Bulgakov's happiness with and devotion to his third wife, to whom he, with failing eyesight, probably dictated *Black Snow* in 1939, are reflected in *The Master and Margarita*. The earliest version of the latter was begun as early as 1928, but Bulgakov destroyed that manuscript in 1929. He continued refining a revised version until his death, in Moscow, on March 10, 1940.

After Bulgakov's death, the official attitude toward his work in the Soviet Union ranged from indifference to hostility, and very few of his writings remained available. During the brief thaw in Soviet cultural repression following Stalin's death, a commission was established to rehabilitate Bulgakov's reputation, and by the late 1960's most of his major works were being published in the Soviet Union for the first time.

ANALYSIS

Mikhail Bulgakov never took advantage of the opportunity to flee Russia during the revolution and its turbulent aftermath, and his fiction is very much a product of Russian life during the first two decades of the Soviet regime. Bulgakov's social commentary is not oblique enough to have averted the ire and the proscription of powerful contemporaries, or to keep later readers from recognizing the quality of roman à clef in much of what he wrote. The key, however, is not simply in details of his own biography—friends, adversaries, and a pet cat persistently transposed into a fictional realm. More important, it is in his ability to render the plight of the creative individual in a system designed to subdue him. Within the carefully limned landscapes of modern Kiev and Moscow, Bulgakov's characters dramatize the limitations and hubris of temporal human power. His books, then, are not merely the frustrated effusions of an author encountering formidable obstacles to his ambitions, nor are they merely perceptive analyses of the kind of community Stalinist social engineering was begetting. Beyond Bulgakov's contempt for contemporary mischief is a veritably religious sense of a universal spiritual force and a conviction that *sic transit gloria mundi*. *The White Guard* thus concludes on a consoling note: "Everything passes away—suffering, pain, blood, hunger and pestilence." It is this spiritual perspective that endows Bulgakov's narratives with more than a parochial sociological or historical interest.

The tone of melancholy that suffuses Bulgakov's works is a consequence of the futility he sees in the artist's struggle against the mighty of this world, and most of his sympathetic characters are more than half in love with easeful death. Creativity, love, and good humor do, nevertheless, triumph. To reduce Bulgakov's fictions to the bare formula of a struggle between sensitivity and brutishness and between eternity and the moment is to miss the mournful exuberance of his *comédies larmoyantes*. Not only *Black Snow*, the subtitle of which proclaims it, but also Bulgakov's other books are theatrical novels. The spirited play of a harried author drawn to and disappointed by the theater, they employ self-conscious devices, such as apostrophes to the reader, impudent violations of verisimilitude, and encased narratives, to enact a liberation not only from the oppressive worlds they depict but also from the literary instrument of emancipation itself. *Black Snow* concludes with a deflationary fictional afterword, and it is night on the final pages of *The White Guard*, *The Master and Margarita*, and *The Heart of a Dog*. Like William Shakespeare's *The Tempest* (pr. 1611) abjuring its own magic, Bulgakov's novels provide bittersweet crepuscular valediction to the powers of temporal authority and to the verbal artifices that their inventive author assembles.

THE WHITE GUARD

Bulgakov's first novel, and the only one to be published (at least in part) in his lifetime, *The White Guard* is set in Kiev in the winter of 1918. It is the moment at which the hetman Pavel Petrovich Skoropadsky, who has ruled with the support of the Germans, flees the city, and the forces of the Ukrainian nationalist Semyon Petlyura prove temporarily triumphant over Whites and Bolsheviks. *The White Guard* is a polyphonic arrangement of a variety of characters and incidents within a brief, dramatic period in the history of modern Kiev. Its focus, however, is on the fate of one family, the Turbins, representative of a venerable way of life that is disintegrating as Ukrainian society undergoes radical change.

The Turbin children have recently buried their mother, and twenty-eight-year-old

Alexei, a physician, his twenty-four-year-old sister Elena, and their seventeen-year-old brother Nikolka, a student, attempt to maintain family traditions and values, which are those of a comfortable Russian intellectual home. Public events make this impossible, however, and the collapse of the kind of humane civilization that the Turbin family exemplifies—with which Bulgakov, whose background was similar, is, despite the censor, sympathetic—is inevitable with the victory of Petlyura's troops.

Captain Sergey Talberg, the opportunistic scoundrel to whom Elena is married, abandons her to seek safety and another woman in Paris. The hetman, in the cowardly disguise of a German officer, likewise deserts Kiev at its moment of greatest danger. Nevertheless, Alexei and Nikolka, along with many others, enlist in the loyalist army in a futile effort to repulse Petlyura's advance into the city. Bulgakov depicts a range of heroism and knavery on all sides during the months of crisis in Kiev. The narrative weaves multiple subplots of combat and domestic drama into a vivid account of an obsolescent society under siege.

Through it all, the Turbin house, number 13 St. Alexei's Hill, remains for the family and its friends a fragile sanctuary. Nikolka barely escapes the violence, and Alexei, who is wounded, miraculously survives battle and an attack of typhus with the gracious assistance of a mysterious beauty named Julia Reiss. Despite the grim situation, gentle comic relief is provided by characters such as the miserly neighbor Vasilisa and the benevolent bumpkin Lariosik, who comes to stay with his relatives, the Turbins.

The apocalyptic tone of *The White Guard* is supported by religious allusions, particularly to the biblical book of Revelation. The music for the opera *Faust* remains open on the Turbin piano from the beginning of the novel to its end, and the reader is reminded of enduring values that transcend the contingencies of politics:

> But long after the Turbins and Talbergs have departed this life the keys will ring out again and Valentine will step up to the footlights, the aroma of perfume will waft from the boxes and at home beautiful women under the lamplight will play the music, because *Faust*, like the Shipwright of Saardam, is quite immortal.

As the novel concludes, Petlyura's victory, too, is ephemeral, as the Bolsheviks advance. Night descends on the Dnieper, and each of several characters dreams of something far beyond the petty intrigues of daylight Kiev. As in all of Bulgakov's fictions, a foregrounded narrative voice, relying on rhetorical questions, playful and ingenious connections and summaries, and an overtly evocative landscape, impels the reader beyond the trifles of wars and words.

BLACK SNOW

Black Snow, an unfinished work, was discovered in 1965 by the commission established during the post-Stalin thaw to rehabilitate Bulgakov. An account of the emergence of an obscure hack named Sergey Leontievich Maxudov as a literary and theatrical celebrity in Moscow, it draws heavily on Bulgakov's own experiences in writing *The White*

Guard and adapting it for the Moscow Art Theater as *Days of the Turbins*. It provides a lively portrait of the artist as a melancholic and misunderstood figure and of a cultural establishment inimical to genuine creativity.

The novel begins with a letter from a producer named Xavier Borisovich Ilchin summoning Maxudov to his office at the Academy of Drama. Ilchin has read Maxudov's unacclaimed novel and is eager for him to adapt it for the stage. Next follows a flashback recounting how Maxudov conceived his book and how, as an obscure employee of the trade journal *Shipping Gazette*, he signed a contract for its publication in *The Motherland* shortly before that magazine folded. The flashback concludes with an account of how Maxudov's life is transformed after he signs a contract for the production of *Black Snow*, his stage version of the novel, by the Independent Theater.

Maxudov soon finds himself a victim of the rivalries and jealousies of figures in the theatrical world. In particular, he is caught between the two directors of the Independent Theater, Aristarkh Platonovich, who is currently off in India, and Ivan Vasilievich; neither has spoken to the other in forty years. Ivan Vasilievich is clearly modeled on Stanislavsky, and grotesque descriptions portray the tyrannical director at work, rehearsing his actors in *Black Snow* with his celebrated "method." The hapless dramatist makes a convincing case that "the famous theory was utterly wrong for my play."

Black Snow employs a sophisticated narrative perspective to distance the reader both from its inept protagonist and from the bizarre characters he encounters. Its two parts are both written by Maxudov himself in the form of a memoir. An afterword, however, introduces a new, anonymous voice who explains how Maxudov sent the manuscript to him shortly before killing himself by jumping off a bridge in Kiev. This second narrator describes the narrative that the reader has just finished as suffering from "slovenly style" and as the "fruit of a morbid imagination." Furthermore, he points out its egregious inaccuracies, among which is the fact that Maxudov never did have anything to do with the theater. The effect of this coda, as of those in Knut Hamsun's *Pan* (1894; English translation, 1920) and director Robert Wiene's film *The Cabinet of Dr. Caligari* (1920), is to cast retrospective doubt on the reliability of everything that precedes it. Is *Black Snow* a caustic mockery of philistine bureaucrats, or is it a case study in the psychopathology of a deluded author manqué? Or perhaps both? Maxudov, distraught over frustrations with the Independent Theater, does admit that he is a melancholic and describes an early suicide attempt, aborted when he heard a recording of *Faust* coming from the apartment downstairs. *Black Snow*, with its examination of the artist as victim—of powerful boors and of himself—and its lucid blend of whimsy and social observation, is a fitting commentary on and companion to Bulgakov's other works.

THE MASTER AND MARGARITA

Perhaps the supreme Russian novel of the twentieth century, and one of the most endearing modern texts in any language, *The Master and Margarita* was first published in abridged form in 1966-1967 and immediately created a sensation. It is a rich fusion of at least four realms and plots: the banal world of contemporary Moscow, containing the Griboyedov House, the Variety Theater, the apartments at 302-b Sadovaya, and a psychiatric hospital; ancient Jerusalem, where Pontius Pilate suffers torment over whether to crucify Yeshua Ha-Nozri; the antics of Woland and his satanic crew, including Koroviev, Azazello, Behemoth, and Hella; and the activities of the Master, utterly devoted to his art, and of Margarita, utterly devoted to him. Throughout, chapters of the novel crosscut from one of these subplots to another and ultimately suggest that perhaps they are not so distinct after all.

What sets the complex machinery of Bulgakov's novel in motion is a four-day visit to Soviet Moscow by the devil, referred to as Woland, and his assistants. They gleefully wreak havoc with the lives of the bureaucrats, hypocrites, opportunists, and dullards they encounter. They do, however, befriend and assist the Master, an alienated writer who has been hospitalized after the worldly failure of his literary efforts. The Master's beloved Margarita consents to serve as hostess at Satan's ball and is rewarded with supernatural powers. An inferior poet named Ivan Homeless finds himself in the same psychiatric clinic as the Master and gradually becomes his disciple. The lifework of the Master is a novel about Pontius Pilate, and chapters from it, with manifest parallels to the situation in contemporary Moscow, are interspersed throughout Bulgakov's novel.

Woland's performance at the Variety Theater is billed as a "black magic act accompanied by a full exposé," and *The Master and Margarita* itself, an absorbing blend of fantasy and verisimilitude presented with subversive self-consciousness, could be similarly described. The playful narrative voice that overtly addresses the reader mocks not only the characters but itself as well. Numerous authors among the *dramatis personae*, including Ivan, the Master, Matthu Levi, and Ryukhin, as well as characters given musical names such as Berlioz, Stravinsky, and Rimsky, foreground the process of fabrication and reinforce one of the novel's persistent themes—the elusive nature of truth.

Most of the characters in Moscow refuse to recognize anything problematic about truth. Arrogantly convinced that human reason is adequate to any cognitive task, they stubbornly deny the supernatural that erupts in the form of Woland or that is evoked in the story of Yeshua. Like the other hack writers who congregate at the Griboyedov House, Ivan Homeless would just as soon take life on the most comfortable terms possible, but his spirit will not permit him to do so. Torn between the material and the spiritual, the temporal and the eternal, the collective and the individual, Ivan is diagnosed as schizophrenic and is hospitalized. His progress as a patient and as a writer will be marked by his success in reconciling opposing realms. Bulgakov, the novelist as master weaver, seems to be suggesting that both artistic achievement and mental health are dependent on a harmony between ostensibly disparate materials.

The Master, like Bulgakov himself, attempted to destroy his book, but, as Woland points out, "manuscripts don't burn." Art survives and transcends the hardships and iniquities of particular places and times. It ridicules the obtuseness of temporal authorities with the example of immortal authority. In one of many echoes of the Faust legend, *The Master and Margarita* chooses as its epigraph Johann Wolfgang von Goethe's reference to "that Power which eternally wills evil and eternally works good." Bulgakov's ambitious novel certainly does not deny the oppressive reality of contemporary society, but its humor is restorative, and it moves toward an exhilarating, harmonious vision that would exclude nothing. It concludes with a benedictory kiss from a spectral Margarita.

THE HEART OF A DOG

The most overt of Bulgakov's statements on the Russian Revolution, *The Heart of a Dog*, though written in 1925, was published in English in 1968 and in Russian in 1969. It is a satiric novella about an experiment performed by the celebrated Moscow surgeon Philip Philipovich Preobrazhensky, who takes a stray mongrel dog, Sharik, and transforms him into a human being named Sharikov. Much of the tale is narrated by Sharikov himself, who is not necessarily better off for his transformation. To perform the operation, Preobrazhensky has inserted the pituitary of a vulgar criminal into the brain of the dog. The result is an uncouth, rowdy human being who, though adept at language and even at repeating the political slogans supplied by the officious house committee chairman, Shvonder, proves incapable of satisfying the standards of civilized behavior demanded by Preobrazhensky. Hence, convinced that the experiment is a fiasco, he reverses it and turns Sharikov back into Sharik.

The Heart of a Dog features Bulgakov's characteristic blend of fantasy and social analysis. It parabolically raises the question of the malleability of human nature and of the possibility of social melioration. Once again, it exposes to ridicule the arrogance of those who would presume to shape others' lives and raises doubts about the efficacy and desirability of social engineering, such as Russia was undergoing in the 1920's. The book suggests a fatal incompatibility between the proletariat and the intelligentsia, implying that the humane values of the latter are threatened by the former. It seems to counsel humble caution in tampering with the arrangements of the world.

Steven G. Kellman

OTHER MAJOR WORKS

SHORT FICTION: *Diavoliada*, 1925 (*Diaboliad, and Other Stories*, 1972); *Traktat o zhilishche*, 1926 (*A Treatise on Housing*, 1972); *Zapiski iunogo vracha*, 1963 (*A Country Doctor's Notebook*, 1975); *Notes on the Cuff, and Other Stories*, 1991.

PLAYS: *Dni Turbinykh*, pr. 1926 (adaptation of his novel *Belaya gvardiya*; *Days of the Turbins*, 1934); *Zoykina kvartira*, pr. 1926 (*Zoya's Apartment*, 1970); *Bagrovy ostrov*, pr. 1928 (adaptation of his short story; *The Crimson Island*, 1972); *Kabala svyatosh*, pr. 1936 (wr. 1929; *A Cabal of Hypocrites*, 1972; also known as *Molière*); *Don Kikhot*, pr. 1941; *Posledniye dni (Pushkin)*, pr. 1943 (wr. 1934-1935; *The Last Days*, 1976); *Beg*, pr. 1957 (wr. 1928; *Flight*, 1969); *Ivan Vasilievich*, pb. 1965 (wr. 1935; English translation, 1974); *Blazhenstvo*, pb. 1966 (wr. 1934; *Bliss*, 1976); *Adam i Eva*, pb. 1971 (wr. 1930-1931; *Adam and Eva*, 1971); *The Early Plays of Mikhail Bulgakov*, 1972; *Rashel*, pb. 1972 (wr. c. 1936; libretto; adaptation of Guy de Maupassant's short story "Mademoiselle Fifi"); *Minin i Pozharskii*, pb. 1976 (wr. 1936; libretto); *Batum*, pb. 1977 (wr. 1938); *Six Plays*, 1991.

NONFICTION: *Zhizn gospodina de Molyera*, 1962 (*The Life of Monsieur de Molière*, 1970).

TRANSLATION: *L'Avare*, 1936 (of Molière's play).

BIBLIOGRAPHY

Barratt, Andrew. *Between Two Worlds: A Critical Introduction to "The Master and Margarita."* New York: Oxford University Press, 1987. Puts forth an imaginative approach to understanding Bulgakov's most important work. Describes the genesis of the novel and its reception inside and outside the Soviet Union.

Curtis, J. A. E. *Manuscripts Don't Burn: Mikhail Bulgakov, a Life in Letters and Diaries.* Woodstock, N.Y.: Overlook Press, 1992. Contains previously unpublished letters and a diary that were believed to be lost. Groups of Bulgakov's letters, diaries, and speeches are arranged in chronological order and interspersed with biographical chapters, providing context for the primary source material.

Drawicz, Andrzej. *The Master and the Devil: A Study of Mikhail Bulgakov.* Translated by Kevin Windle. Lewiston, N.Y.: Edwin Mellen Press, 2001. Analyzes all of Bulgakov's prose and dramatic works, placing them within the context of the author's life and times. The initial chapters focus on Bulgakov's life, providing new biographical information, and subsequent chapters concentrate on his novels and other writings.

Haber, Edythe C. *Mikhail Bulgakov: The Early Years.* Cambridge, Mass.: Harvard University Press, 1998. Discusses Bulgakov's early life and career, describing how his novels and other works arose from his experiences during the Russian Revolution, civil war, and early years of Communism. Traces the themes and characters of his early works and demonstrates how he perfected these fictional elements in *The Master and Margarita*.

Milne, Lesley. *Mikhail Bulgakov: A Critical Biography.* New York: Cambridge University Press, 1990. Describes some of the features that are essential to understanding Bulgakov's outlook on life and the themes and techniques of his works. Includes detailed and original interpretations of some of Bulgakov's earliest works as well as a serious examination of *The Master and Margarita*.

_____, ed. *Bulgakov: The Novelist-Playwright.* New York: Routledge, 1996. Collection of twenty-one essays surveys Bulgakov's works from a wide variety of perspectives. Several essays examine *The Master and Margarita*, including one that compares the novel to Salman Rushdie's *The Satanic Verses* (1988). Includes an index of Bulgakov's works.

Proffer, Ellendea. *Bulgakov: Life and Work*. Ann Arbor, Mich.: Ardis, 1984. Comprehensive treatment of Bulgakov's career provides information and analysis of some early works that previously received little scholarly attention. Proffer's portrait of Bulgakov contrasts with that of other critics, who depict him as being a suppressed and haunted author under the Stalinist regime.

Weir, Justin. *The Author as Hero: Self and Tradition in Bulgakov, Pasternak, and Nabokov*. Evanston, Ill.: Northwestern University Press, 2002. Analyzes novels by three Russian authors—Bulgakov's *The Master and Margarita*, Boris Pasternak's *Doktor Zhivago* (1957; *Doctor Zhivago*, 1958), and Vladimir Nabokov's *Dar* (1952; *The Gift*, 1963)—to describe how these authors reveal themselves through their writing, transforming the traditional authors into the heroes of their novels.

Wright, A. Colin. *Mikhail Bulgakov: Life and Interpretations*. Toronto, Ont.: University of Toronto Press, 1978. Thorough critical biography examines *The Master and Margarita* and other works and places them within the context of Bulgakov's life. Includes indexes and bibliography.

FYODOR DOSTOEVSKI

Born: Moscow, Russia; November 11, 1821
Died: St. Petersburg, Russia; February 9, 1881
Also known as: Fyodor Mihaylovich Dostoevski; Feodor Dostoyevsky; Feodor
Dostoevsky

PRINCIPAL LONG FICTION

Bednye lyudi, 1846 (*Poor Folk,* 1887)
Dvoynik, 1846 (*The Double,* 1917)
Netochka Nezvanova, 1849 (English translation, 1920)
Unizhennye i oskorblyonnye, 1861 (*Injury and Insult,* 1886; also known as *The
Insulted and Injured*)
Zapiski iz myortvogo doma, 1861-1862 (*Buried Alive: Or, Ten Years of Penal
Servitude in Siberia,* 1881; better known as *The House of the Dead*)
Zapiski iz podpolya, 1864 (*Letters from the Underworld,* 1913; better known as
Notes from the Underground)
Igrok, 1866 (*The Gambler,* 1887)
Prestupleniye i nakazaniye, 1866 (*Crime and Punishment,* 1886)
Idiot, 1868 (*The Idiot,* 1887)
Vechny muzh, 1870 (*The Permanent Husband,* 1888; also known as *The Eternal
Husband*)
Besy, 1871-1872 (*The Possessed,* 1913; also known as *The Devils*)
Podrostok, 1875 (*A Raw Youth,* 1916)
Bratya Karamazovy, 1879-1880 (*The Brothers Karamazov,* 1912)
The Novels, 1912 (12 volumes)

OTHER LITERARY FORMS

The collected works of Fyodor Dostoevski (dahs-tuh-YEHF-skee) are available in
many Russian editions, starting from 1883. The most carefully prepared of these, comprising some thirty volumes, is the Leningrad Nauka edition, which began publishing in
1972. A wide variety of selected works are also available in English. While the novels
dominate Dostoevski's later creative period, he began his career with sketches, short stories, and novellas, and he continued to write shorter pieces throughout his working life.
These works do not exhibit the same unity of theme as the major novels, though many of
them in one way or another involve Dostoevski's favorite topic, human duality.

Dostoevski's nonfictional writing is diverse. In his monthly *Dnevnik pisatelya* (1876-
1877, 1880-1881; *The Diary of a Writer,* 1949), he included commentary on sociopolitical issues of the time, literary analyses, travelogues, and fictional sketches. He also
contributed many essays to his own journals and other publications. The nonfictional

Fyodor Dostoevski
(Library of Congress)

writings often clash with the views expressed in the novels and consequently enjoy wide circulation among specialists for comparative purposes. Equally popular is his correspondence, comprising several volumes in his collected works. The notebooks for the major novels, as well as other background comments, are also included in the collection. They became available in English in editions published by the University of Chicago Press during the 1960's and 1970's.

ACHIEVEMENTS

Both Leo Tolstoy and Fyodor Dostoevski, the giants of the Russian novel during the era preceding the 1917 October Revolution, are firmly part of the Western literary tradition today, but whereas Tolstoy's outlook is solidly rooted in the nineteenth century, Dostoevski's ideas belong to modern times. His novels go far beyond the parameters of aesthetic literature; they are studied not only by literary historians and critics but also by psychologists, philosophers, and theologians the world over. Each discipline discerns a different drift in Dostoevski's work, and few agree on what the author's basic tenets are, but all claim him as their hero. His contemporaries, too, were at a loss to categorize him, primarily because his style and subject matter had little in common with accepted literary norms. Russia's most prominent writing, as espoused by Ivan Turgenev and Tolstoy, was smooth and lyric. While Turgenev analyzed topical social problems in a restrained, faintly didactic manner, and Tolstoy presented panoramic visions of certain Russian social classes and their moral problems, Dostoevski brought an entirely new style and content to Russian writing. He disregarded his colleagues' logically progressing, chronological narrative mode and constructed his stories as mosaics or puzzles, often misleading the audience, experimenting with peculiar narrative voices, allowing his pathological figures to advance the plot in disconcertingly disorienting ways, and in general forcing the reader to reevaluate and backtrack constantly. Dostoevski was also revolutionary in his choice of subjects, introducing characters whose perception of outside reality essentially mirrored their own skewed personalities.

Dostoevski thus rendered obsolete both his contemporaries' classical realism and the prevailing superficial treatment of the human psyche. In his choice of settings, he disdained the poetic landscapes preferred by others and concentrated on the teeming of the city or the starkly barren aspects of the countryside. Because of this preference for the seamy side of life, he is often linked to Nikolai Gogol, but Dostoevski's descriptions of deviant behavior have a decidedly more modern flavor than do Gogol's. During his enforced proximity to criminals, Dostoevski applied his powers of observation to their perverted worldview and, in the process, developed a new approach to literary portraiture; Sigmund Freud praised him for anticipating modern psychological approaches, and twentieth century psychologists on the whole have accepted Dostoevski's observations as valid.

Dostoevski tended to be conservative and didactic in his nonfictional writings, though his often cantankerous and controversial assertions contributed to the lively journalistic interplays of the time; to this day, there is disagreement over whether he affected a conservative public stance in order to be trusted with censorially sensitive material in his fiction or whether conflicting elements were actually integral to his personality. In either case, Dostoevski is responsible for leading Russian literature away from its often tranquilly harmonious narratives, with their clearly discernible authorial points of view, to a polyphonic plane.

During Joseph Stalin's reign as leader of the newly formed Soviet Union, severe censorial strictures limited the average Soviet reader's access to Dostoevski, yet interest in him remained undiminished, and he returned to his prominent place after Stalin's death. Outside his homeland, Dostoevski's influence has been immeasurable. Albert Camus—to cite only one among countless examples of twentieth century writers awed by the power of Dostoevski's metaphysical dialectics—transformed *The Possessed* into a gripping play, *Les Possédés* (pr., pb. 1959; *The Possessed*, 1960), because he saw in Dostoevski's tortured protagonists the forerunners of today's existentialist heroes. Dostoevski's work thus has remained topical and continues to appeal to widely divergent views.

BIOGRAPHY

There was little in the childhood of Fyodor Mihaylovich Dostoevski to presage his achievements as a writer of world-famous novels. Born into a middle-class family of few cultural pretensions, he received a mediocre education. His father, a physician at a Moscow hospital for the poor, ruled the family with a strict hand and enforced observance of Russian Orthodox ritual at home. When Dostoevski entered the St. Petersburg Military Engineering School in 1838, he found himself unprepared for academic life; nevertheless, he enjoyed his first exposure to literature and soon immersed himself in it. The elder Dostoevski's murder at the hands of his serfs (he had in the meantime become a modest landowner) and the first signs of his own epilepsy upset Dostoevski's academic routine, delaying his graduation until 1843.

Dostoevski worked only briefly as a military engineer before deciding to pursue a literary career. When the efforts of acquaintances resulted in the publication of his first fictional work, *Poor Folk*, his excitement knew no bounds, and he envisioned a promising writing career. His initial success led easily to publication of several additional pieces, among them the uncompleted *Netochka Nezvanova* and the psychologically impressive *The Double*. While these works are not considered primary by Dostoevski scholars, they hint at what was to become the author's fascination with humankind's ambiguous inner world.

The perfecting of this artistic vision was interrupted by Dostoevski's encounter with the realities of czarist autocracy under Nicholas I. Dostoevski was active in the Petrashevsky Circle, one of many dissident groups engaged in underground dissemination of sociopolitical pamphlets. Dostoevski's arrest and death sentence in 1849, commuted at the last moment to prison and exile, initiated a terrible period for the young author. On Christmas Eve of that year, he left St. Petersburg in chains to spend four years in the company of violent criminals in Omsk, Siberia. The inhuman conditions of his imprisonment severely taxed his mental stability, especially because he was forbidden to write or even read anything, except religious matter. He later recorded these experiences graphically in *The House of the Dead* (initially translated as *Buried Alive: Or, Ten Years of Penal Servitude in Siberia*), immediately catching public attention for his psychological insight into pathological and criminal behavior. He spent an additional five years (1854-1859) as a political exile in a Siberian army contingent.

In 1857, after recovering somewhat from the ravages of incarceration, which had exacerbated his epilepsy, Dostoevski married a widow, Maria Isayeva, and hesitantly resumed his writing career. Upon his return to St. Petersburg in 1859, he was drawn into a hectic pace of literary activity. Turgenev and Tolstoy occupied first place among writers, leaving the unfortunate ex-convict to rebuild his career almost from scratch. To facilitate the serial printing of his work, he ventured into publishing. Together with his brother Mikhail, he started the journal *Vremya* in 1861, using it as a vehicle to publish his not very successful novel *The Insulted and Injured*, which he had written primarily to alleviate financial pressures. When he visited Western Europe for the first time in 1862, his observations also appeared in *Vremya* as "Zimnie zametki o letnikh vpechatleniyakh" (1863; "Winter Notes on Summer Impressions," 1955). Before he could reap substantial material benefit from his enterprise, government censors closed the magazine in 1863 because a politically sensitive article on Russo-Polish affairs had appeared in its pages.

At this inopportune moment, Dostoevski indulged himself somewhat recklessly by revisiting Europe on borrowed funds in order to pursue a passionate love interest, Apollinaria Suslova, and to try his luck at German gaming tables. Unsuccessful in both pursuits, he returned to Russia in 1864 to risk another publishing venture, the periodical *Epokha*, which folded in less than a year, though he managed to print in it the initial installments of his first successful longer fiction, *Notes from the Underground*, before its demise. His personal life, too, did not proceed smoothly. The deaths of his wife, with whom he had shared seven unhappy years, and of his brother and business partner Mikhail in 1864 brought enormous additional debts and obligations, which led him to make hasty promises of future works. To extricate himself from one such contract, he interrupted work on *Crime and Punishment* and hastily put together a fictional version of his gambling experiences and his torrid love affair with Suslova. To speed the work, he dictated the text to a twenty-year-old stenographer, Anna Snitkina. With her expert help, *The Gambler* was delivered on time. Dostoevski and Snitkina married in 1867, and she is generally credited with providing the stability and emotional security that permitted the author to produce his last four novels at a more measured pace.

Despite the success of *Crime and Punishment*, Dostoevski still ranked below Turgenev and Tolstoy in popular esteem by the end of the 1860's, partly because their wealth allowed them leisure to compose carefully edited works that appealed to the public and their gentry status opened influential doors, and partly because Dostoevski's writings were uneven, alternating between strange psychological portraits and journalistic polemics, all produced in a frantic haste that seemed to transmit itself to the text. Dostoevski spent the first four years after his marriage to Snitkina in Europe, largely to escape creditors but also to feed his gambling mania, which kept the family destitute. He completed *The Idiot* abroad and accepted a publisher's large advance in 1871 to facilitate return to his homeland. His remaining ten years were spent in more rational pursuits.

Between 1873 and 1874, he edited the conservative weekly *Grazhdanin* and initiated a popular column, *Diary of a Writer*, which in 1876 he turned into a successful monthly. The appearance of the politically provocative *The Possessed* and of *A Raw Youth* kept him in the public eye, and he was finally accorded some of the social acknowledgments previously reserved for his rivals Turgenev and Tolstoy. The duality of his writings, at once religiously conservative and brilliantly innovative, made him acceptable to government, Church, and intellectuals alike. This philosophical dichotomy remained characteristic of Dostoevski to the end. In 1880, he delivered an enthusiastically received speech during the dedication of the Alexander Pushkin monument in Moscow, in which he reiterated patriotic sentiments of a rather traditional tenor. At the same time, his last novel, *The Brothers Karamazov,* expressed doubts about a single, traditional view of life. When he died two months after completing the novel, an impressive public funeral attested his stature as a major Russian writer.

ANALYSIS

Fyodor Dostoevski's creative development is roughly divided into two stages. The shorter pieces, preceding his imprisonment, reflect native and foreign literary influences, although certain topics and stylistic innovations that became Dostoevski's trademarks were already apparent. The young author was fascinated by Gogol's humiliated St. Petersburg clerks and their squalid surroundings, teeming with marginal, grotesque individuals. These elements are so abundant in all of Dostoevski's fiction that he labeled himself a disciple of Gogol. Traces of E. T. A. Hoffmann's fantastic tales are evident in the young Dostoevski's preference for gothic and Romantic melodrama. What distinguishes Dostoevski from those influences is his carnivalistically exaggerated tone in describing or echoing the torments of members of the lower classes. He not only imbues them with frantic emotional passions and personality quirks in order to make them strangers to their own mediocre setting but also endows them with precisely the right balance between eccentricity and ordinariness to jar the reader into irritated alertness. While other writers strove to elicit public sympathy for the poor, Dostoevski subtly infused an element of ridiculousness into his portrayals, thereby reducing the social efficacy of the genre while enhancing the complexity of literary expression.

In Dostoevski's later, post-Siberian novels, this delicate equilibrium between empathy and contempt for the downtrodden is honed to perfection. The author supplements his gallery of mistreated eccentrics with powerful, enigmatic, ethically neutral supermen— highly intelligent loners whose philosophies allow simultaneously for self-sacrifice and murder. Other favorite types are passionate females, aborting good impulses with vicious inclinations, and angelic prostitutes, curiously blending religious fanaticism with coarseness.

This multiplicity is the dominant characteristic of Dostoevski's style. It is for the most part impossible to discern in his works an authorial point of view. By using a polyphonic approach, Dostoevski has characters arguing diametrically opposed concepts so convincingly and in such an intellectually appealing fashion that readers are prevented from forming simplistic judgments. Most readers are held spellbound by the detective quality of Dostoevski's writing. On the surface, the novels appear to be thrillers, exhibiting the typical tricks of that genre, with generous doses of suspense, criminal activity, confession, and entrapment by police or detectives. While viewing the works from this angle alone will not yield a satisfactory reading, it eases the way into the psychologically complex subtext. Not the least of Dostoevski's appeal lies in his original development of characters, prominent among them frantically driven types who bare their psyches in melodramatic confes-

sions and diaries while at the same time confusing the reader's expectations by performing entirely contradictory deeds. Superimposed on these psychological conflicts are other
metaphysical quandaries, such as passionate discussions about good and evil, church and
state, Russia and Western Europe, free will and determinism. These struggles often crowd
the plot to the point of symbolic overload, thereby destroying any semblance of harmony.

That Dostoevski is avidly read by the general public and specialists alike attests his genius in fusing banalities with profound intellectual insights. Nevertheless, a certain un-
evenness in language and structure remains. The constant pressure under which Dostoevski worked resulted in incongruities and dead spots that are incompatible with expert
literary craftsmanship, while the installment approach forced him to end segments with
suspense artificially built up to ensure the reader's continuing interest. Some of these
rough spots were edited out in later single-volume editions, but the sense of rugged style
persists, and reading Dostoevski is therefore not a relaxing experience. No reader, however, can easily forget the mental puzzles and nightmarish visions generated by Dostoevski's work.

NOTES FROM THE UNDERGROUND

Notes from the Underground, Dostoevski's first successful longer work, already contained many elements found in the subsequent novels. The nameless underground man is
a keenly conscious misogynist who masks excessive pride with pathological submissive-
ness. In his youth, his need for self-esteem led him into disastrous social encounters from
which he usually emerged the loser. For example, his delusion of being ignored by a social
superior, who is not even aware of him, has caused him to spend years planning a ridiculous, and in the end miscarried, revenge. Dostoevski liked to use noncausal patterning in
his compositional arrangements to enhance a sense of discontinuity. Thus, *Notes from the
Underground* begins with the forty-year-old protagonist already withdrawn from society,
spewing hatred, bitter philosophy, and ridicule at the imaginary reader of his journals.
Only in the second part of the novel, which contains the underground man's actual confrontations, does it become clear that he has no choice but to hide himself away, because
his twisted personality is incapable of even a casual positive human interaction. His very
pronouncement is a contradiction, uttered in a continuous stream without developing a
single argument, so that the overall effect is one of unordered dialectical listing.

On one level, *Notes from the Underground* was written to counter Nikolay Chernyshevsky's *Chto delat'?* (1863; *What Is to Be Done?*, c. 1863), which stresses the benefits
of scientific thinking and considers self-interest beneficial to all society. Through the underground man's irrational behavior and reasoning, Dostoevski ridicules Chernyshevsky's assumptions. He makes his hero a living refutation of scientific approaches. If human logic can be corrupted by the mind's own illogic, no strictly logical conclusions are
possible. By indulging in actions injurious to himself, the underground man proves that
human beings do not act solely out of self-interest, that they are, in part at least, intrinsi-

cally madcap. Thus, any attempt to structure society along scientific lines, as suggested by Chernyshevsky, is doomed to failure. The duality of the hero is such, however, that rational assertions, too, receive ample exposure, as the underground man refutes his own illogic and spins mental webs around the imaginary listener. *Notes from the Underground* is difficult to read, especially for those unfamiliar with Chernyshevsky's novel. The unprogressively flowing illogicalities, coupled with an elusive authorial voice, render the narrative undynamic and tax even the intellectually committed reader. Dostoevski himself realized an insufficiency in the work but blamed it partly on censorial editing of an obscure religious reference, according to which the hero saw a glimmer of hope for himself in Christianity. The deleted comments, however, do not carry such a weighty connotation, and Dostoevski made no effort to restore the cut text later, when he might have done so. In its emphasis on the dual qualities of human endeavor, *Notes from the Underground* is firmly linked to the subsequent novels, in which this theme is handled with more sophistication.

CRIME AND PUNISHMENT

The wide appeal of *Crime and Punishment* results partly from its detective-story elements of murder, criminal investigation, evasion, confession, and courtroom drama. Dostoevski immediately broadens the perspective of the genre, however. Readers not only know from the outset who the murderer is but also are at once made part of his thinking process, so that his reasoning, motivations, and inclinations are laid bare from the start. The enigmatic element enters when readers come to realize, along with the murderer, and as slowly and painfully as the murderer, that he cannot assign a purpose to the crime, that human motivation remains, in the end, an unsolved mystery.

The very name of the hero, Raskolnikov, is derived from the Russian word for "split," and his entire existence is characterized by a swiftly alternating, unsettling duality. Raskolnikov is introduced as an intense former student who is about to put a carefully constructed theory into action. The opening chapters chronicle the confused state of his mental processes. He plans to rid the world of an evil by killing a pawnbroker who is gradually ruining her customers, Raskolnikov among them, and plans to use her hoarded wealth for philanthropical purposes in justification of the crime. Almost immediately, other motives call the first into question. Raskolnikov's mother threatens to sacrifice her daughter to ensure his financial well-being. An encounter with a derelict drunkard, Marmeladov, strengthens Raskolnikov in his resolve to kill, for Marmeladov keeps himself in drink and out of work by drawing on the pitiful earnings of his young daughter, Sonia, whom he has sent into prostitution. Raskolnikov notes in horror that he may force his sister into a similar situation through the legal prostitution of a sacrificial marriage. The crime itself renders all of Raskolnikov's musings invalid. He brutally murders a second, innocent victim, takes very little money, does not spend what he does steal, and will have nothing to do with his family.

From this point on, the novel focuses on Raskolnikov's struggle within himself. His prominently present but long repressed humanity asserts itself against his will to demolish arguments against confession provided by the proud part of his personality. Dostoevski uses the device of multiple alter egos in projecting Raskolnikov's dichotomy onto other characters. At one extreme pole stands the personification of Raskolnikov's evil impulses, the suspected killer and seducer Svidrigaïlov. Time and again, Raskolnikov confronts the latter in attempts to develop a psychological affinity with him. Raskolnikov's subconscious moral restraints, however, prevent such a union. Svidrigaïlov, and by extension Raskolnikov, cannot bring himself to perform planned abominations or live peacefully with already committed ones. Svidrigaïlov exits through suicide at about the same time that Raskolnikov is more urgently drawn to his other alter ego, the self-sacrificing, gentle prostitute Sonia.

Whereas Svidrigaïlov is a sensually vibrant figure, Sonia is basically colorless and unbelievable, but as a symbol of Raskolnikov's Christian essence, she turns out to be the stronger influence on him. She is not able to effect a moral transformation, yet she subtly moves into the foreground the necessity of confession and expiation. Raskolnikov never truly repents. He has, however, been forced to take a journey into his psyche, has found there an unwillingness to accommodate murder, and, almost angrily, has been forced to acknowledge that each life has its own sacramental value and that transgression of this tenet brings about psychological self-destruction. The final pages hint at Raskolnikov's potential for spiritual renewal, a conclusion that many critics find artistically unconvincing.

Intertwined with this primary drama are related Dostoevskian themes. Raskolnikov, in one of his guises, imagines himself a Napoleonic superman, acting on a worldwide stage on which individual killings disappear in the murk of historical necessity. On another plane, Dostoevski weaves Raskolnikov's mother, his landlady, and the slain pawnbroker into a triangle that merges the figures in Raskolnikov's confused deliberations, so that murderous impulses toward one are sublimated and redirected toward another. Similarly, the figures of Sonia, Raskolnikov's sister Dounia, and the pawnbroker's sister Lizaveta, also killed by Raskolnikov, are symbolically linked. Raskolnikov directs Dounia away from his lecherous alter ego Svidrigaïlov toward his proper, good-hearted embodiment and friend, Razumihin, while he himself, in expiation for killing Lizaveta, becomes a brotherly friend to Sonia. An important and cleverly presented role is reserved for the detective Porfiry, whose cunning leads Raskolnikov to confess a moral as well as a legal transgression. *Crime and Punishment* remains Dostoevski's most popular novel.

THE IDIOT

The author's narrative mode does not differ drastically in the remaining novels. Though each work is built on a different drama, all are developed along Dostoevski's favorite lines of human duality, alter ego, and authorial ambiguity. These qualities find expression in a most controversial way in *The Idiot*, the incongruous, almost sacrilegious portrayal of a Christlike figure. While the devout and selfless Sonia of *Crime and Punishment* occupies a position secondary to that of the central hero and thus lacks extensive development, Dostoevski makes the similarly self-sacrificing Prince Myshkin into the pivotal character of *The Idiot*. Through him, the author unfolds the notion that compassion and goodness, no matter how commendable on a theological plane, are insufficient to counter the less desirable aspects of reality.

The manner of Myshkin's presentation immediately challenges the reader's expectation of a "perfectly beautiful human being," as Dostoevski called his hero in preparatory notes. Myshkin—the name derives from the root of the Russian word for "mouse"—enters the novel as an insecure, epileptic, naïve young man, characterized by boundless goodwill, an immense capacity for humiliation, and a willingness to take the blame for the loathsome actions of others. He is a rather vapid personality, totally out of tune with existing human realities. Socially inept because of a long absence from Russia, ill at ease and inexperienced in confrontation with women, Myshkin is unable to establish satisfactory relationships. His kindness and empathy with suffering cause him to intervene repeatedly in other affairs, only to run afoul of the intense passions motivating his friends, and his interventions eventually lead to tragedy all around. Far from serving as counselor and redeemer, Myshkin is the cause of several calamities. Unversed in the intricacies of human interaction, created insufficiently incarnate by Dostoevski, the hapless protagonist leaves a path of misery and destruction before sinking totally into idiocy.

As he blunders his way through many unhappy encounters, several other themes emerge. The virginal hero actually has a sexually vicious and otherwise offensive double in Rogozhin, with whom he retains a close bond to the end, when both seemingly merge into one over the body of their mutual love, Nastasya Filipovna, freshly murdered by Rogozhin. Dostoevski assured outraged moralist critics that he had intended to create a perfect saint in Myshkin and implied that he had perhaps failed to create believable separate identities for Myshkin and Rogozhin, but Dostoevski's public assertions often contradicted the thrust of his novels, and it is more likely that here, too, he employed his favorite device of embodying the multifaceted human psyche in diametrically opposed figures.

In most of Dostoevski's novels, male characters are placed at center stage, leaving women to embody a given alter ego, highlight certain aspects of the protagonist, or echo other major concerns. *The Idiot* differs in presenting Nastasya Filipovna as Myshkin's primary antagonist. She is given scope and complexity in bringing to the surface Myshkin's temperamental inadequacy; in revenging herself for having been made concubine to the man appointed to be her guardian; in being torn by pride, guilt, and frustration; in vacillating between Myshkin and Rogozhin; and finally in orchestrating her own destruction. The other major female, Aglaya, receives less psychological expansion, but even here Dostoevski gives an interesting portrayal of a goodly woman unable to accept the humiliations associated with being Myshkin's companion. Dostoevski favored females of devious intensity, as typified by Nastasya Filipovna. In *Crime and Punishment* and *The Brothers Karamazov*, this type is marked by the identical name of "Katerina Ivanovna." Analysts interested in linking biography to plot perceive in these women an echo of Dostoevski's equally cruel and passionate friend, Apollinaria Suslova, as well as traits of his first wife, Maria Isayeva.

The preparatory notes to the novel reveal that Dostoevski changed perspective several times in shaping his guiding theme. In early drafts, Myshkin is a genuine double, possessed of many violent traits later transferred to Rogozhin. As Myshkin is stripped of negative features in later versions, he acquires the characteristics of a "holy fool," a popular type in pre-nineteenth century Russian literature, the mental defective as sweet, innocent, and specially favored by God. In the end, however there emerges the idea that an overflow of goodwill cannot vouchsafe positive results and can easily have the opposite effect. A certain meandering in the second part of the novel still reflects the author's hesitation in deciding on a direction. Earlier scholarship, unwilling to accept the fact that Dostoevski had depicted a failed saint in such a controversial manner, saw in *The Idiot* an unsuccessful attempt to portray a wholly Christian figure, but careful study of the text and background material reveals an intentional and original portrayal of a Christian dilemma. In succeeding works, too, Dostoevski's integrity as novelist took precedence over personal theological convictions.

THE POSSESSED

In *The Possessed*, Dostoevski centered his attention on a very different type, the emerging Russian nihilist-atheist generation of the latter half of the nineteenth century. While the political aspect of the work occupies the general background, metaphysical and moral issues soon find their way into the narrative, as do satiric portraits of prominent Russians, among them a caricature of Turgenev, depicted in the ridiculous figure of Karmazinov. On the political level, Dostoevski demonstrates that revolutionary nihilism inevitably turns into a greater despotism than the order it intends to replace. One unscrupulous gang member, Shigalev, advocates a dictatorship of select revolutionaries and absolute submission on the part of the governed. For this reason, *The Possessed* faced long censorial repression in the Soviet Union, and former Soviet critics still find it awkward to present credible analyses of the novel.

The novelistic conspiracy is headed by a bloodthirsty degenerate, Pyotr Verkhovensky. Like Raskolnikov's murder in *Crime and Punishment*, Verkhovensky's killing is based on an actual event, the extermination of a student by the political terrorist Sergey Nechayev in 1869. Dostoevski's correspondence reveals that he was disturbed by the perverse publicity attending Nechayev's notoriety and intended to incorporate the incident into *The Possessed* for the purpose of deglamorizing such nihilistic misdeeds. In this he succeeded without question. Verkhovensky is shown to manipulate followers whose brutality and narrow-mindedness easily fashion them into blindly obedient puppets.

The focus of the novel, however, is on an enigmatic atheist, Stavrogin, who is only passively interested in external events. Stavrogin has no plans, preferences, illusions, beliefs, or passions, and his actions are accordingly illogical. For example, he engages in duels although he does not believe in them; marries a mental defective on a wager; bites his host, the governor of the province, on the ear; and calmly accepts a slap in the face from a subordinate. His very indifference to everyone and everything has made him into a charismatic figure whom Verkhovensky and his revolutionaries revere as a deity.

Stavrogin is depicted in such a shadowy manner that no coherent portrait emerges. The notebooks for *The Possessed* record the author's difficulties in creating the character: In early versions, Stavrogin is more fleshed out and clarified, but in the end Dostoevski chose to present him as a riddle, to demonstrate that an incorporeal image, by its very nature, exacts the deepest loyalties. Stavrogin's disinterest in the world eventually leads to inner dissatisfaction and suicide. An interesting part of his portrayal, his confession to a priest that he is responsible for the death of a child whom he raped, was excised by the censors and never restored by Dostoevski. Omission of this episode strips Stavrogin of the feeling of regret implied in the confession and intensifies the impression of absolute ethical neutrality assigned to his personality. Stavrogin is the opposite of Prince Myshkin in every respect—uninvolved rather than concerned, bored rather than active, cruel and unpredictable rather than steadfastly compassionate—yet their endeavors lead to the same tragic end. Neither manages to cope with reality and both abandon the world, Myshkin through madness, Stavrogin through suicide.

Another major character carrying a symbolic burden is Kirillov, whose inner conflicts about the existence or nonexistence of God also drive him to self-extinction. Kirillov is Western-educated, influenced by the scientific discoveries of the age; an avowed atheist, he transfers godlike attributes to himself. As Dostoevski traces Kirillov's inner reasoning, he reveals Kirillov to be a philosophical extremist. Because he no longer believes in an afterlife but is inexplicably afraid of death, he conquers that fear by annihilating himself. His opposite, Shatov, a believer in the Orthodox Church and in the special status of the Russian people, ends as a victim of the conspirators; once more, the author's plot line follows two diametrically opposed figures to the same fatal end.

Both *The Idiot* and *The Possessed* lack a hopeful view of the future. The society and mores in which the major figures operate reflect moral confusion and material corruption, a Babylonian atmosphere that Dostoevski subtly ascribes to erosion of faith. As always, it is difficult to say exactly where the author stands. Clearly, he refutes the terrorism exercised by Verkhovensky and his gang. Their political intrigue assumes the metaphysical quality of biblical devils "possessed" by love of ruin and chaos. The grisly demise of the other major characters suggests that Dostoevski also considered their approaches inadequate. The philosophical arguments, however, are presented with such conviction and honesty that no point of view is totally annihilated.

For most of the 1870's, Dostoevski was able to work at a leisurely pace, free from the material wants and deadline pressure of the preceding decades. It is all the more surprising, then, that *A Raw Youth*, composed in those tranquil years, is his least successful major novel. The reasons are painfully clear. The author overloaded the plot with poorly integrated, unrelated themes. What is worse, he let the rhetorical expression of his pet ideas overwhelm the artistic structure. The basic story deals with the illegitimate "raw youth" Arkady Dolgoruky, who is engaged in winning some recognition or affection from his biological father, Versilov. The narrative soon shifts to Versilov, a typical Dostoevskian dual type, motivated simultaneously by cruel passions and Christian meekness. Versilov carries additional symbolic burdens relating to Russia's alleged spiritual superiority over Western Europe. While Dostoevski fails to tie the many strands into a believable or even interesting panorama, he does attempt a symbolic scheme. Arkady's mother, Sofia, embodies "Mother Russia." She is on one side linked by marriage to a traditional peasant, Makar Ivanitch. At the same time, Sofia has been seduced by and continues to be involved with Versilov, the representative of the Western-educated nobility. The hapless Arkady, the disoriented offspring of this unconsecrated union, is driven to drastic schemes in an effort to find his place in life.

THE BROTHERS KARAMAZOV

Together with *Crime and Punishment*, *The Brothers Karamazov* continues to be Dostoevski's most widely read and discussed work. The author introduces no new concepts or literary devices in the novel, but this time he is successful in casting his themes into a brilliantly conceived construct. The conflict between a cruelly uncaring father and his vengeance-bound sons receives the artistic treatment missing in *A Raw Youth*. The metaphysical arguments, especially the dialectic between atheism and Christianity, are dealt with at length. Finally, the behavioral complexities of bipolar personalities are depicted in a most sophisticated manner.

The plot of the novel revolves around parricide. Four brothers, one illegitimate, have been criminally neglected by their wanton father, Fyodor Pavlovich, and subconsciously strive to avenge this transgression. The abominations of old Karamazov, some brutally indulged in the children's presence and partly involving their respective mothers, settle in the brothers' subconscious and motivate all of their later actions and behaviors. For most of the novel, none of the adult brothers is ever completely aware of the now-sublimated parricidal impulses, but all silently play their parts in seeing the old man murdered. The three legitimate brothers cope by nurturing father substitutes with whom they enter into complicated relationships. The oldest, Dmitri, fights his surrogates, almost murdering one, while the youngest, Alyosha, a novice, faces deep mental anguish in cultivating a father figure in his spiritual superior, Father Zossima. Ivan, the middle brother, has transferred his hatred of his father to a metaphysical plane, where he spars with a cruel God about the injustice of permitting mistreatment of children. In his prose poem "The Legend of the Grand Inquisitor," Ivan creates a benevolent father figure who shields his human flock from such suffering. Only Smerdyakov, the illegitimate offspring, keeps his attention focused on the primary target and actually kills old Karamazov, though his inner understanding of the factors motivating him is equally fuzzy. In desperation at not being fraternally acknowledged by his brothers, even after murdering for them, Smerdyakov implicates them in the crime and removes himself through suicide. The other three undergo painful self-examination from which they emerge as better human beings but not victorious. Dmitri, officially convicted of the crime, faces long imprisonment; Ivan's mind has given way as hallucinations plague him; and Alyosha seeks ways to combine his faith in a merciful God with the catastrophes of his actual experience.

Dostoevski has the major characters respond in different ways to their situation, developing each in terms of a specific psychological or metaphysical problem. Through Ivan, the author demonstrates the inadequacy of intellect where subconscious motivation is concerned. Ivan is educated, rational, atheistic, given to abstraction, loath to enter into close personal relationships, and proud of his intellectual superiority. Yet his wish to see his father dead is so powerful that it leads him into a silent conspiracy with Smerdyakov, whom he despises on a rational plane. The author attaches a higher moral value to Dmitri's type of personality. Dmitri represents an emotionally explosive spirit, quick to engage in melodramatic outbursts and passionate displays of surface sentiment. He instinctively grasps the moral superiority of the earthy, morally lax Grushenka to the socially superior, moralizing Katerina Ivanovna. His reckless nature leads him into many transgressions and misjudgments, but at a crucial point, when he has sought after opportunity to murder his parent, a deeply embedded reverence for life stays his hand. Alyosha acts as Dostoevski's representative of the Christian faith, and, like all other Dostoevskian Christian heroes, he is subjected to severe spiritual torments. His faith is tested as the externals and rituals of religion to which he clings prove elusive, if not false, and he is made to reach for a more profound Christian commitment within himself in order to survive the violence engendered by the Karamazov heritage. He is given the privilege, rare among Dostoevskian heroes, of affecting his environment in a wholesome fashion, especially at the end of the novel.

Each of the three brothers is rendered more complex in the course of his spiritual odyssey. The atheistic Ivan defends the cause of the Orthodox Church in his formal writings and in the end loses all pride and reason as he humbles himself in a futile attempt to save the innocent Dmitri from imprisonment. Dmitri acquires a measure of philosophical introspection as he learns to accept punishment for a murder he ardently desired but did not commit. Alyosha, too, despite largely positive patterning, is shown to let hidden desire neutralize religious conviction. Charged by Father Zossima with acting as Dmitri's keeper, the otherwise conscientious and compassionate Alyosha simply "forgets" the obligation and thereby fails to prevent his father's murder and his brother's entrapment. Dostoevski envisioned a larger role for Alyosha in a sequel to *The Brothers Karamazov* that never materialized. For this reason, Alyosha exits the work somewhat incomplete, incongruously engaged to a cunning, cruel cripple, Liza, who serves as his own unholy alter ego in the parricidal scheme.

The work abounds in secondary plots and figures, all interconnected and echoing the primary drama in intricate ways. Prominent among these plots is the legend of the Grand Inquisitor and the refutation of the legend by Father Zossima. Through the Grand Inquisitor, Dostoevski argues that Christian ideals are set too high for ordinary mortals, who prefer security and comfort to difficult individual choices. The Grand Inquisitor, in a dramatic encounter with Christ, thoroughly defends a benign kingdom on earth as most suitable for the masses. This argument is countered by Zossima's restatement of basic Christian theology, which does not answer the Grand Inquisitor's charges but simply offers traditional belief and practice of Christian tenets as an alternative perspective. The very type of behavior that proved ruinous to Prince Myshkin is in Zossima's actions converted into a richly beneficial model. By presenting the discourse in this fashion, Dostoevski cleverly juxtaposed humanistic and Christian arguments without resolving them. He thus once more implied that all so-called issues contain their own contradictions, that life and truth are indeed multiple.

By devoting his novels to the exploration of the mind, Dostoevski extended the intellectual horizons of his day. Although publicly a conservative of Russian Orthodox conviction, Dostoevski produced works that continuously challenge the notion that atheism inevitably engenders wanton amorality. It is this recognition of human complexity, coupled with a fascinating narrative style, that gives Dostoevski his modern flavor.

Margot K. Frank

OTHER MAJOR WORKS

SHORT FICTION: *Sochineniya,* 1860 (2 volumes); *Polnoye sobraniye sochineniy,* 1865-1870 (4 volumes); *Povesti i rasskazy,* 1882; *The Gambler, and Other Stories,* 1914; *A Christmas Tree and a Wedding, and an Honest Thief,* 1917; *White Nights, and Other Stories,* 1918; *An Honest Thief, and Other Stories,* 1919; *The Short Novels of Dostoevsky,* 1945.

NONFICTION: "Zimniye zametki o letnikh vpechatleniyakh," 1863 ("Winter Notes on Summer Impressions," 1955); *Dnevnik pisatelya,* 1876-1877, 1880-1881 (2 volumes; *The Diary of a Writer,* 1949); *Pisma,* 1928-1959 (4 volumes); *Iz arkhiva F. M. Dostoyevskogo: "Idiot,"* 1931 (*The Notebooks for "The Idiot,"* 1967); *Iz arkhiva F. M. Dostoyevskogo: "Prestupleniye i nakazaniye,"* 1931 (*The Notebooks for "Crime and Punishment,"* 1967); *F. M. Dostoyevsky: Materialy i issledovaniya,* 1935 (*The Notebooks for "The Brothers Karamazov,"* 1971); *Zapisnyye tetradi F. M. Dostoyevskogo,* 1935 (*The Notebooks for "The Possessed,"* 1968); *Dostoevsky's Occasional Writings,* 1963; *F. M. Dostoyevsky v rabote nad romanom "Podrostok,"* 1965 (*The Notebooks for "A Raw Youth,"* 1969); *Neizdannyy Dostoyevsky: Zapisnyye knizhki i tetradi 1860-1881,* 1971 (3 volumes; *The Unpublished Dostoevsky: Diaries and Notebooks, 1860-1881,* 1973-1976); *F. M. Dostoyevsky ob iskusstve,* 1973; *Selected Letters of Fyodor Dostoyevsky,* 1987.

TRANSLATION: *Yevgeniya Grande*, 1844 (of Honoré de Balzac's novel *Eugénie Grandet*).

MISCELLANEOUS: *Polnoe sobranie sochinenii v tridtsati tomakh*, 1972-1990 (30 volumes).

BIBLIOGRAPHY

Adelman, Gary. *Retelling Dostoyesvky: Literary Responses and Other Observations.* Lewisburg, Pa.: Bucknell University Press, 2001. Provides information on Dostoevski's life and works by examining how nine twentieth century authors re-created *Crime and Punishment* and other Dostoevski novels. Describes how Dostoevski deeply influenced Joseph Conrad, Richard Wright, Vladimir Nabokov, Bernard Malamud, David Storey, Leonid Leonov, J. M. Coetzee, Frank Herbert, and Albert Camus.

Bloom, Harold, ed. *Fyodor Dostoevsky.* New York: Chelsea House, 2005. Collection of essays includes a biography, analyses of Dostoevski's works, and discussions about the characters in *The Brothers Karamazov* and Dostoevski's detractors and defenders. Also reprints "The Idea in Dostoevsky," an essay by Russian philosopher and literary critic Mikhail Bakhtin.

Catteau, Jacques. *Dostoevsky and the Process of Literary Creation.* Translated by Audrey Littlewood. New York: Cambridge University Press, 1989. Excellent resource offers detailed textual analysis and factual information on Dostoevski. Provides a thematic overview of the pressures and inspirations that motivated the author. Includes extensive notes, bibliography, and index.

Frank, Joseph. *Dostoevsky: The Seeds of Revolt, 1821-1849.* Princeton, N.J.: Princeton University Press, 1976.

_____. *Dostoevsky: The Years of Ordeal, 1850-1859.* Princeton, N.J.: Princeton University Press, 1983.

_____. *Dostoevsky: The Stir of Liberation, 1860-1865.* Princeton, N.J.: Princeton University Press, 1986.

_____. *Dostoevsky: The Miraculous Years, 1865-1871.* Princeton, N.J.: Princeton University Press, 1995.

_____. *Dostoevsky: The Mantle of the Prophet.* Princeton, N.J.: Princeton University Press, 2002. Monumental five-volume biography is one of the best sources on Dostoevski's life and art available in English. Frank subordinates details about the writer's private life in favor of tracing his connection to the social and cultural history of his time.

Kjetsaa, Geir. *Fyodor Dostoevsky: A Writer's Life.* Translated by Siri Hustvedt and David McDuff. New York: Viking Press, 1987. Thorough and compelling work on Dostoevski's life seeks to shed light on the creation of his fiction, citing letters and notes as artistic points of departure for the author.

Leatherbarrow, W. J., ed. *The Cambridge Companion to Dostoevskii.* New York: Cambridge University Press, 2006. Collection of essays examines the author's life and works, discussing his relationship to Russian folk heritage, money, the intelligentsia, psychology, religion, the family, and science, among other topics. Includes chronology and bibliography.

McReynolds, Susan. *Redemption and the Merchant God: Dostoevsky's Economy of Salvation and Antisemitism.* Evanston, Ill.: Northwestern University Press, 2008. Argues that readers cannot fully understand Dostoevski's writings without understanding his obsession with the Jews. Analyzes not only the elements of anti-Semitism in his works but also examines his views of the Crucifixion, Resurrection, morality, and other aspects of Christian doctrine.

Miller, Robin Feuer. *Dostoevsky's Unfinished Journey.* New Haven, Conn.: Yale University Press, 2007. Examines Dostoevski's works from numerous perspectives, analyzing the themes of conversion and healing in his fiction, questioning his literary influence, and exploring what happens to *Crime and Punishment* when it is taught in the classroom.

Scanlan, James P. *Dostoevsky the Thinker: A Philosophical Study.* Ithaca, N.Y.: Cornell University Press, 2002. Analyzes Dostoevski's novels, essays, letters, and notebooks to provide a comprehensive account of his philosophy, examining the weakness as well as the strength of Dostoevski's ideas. Concludes that Dostoevski's thought was shaped by anthropocentrism—a struggle to define the very essence of humanity.

Straus, Nina Pelikan. *Dostoevsky and the Woman Question: Rereadings at the End of a Century.* New York: St. Martin's Press, 1994. Argues that Dostoevski's compulsion to depict men's cruelties to women is an important part of his vision and his metaphysics. Maintains that Dostoevski attacks masculine notions of autonomy and that his works evolve toward "the death of the patriarchy."

NIKOLAI GOGOL

Born: Sorochintsy, Ukraine, Russian Empire (now in Ukraine); March 31, 1809
Died: Moscow, Russia; March 4, 1852
Also known as: Nikolai Vasilyevich Gogol

PRINCIPAL LONG FICTION
Myortvye dushi, 1842, 1855 (2 parts; *Dead Souls*, 1887)
Taras Bulba, 1842 (revision of his 1835 short story; English translation, 1886)

OTHER LITERARY FORMS

Nikolai Gogol (GAW-guhl) authored many short stories, most of which are part of his "Ukrainian cycle" or his later "Petersburg cycle." He also wrote many plays, including *Revizor* (pr., pb. 1836; *The Inspector General*, 1890) and *Zhenit'ba* (pr., pb. 1842; *Marriage: A Quite Incredible Incident*, 1926), as well as a great deal of nonfiction, much of it collected in *Arabeski* (1835; *Arabesques*, 1982) and *Vybrannye mesta iz perepiski s druzyami* (1847; *Selected Passages from Correspondence with Friends*, 1969). Gogol's *Polnoe sobranie sochinenii* (1940-1952; collected works), which includes unfinished works and drafts as well as his voluminous correspondence, fills fourteen volumes. All of Gogol's finished works, but not his drafts or correspondence, are available in English translation.

ACHIEVEMENTS

Nikolai Gogol's first collection of short stories, *Vechera na khutore bliz Dikanki* (1831, 1832; *Evenings on a Farm near Dikanka*, 1926), made him famous, and his second collection, *Mirgorod* (1835; English translation, 1928), highlighted by the story "Taras Bulba," established his reputation as Russia's leading prose writer. While Gogol's early stories, set in the Ukraine, are for the most part conventionally Romantic, his later Petersburg cycle of short stories, among which "Zapiski sumasshedshego" ("Diary of a Madman") and "Shinel" ("The Overcoat") are two of the best known, marks the beginning of Russian critical realism. Gogol's comedic plays are classics and are as popular on the stage (and screen) today as they were in Gogol's lifetime.

Gogol's novel *Dead Souls* is rivaled only by Leo Tolstoy's *Voyna i mir* (1865-1869; *War and Peace*, 1886) as the greatest prose work of Russian literature. Russian prose fiction is routinely divided into two schools: the Pushkinian, which is objective, matter-of-fact, and sparing in its use of verbal devices; and the Gogolian, which is artful, ornamental, and exuberant in its use of ambiguity, irony, pathos, and a variety of figures and tropes usually associated with poetry. Tolstoy and Ivan Turgenev belong to the Pushkinian school; Fyodor Dostoevski, to the Gogolian. In his historical, critical, and moral essays, but especially in *Selected Passages from Correspondence with Friends*, Gogol established

Nikolai Gogol
(Library of Congress)

many of the principles of Russian conservative thought, anticipating the ideas of such writers as Dostoevski and Apollon Grigoryev.

BIOGRAPHY

Nikolai Vasilyevich Gogol, the son of a country squire, was born and educated in the Ukraine. Russian was to him a foreign language, which he mastered while attending secondary school in Nezhin, also in the Ukraine. After his graduation in 1828, Gogol went to St. Petersburg, where he joined the civil service. His first literary effort, "Hans Küchelgarten" (1829), a sentimental idyll in blank verse, was a failure, but his prose fiction immediately attracted attention. After the success of *Evenings on a Farm near Dikanka*, Gogol decided to devote himself entirely to his literary career. He briefly taught medieval history at St. Petersburg University (1834-1835) and thereafter lived the life of a freelance writer and journalist, frequently supported by wealthy patrons. The opening of his play *The Inspector General* at the Aleksandrinsky Theater in St. Petersburg on April 19, 1836, attended and applauded by Czar Nicholas I, was a huge success, but it also elicited vehement attacks by the reactionary press, enraged by Gogol's spirited satire of corruption and stupidity in the provincial administration, and Gogol decided to go abroad to escape the controversy.

From 1836 to 1848, Gogol lived abroad, mostly in Rome, returning to Russia for brief periods only. The year 1842 marked the high point of Gogol's career with the appearance of the first part of *Dead Souls* and the publication of a four-volume set of collected works, which contained some previously unpublished pieces, in particular the great short story "The Overcoat." After 1842, Gogol continued to work on part 2 of *Dead Souls*, but he was becoming increasingly preoccupied with questions of religion and morality. His book *Selected Passages from Correspondence with Friends*, actually a collection of essays in which Gogol defends traditional religious and moral values as well as the social status quo (including the institution of serfdom), caused a storm of protest, as liberals felt that it was flagrantly and evilly reactionary, while even many conservatives considered it to be unctuous and self-righteous.

Sorely hurt by the unfavorable reception of his book, Gogol almost entirely withdrew from literature. He returned to Russia for good in 1848 and spent the rest of his life in religious exercise and meditation. Shortly before his death, caused by excessive fasting and utter exhaustion, Gogol burned the final version of part 2 of *Dead Souls*. An earlier version was later discovered and published in 1855.

ANALYSIS

The cover of the first edition of *Dead Souls*, designed by Nikolai Gogol himself, reads as follows: "*The Adventures of Chichikov or Dead Souls. A Poem by N. Gogol. 1842.*" "The Adventures of Chichikov" is in the smallest print, "Dead Souls" is more than twice that size, and "A Poem" is twice again the size of "Dead Souls." The word "or" is barely legible. The fact that "The Adventures of Chichikov" was inserted at the insistence of the censor, who felt that "Dead Souls" alone smacked of blasphemy, accounts for one-half of this typographical irregularity. The fact that "A Poem" (Russian *poema*, which usually designates an epic poem in verse) dominates the cover of a prose work that at first glance is anything but "poetic" also had its reasons, as will be seen.

DEAD SOULS

The plot structure of *Dead Souls* is simple. Chichikov, a middle-aged gentleman of decent appearance and pleasing manners, travels through the Russian provinces on what seems a mysterious quest: He buys up "dead souls," meaning serfs who have died since the last census but are still listed on the tax rolls until the next census. Along the way, he meets various types of Russian landowners: the sugary and insipid Manilov; the widow Korobochka, ignorant and superstitious but an efficient manager of her farm; the dashing Nozdryov, a braggart, liar, and cardsharp; the brutish but shrewd Sobakevich; and the sordid miser Plyushkin. Having returned to the nearby provincial capital to obtain legal title to his four-hundred-odd "souls," Chichikov soon comes under a cloud of suspicion and quickly leaves town. Only at this stage does the reader learn about Chichikov's past and the secret of the dead souls. A civil service official, Chichikov had twice reached the threshold of prosperity through cleverly devised depredations of the state treasury, but each time he had been foiled at the last moment. After his second fiasco, he had been allowed to resign with only a small sum saved from the clutches of his auditors. Undaunted, he had conceived yet another scheme: He would buy up a substantial number of "dead souls," mortgage them at the highest rate available, and disappear with the cash.

The plot of part 1 takes the story only this far. In what is extant of part 2, Chichikov is seen not only trying to buy more dead souls but also getting involved in other nefarious schemes. It also develops, however, that Chichikov is not happy with his sordid and insecure existence and that he dreams of an honest and virtuous life. He would be willing to mend his ways if he could only find a proper mentor who would give him the right start. There is reason to believe that Gogol planned to describe Chichikov's regeneration and return to the path of rightenousness in part 3. The whole plot thus follows the pattern of a picaresque novel, and many details of *Dead Souls* are, in fact, compatible with this genre, which was well established in Russian literature even before Gogol's day.

Actually, part 1 of *Dead Souls* is many things in addition to a picaresque novel: a humorous novel after the fashion of Charles Dickens's *Pickwick Papers* (1836-1837, serial; 1837, book), with which it was immediately compared by the critics; a social satire attacking the corruption and inefficiency of the imperial administration and the crudity and mental torpor of the landed gentry; a moral sermon in the form of grotesque character sketches; and, above all, an epic of Russia's abjection and hoped-for redemption. The characters of part 2, while copies, in a way, of those encountered in part 1, have redeeming traits and strike the reader as human beings rather than as caricatures. The landowner Tentetnikov, in particular, is clearly a prototype of Oblomov, the hero of Ivan Goncharov's immortal novel of that title (1859; English translation, 1915), and, altogether, part 2 of *Dead Souls* is a big step in the direction of the Russian realist novel of the 1850's and 1860's. The following observations apply to part 1, unless otherwise indicated.

The structure of *Dead Souls* is dominated by the road, as the work begins with a description of Chichikov's arrival at an inn of an unidentified provincial capital and ends with him back on the road, with several intervening episodes in which the hero is seen on his way to his next encounter with a potential purveyor of dead souls. Chichikov's tippling coachman, Selifan, and his three-horse carriage (*troika*) are often foregrounded in Gogol's narrative, and one of the three horses, the lazy and stubborn piebald, has become one of the best-known "characters" in all of Russian fiction. The celebrated *troika* passage concludes part 1. Vladimir Nabokov has written that critic Andrey Bely saw "the whole first volume of *Dead Souls* as a closed circle whirling on its axle and blurring the spokes, with the theme of the wheel cropping up at each new revolution on round Chichikov's part."

When Chichikov is not on the road, the narrative becomes a mirror, as each new character is reflected in Chichikov's mind with the assistance of the omniscient narrator's observations and elucidations. One contemporary critic said that reading *Dead Souls* was like walking down a hotel corridor, opening one door after another—and staring at another human monster each time.

The road and the mirror by no means exhaust Gogol's narrative attitudes. *Dead Souls* features some philosophical discussions on a variety of topics; many short narrative vignettes, such as when Chichikov dreamily imagines what some of his freshly acquired dead souls may have been like in life; an inserted novella, *The Tale of Captain Kopeikin*, told by the local postmaster, who suspects that Chichikov is in fact the legendary outlaw Captain Kopeikin; repeated apostrophes to the reader, discussing the work itself and the course to be taken in continuing it; and, last but not least, Gogol's much-debated lyric digressions. Altogether, while there is some dialogue in *Dead Souls*, the narrator's voice dominates throughout. In fact, the narrative may be described as the free flow of the narrator's stream of consciousness, drifting from observation to observation, image to image, and thought to thought. It is often propelled by purely verbal associations. A common instance of the latter is the so-called realized metaphor, such as when a vendor of hot mead, whose large red face is likened to a copper samovar, is referred to as "the samovar"; when Chichikov, threatened with bodily harm by an enraged Nozdryov and likened to a fortress under siege, suddenly becomes "the fortress"; or when the bearlike Sobakevich is casually identified as a "fair sized bear" in the role of landowner. It is also verbal legerdemain that eventually turns Sobakevich's whole estate into an extension of its owner: "Every object, every chair in Sobakevich's house seemed to proclaim: 'I, too, am Sobakevich!'"

Hyperbole is another device characteristic of Gogol's style. Throughout *Dead Souls*, grotesque distortions and exaggerations are presented as a matter of course—for example, when the scratching of the clerks' pens at the office where Chichikov seals his purchase of dead souls is likened to "the sound of several carts loaded with brushweed and driven through a forest piled with dead leaves a yard deep." Often the hyperbole is ironic, such as when the attire of local ladies is reported to be "of such fashionable pastel shades that one could not even give their names, to such a degree had the refinement of taste attained!"

A sure sign of the author's own point of view surfaces in frequent literary allusions and several passages in which Gogol digresses to discuss the theory of fiction—for example, the famous disquisition, introducing chapter 7, on the distinction between the writer who idealizes life and the writer who chooses to deal with real life. Gogol, who fancies himself to be a realist, wryly observes that "the judgment of his time does not recognize that much spiritual depth is required to throw light upon a picture taken from a despised stratum of life, and to exalt it into a pearl of creative art" but feels "destined by some wondrous power to go hand in hand with his heroes, to contemplate life in its entirety, life rushing past in all its enormity, amid laughter perceptible to the world and through tears that are unperceived by and unknown to it!" The phrases "to exalt it into a pearl of creative art" and "amid laughter perceptible to the world and through tears that are unperceived by and unknown to it" have become common Russian usage, along with many others in *Dead Souls*.

Dead Souls is studded with many outright digressions. It must be kept in mind, however, that the mid-nineteenth century novel was routinely used as a catchall for miscellaneous didactic, philosophical, critical, scholarly, and lyric pieces that were often only superficially, if at all, integrated into the texture of the larger work. Still, the number and nature of digressions in *Dead Souls* are exceptional even by the standards of a *roman feuilleton* of the 1840's. As described by Victor Erlich, two basic types of digressions are found in *Dead Souls:* "the lateral darts and the upward flights." The former are excursions into a great variety of aspects of Russian life, keenly observed, sharply focused, and always lively and colorful. For example, having observed that Sobakevich's head looks quite like a pumpkin, Gogol, in one of his many "Homeric similes," veers off into a village idyll about a peasant lad strumming a balalaika made from a pumpkin to win the heart of a "snowy-breasted and snowy-necked Maiden."

Gogol's upward flights are of a quite different order. They permit his imagination to escape the prosaic reality of Chichikov's experience and allow him to become a poet who takes a lofty view of Russia and its destiny. In several of these passages, Gogol's imagination becomes quite literally airborne. One of them, at the conclusion of chapter 5, begins with a lofty aerial panorama: "Even as an incomputable host of churches, of monasteries, with cupolas, bulbous domes, and crosses, is scattered all over holy and devout Russia, so does an incomputable multitude of tribes, generations, peoples swarm, flaunt their motley and scurry across the face of the earth." It ends in a rousing paean to "the Russian word which, like no other in the world, would burst out so, from out the very heart, which would seethe so and quiver and flutter so much like a living thing."

Early in chapter 11, Gogol produces another marvelous panoramic vision of Russia, apostrophized in the famous passage, "Russia, Russia! I behold thee—from my alien, beautiful, far-off vantage point I behold thee." (Gogol wrote most of *Dead Souls* while living in Italy.) The conclusion of this, the final chapter of part 1, then brings the most famous lines of prose in all of Russian literature, the *troika* passage in which a speeding three-horse carriage is elevated to a symbol of Russia's historical destiny. The intensity and plenitude of life and emotion in these and other airborne lyric passages stand in stark contrast to the drab world that is otherwise dominant in *Dead Souls*. These lyric digressions were challenged as incongruous and unnecessary even by some contemporary critics who, as do many critics today, failed to realize that Gogol's is a dual vision of manic-depressive intensity.

As a *poema* (epic poem), *Dead Souls* is a work that Gogol perceived as the poetic expression of an important religious-philosophical conception—that is, something on the order of Dante's *La divina commedia* (c. 1320; *The Divine Comedy*, 1802) or John Milton's *Paradise Lost* (1667, 1674). Incidentally, there is one rather inconsequential allusion to Dante in chapter 7, where one reads that a collegiate registrar "served our friends even as Virgil at one time had served Dante, and guided them to the Presence."

Immediately after the appearance of *Dead Souls*, critics were split into two camps: those who, like Konstantin Aksakov, greeted the work as the Russian national epic, found numerous Homeric traits in it, and perceived it as a true incarnation of the Russian spirit in all of its depth and plenitude, and those who, like Nikolai Alekseevich Polevoi and Osip Ivanovich Senkovsky, saw it as merely an entertaining, though rather banal and in places pretentious, humorous novel. The latter group—which included even the great critic Vissarion Belinsky, who otherwise felt that *Dead Souls* was a perfect quintessence of Russian life—found Gogol's attempts at philosophizing and solemn pathos merely pompous and false. There has never been agreement in this matter. Nevertheless, several passages in part 1, the whole drift of part 2, and a number of quite unequivocal statements made by Gogol in his correspondence (in *Selected Passages from Correspondence with Friends* and in his posthumous "Author's Confession") all suggest that Gogol did indeed perceive *Dead Souls* as a *Divine Comedy* of the Russian soul, with part 1 its *Inferno*, part 2 its *Purgatory*, and part 3 its *Paradise*.

How, then, is part 1 in fact an *Inferno*, a Russian Hell? It is set in a Hades of dead souls, of humans who lead a shadowy phantom existence bereft of any real meaning or direction. Thus, it must be understood that in the Romantic philosophy of Gogol's time, the "normal" existence of a European philistine was routinely called "illusory," "unreal," and even "ghostly," while the ideal quest of the artist or philosopher was considered "substantial," "real," and "truly alive." As Andrey Bely demonstrated most convincingly, all of part 1 is dominated by what he calls "the figure of fiction." Whatever is said or believed to be true is from beginning to end a fiction, as unreal as Chichikov's financial transactions. For example, when the good people of N. begin to suspect that something is wrong with Chichikov, some of them believe that he plans to abduct the Governor's daughter, others conjecture that he is really Captain Kopeikin, a highway robber of legendary fame, and some actually suspect that he is Napoleon escaped from his island exile, but nobody investigates his motive for buying dead souls. As Bely also demonstrated, even time and space in *Dead Souls* are fictitious: The text will not even allow one to determine the season of the year; Chichikov's itinerary, if methodically checked, is physically impossible; and so on. Behind the figure of fiction, there looms large the message that all earthly experience and wisdom are in fact illusory, as Gogol makes explicit in a philosophical digression found in chapter 10.

In this shadowy world of fiction there exist two kinds of dead souls. There are the dead serfs who are sold and mortgaged and who, in the process, acquire a real semblance of life. Mrs. Korobochka, as soon as she has understood that Chichikov is willing to pay her some money for her dead serfs, is afraid that he may underpay her and somewhat timidly suggests that "maybe I'll find some use for them in my own household." Sobakevich, who haggles about the price of each dead soul, insists on eloquently describing their skills and virtues, as though it really mattered. Chichikov himself firmly rejects an offer by the local authorities to provide him with a police escort for the souls he has purchased, asserting that "his peasants are all of eminently quiet disposition." The same night, however, when he returns home from a party thrown by the local police chief to honor the new owner of four hundred souls, he actually orders Selifan "to gather all the resettled peasants, so he can personally make a roll call of them." Selifan and Petrushka, Chichikov's lackey, barely manage to get their master to bed.

The humanitarian message behind all of this is obvious: How could a person who finds the buying and selling of dead souls "fantastic" and "absurd" have the effrontery to find the same business transactions involving living souls perfectly normal? This message applies not only to Russia in the age of serfdom (which ended only in 1861—that is, at about the same time formal slavery ended in the United States) but also to any situation in which human beings are reduced to their social or economic function.

The other dead souls are the landowners and government officials whom we meet in *Dead Souls*. As the critic Vasily Rozanov observed, the peculiar thing about Gogolian characters is that they have no souls; they have habits and appetites but no deeper human emotions or ideal strivings. This inevitably deprives them of their humanity and renders them two-dimensional personifications of their vices—caricatures. Sobakevich is a very shrewd talking bear. Nozdryov is so utterly worthless that he appears to be a mere appendage of his extraordinarily handsome, thick, and pitch-black sideburns, thinned out a bit from time to time, when their owner is caught cheating at cards and suffers a whisker pulling. Plyushkin's stony miserliness has deprived him of all feeling and has turned him, a rich landowner, into a beggar and an outcast of society. *Dead Souls* has many such caricatures, which have been likened to Brueghelian grotesque paintings. This analogy applies to the following passage in chapter 11, for example: "The clerks in the Treasury were especially distinguished for their unprepossessing and unsightly appearance. Some had faces for all the world like badly baked bread: one cheek would be all puffed out to one side, the chin slanting off to the other, the upper lip blown up into a big blister that, to top it all off, had burst."

As early as 1842, the critic Stepan Shevyrev suggested that *Dead Souls* represented a mad world, thus following an ancient literary and cultural tradition (which today is often referred to as that of the "carnival"). The massive absurdities, non sequiturs, and simply plain foolishness throughout the whole text could, for Gogol and for many of his readers, have only one message: That which poses for "real life" is in fact nothing but a ludicrous farce. The basic course of Gogol's imagination is that of a descent into a world of ridiculous, banal, and vile "nonbeing," from which it will from time to time rise to the heights of noble and inspired "being."

TARAS BULBA

While *Dead Souls* is unquestionably Gogol's masterpiece, his only other work of long fiction, *Taras Bulba*, is not without interest. The 1835 version of this work is a historical novella; the 1842 version, almost twice as long and thus novel-sized, has many digressions and is at once more realistic and more gothic but also more patriotic, moralizing, and bigoted. The plot is essentially the same in both versions.

Taras Bulba is a Ukrainian Cossack leader, so proud of his two fine sons recently back from school in Kiev that he foments war against the hated Poles, so that Ostap and Andriy can prove their manhood in battle. The Cossacks are initially successful, and the Poles are driven back to the fortress city of Dubno. The Cossacks lay siege to it, and the city seems ready to fall when Andriy is lured to the city by a messenger from a beautiful Polish maiden with whom he had fallen in love as a student in Kiev. Blinded by her promises of love, Andriy turns traitor. The Cossacks' fortunes now take a turn for the worse. They are pressed hard by a Polish relief force. On the battlefield, Taras meets Andriy (now a Polish officer), orders him to dismount, and shoots him. The Cossacks, however, are defeated, and Ostap is taken prisoner. Old Taras makes his way to Warsaw, hoping to save him, but can only witness his son's execution. Having returned to the Ukraine, Taras becomes one of the leaders of yet another Cossack uprising against the king of Poland. When peace is made, Taras alone refuses to honor it. He continues to wreak havoc on the Poles all over the Ukraine but is finally captured by superior Polish forces. He dies at the stake, prophesying the coming of a Russian czar against whom no power on earth will stand.

There is little historical verity in *Taras Bulba*. Different details found in the text point to the fifteenth, sixteenth, and seventeenth centuries as the time of its action. It is thus an epic synthesis of the struggle of the Orthodox Ukraine to retain its independence from Catholic Poland. The battle scenes are patterned on those in the works of Vergil and Homer, and there are many conventional epic traits throughout, such as scores of brief scenes of single combat, catalogs of warriors' names, extended Homeric similes, orations, and, of course, the final solemn prophecy. Taras Bulba is a tragic hero who expiates his hubris with the loss of his sons and his own terrible death.

The earlier version of *Taras Bulba* serves mostly the glorification of the wild, carefree life at the Cossack army camp. In the later version, this truly inspired hymn to male freedom is obscured by a message of Russian nationalism, Orthodox bigotry, and nostalgia for a glorious past that never was. The novel features almost incessant baiting of Poles and Jews. Gogol's view of the war is a wholly unrealistic and romantic one: The reader is told of "the enchanting music of bullets and swords" and so on. From a literary viewpoint, *Taras Bulba* is a peculiar mixture of the historical novel in the manner of Sir Walter Scott and the gothic tale. The narrator stations himself above his hero, gently faulting him on some of his uncivilized traits, such as the excessive stock Taras puts in his drinking prowess or his maltreatment of his long-suffering wife. Rather often, however, the narrator descends to the manner of the folktale. His language swings wildly from coarse humor and naturalistic grotesque to solemn oratory and lyric digressions. Scenes of unspeakable atrocities are reported with relish, but some wonderful poems in prose are also presented, such as the well-known description of the Ukrainian steppe in the second chapter.

Altogether, *Taras Bulba* contains some brilliant writing but also some glaring faults. It immediately became a classic, and soon enough a school text, inasmuch as its jingoism met with the approval of the czar—and eventually of Soviet school administrators. Several film versions, Russian as well as Western, have been produced.

Although Gogol's production of fiction was quite small by nineteenth century standards, both his novels and his short stories have had extraordinary influence on the development of Russian prose—an influence that was still potent at the end of the twentieth
century, as witnessed by the works of Andrei Sinyavsky and other writers of the Third
Emigration.

Victor Terras

OTHER MAJOR WORKS

SHORT FICTION: *Vechera na khutore bliz Dikanki*, 1831, 1832 (2 volumes; *Evenings on
a Farm near Dikanka*, 1926); *Arabeski*, 1835 (*Arabesques*, 1982); *Mirgorod*, 1835 (English translation, 1928); *The Complete Tales of Nikolai Gogol*, 1985 (2 volumes; Leonard J.
Kent, editor).

PLAYS: *Revizor,* pr., pb. 1836 (*The Inspector General*, 1890); *Utro delovogo cheloveka*,
pb. 1836 (revision of *Vladimir tretey stepeni*; *An Official's Morning*, 1926); *Igroki*, pb.
1842 (*The Gamblers*, 1926); *Lakeyskaya*, pb. 1842 (revision of *Vladimir tretey stepeni*;
The Servants' Hall, 1926); *Otryvok*, pb. 1842 (revision of *Vladimir tretey stepeni*; *A Fragment*, 1926); *Tyazhba*, pb. 1842 (revision of *Vladimir tretey stepeni*; *The Lawsuit*, 1926);
Vladimir tretey stepeni, pb. 1842 (wr. 1832); *Zhenit'ba,* pr., pb. 1842 (wr. 1835; *Marriage:
A Quite Incredible Incident*, 1926); *The Government Inspector, and Other Plays*, 1926.

POETRY: *Hanz Kuechelgarten*, 1829.

NONFICTION: *Vybrannye mesta iz perepiski s druzyami*, 1847 (*Selected Passages from
Correspondence with Friends*, 1969); *Letters of Nikolai Gogol*, 1967.

MISCELLANEOUS: *The Collected Works*, 1922-1927 (6 volumes); *Polnoe sobranie
sochinenii*, 1940-1952 (14 volumes); *The Collected Tales and Plays of Nikolai Gogol*,
1964.

BIBLIOGRAPHY

Bojanowska, Edyta M. *Nikolai Gogol: Between Ukrainian and Russian Nationalism.*
Cambridge, Mass.: Harvard University Press, 2007. Analyzes Gogol's life and works
in terms of his conflicted national identity. Gogol was born in Ukraine when it was a
part of the Russian empire; Bojanowska describes how he was engaged with questions
of Ukrainian nationalism and how his works presented a bleak and ironic portrayal of
Russia and Russian themes.

Erlich, Victor. *Gogol.* New Haven, Conn.: Yale University Press, 1969. Provides an accessible and evenhanded discussion of Gogol for nonspecialists. Focuses on Gogol's
oeuvre, dealing with much of the "myth" about the author, and supplies interesting
background to the making of Gogol's works.

Fanger, Donald L. *The Creation of Nikolai Gogol.* Cambridge, Mass.: Belknap Press of
Harvard University Press, 1979. Digs deeply into background material and includes
discussion of Gogol's works both published and unpublished in an effort to reveal the

genius of Gogol's creative power. Worthwhile in many respects, particularly for the wealth of details provided about Gogol's life and milieu. Includes endnotes and index.

Gippius, V. V. *Gogol*. Translated by Robert Maguire. Ann Arbor, Mich.: Ardis, 1981. Originally written in 1924, this famous monograph supplies not only the view of a fellow countryman but also a vast, informed, and intellectual analysis of both the literary tradition in which Gogol wrote and his innovation and contribution to that tradition. Vastly interesting and easily accessible. Includes notes and a detailed list of Gogol's works.

Luckyj, George Stephen Nestor. *The Anguish of Mykola Hohol a.k.a. Nikolai Gogol*. Toronto, Ont.: Canadian Scholars' Press, 1998. Explores Gogol's life and discusses how it affected his work. Includes bibliographical references and index.

Maguire, Robert A. *Exploring Gogol*. Stanford, Calif.: Stanford University Press, 1994. One of the most comprehensive studies of Gogol's ideas and entire writing career available in English. Includes chronology, detailed notes, and extensive bibliography.

_____, ed. *Gogol from the Twentieth Century: Eleven Essays*. Princeton, N.J.: Princeton University Press, 1974. Collection of essays represents some of the most famous and influential opinions on Gogol in the twentieth century. Following a lengthy introduction by the editor and translator, the contributors address and elucidate some of the most problematic aspects of Gogol's stylistics, thematics, and other compositional elements. Includes bibliography and index.

Setchkarev, Vsevolod. *Gogol: His Life and Works*. Translated by Robert Kramer. New York: New York University Press, 1965. Standard work on Gogol is still often recommended in undergraduate courses. Concentrates on both the biography and the works, seen individually and as an artistic system. Very straightforward and easily readable.

Spieker, Sven, ed. *Gogol: Exploring Absence—Negativity in Nineteenth Century Russian Literature*. Bloomington, Ind.: Slavica, 1999. Collection of essays focuses on the negativity in *Dead Souls* and Gogol's other works and in the works of other Russian writers. Includes bibliography and index.

Troyat, Henri. *Divided Soul*. Translated by Nancy Amphoux. Garden City, N.Y.: Doubleday, 1973. Provides perhaps the most information on Gogol's life available in English in a single volume. Demonstrates masterfully how Gogol's life and work are inextricably intertwined and does not neglect the important role that "God's will" played in Gogol's life, as the thread that lends the greatest cohesion to the diverse developments in his creative journey. Includes some interesting illustrations as well as bibliography, notes, and index.

Weiner, Adam. "The Evils of *Dead Souls*." In *By Authors Possessed: The Demonic Novel in Russia*. Evanston, Ill.: Northwestern University Press, 1998. Chapter focusing on *Dead Souls* is included in a wider analysis of nineteenth and twentieth century Russian "demonic novels," defined as novels in which the protagonists are incarnated with the evil presence of the Devil.

IVAN GONCHAROV

Born: Simbirsk, Russia; June 6, 1812
Died: St. Petersburg, Russia; September 15, 1891
Also known as: Ivan Alexandrovich Goncharov

PRINCIPAL LONG FICTION

Obyknovennaya istoriya, 1847 (*A Common Story*, 1890)
Oblomov, 1859 (English translation, 1915)
Obryv, 1869 (*The Precipice*, 1916)

OTHER LITERARY FORMS

The early stories and poems of Ivan Goncharov (gon-chah-RAHF) were considered mediocre by the author himself as well as the public and have long been out of print. Goncharov's first significant piece was the sketch "Ivan Savich Podzhabrin," available in *Sobranie sochinenii* (1883, 1888, 1952; collected works). Still widely published and read is the travelogue *Fregat Pallada* (1858; *The Voyage of the Frigate Pallada*, 1965). During the final two decades of his life, Goncharov concentrated on critical essays, reminiscences, and polemical articles. "Mil'yon terzaniy" (1872), his analysis of Alexander Griboyedov's *Gore ot uma* (1825, 1831; English translation, 1857), and his autobiographical memoir "Luchshe pozdno, chem nikogda" (1879; better late than never) have limited circulation, even among literary specialists.

ACHIEVEMENTS

Ivan Goncharov's novels mark the transition from Russian Romanticism to a much more realistic worldview. They appeared at a time when sociological criteria dominated analysis and when authors were expected to address the injustices of Russian life. The critic Nikolay Dobrolyubov derived the term *Oblomovism* from Goncharov's most famous novel, using it to denote the physical and mental sluggishness of Russia's backward country gentry. Thus, Goncharov is credited with exposing a harmful national type: the spendthrift serf-holding landowner who contributed nothing to the national economy and resisted progress for fear of destroying his carefree existence.

By presenting this type in his rather ordinary surroundings and endeavors, stripped of the Romantic aura with which Alexander Pushkin's classical and Mikhail Lermontov's Romantic verse had imbued him, Goncharov gained renown as a critical realist. While all three of his novels remain popular classics in his homeland, only *Oblomov* has found a wide readership and critical acclaim abroad. Emphasis on that work has caused modern Western scholars to value Goncharov as highly for his artful psychological portraits of stunted adults adrift in a changing world as for his sociological contribution.

Oblomov's "return to the womb" predates Sigmund Freud by several decades. On the artistic level, Goncharov far transcends the realistic label often applied to him. His talent for transforming an endlessly mundane provincial existence into a delicate poetic network of pre-Petrine Russian values set standards for the budding Russian novel; his stream-of-consciousness approach points ahead to James Joyce and Marcel Proust. Goncharov has firmly established a place for himself within the genre of the modern psychological novel.

BIOGRAPHY

Ivan Goncharov was born Ivan Alexandrovich Goncharov on June 18, 1812, in remote Simbirsk (now Ulyanovsk) on a country estate of the type featured in his novels. After losing his merchant father at age seven, he was reared in the old tradition by his strong-willed mother and her landowning companion. This heritage of easygoing manor life and progressive mercantile activity characterizes Goncharov's own outlook and that of his major fictional characters. Encouraged to follow in his father's footsteps, he languished for eight years in a school of commerce without graduating. From 1831 to 1834, he attended Moscow University, without taking an active part in the famous philosophical student circles of the time. Instead, he entered the literary world as a tutor in the culturally sophisticated Maikov family, using this experience to produce his first poems and stories.

Goncharov's rise to fame was slow, and he was trapped in a civil service career spanning more than thirty years, almost half of which was spent uneventfully as a translator in the finance ministry. Goncharov's private existence turned out to be equally monotonous. Although he was attracted to a number of women, his courtships were not successful, and he never married. The frustrations of his relationships with women are prominently mirrored in all three novels.

The success of his first novel, *A Common Story*, did not alleviate Goncharov's self-doubt, and he remained fettered to extraliterary activity. A worldwide sailing tour on behalf of the trade ministry in the 1850's yielded material for his travel sketches. The same period brought an appointment to the literary censorship board, a result of Czar Alexander II's relaxed attitude. Goncharov followed a middle-of-the-road philosophy in this post, often enraging progressive writers, whose harsh judgments of conservative ideals he would not accept. He secured his own literary fame with *Oblomov* but felt too insecure to devote himself exclusively to literature. After a brief try at editing the official newspaper *Severnaya pchela* in the 1860's, he returned to a censorial post in the influential Press Council. His civic duties earned for him the Order of Vladimir, third class, prior to retirement in 1868.

Meanwhile, Goncharov's mental state had gradually deteriorated. Ivan Turgenev's literary success easily eclipsed that of Goncharov, and when Turgenev's *Dvoryanskoe gnezdo* (1859; *Liza: Or, "A Nest of Nobles,"* 1869; better known as *A House of Gentlefolk*, 1959) superseded *Oblomov* in critical acclaim, Goncharov accused his rival of plagiarism. Arbitration found Turgenev innocent, and the writers reconciled, but in private, the increasingly neurotic Goncharov continued the accusations, venting on Turgenev all the frustrations of his own unsatisfactory existence. Philosophically, Goncharov moved from a modestly progressive stance to a firm defense of the traditional values of the landed gentry. These sentiments found expression in *The Precipice*, in which moral regeneration is embedded in the unchanging order of provincial Russia.

Goncharov died on September 15, 1891, a stranger to the swiftly moving social currents of the latter part of the century. His later published works chronicle his artistic decline. A complete recluse, he burned his letters and manuscripts. He spent his final days not unlike his major hero, Oblomov, in a St. Petersburg flat, looked after by a kindly woman and her children.

ANALYSIS

"My life began flickering out from the very first moment I became conscious of myself." Thus, Ilya Oblomov explains his arrested development to his successful business friend, Stolz, who is making a last try to rouse Oblomov from his fatal lethargy, and thus Goncharov points the reader to the cause of Oblomov's inertia: his childhood in a sleepy, backward manor house, attended by an army of serfs, every moment structured to reinforce an existence of indolently blissful inactivity, a paradise to which the adult strives all of his life to return. Oblomov's failure as a man and his search for a surrogate childhood in a simple St. Petersburg family fit perfectly the scheme of the psychological novel. From this perspective, the seemingly typical Russian landowner Oblomov becomes a universal figure, and the old-fashioned Russian village becomes merely background.

Such a perspective, however, has its drawbacks. If one considers *Oblomov* apart from Goncharov's other novels, as is often the case in the West, the wider artistic sweep of his fiction is neglected. Each of his novels gives expression to a different facet of the contradictions encountered by the Russian patriarchal order as it confronted sociopolitical reform. Goncharov's characters can be said to embody the two warring dominant philosophies of nineteenth century Russia: Slavophilism and Westernization. The author's own struggle between these two opposing forces is cast into sharp focus in the novels, as his progress-oriented mind gradually loses ground to his tradition-loving, Slavophile heart.

Neither Goncharov's personal dissatisfactions nor his conservative turn impair his stature as an accomplished novelist. The expert use of several literary devices contributes to this renown. There is, first of all, his power of observation, the ability to create such a lifelike image of an ordinary event through accumulation of detail that his scenes are compared to Flemish interiors. Authorial ambiguity also enriches the narrative. The first two novels conceptually demonstrate the advantages of a progressive economy and the futility of perpetuating serfdom, but Goncharov presents a dying way of life with such a wealth of attractive imagery that social indifference, indeed exploitation, infantilism, and stagnation, are turned into a languidly cozy, almost noble way of life, feeding on nostalgia and winning sympathy for its prejudices.

No less impressive is Goncharov's skill in suggesting the delusions of the regressive personality. Oblomov's insecure psyche reshapes his ordinary village into a harmless, safe refuge, smoothing craggy mountains into gentle hillocks, swift rivers into murmuring brooks, extremes of climate into eternally pleasant weather, passions into lethargy. Readers are scarcely aware that the descriptions are no longer objective, but the distortions of a frightened mind.

Finally, Goncharov excels in drawing exquisite female portraits; his women also symbolize the synthesis between the old and new. In *A Common Story*, Lizaveta is able to balance the contradictory forces that pull the male characters into adversary position; in *Oblomov*, Olga combines the best of old Russia, its cultural heritage, with an inquisitive mind and an active personality; in *The Precipice*, Vera eventually unites the positive features of her patriarchal upbringing with the progressive forces of a commercially enterprising spouse.

In his final novel, Goncharov's moralizing instincts undermine his mastery of style, as didactic elements intrude too explicitly. The author's own estrangement from the present and his nostalgia for a less complex existence color his perceptions. His slow-paced upbringing, his later insecurities, his realization that progress was necessary, his struggle between old and new, and his final withdrawal from society are the building blocks of all of his works. He delicately managed to balance these elements before yielding to his own preferences.

A Common Story

The unstinting praise of Russia's foremost social critic, Vissarion Belinsky, assured the success of *A Common Story* the moment it appeared in the literary journal *Sovremennik*. Ironically, the work was hailed as an exposé of the degenerate gentry class and a call for modernization. Critics and readers alike noted only the main character Alexander Aduev's final acceptance of St. Petersburg's progressive lifestyle, not his mentor-uncle's disillusionment with it. They also overlooked the author's cautious suggestion that the city's competitive utilitarianism was no more satisfying than the monotony of the backward village.

This misperception attests Goncharov's balancing skill. Alexander is lured from his peaceful, idyllic estate, lovingly presented in the fragrance of its lilacs, berries, bushes, and forests, by visions of cosmopolitan dazzle. Once he is taken in hand by a "new man," his coldly efficient, philistine uncle, Peter, one disappointment succeeds another. Like an early Oblomov, Alexander adjusts only superficially, never able to integrate his rustic values with St. Petersburg's diverse phenomena. Like a young Goncharov, Alexander blunders from one unsuccessful love affair to another. His literary endeavors, characterized by overblown sentimental clichés, are equally fruitless. Despite all efforts by Peter, he turns into a rather ridiculous figure, an out-of-place relic in the bustling city. Goncharov's ambiguous attitude, however, gives enough scope to elicit a measure of pity from the reader, to mark the young man's discomforts and his inability to cope.

Peter's young wife, Lizaveta, compassionately brings out Alexander's positive traits.

When all attempts at acclimatization end in failure, he returns to his quiet country home and recovers his bearings. yet the lessons of the city are not lost. At a distance, its hectic multiplicity develops into a fair alternative to the boring idyll of the placid province. In the end, Alexander sets out for St. Petersburg once more, cured of his romantic expectations, determined to copy his uncle's career through realistic adaptation and lowered sights. His success is presented in the epilogue. He parallels Peter faithfully: fat and balding, engaged to a young heiress, adjusted, mature, eager for progressive endeavors.

While this conclusion heartened liberal critics, Goncharov's reservations are apparent in the incompletely dramatized and therefore unconvincing psychological transformation of Alexander. The artistically unmotivated ending causes a change of focus. The carefully developed juxtaposition of old versus new, village versus city, Slavophile versus Westernizer assumes the outline of a bildungsroman. Peter and Alexander represent two stages of identical development. Alexander's romantic striving mirrors Peter's own youthful immaturity, while Peter's rational, mature stage serves as a marker for Alexander's similar destiny. At the moment of Alexander's arrival at that stage, Peter's dry and joyless stance casts doubt on the wisdom of these very accomplishments, foreshadowing eventual disillusionment for his nephew. The general inattention to this downbeat element is a result of the shortage of bourgeois heroes in Russian literature.

The Romantic characters of Pushkin, Lermontov, and the early Turgenev are immobile, purposeless, and contemptuous of practical activity. Liberal critics had long called for a positively depicted, businesslike nobleman, and they accepted Alexander in his final guise enthusiastically as such. The careful reader is left questioning both men's aspirations and sharing Lizaveta's wistful awareness that St. Petersburg's progress is far from ideal. The alternative of seeking that ideal in Russia's past surfaces only in Goncharov's later works, although the absence of a critical stand against serfdom and landowner privileges already serves to modify the seeming victory of Westernization.

OBLOMOV

Turgenev's popular *A Nest of Gentlefolk* threatened to overshadow *Oblomov*, which was first printed in *Otechestvennye zapiski*, until critic Dobrolyubov's 1859 article "Chto takoyo Oblomovshchina?" ("What Is Oblomovism?") swiftly drew national attention to the work. Following Dobrolyubov's cue, most readers and succeeding generations saw in *Oblomov* the hero's inertia the psychological consequence of total dependence on serf labor. By lavishing endless pages on the harmful effects of Oblomovism and the virtues of Stolz, a Western-influenced business type, Goncharov seemed to strike a forceful blow at the roots of Russia's economic and social evils.

Oblomov appears as the epitome of the superfluous nobleman, the lazy, alienated dreamer who cannot adjust to change or find a place for himself in the present. Different embodiments of this type exist in Pushkin's Onegin, Lermontov's Pechorin, and Turgenev's Rudin. Oblomov differs from these characters in that he rejects even the search for an alternative, preferring instead the never-changing ways of his childhood Oblomovka. The location of this estate on the Asian border aptly suggests the Asian fatalism and circular philosophy that represent Oblomov's and, by extension, Russia's Eastern Tartar heritage. The hero's Asian dressing gown, serving as his security blanket and finally his shroud, is an equally fitting symbol.

The reader is initiated into all the details of Russian provincial backwardness through Oblomov's lengthy dream of his sleepy backwater. The dream, a thematic outline of the work and its centerpiece, had been published separately as a sort of overture as early as 1849. The finished novel shows the deadening effect of this "blessed spot" on those who cannot free themselves from the dependencies it fosters. Little Ilya was born a normal child, willing to experiment, to rough it, to develop. The atmosphere of Oblomovka snuffed out all of these inclinations. Tradition stipulates that a Russian gentleman sit, surrounded by hordes of serfs who attend to his every whim, that he eat and doze most of the day, phlegmatically observe the seasonal and ecclesiastical rituals, ignore any attempt at change, be it literacy or postal service, and hope that the waves of Peter the Great's Westernizing reforms never reach his quiet hamlet. Inevitably, they do reach Oblomovka, and the product of its upbringing must serve his term in St. Petersburg.

The innumerable ways in which the transplanted Oblomov manages to ignore the city's reality take up a good portion of the narrative. Each failure on the realistic plane is paralleled by a success on the imaginary level, which always features a happy Oblomov in a paradisiacal Oblomovka. Eventually, Oblomov gains a questionable victory. A motherly widow's shabby lodging transforms itself into a blissful surrogate of Oblomovka for the by-now infantile hero. He has returned to the womb and lives out a short but happy span, until mental stagnation and greedy overeating end his life. Two people try their best to save Oblomov. First Stolz, the half-German entrepreneur, as lean as an English racehorse where Oblomov is fat and flabby, uses reason and intellectual appeal to convince Oblomov to change. Then Olga, already adapted to a modern intelligentsia but preserving a deep love for Russia's cultural past, lures him with promises of selfless love. Sexually aroused, Oblomov briefly responds to her, but when he finds that Olga also demands intellectual arousal, constant mental awareness, he takes flight. The equally dull-witted widow offers both maternal and mistress services without the necessity of mental effort.

Stolz and Olga, who eventually marry, represent the best of traditional Russia fused with the best of imported progressive behavior. Stolz is an improved version of Peter Aduev. The latter's negative traits and final pessimistic outlook have been replaced by Stolz's cheerfulness and compassion. Even here, however, the author's descriptive talents hover lovingly over the blubbery Oblomov—over his dreams, his reflections, his blunders—while Stolz comes across as artificial and wooden, the victim of uninspired portrayal. Olga, who loves and appreciates Oblomov's values, is a more credible figure, and it is she who embodies and carries into the future the reconciliation of the conflict. In some respects, she acts as Goncharov's mouthpiece. Her dissatisfactions, even with the faultless

Stolz, echo the author's own inability to believe fully in the spiritual benefits of a forward-moving Russia.

Goncharov had no such reservations when it came to praising the charms of Oblomovka. Its oneness with nature renders each inhabitant a paragon of virtue. No passionate outbursts or personal animosities mar the peacefulness. Serfs are not slaves, but content to be reflections of their masters. Their sloth and their ample participation in all the feasting, indulged by benevolent owners, help to deplete Oblomovka's reserves. When this slothful behavior is transplanted to St. Petersburg in the person of Oblomov's loyal valet Zakhar, it loses much of its bucolic enchantment, yet the touching interdependence of master and servant redeems the ineptness. It was simply impossible for Goncharov to carry to its logical conclusion his commonsense understanding that radical Slavophilism would result in national stagnation and regression.

THE PRECIPICE

Goncharov's unwillingness to endow his progressive characters with the vitality necessary to make them convincing and interesting asserts itself more fully in his last major work, *The Precipice*. It appeared in *Vestnik Evropy* at a time when emancipation was a fact, when Alexander II's liberalism gave wide scope to social commentators, when literature closely echoed the zeitgeist of reform. Goncharov's liberal representative is the political exile Volokhov, who, like Turgenev's nihilist Bazarov, spreads unrest in a deeply conservative village. Volokhov's positive qualities are quickly neutralized by his seduction of a virtuous country woman, Vera, who naïvely tries to straighten him out. Vera is also a link to the other male principal, Raisky, a St. Petersburg intellectual, who has failed to find a purpose in life and returns to his country estate in search of a footing. It is easy to see in him yet another embodiment of Goncharov's favorite type: the neurotic male whose interests, convictions, and common sense pull him toward reform but whose temperament and deep-seated impulses chain him to the past. In each of these split personalities, Goncharov's own schism finds expression. As before, he reserves the best of his descriptive talents for the backwoods, symbolized by the figure of the grandmother. It is in this traditional setting that the abused Vera finds regeneration and mental recovery; it is the rural past that bequeaths stability, sanity, and direction for the future.

Goncharov had once again drawn an exquisite cameo of old Russia, once again contrasted the conflicting values of old and new, once again pictured an artistically masterful "homecoming." Despite the popularity of the somewhat meandering work, Goncharov's point of view drew heavy moral indignation. Liberal critics were quick to point out that Goncharov had come down on the side of rural conservatism, that he favored the Slavophiles. Obviously and painfully out of step with the tenor of the time, and psychologically unable and unwilling to recapture his artistic independence, Goncharov withdrew. His subsequent writings did not approach the stature of his novels.

Goncharov's significance in the development of the Russian novel and Russian intellectual history remains great. He brought to life the characters of old Russia, with a style peculiarly his own, at a time when that patriarchal order began to disintegrate. In his portraits of Slavophiles and Westernizers, he elaborated on the dominant conflict of mid-century Russia. He was the first Russian author to integrate psychological complexities successfully and expertly into his plots, and thereby he created universal types.

Margot K. Frank

OTHER MAJOR WORKS

SHORT FICTION: "Ivan Savich Podzhabrin," 1848; "Slugi starogo veka," 1888.

NONFICTION: *Fregat Pallada*, 1858 (*The Voyage of the Frigate Pallada*, 1965); "Mil'yon terzaniy," 1872; "Luchshe pozdno, chem nikogda," 1879; "V universitete," 1887; "Na rodine," 1888; "Neobyknovennaya istoriya," 1924.

MISCELLANEOUS: *Sobranie sochinenii*, 1883, 1888, 1952 (8 volumes).

BIBLIOGRAPHY

Diment, Galya. "The Two Faces of Ivan Goncharov: Autobiography and Duality in *Obyknovennaia Istorija*." *Slavic and East European Journal* 32 (Fall, 1988). Diment discusses Goncharov's use of autobiographical facts in his writings, focusing on his novel *A Common Story*.

_____, ed. *Goncharov's "Oblomov": A Critical Companion*. Evanston, Ill.: Northwestern University Press, American Association of Teachers of Slavic and East European Languages, 1998. Collection of essays analyzing various aspects of the novel, including its questions of heroism; themes of mistaken identities and "food, eating, and the search for communion"; and its Freudian perspectives.

Ehre, Milton. *Oblomov and His Creator: The Life and Art of Ivan Goncharov*. Princeton, N.J.: Princeton University Press, 1973. A literary biography and a deep analysis of Goncharov's works. An excellent starting point for research.

Frank, Joseph. "Being and Laziness." *The New Republic*, January 29, 2007. Frank, a professor of comparative literature and Slavic languages and literature at Stanford University, provides a detailed discussion of both Goncharov's life and the novel *Oblomov* in response to the publication of a new translation of the work.

Lyngstad, Alexandra, and Sverre Lyngstad. *Ivan Goncharov*. New York: Twayne, 1971. A psychological sketch of the author and a discussion of his literary works, including separate chapters analyzing *Oblomov* and "The Art of Goncharov." Includes notes, references, and an index.

Maguire, Robert A. "The City." In *The Cambridge Companion to the Classic Russian Novel*, edited by Malcolm V. Jones and Robin Feuer Miller. New York: Cambridge University Press, 1998. Maguire's essay about the theme of the city in *Oblomov* and novels by other authors places Goncharov's work within the broader context of the development of the Russian novel.

Platonov, Rachel S. "Remapping Arcadia: 'Pastoral Space' in Nineteenth-Century Russian Prose." *Modern Language Review* 102, no. 4 (October, 2007): 1105-1121. An examination of the role of space and spatiality in *Oblomov* and three other Russian prose pastorals. Platonov argues that Russian culture gives a particular significance to the notion of boundaries, which explains, in part, why Russian writers' depictions of pastoral paradises are "particularly prone to disintegration and self-destruction."

MAXIM GORKY

Born: Nizhny-Novgorod, Russia; March 28, 1868
Died: Gorki, near Moscow, Russia, Soviet Union (now Nizhny Novgorod, Russia); June 18, 1936
Also known as: Aleksey Maksimovich Peshkov; Maksim Gorky; Maxim Gorki

PRINCIPAL LONG FICTION

Goremyka Pavel, 1894 (novella; *Orphan Paul*, 1946)
Foma Gordeyev, 1899 (English translation, 1901)
Troye, 1901 (*Three of Them*, 1902)
Mat, 1906 (serial), 1907 (book; *Mother*, 1906)
Ispoved, 1908 (*The Confession*, 1909)
Zhizn Matveya Kozhemyakina, 1910 (*The Life of Matvei Kozhemyakin*, 1959)
Delo Artamonovykh, 1925 (*Decadence*, 1927; better known as *The Artamonov Business*, 1948)
Zhizn Klima Samgina, 1927-1936 (*The Life of Klim Samgin*, 1930-1938; includes *The Bystander*, 1930, *The Magnet*, 1931, *Other Fires*, 1933, and *The Specter*, 1938)

OTHER LITERARY FORMS

Maxim Gorky (GAWR-kee) wrote a total of fifteen plays, only three of which were staged during his lifetime: *Na dne* (pr., pb. 1902; *The Lower Depths*, 1912), *Vassa Zheleznova* (pb. 1910; English translation, 1945), and *Yegor Bulychov i drugiye* (pr., pb. 1932; *Yegor Bulychov and Others*, 1937). His other plays include *Meshchane* (pr., pb. 1902; *Smug Citizen*, 1906), *Dachniki* (pr., pb. 1904; *Summer Folk*, 1905), *Deti solntsa* (pr., pb. 1905; *Children of the Sun*, 1906), *Varvary* (pr., pb. 1906; *Barbarians*, 1906), *Vragi* (pb. 1906; *Enemies*, 1945), *Chudake* (pr., pb. 1910; *Queer People*, 1945), *Falshivaya moneta* (pr., pb. 1927, wr. 1913; the counterfeit coin), *Zykovy* (pb. 1914; *The Zykovs*, 1945), *Starik* (pr. 1919, wr. 1915; *Old Man*, 1924), and *Dostigayev i drugiye* (pr., pb. 1933; *Dostigayev and Others*, 1937). All are available in Russian in the thirty-volume *Polnoe sobranie sochinenii* (1949-1955; complete works), in the twenty-five-volume *Polnoe sobranie sochinenii* (1968-1976), and in English in *Seven Plays* (1945), *Five Plays* (1956), and *Plays* (1975). The eight-volume *Collected Works of Maxim Gorky* (1979-1981), is also available.

Gorky wrote about three hundred short stories. Among the most important are "Makar Chudra" (1892; English translation, 1901), "Chelkash" (1895; English translation, 1901), "Starukha Izergil" (1895; "The Old Woman Izergil"), "Malva" (1897; English translation), "V stepi" (1897; "In the Steppe"), "Dvadtsat' shest' i odna" (1899; "Twenty-six Men and a Girl," 1902), "Pesnya o burevestnike" (1901; "Song of the Stormy Petrel"),

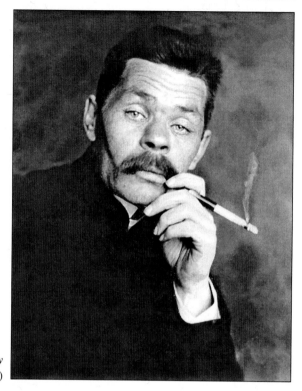

Maxim Gorky
(Library of Congress)

"Pesnya o sokole" (1908; "Song of the Falcon"), and the collections *Po Rusi* (1915; *Through Russia*, 1921) and *Skazki ob Italii* (1911-1913; *Tales of Italy*, 1958?). A three-volume collection of his stories, *Ocherki i rasskazy*, was first published in Russian in 1898-1899. The short stories are available in the collected works; some of the best of them are available in English in *Selected Short Stories* (1959), introduced by Stefan Zweig.

Among Gorky's numerous essays, articles, and nonfiction books, the most important are "O Karamazovshchine" (1913; "On Karamazovism"), "Revolyutsia i kultura" (1917; "Revolution and Culture"), *Vladimir Ilich Lenin* (1924; *V. I. Lenin*, 1931), and "O mesh-chanstve" (1929; "On the Petty Bourgeois Mentality"). The collection *Untimely Thoughts: Essays on Revolution, Culture, and the Bolsheviks* (1968) includes many of these essays in English translation.

ACHIEVEMENTS

Hailed by Soviet critics as a true proletarian writer and the model of Socialist Realism, Maxim Gorky is one of few authors to see their native towns renamed in their honor. Many schools, institutes, universities, and theaters bear his name, as does one of the main streets in Moscow. These honors, says Helen Muchnic, resulted from the fact that Gorky, along with Vladimir Ilich Lenin and Joseph Stalin, "shaped and disseminated the country's official philosophy." Stalin admired Gorky greatly, awarding him the coveted Order of Lenin. As chair of the All-Union Congress of Soviet Writers in 1934, Gorky delivered an address in which he defined Socialist Realism, a doctrine that was to be interpreted in a manner different from what he intended or practiced; the *Soviet Encyclopedia* (1949-1958) calls him "the father of Soviet literature . . . the founder of the literature of Socialist Realism."

Although Gorky's novels are not among the best in Russian literature, they did inaugurate a new type of writing, revealing to the world a new Russia. In contrast to the countless fin de siècle evocations of the tormented Russian soul, with their gallery of superfluous men, Gorky offered a new hero, the proletarian, the revolutionary, such as Pavel Vlassov and his mother, Pelagea Nilovna, in the poorly constructed but ever-popular *Mother.* Indeed, Richard Hare argues that even today *Mother* is the prototype for the socially tendentious novel in the Soviet Union, with its crude but determined effort to look into the dynamism of social change in Russia.

Gorky's highest artistic achievements, however, are his literary portraits; the best, says Muchnic, are those that he drew from life, especially of Leo Tolstoy and Anton Chekhov. Also notable is Gorky's affectionate portrait of his grandmother. Gorky had a strong visual sense, the gift of astute observation, and the ability to translate these insights into sparkling dialogue. He created an entire portrait gallery of vignettes, most of which can be traced to people he met in his endless wanderings through Russia and abroad.

The child of a lower-middle-class family that faced rapid impoverishment, a self-taught student, a young man whose universities were the towns along the Volga and the steamers that made their way along its mighty waters, Gorky was nevertheless sympathetic to culture. He devoured books voraciously and indiscriminately and encouraged others to study. From 1918 to 1921, not wholly in favor with the new regime, he worked tirelessly to save writers and intellectuals from starvation and from censorship. He befriended the Serapion Brothers (a group of young Russian writers formed in 1921) and later Mikhail Sholokhov, always encouraging solid scholarship.

Estimates of Gorky even now depend on political ideology, for he is closely associated with the Russian Revolution. His vision, however, is broader than that of any political movement. He repeats often in his autobiographical works his dismay at the ignorance of people and their lack of desire for a better life, and he felt keenly the injustice done to the innocent. His writing is permeated by the desire to bring people from slavery to freedom, to build a good life; he believed in the power of human beings to change their world. Courageous, generous, and devoted to the public good, Gorky was timid, lacking in self-confidence, and infinitely modest. His commitment to social justice is unquestionable. These qualities may be what Chekhov had in mind when he said that Gorky's works might be forgotten, but that Gorky the man would never be.

BIOGRAPHY

Maxim Gorky, champion of the poor and the downtrodden, was born Aleksey Maksimovich Peshkov in Nizhny-Novgorod (a town that would bear the name Gorki after 1932), on March 28, 1868. His father, who died three years later from cholera, was a joiner-upholsterer and later a shipping agent; his mother's family, the Kashirins, were owners of a dyeing establishment. After his father's death, Gorky's mother left young Gorky to be reared by her parents, with whom he lived until the age of eleven, when his recently remarried mother died. Gorky recounts his childhood experiences in brilliant anecdotes and dialogue in his autobiographical *Detstvo* (1913; *My Childhood*, 1915). The influence of his grandparents was great: His grandfather was a brutal, narrowly religious man, while his grandmother was gentle and pious; her own peculiar version of a benevolent God, sharply in contrast to the harsh religiosity of her husband, marked the impressionable child.

The frequent wanderers in Gorky's works are a reflection of his own experience. In 1879, his grandfather sent him "into the world." He went first to the family of his grandmother's sister's son, Valentin Sergeyev, to whom he was apprenticed as a draftsman. Gorky hated the snobbishness and avarice of this bourgeois family, which became the prototype of the Gordeyevs and the Artamonovs in his fiction. For the next ten years, he filled many other minor posts, from messboy on a Volga steamer to icon painter, reading when and where he could. Other than an idealistic admiration for a neighbor whom he named Queen Margot, there were few bright spots in this period, which he describes in *V lyudyakh* (1916; *In the World*, 1917).

In 1889, after an unsuccessful suicide attempt that left him with a permanently weakened lung, Gorky met the Populist revolutionary Mikhail Romas, who helped him to clarify his confused ideas. At the same time, his acquaintance with the writer Vladimir Korolenko aided his literary development, as Tolstoy and Chekhov were to do in later years. In 1892, Gorky published his first story, "Makar Chudra," assuming at that time the pen name Maxim Gorky, meaning "the bitter one," a reflection of his painful childhood. Gorky wandered through Russia, wrote, and began a series of unsuccessful romantic involvements, first with Olga Kaminskaya, an older woman of some sophistication with whom he lived from 1892 to 1894, and then with Ekaterina Pavlovna Volzhina, a proofreader on the newspaper for which he was working. Gorky married Volzhina in 1896; the couple had two children, Maxim and Ekaterina. Imprisoned several times, Gorky was seldom free of police surveillance. In 1899, he became literary editor of the Marxist newspaper *Zhizn* and directed his attention to the problems of social injustice.

In 1905, Gorky's violent protests of government brutality in suppressing the workers' demonstrations on Bloody Sunday once again brought him imprisonment, this time in the Peter-Paul Fortress. By then, however, Gorky was famous, and celebrities all over Europe and the United States protested the sentence. Upon his release, he once again began to travel, both for political reasons and for his health. He visited New York, which he called "the city of the yellow devil," in 1906, where he attacked the United States for its inequalities and the United States attacked him for the immorality of his relationship with Maria Fyodorovna Andreyeva, an actor of the celebrated Moscow Art Theater. After six months in the United States, he spent seven years in Italy, settling in Capri, where his Villa Serafina became a center of pilgrimage for all revolutionaries, including Lenin.

Gorky returned to Russia in 1913. When the Revolution broke out in 1917, he was not at first among its wholehearted supporters, although he served on many committees, working especially to safeguard culture. In 1921, for reasons of health, he went to Sorrento, Italy, where he spent his time writing. Although he made periodic visits to his homeland beginning in 1928, it was not until 1932 that he returned to the Soviet Union for good; in that same year, Stalin awarded him the Order of Lenin. In 1934, he was elected chair of the All-Union Congress of Soviet Writers; during this period, he became increasingly active in cultural policy making. Although he continued to write, he produced nothing noteworthy; his four-novel cycle *The Life of Klim Samgin*, the last volume of which he did not live to complete, is an artistic failure. Gorky's death in 1936 was surrounded by mysterious circumstances, although official autopsy reports attribute it to tuberculosis and influenza.

ANALYSIS

Although Soviet critics tend to exalt the realism of Maxim Gorky's works, D. S. Mirsky said that Gorky never wrote a good novel or a good play, while Tolstoy remarked that Gorky's novels are inferior to his stories and that his plays are even worse than his novels. Maintaining that Gorky's "tremendous heroic emotions ring false," Tolstoy criticized Gorky's lack of a sense of proportion, as Chekhov had noted Gorky's lack of restraint. It is obvious that Gorky did not know how to limit his stories, that he piles up details along with extraneous dialogue. His narrative technique consists in recounting the life story of a single protagonist or the saga of a family. His narratives are always linear, often proceeding from birth to death; the main character yearns for a new life and struggles with a stagnant environment, sometimes experiencing flashes of light. Thus, the typical Gorky novel is a tireless and often tiresome documentary on a single theme.

Gorky's weak narrative technique is counterbalanced by excellent characterization. True, he is guilty of oversimplification—his characters are types rather than individuals, figures from a modern morality play—but he introduced into Russian fiction a wide range of figures from many different walks of life rarely or never treated by earlier novelists. Though not highly individualized, Gorky's characterizations are vivid and convincing, imbued with his own energy.

Gorky sees people as social organisms, and therefore he is especially conscious of their role in society. He was particularly familiar with the merchant class or the *meshchane*, because he grew up among them, in the Kashirin and Sergeyev households. They form some of his most successful portraits, representing not only the petty bourgeoisie but also the barge owners, grain dealers, mill owners, and textile manufacturers, the Gordeyevs, Artamonovs, and Kozhemyakins. Gorky represents them as self-centered individualists, characterized by envy, malice, self-righteousness, avarice, and intellectual and spiritual torpor. Their decadence is symbolic of the malady that ravages prerevolutionary Russia.

In contrast to the merchants are the lonely and downtrodden, not always idealized as in the novels of Fyodor Dostoevski but presented, rather, as the ignorant victims of society and its lethargic sycophants. The corrupt and indifferent town of Okurov in *The Life of Matvei Kozhemyakin* symbolizes Russia's decadence, as do the thieves and vagabonds of Kazan, the flophouse of *The Lower Depths*, and the orgies of the theology students in the houses of prostitution. More Dostoevskian are the *bosyaki*, the barefoot tramps, such as Chelkash and Makar Chudra, who are the heralds of the future. Along with them, yet very different in spirit, is the revolutionary intelligentsia, the new heroes created by Gorky. They are Pelagea Nilovna, the "mother"; her son, Pavel; and his friends, Mansurova in *The Life of Matvei Kozhemyakin* and Derenkov and Romas in Gorky's own life. It is for such characters that Gorky is exalted by the Soviets, though to foreign readers they are usually the least attractive.

Gorky's best characters are presented without excessive ideological trappings. They range from his saintly grandmother, Akulina Kashirina, perhaps his most unforgettable character, to Queen Margot, the idol with clay feet. They include Smoury, the cook on the steamer, who first encouraged Gorky to read, and many other simple people whom Gorky was to meet, "kind, solitary, and broken off from life." They also take the form of figures such as the merchant Ignat Gordeyev, the image of the Volga, vital, seething, creative, generous, and resolute.

Most of Gorky's women are victims of violence, beaten by their husbands and unappreciated by their families, such as Natasha Artamonova and the wife of Saveli Kozhemyakin, who is beaten to death by him. Love in Gorky's novels is either accompanied by violence and brutality or idealized, as in Queen Margot or Tanya in the story "Twenty-six Men and a Girl." It ranges from tender devotion in *Mother* to drunken orgies on Foma Gordeyev's Volga steamer. Gorky's own experience of love was unhappy, and he was ill at ease when portraying sexual scenes. Even his coarsely erotic scenes seem to be tinged with a moralizing intent.

Against a background of resplendent nature, the Volga, the sea, or the steppe, Gorky depicts the eruptions of violence and brutality, the orgies and the squalor, the pain and the harshness that, says Muchnic, are at the heart of his work. One has only to read the opening pages of *My Childhood* to feel its force. His own weight of harsh experience impelled him to force others to look at the bestiality that he saw rampant in Russia and to urge them to exterminate it. Ever the champion of social justice, Gorky felt the need to fight ignorance, cruelty, and exploitation.

FOMA GORDEYEV

Gorky's first and best novel, *Foma Gordeyev*, is set along the banks of the Volga, a region well known to the author. It is the story of the Volga merchants, represented here by the Gordeyev and Mayakin families. Rich, greedy, and passionate, both families represent the iron will and the domination of the merchant class. Gorky's merchants are of peasant origin, unsophisticated and uneducated. In Foma's revolt, Gorky shows the decay of society at the end of the nineteenth century and the impending Revolution, as yet only dimly anticipated.

Foma, the only son of Ignat Gordeyev, a self-made barge owner and one of Gorky's richest character sketches, is brought up by his godfather and his father's business colleague, Yakov Mayakin, whose family has owned the local rope works for generations. Foma shows no talent for or interest in business and, after his father's death, wastes his money on debauchery, drink, and wanton destruction. At first dimly attracted to Lyubov Mayakina, he is unable to conform to her educated tastes, and she, in obedience to her father's wishes, marries the respectable and highly Europeanized Afrikan Smolin. Foma continues his wild rebellion, actually a search for self and meaning, not unlike that of Mikhail Lermontov's Pechorin. Finally institutionalized for apparent insanity, Foma becomes an enlightened vagabond.

Foma Gordeyev follows the story line generally adopted by Gorky: the life story of the hero from birth to a crisis. Although it is weak in plot and characterization, it is readable, especially powerful in its evocation of the Volga, the elemental force that intoxicated the wealthy Ignat. Ignat is a finished portrait of the boisterous, dynamic businessman Gorky knew so well—vital, creative, and resolute. He is one of Gorky's most sympathetic portraits, along with Yakov Mayakin, who shows the characteristic traits of the Russian merchant that go back to the sixteenth century *Domostroy* (a book on social conduct). Foma, though not so well drawn, represents the rift in generations and the universally disturbed mood that pervaded Russia on the eve of the abortive Revolution of 1905. The whole novel attempts to assess the flaws in the capitalistic system and thus is very modern in spirit.

MOTHER

Mother, written while Gorky was in the United States after the 1905 Revolution, reflects his disillusionment with both czarist and capitalistic social structures and his desire "to sustain the failing spirit of opposition to the dark and threatening forces of life." The novel was published first in English, in 1906, by *Appleton's Magazine* in New York, and then in Russian in Berlin. It became the symbol of the revolutionary cause and was widely read and acclaimed, even after the Revolution, as a model of the socialist novel. Translated into many languages, it became the basis for other novels and plays, such as Bertolt Brecht's *Mutter Courage und Ihre Kinder* (1941; *Mother Courage and Her Children*, 1941). As a novel, it is one of Gorky's weakest in characterization and plot, yet its optimistic message and accessible style have assured its continuing popularity.

Written in the third person, through the eyes of the courageous mother, Pelagea Nilovna Vlassova, the novel relates her encounter with the Social Democratic Party, inspired by her son, Pavel. Pelagea suffered mistreatment from her husband and seems destined to continue in the same path with her son until his "conversion" to socialism. Pavel becomes a champion of the proletarian cause, the acknowledged leader of a small group of fellow revolutionaries who study forbidden books and distribute literature among the factory workers in their village. After Pavel's arrest, the illiterate Pelagea continues Pavel's work, stealthily distributing pamphlets and becoming a mother to the other members of the group: Sasha, who is secretly in love with Pavel; the "God-builder" Rybin; Andrei, the charming and humorous *khokhol*; the misanthropic Vesovshchikov; and the open-hearted urban intellectual Nikolai. Pavel's release from prison is immediately followed by his bold leadership in the May Day demonstration, for which he is again imprisoned. The mother's work becomes more daring and widespread as she passes to other villages like the holy wanderers so common in Gorky's early work. After Pavel's condemnation to exile in Siberia, Pelagea herself is arrested as she prepares to distribute the speech her son made prior to his sentence.

The best portrait in this weak novel is that of the mother, the only character to show psychological development. Yet Pelagea passes from one type of religious fervor to another, and her socialist convictions are simply the transferral of her Orthodox beliefs to the kingdom of this world. Even the revolutionaries invoke Christ and compare their work to his. The austere Pavel remains remote and unconvincing, while maternal love is the dominant force in the affectionate and almost mystical Pelagea.

THE ARTAMONOV BUSINESS

Written in 1924 and 1925 while Gorky was living abroad in Sorrento, *The Artamonov Business* is a retrospective novel on the causes of the 1917 Revolution. Encompassing three generations and covering the period from 1863 to 1917, it has a much broader base than most of Gorky's works. Although here, as elsewhere, Gorky fills his narrative with extraneous detail, he draws many convincing portraits of the demoralized merchant class at the turn of the century. Frank M. Borras singles out Gorky's interweaving of the historical theme with the characters' personal destinies as one of the merits of the novel.

Ilya Artamonov is the patriarch of the family, a passionate and dynamic freed serf who establishes a linen factory in the sleepy town of Dryomov. His son, Pyotr, inherits his father's sensuality but not his business skill, and the narrative of his debauchery and indifference to his workers occupies the greater part of the novel. The Artamonov family also includes the more businesslike and adaptable Aleksei and the hunchback Nikita, who becomes a monk though he has lost his faith in God. The women in the novel occupy a secondary and passive role, existing mainly for the sensual gratification of the men, both attracting and repelling them.

Pyotr has two sons and two daughters. The eldest son, Ilya, leaves home to study and, as in Chekhov's stories, becomes an unseen presence, presumably joining the revolutionary Social Democratic Party. Yakov, the second son, is a sensualist, indifferent to business, and is killed by revolutionaries as he escapes in fear of them. Miron, Aleksei's son, though physically weak, shows, like his father, an aptitude for commerce. Yet none is strong enough to save the family's ailing business, weakened by the corruption and indifference of its managers.

Gorky's symbolism is evident in his characterization of Tikhon Vialov (the quiet one), an enigmatic ditchdigger, gardener, and ubiquitous servant of the Artamonov family. It is Tikhon who at the very end of the story proclaims the Revolution, calling for revenge for the injustices that he has suffered at the hands of the Artamonovs. Quite obviously he symbolizes the proletariat, victim of the bourgeoisie. Aside from Tikhon, Gorky emphasizes much less the oppression of the workers than the empty, selfish, and superfluous lives of the factory owners.

Alternating wild episodes of debauchery, cruelty, and murder with scenes of boredom and superfluous dialogue, *The Artamonov Business* is both a modern novel and a return to Dostoevskian melodrama. Gorky had planned to write the novel as early as 1909 but was advised by Lenin to wait for the Revolution, which would be its logical conclusion. This story of the progressive deterioration of a family is also a profound study in the consequences of the failure of human relationships.

Gorky was less a man of ideas and reason than one of instinct and emotion. His best works are based on intuition and observation. His truth and reality are humanistic, not metaphysical; they deal with the useful and the practical. Unlike Honoré de Balzac, whom he admired, Gorky did not succeed in investing the sordid with mystery or the petty with grandeur. He wrote a literature of the moment, "loud but not intense," as Muchnic describes it. It is, however, a literature of the people and for the people, accessible and genuine. Although some of his works are monotonous to today's Western reader, and no doubt to the Russian reader as well, at their best they are honest portrayals of people, inspiring confidence in humanity's power to change the world.

Irma M. Kashuba

OTHER MAJOR WORKS

SHORT FICTION: "Makar Chudra" (1892; English translation, 1901); "Chelkash," 1895 (English translation, 1901); "Byvshye lyudi," 1897 ("Creatures That Once Were Men," 1905); *Ocherki i rasskazy,* 1898-1899 (3 volumes); "Dvadtsat' shest' i odna," 1899 ("Twenty-six Men and a Girl," 1902); *Orloff and His Wife: Tales of the Barefoot Brigade,* 1901; *Rasskazy i p'esy,* 1901-1910 (9 volumes); *Skazki ob Italii,* 1911-1913 (*Tales of Italy,* 1958?); *Tales of Two Countries,* 1914; *Chelkash, and Other Stories,* 1915; *Po Rusi,* 1915 (*Through Russia,* 1921); *Stories of the Steppe,* 1918; *Zametki iz dnevnika: Vospominaniia,* 1924 (*Fragments from My Diary,* 1924); *Rasskazy 1922-1924 godov,*

1925; *Selected Short Stories*, 1959; *A Sky-Blue Life, and Selected Stories*, 1964; *The Collected Short Stories of Maxim Gorky*, 1988.

PLAYS: *Meshchane*, pr., pb. 1902 (*Smug Citizen*, 1906); *Na dne*, pr., pb. 1902 (*The Lower Depths*, 1912); *Dachniki*, pr., pb. 1904 (*Summer Folk*, 1905); *Deti solntsa*, pr., pb. 1905 (*Children of the Sun*, 1906); *Varvary*, pr., pb. 1906 (*Barbarians*, 1906); *Vragi*, pb. 1906 (*Enemies*, 1945); *Posledniye*, pr., pb. 1908; *Chudake*, pr., pb. 1910 (*Queer People*, 1945); *Vassa Zheleznova* (first version), pb. 1910 (English translation, 1945); *Zykovy*, pb. 1914 (*The Zykovs*, 1945); *Starik*, pr. 1919 (wr. 1915; *Old Man*, 1924); *Falshivaya moneta*, pr., pb. 1927 (wr. 1913); *Yegor Bulychov i drugiye*, pr., pb. 1932 (*Yegor Bulychov and Others*, 1937); *Dostigayev i drugiye*, pr., pb. 1933 (*Dostigayev and Others*, 1937); *Vassa Zheleznova* (second version), pr., pb. 1935 (English translation, 1975); *Seven Plays*, 1945; *Five Plays*, 1956; *Plays*, 1975.

NONFICTION: *Detstvo*, 1913 (*My Childhood*, 1915); *V lyudyakh*, 1916 (*In the World*, 1917); *Vozpominaniya o Lev Nikolayeviche Tolstom*, 1919 (*Reminiscences of Leo Nikolaevich Tolstoy*, 1920); *Moi universitety*, 1923 (*My Universities*, 1923); *Vladimir Ilich Lenin*, 1924 (*V. I. Lenin*, 1931); *Reminiscences of Tolstoy, Chekhov, and Andreyev*, 1949; *Untimely Thoughts: Essays on Revolution, Culture, and the Bolsheviks*, 1968; *Selected Letters*, 1997 (Andrew Barratt and Barry P. Scherr, editors); *Gorky's Tolstoy and Other Reminiscences: Key Writings by and About Maxim Gorky*, 2008 (Donald Fanger, editor).

MISCELLANEOUS: *Polnoe sobranie sochinenii*, 1949-1955 (30 volumes); *Polnoe sobranie sochinenii*, 1968-1976 (25 volumes); *Collected Works of Maxim Gorky*, 1979-1981 (8 volumes).

BIBLIOGRAPHY

Borras, F. M. *Maxim Gorky the Writer: An Interpretation*. Oxford, England: Clarendon Press, 1967. One of the more astute interpretations of Gorky's works, especially his novels and plays. Unlike many other books that concentrate on either biography or political issues, Borras's book emphasizes Gorky's artistic achievements.

Hare, Richard. *Maxim Gorky: Romantic Realist and Conservative Revolutionary*. New York: Oxford University Press, 1962. The first substantial study of Gorky in English since Alexander Kaun's 1931 book. Hare combines the political aspects of Gorky's biography with critical analyses of his works, with the latter receiving the short end. Contains some interesting observations obtained from anonymous people who knew Gorky well.

Kaun, Alexander. *Maxim Gorky and His Russia*. New York: Jonathan Cape and Harrison Smith, 1931. The first book on Gorky in English, written while Gorky was still alive and supported by firsthand knowledge about him. Covers literary and nonliterary life in Russia and the atmosphere in Gorky's time. Still one of the best biographies, despite some outdated facts later corrected by history.

Levin, Dan. *Stormy Petrel: The Life and Work of Maxim Gorky*. New York: Schocken

Books, 1985. This reprint of the author's 1965 work contains the detailed notes he excised from the original edition. An engrossing biographical and literary interpretation of Gorky's life and work.

Morris, Paul D. *Representation and the Twentieth-Century Novel: Studies in Gorky, Joyce, and Pynchon.* Würzburg, Germany: Königshausen & Neumann, 2005. A critical interpretation of Gorky's *Mother*, as well as James Joyce's *Ulysses* and Thomas Pynchon's *Gravity's Rainbow*, discussing how each novel represents a different literary tradition. Morris views Gorky's book as a paradigm of the Socialist Realist novel. For advanced students.

Scherr, Barry P. *Maxim Gorky.* Boston: Twayne, 1988. Chapters on the writer and revolutionary, his literary beginnings, his career as a young novelist, his plays, his memoirs, and his final achievements. Includes a chronology, detailed notes, and an annotated bibliography. Still the best introductory study.

Troyat, Henri. *Gorky.* Translated by Lowell Bair. New York: Crown, 1989. A translation of a French biography, written by a well-regarded literary biographer, which discusses Gorky's life and works. Includes a bibliography and an index.

Valentino, Russell Scott. *Vicissitudes of Genre in the Russian Novel: Turgenev's "Fathers and Sons," Chernyshevsky's "What Is to Be Done?," Dostoevsky's "Demons," Gorky's "Mother."* New York: Peter Lang, 2001. Analyzes Russian fictional works from the 1860's that are examples of the "tendentious novel" of this period. Describes how these novels influenced twentieth century literature.

Weil, Irwin. *Gorky: His Literary Development and Influence on Soviet Intellectual Life.* New York: Random House, 1966. One of the most scholarly books on Gorky in English, skillfully combining biography with critical analysis. Valuable especially for the discussion of Soviet literary life and Gorky's connections with, and influence on, younger Soviet writers. Contains a select but adequate bibliography.

Yedlin, Tova. *Maxim Gorky: A Political Biography.* Westport, Conn.: Praeger, 1999. Yedlin's biography focuses on Gorky's political and social views and his participation in the political and cultural life of his country. Includes a bibliography and an index.

MIKHAIL LERMONTOV

Born: Moscow, Russia; October 15, 1814
Died: Pyatigorsk, Russia; July 27, 1841
Also known as: Mikhail Yurievich Lermontov

PRINCIPAL LONG FICTION

Geroy nashego vremeni, 1839 (serial), 1840 (book; *A Hero of Our Time*, 1854)
Vadim, 1935-1937 (wr. 1832-1834; in *Polnoe sobranie sochinenii v piati tomakh*; English translation, 1984)
Knyaginya Ligovskaya, 1935-1937 (wr. 1836-1837; in *Polnoe sobranie sochinenii v piati tomakh*; *Princess Ligovskaya*, 1965)

OTHER LITERARY FORMS

Mikhail Lermontov (LYAYR-muhn-tuhf) is as well known for his poetry as for his prose writings. In his homeland, his lyric verse and narrative poems enjoy continuous publication and are liberally included in the educational curricula. Abroad, his poetic renown is less well established. English translations of his verse are available in *The Demon, and Other Poems* (1965), in *Michael Lermontov: Biography and Translation* (1967), in *Mikhail Lermontov: Major Poetical Works* (1983), and in anthologies. Lermontov also tried his hand at drama. *Maskarad* (pb. 1842; *Masquerade*, 1973) is still occasionally performed in Russia as well as in other nations, as is *Dva brata* (pb. 1880; *Two Brothers*, 1933). Lermontov's collected works, *Sochtsnentsya M. Ya. Lermontova* (1889-1891), first issued in six volumes, remained in print in Russia for more than a century.

ACHIEVEMENTS

Mikhail Lermontov is still one of the most popular Russian writers, joined in this respect by Alexander Pushkin. His talent and unusual circumstances catapulted him to instant fame despite his brief creative span. He continues to capture the public's imagination, undimmed by revolutionary upheaval and changing cultural values. The acclaim is not undeserved. With *A Hero of Our Time*, Lermontov made the difficult shift from verse to prose that had eluded his predecessors. Pushkin recognized the novel as Russia's undeveloped genre but cast his own novel *Evgeny Onegin* (1825-1832, 1833; *Eugene Onegin*, 1881) in verse, in frustrating admission that accomplished lengthy fictional prose was beyond his reach. Lermontov, too, was already an accomplished poet when he made the transition successfully, thereby giving to Russian literature its first aesthetically credible novel. Lermontov is also considered the greatest Russian Romantic, a Slavic Lord Byron, Childe Harold in a Russian cloak.

At the beginning of the nineteenth century, Russian literature still drew heavily on foreign models. Pushkin had adopted France's strict neoclassical verse form for his works,

Mikhail Lermontov
(Library of Congress)

carefully avoiding emotional and diffuse outpourings. Lermontov, by nature a Romantic, imported Byron's Romantic style and content and grafted them artfully into Russian verse and prose. His characters contemptuously reject civilization to seek contemplation and noble savages in the wild region of the Caucasus; they turn melancholy, seek nature, become alienated, die young, and, in general, possess all the major qualities of the Western Romantic hero.

Lermontov's career was exemplary in another sense as well. The participation of many writers in the 1825 Decembrist uprising induced Czar Nicholas I to muzzle liberal sentiments as strongly in literature as elsewhere, and Lermontov's forceful poems, boldly bypassing the censors, marked him as a courageous defender of a less repressive way of life, a proponent of reform, at a time when such defenders were scarce because of swift retribution. Lermontov himself paid the price through several incarcerations and exiles. In the late 1830's, when continuing repression cast a gloom over Russia's creative mood, Lermontov again caught the zeitgeist by mirroring the doubts, despair, and resignation in his work.

As general withdrawal from public endeavors directed writers to private affairs, Lermontov created a new "hero of the time" in the character Pechorin, showing how frustrated and wasted creative energies wreak havoc on the psychological development of the intelligent individual. Lermontov's own frustrations served his literary development well. He presented Russian readers with the first hero whose nature is minutely analyzed. Not only psychological introspection but also a psychically ruinous unwillingness to correct moral defects characterizes the Lermontov hero. Whereas previous authors had passed some measure of judgment on ethical offenders, Lermontov coolly showed that destructive malice is as credible an authorial point of view as virtuous aspiration. The czar furiously denounced Pechorin's misanthropic stance and impure actions, refusing to acknowledge that such dark probings of the mind had a right to fictional existence. Lermontov, thus, fought a brief but fierce and successful battle to broaden Russian literary expression.

BIOGRAPHY

Mikhail Yurievich Lermontov, born October 15, 1814, in Moscow, had a diverse ancestry. His mother's family was related to the influential aristocratic Stolypins, while his father traced his origins back to the Learmonths of Scotland. Lermontov's childhood, however, was traumatic, extending its insecurities into most of his works. His mother died when he was three years old, and his maternal grandmother bribed her philandering son-in-law to leave the boy's upbringing to her. The ensuing discord, as both sides battled for the child's affection, left traces of bitterness in Lermontov that are reflected in his major characters. Pechorin, in *A Hero of Our Time*, especially echoes the author's inability to express emotion.

Lermontov's alienation from society and from individuals grew as he matured, despite wealth, elevated social position, and excellent education. He fell deeply in love a number of times without being able to establish a lasting bond. Like the female-hating Pechorin, Lermontov tricked and offended several young women he had earlier admired. As Pechorin rebuffs male friendships, so did the author keep aloof, despising schoolmates, professors, and fellow officers alike. His years at Moscow University's Department of Literature, from 1830 to 1832, and the proximity of many famous literati, did not significantly further his talents, for he haughtily refused to be influenced. He had his first poems in print at age sixteen, and he relied on self-developed abilities for inspiration. An avid student of English because of pride in his Scottish ancestry, he was much under the influence of Byron, whose works he read extensively in the original. Bored at the university, he entered the School of Guard Ensigns and Cavalry Cadets and joined the Guard Hussars in 1834. His irregular and frivolous life as a rich, spoiled cadet earned for him the reputation of an *enfant terrible*.

Lermontov also directed his malice toward Nicholas I's harsh regime, and by 1837, his challenges brought reprisals. Pushkin's death in a duel at the hands of a court fop caused

Lermontov to write and distribute a poem, "Smert poeta" ("Death of a Poet"), filled with accusations against the imperial circle. Nicholas's censors had already warned Lermontov by banning his drama *Masquerade* (which he wrote in 1834-1835) because of its critical attitude toward St. Petersburg high society. The czar perceived the Pushkin-inspired poem as a revolutionary challenge by a liberal hothead, and from that time on he took a personal interest in keeping the writer absent from the capital. Lermontov's poetic dare resulted in his exile to the Caucasus, where Russian regiments sporadically tangled with rebellious non-Russian tribes. This majestic mountain range subsequently served as Lermontov's primary literary inspiration. It is the locale of all the episodes in *A Hero of Our Time*, and many events in the novel are taken directly from Lermontov's experiences in that region: His encounter with smugglers in Taman is faithfully reproduced in the chapter "Taman"; the holidays in the spa of Pyatigorsk are incorporated into the primary section, "Princess Mary"; the service at the Grozny fortress provides the background for the first episode, "Bela"; and his capers with native adventurers and outlaws run through the entire novel.

By 1839, having produced several poetic masterpieces and successfully started his prose career, Lermontov found that his literary fame outstripped his unsavory reputation as a malicious rich boy. His influential grandmother's intercession yielded periodic lifting of exiles, but Lermontov each time managed to incur the czar's wrath anew and was imprisoned or banned again—for dueling, insulting courtly personages, or leaving his regiment. In the spring of 1841, Nicholas gave the order for Lermontov to be sent speedily to a particularly dangerous spot on the Black Sea coast to serve in a regiment famous for its heavy casualties. Lermontov, enraged and bitter, evaded the order by arranging sick leave for himself en route, in the fashionable resort Pyatigorsk. His behavior there closely parallels that of Pechorin in *A Hero of Our Time*. Lermontov immediately and deliberately enraged an overblown officer—Grushnitsky in the narrative—to the point of dueling. The duel, too, was almost a replica of the shoot-out in the novel, as if Lermontov had meant to transfer literature to life. The fates, however, refused to humor him this time. Whereas Pechorin kills his rival and walks away from the duel unharmed, Lermontov fell mortally wounded without firing a shot, on July 27, 1841, several months short of his twenty-seventh birthday. The circumstances of his death; his succession to both Pushkin's fame and his destiny; his close affinities with his hero, Pechorin; his fame as a political teaser and daredevil; and his general Romantic demeanor—all combined to elevate Lermontov to a high position in Russian literature.

ANALYSIS

Mikhail Lermontov wrote during the most restrictive period of the nineteenth century in Russia, the reign of Nicholas I. The educated citizen could question neither serfdom nor autocracy, was limited in individual development and expression, and was hemmed in on all sides by suspicious overseers and a mediocre, lethargic ruling class. Reflecting the realities of the time, Lermontov created talented heroes who are stifled by the oppressive atmosphere and are driven to release their creative energies in destructive outbursts. His young intellectuals, their career possibilities limited to a highly ossified civil service, an equally conservative priesthood, and a physically active but mentally stagnant military life, are deprived of stimulating social outlets and consider themselves superfluous. Their attitude is highly cynical, coupled with a willful determination to revenge themselves. Unable to challenge the autocracy, they torment others and themselves in disastrous individual encounters.

Lermontov was fascinated by this alienated social category and expanded its portrait to include exploration of the psychological complexities embedded in misanthropic behavior. His characters are acutely self-conscious but frustrated, because they can neither pinpoint the cause of their destructive impulses nor overcome those impulses. Lermontov's perceptive understanding of such psychic behavior caused him to treat his aberrant protagonists sympathetically, as lost souls craving human contact yet tragically unable to sustain normal relationships. Such psychological probing, entirely new to Russian literature, engendered lively criticism. It also challenged and broadened the prevailing narrow limits of literary expression. The author's daring resulted in several official reprisals.

Stylistically, Lermontov made a significant contribution to the development of Russian prose. Himself a talented poet, he incorporated many lyrical features into his narratives. His overall novelistic technique is far from perfect, yet it stands out when judged against the general low level of Russian prose at that time. Of equal and perhaps greater significance is Lermontov's character development along modern psychological lines, one of the primary reasons for his continuing popularity.

More than a century after his death, Lermontov's dual talents as poet and novelist inspired another Russian poet-novelist, Boris Pasternak. In Pasternak's view, Lermontov's art laid the foundation for the great achievements of modern Russian poetry and prose, while his life embodied the principle of creative freedom. When, in *Doktor Zhivago*, 1957 (*Doctor Zhivago*, 1958), Pasternak attempted to find new approaches to the well-worked-over novelistic genre through the use of poetic prose and the inclusion of Zhivago's poems in the novel, he was following the example of Lermontov, who, taking part in the creation of the genre on Russian soil, could not bring himself to keep poetic devices out. *A Hero of Our Time* contains lyrics in the form of a song, lyrical outbursts describing natural phenomena, incomplete transitions between sections, and, in general, a loose structure typical of poetry.

VADIM

Though Lermontov's fame as a novelist rests on *A Hero of Our Time*, he moved into novel writing as early as 1832 with the unfinished *Vadim*. The author's immaturity—he was eighteen at the time—is painfully evident in this work. Elements of the popular historical tale alternate with gothic features. A vaguely described peasant rebellion under Catherine the Great serves as a backdrop for the narrative, though no actual historical personages appear. The action is less centered on battle than on the bloody goings-on of bizarre individuals. The incestuous longings of the physically disfigured Vadim, his overwhelming desire for revenge, and his murderous schemes are all presented with a rather grotesque sentimentality. Though the misshapen Vadim is believed to be modeled on Byron's Arnold, the hero of the unfinished poetic drama *The Deformed Transformed* (pb. 1824), Lermontov's tale never approaches Byron's craftsmanship.

Vadim does, however, point ahead to *A Hero of Our Time* in several respects. Lermontov's loose integration of biographical events is present in both works. Vadim and Pechorin are both bitter, alienated types who quickly turn into villains and remain villains, although the frantic, flowery, emotional outpourings that accompany Vadim's activity are absent in *A Hero of Our Time*. The glaring shortcomings of this youthful work are partly redeemed by nature and locale descriptions of a much higher quality, the work of a credible poet. In the same manner, the uneven features of *A Hero of Our Time* contrast sharply with the novel's accomplished poetic passages. In the end, Vadim's transformation into a macabre monster did not mesh with the rest of the clumsily fragmented settings, and Lermontov abandoned the work.

PRINCESS LIGOVSKAYA

Lermontov's next attempt, *Princess Ligovskaya*, written in the period 1836-1837 and then put aside unfinished, shows remarkable improvement. The structure of the narrative mirrors the already popular society tale, which chronicled the mores of the upper classes, frequently from a satiric point of view. The resulting tone ridiculed the empty, superficial activities of the rich. Superimposed on this setting was a love intrigue, usually featuring a wealthy female aristocrat and her lower-class admirer. Lermontov's tale has all of these elements and adds autobiographical notes by reflecting his romantic involvements with Varvara Lopukhina and Ekaterina Sushkova.

Princess Ligovskaya also points strongly to *A Hero of Our Time*. The Princess Vera of the former becomes the Princess Mary of the latter, and the introspective officer Pechorin of this work is clearly a prototype for Lermontov's major hero of the same name. What makes *Princess Ligovskaya* noteworthy is the quality of character portrayal, which rises far above the rudimentary efforts of the Russian tale of manners and morals. Lermontov fleshes out his protagonist, detailing his lifestyle in a way that no Russian author before him had been able to do. The description of the tensions attending infiltration of a higher social class is excellent, judged by the standards of the time. The author still had difficulties with believable plot development, however, and other insufficiencies are also evident in the novel. With prolonged exile in the Caucasus, Lermontov turned his attention to other issues and places. He left *Princess Ligovskaya* incomplete and transferred the best of it to *A Hero of Our Time*.

A HERO OF OUR TIME

The tendency of nineteenth century Russians to see in literature an ideological weapon colored the reception of *A Hero of Our Time* from the start. Guided by the eminent social critic Vissarion Belinsky, readers first and foremost scanned each new literary work for its hidden political connotations. The practice of imparting such challenges even to works that did not seem to contain them found wide acceptance, inasmuch as it was taken for granted that authors had to mask their ideological intent from strict censorial probings by clothing it in innocuous fictional garb. Thus the radical critics, led by Belinsky, fit *A Hero of Our Time* to their expectation by ascribing Pechorin's psychological defects to the shortcomings of Nicholas I's regime. Pechorin was seen as the typical intelligent young man of his time, lacking all opportunity to use his talents and thus forced to waste his creative energies in petty intrigues of a personal nature. Lermontov's own rebellious temperament and his criticism of high society in previous prose and a number of provocative poems supported a tendentious understanding of the novel. Indeed, when sections of it first appeared in the journal *Otechestvennye zapiski* in 1839-1840, Lermontov was on his way to exile in the Caucasus. The text itself, however, goes far beyond a political interpretation to reveal a tortured individual at odds with himself.

Lermontov's originality in unfolding his hero's complex personality is one of the principal strengths of the novel. The stylistically diverse, seemingly unconnected sections not only present a successful merging of several short prose genres—travel sketch, society tale, military adventure story, diary—but also illuminate Pechorin's character from different angles. At first, Pechorin is a hearsay figure, rendered enigmatic by the kind but unsophisticated staff captain Maxim Maximych, whose own conservative mentality does not grasp the depth of the hero's personality. Maxim Maximych is, on one hand, attracted to Pechorin's exceptional unconventionality; on the other hand, he is puzzled and put on guard by Pechorin's cruelty, a duality experienced by all who encounter Pechorin. The staff captain's secondhand account leaves the impression that Pechorin has carelessly abducted a local girl, Bela, charmed her into falling in love with him, abandoned her, and shrugged off her subsequent death with an indifferent smile. The fact that this behavior masks an inability to express emotion, that Pechorin actually suffers deeply, escapes the simple Maxim Maximych.

The reader receives a fragmented but psychologically more correct view from the educated editor of Pechorin's journal. In contrast to the careless daredevil portrayed by Maxim Maximych, the editor's Pechorin is a delicate, reticent person, almost feminine and vulnerable. His childlike countenance, however, is belied by steely, cold eyes that warn others to keep their distance. With reader interest thus firmly established, Lermontov moves to unfold his hero's character further through the latter's own view of himself in diary form.

This self-view has many facets because of Pechorin's unwillingness and inability to analyze himself completely and honestly. Initially, Pechorin keeps readers at bay as he coolly relates his encounter with smugglers and the plot to kill him. He briefly acknowledges his own provocations and recognizes that he has destroyed the livelihood of simple people whose customs he did not understand. What he cannot do, then or later, is accept a share in the guilt. Instead, he hides behind the superiority of the Russian officer: "What have the joys and sorrows of humankind to do with me, a military man, moving through on official business." In the "Princess Mary" section, long monologues facilitate a more probing self-analysis. Pechorin is aware that he is out of tune with his surroundings. He ascribes this disharmony to his intellectual superiority, his recognition that people around him are boring and shallow. With deft perception, Pechorin exposes the spa's population as ridiculous, pinpointing and deflating the social pretensions of others. His continuous questioning of his own motives, childhood influences, feelings, and judgments raises him far above his environs in the reader's discernment.

Lermontov's achievements, however, are not complete with the creation of this introspective character, a new kind of character in Russian literature. The author also prompts his readers to see the inadequacies of Pechorin's skepticism, to witness a demoniac personality's avoidance of probing too deeply. Pechorin's misanthropic behavior is balanced by a profound need to interact with people. Unable to express his feelings for fear of rendering himself vulnerable, Pechorin relates to others through destructive acts.

It is immaterial whether men and women love him, like him, hate him, or ignore him. All are, in the end, recipients of his malice. He ruins the petty smugglers' wretched business, rebuffs the friendship offered by both the simple staff captain and the sophisticated Dr. Werner, brutally victimizes the naïve Princess Mary, equally brutally repays Vera's loyalty by ruining her a second time, causes Bela's death, and kills Grushnitsky in a duel. After each encounter, he mournfully reflects, accuses himself, cries, and once more retreats into his lonely, miserable existence. Each time, this withdrawal is of limited duration, for the drive to reach out to others soon asserts itself with an intensity he cannot control. Pechorin's attempts at normal relationships, as with Vera and Dr. Werner, cannot be sustained. His innate fear of exposing himself in honest friendship soon forces him into an adversary position, from which he must assert his superiority. He cannot rest until he has devastated his partner in some manner. Though he analyzes his malice at length, he is unable to decipher the impulses that drive him. The fact that not all the nuances of Pechorin's character are explored also attests the author's skill. The causes of Pechorin's alienation are, in the end, unknowable—both to himself and to others.

Such a perceptive rendering of the mysteries of human behavior had not been presented in Russian literature before, and this achievement far outweighs the novel's rough spots. It must be kept in mind that Lermontov's stylistic innovations are exceptional only when seen against the background of Russian fiction in the first decades of the nineteenth century. Judged by today's standards, the novel is much less impressive. Plot advancement proceeds primarily through the device of having Pechorin eavesdrop on crucial conversations. Good descriptive passages alternate with florid clichés reminiscent of sentimental Romanticism. Pechorin's attachment to Vera, a carryover from *Princess Ligovskaya*, is improperly motivated and explained. The "Fatalist" episode is poorly integrated. Liberal allusions to Western and earlier Russian literature make the narrative top-heavy, as do casually inserted autobiographical references. A host of other minor problems remind the reader that Lermontov is not a novelist par excellence.

Within the development of the Russian novel, however, the author occupies an impressive place. The unchronological arrangement of sections of the novel—similar to the sectioning in William Faulkner's *The Sound and the Fury* (1929)—for the purpose of heightening reader tension and adding complexity is a technique that was not used by other authors until much later. In addition, Lermontov artfully integrates descriptions of nature into the work; for example, Pechorin's inner turmoil is echoed in natural phenomena. On a larger scale, the harmony and magnificence of the Caucasus mountains are in jarring discord with the spiritual emptiness of the spa's high society and the machinations of its villains. In this respect, Lermontov outstrips his own Romantic borrowings from Byron and Jean-Jacques Rousseau. Neither nature nor intimate contact with simple tribes regenerates the disillusioned hero. On the contrary, Pechorin skillfully devastates civilized and untamed adversary alike. Seen from this perspective, Lermontov transcends the Romantic era with which his name is connected and widens its scope to include a hesitant realism.

On a contextual level, too, Lermontov made a significant contribution. The collision of Europeanized Russia with subjugated "primitive" cultures is cast into sharp focus in this novel. In line with the preferences of Romanticism, the exotic pagans often appear ethically superior or at least equal to their civilized conquerors. While *A Hero of Our Time* has much in common with Byron's verse play *Manfred* (pb. 1817), Lermontov goes beyond the typically Romantic tragedy of Byron's hero to reveal a much more modern understanding of the psyche. The psychologically split nature of Pechorin's character, as he coldly manipulates people's emotions as though they were marionettes while at the same time crying out silently for help and pity, bears a decidedly modern and universal stamp and explains the continuing appeal of this work.

The arguments about the philosophical orientation of the novel also continue. When it was first serialized, social critics, seeing in Pechorin the despairing intellectual of their time, battled conservatives, who labeled Pechorin un-Russian, satanic, and unreal and accused Lermontov of transferring his own abominable excesses to his fiction. Lermontov entered the fray in a foreword to the novel's first appearance in book form, in 1840, accusing his readers of immaturity and simplicity. In subsequent decades, the richness of the novel began gradually to be understood, but in the mid-1970's Soviet critics were still charging one another, in treatises far exceeding the length of the original work, with misunderstanding Lermontov's intentions. The novel itself remains a favorite at home and abroad.

Margot K. Frank

OTHER MAJOR WORKS

PLAYS: *Ispantsy*, pb. 1935 (wr. 1830; verse play); *Menschen und Leidenschaften*, pb. 1935 (wr. 1830); *Stranny chelovek*, pb. 1935 (wr. 1831; verse play; *A Strange One*, 1965); *Tsigany*, pb. 1935 (wr. 1830); *Maskarad*, pb. 1842 (wr. 1834-1835; *Masquerade*, 1973); *Dva brata*, pb. 1880 (wr. 1836; *Two Brothers*, 1933).

POETRY: *Pesnya pro tsarya Ivana Vasilyevicha, molodogo oprichnika i udalogo kuptsa Kalashnikova*, 1837 (*A Song About Tsar Ivan Vasilyevitch, His Young Body-Guard, and the Valiant Merchant Kalashnikov*, 1911); *Stikhotvoreniya M. Lermontova*, 1840; *Demon*, 1841 (*The Demon*, 1875); *The Demon, and Other Poems*, 1965; *Mikhail Lermontov: Major Poetical Works*, 1983.

MISCELLANEOUS: *Sochtsnentsya M. Ya. Lermontova*, 1889-1891 (6 volumes); *Polnoe sobranie sochinenii v piati tomakh*, 1935-1937 (5 volumes; prose and poetry); *Polnoe sobranie sochinenii v shesti tomakh*, 1954-1957 (6 volumes; prose and poetry); *A Lermontov Reader*, 1965 (includes *Princess Ligovskaya, A Strange One*, and poetry); *Michael Lermontov: Biography and Translation*, 1967; *Selected Works*, 1976 (prose and poetry).

BIBLIOGRAPHY

Allen, Elizabeth Cheresh. *A Fallen Idol Is Still a God: Lermontov and the Quandaries of Cultural Transition*. Stanford, Calif.: Stanford University Press, 2007. Takes a critical look at Lermontov's writing, applying literary theories and placing the work within the context of the author's time and culture. Portrays Lermontov as a writer who defies categorization, straddling the line between Romanticism and realism. Provides thorough analysis of Lermontov's works, especially his novel *A Hero of Our Time*. Focuses on his narration and characterization as defining qualities of his writing style.

Bagby, Lewis, ed. *Lermontov's "A Hero of Our Time": A Critical Companion*. Evanston, Ill.: Northwestern University Press, 2002. Provides background information to help readers better understand Lermontov's novel, including translated essays by Russian literary critics Boris Eikhenbaum and Vissarion Belinsky and discussions of the novel's portrayals of women. Also reprints some contemporary reviews of the novel.

Eikhenbaum, Boris. *Lermontov*. Translated by Ray Parrot and Harry Weber. Ann Arbor, Mich.: Ardis, 1981. A translation of a monograph by a leading Russian critic of the 1920's, this thorough study of Lermontov's prose and poetry remains the seminal work on him. Includes many of Lermontov's poems in both Russian and English.

Garrard, John. *Mikhail Lermontov*. Boston: G. K. Hall, 1982. Discusses Lermontov and his works meticulously in a concise, easy-to-understand fashion. Provides a good foundation from which students can approach more ambitious studies of Lermontov in any language.

Golstein, Vladimir. *Lermontov's Narratives of Heroism*. Evanston, Ill.: Northwestern University Press, 1998. Tackles Lermontov's use of the topic of heroism, which is prevalent in his works. Focuses on the character of Pechorin in *A Hero of Our Time* as well as on the poems "The Demon" and "The Song." Bibliography includes works in both Russian and English.

Kelly, Laurence. *Lermontov: Tragedy in the Caucasus.* 1977. Reprint. London: Tauris Parke, 2003. Colorfully illustrated biography of Lermontov covers his childhood in the "wild" East, his education, his rise and fall in society, and his attitudes toward war as reflected in his works.

Mersereau, John, Jr. *Mikhail Lermontov.* Carbondale: Southern Illinois University Press, 1962. Very concise biography manages to include much valuable detail. The focus is distinctly on Lermontov's development of a prose style, with more than half of the book devoted to an examination of *A Hero of Our Time*.

Powelstock, David. *Becoming Mikhail Lermontov: The Ironies of Romantic Individualism in Nicholas I's Russia.* Evanston, Ill.: Northwestern University Press, 2005. Argues that Lermontov had a coherent worldview, termed here "Romantic individualism," and refers to this philosophy to explain contradictions in the writer's life and works.

Reid, Robert. *Lermontov's "A Hero of Our Time."* London: Bristol Classical Press, 1997. Approaches the novel from the perspective of modern literary criticism, analyzing its plot, its representation of ethnicity, and other elements. Also provides a history of the book's critical reception. Includes bibliographical references.

Turner, C. J. G. *Pechorin: An Essay on Lermontov's "A Hero of Our Time."* Birmingham, England: University of Birmingham, 1978. Offers a pithy discussion of various aspects of Lermontov's main character, analyzing the relationships between the narrator and the reader, the narrator and the hero, the hero and himself, the hero and the author, and the hero and the reader.

DMITRY MEREZHKOVSKY

Born: St. Petersburg, Russia; August 14, 1865
Died: Paris, France; December 9, 1941
Also known as: Dmitry Sergeyevich Merezhkovsky

PRINCIPAL LONG FICTION

Smert bogov: Yulian Otstupnik, 1896 (*The Death of the Gods,* 1901; also known
    as *The Death of the Gods: Or, Julian the Apostate,* 1929)
Khristos i Antikhrist, 1896-1905 (collective title for *Smert bogov, Voskresshiye
    bogi,* and *Antikhrist; Christ and Antichrist,* 1901-1905)
Voskresshiye bogi: Leonardo da Vinci, 1901 (*The Forerunner,* 1902; better
    known as *The Romance of Leonardo da Vinci,* 1928, 1953)
Antikhrist: Pyotri Aleksey, 1905 (*Peter and Alexis,* 1905)
Aleksandr I, 1913
Chetyrnadtsatoye dekabrya, 1918 (*December the Fourteenth,* 1923)
Rozhdeniye bogov: Tutankamon na Krite, 1925 (*The Birth of the Gods,* 1925)
Messiya, 1926-1927 (*Akhnaton, King of Egypt,* 1927)

OTHER LITERARY FORMS

Although famous in the Western world primarily for his historical romances, Dmitry
Merezhkovsky (mehr-ehsh-KAWF-skee) was known among his Russian peers as a critic
as well—and a particularly harsh one at that. His first critical work, a collection of essays
published under the title *O prichinakh upadka i o novykh techeniyakh sovremennoy
russkoy literatury* (1893; on the causes of the present decline and the new currents of contemporary Russian literature), was followed a decade later by perhaps his most important
work of criticism and nonfiction, *L. Tolstoy i Dostoyevsky* (1901-1902; *Tolstoi as Man and
Artist, with an Essay on Dostoievski,* 1902).

Throughout his life, Merezhkovsky would remain an essayist and critic, choosing as
his subjects such wide and varied topics as the Acropolis, Michel de Montaigne, Marcus
Aurelius, Gustave Flaubert, Henrik Ibsen, Alexander Pushkin, and Maxim Gorky. After
the Bolshevik Revolution, his criticism became especially vitriolic, culminating in
Tsarstvo Antikhrista (1921, with Z. N. Gippius and others), an indictment of Russia as a
whole.

In addition, Merezhkovsky was a classicist, thus enabling him to translate Longus's
idyll *Daphnis and Chloë* (c. mid-second century C.E.) as well as numerous tragedies of
Aeschylus, Sophocles, and Euripides, into Russian for the first time. Finally, in the early
stages of his career, Merezhkovsky published two collections of poetry, *Stikhotvoreniya,
1883-1887* (1888) and *Simvoly* (1892), and one play, *Pavel I* (1908).

ACHIEVEMENTS

To understand Dimitry Merezhkovsky's importance, one must look beyond the source of his international reputation, his historical romances, into prerevolutionary Russia itself, for in a confused yet profound way, he reflected a current of thought and belief common to members of the intelligentsia of that day. Steeped in years of czarist tyranny, prey to feelings of cultural inferiority brought on by the legacy of Russian isolationism, trying desperately to discover and solidify a national identity, trapped within the heated polemics of the Westerners, who followed the lead of their patron saint, Peter the Great, and the Slavophiles, who refused to have anything to do with Europe's cultural "corruption," it was no wonder that the artists and writers of turn-of-the-century Russia should accuse themselves and one another of floundering in history and finally standing still. This was not only a political crisis but also a deeply felt spiritual one. Was Russia merely a reflection of Europe with nothing original to say? Or was it blessed with a culture and message of its own that would save its own land, Europe, and eventually the world?

Concurrent with this was the central position of the Russian Orthodox Church in shaping the philosophy and action of its homeland. From time immemorial, the Russian Church had existed in a kind of grand and splendid isolation from Western Christianity; after the fall of Constantinople to the Turks in 1453, however, a belief arose that would show itself, with slight modifications, time and again—the conception of Moscow as the third Rome, the spiritual center of a Russia that would lead the world out of sin and darkness. This notion caused the Russian Church to regard "heretical" Europe with pride, condescension, and fear.

Finally, in the 1890's—the decade of Merezhkovsky's rise to fame—changes inspired by literary experimentation and new aesthetic trends were in the wind. Stéphane Mallarmé, Paul Verlaine, Arthur Rimbaud, and Charles Baudelaire were the ascendant stars, yet, simultaneously, a renewed interest in Fyodor Dostoevski and everything Russian could not help but modify such "decadent" foreign trends. These early modernists were quickly superseded by the Russian Symbolists, who sought to transform art into a mystical theurgy—the ultimate purpose of which was the transfiguration of consciousness for humans and humankind. In time, even this would be replaced—by Maxim Gorky and his Znaniye school of violent Social Realists.

From a historical perspective, Merezhkovsky stands in the center of this whirlwind. Though never actually considered a literary great, he was, for nearly a decade, the central figure of Russia's early modern period; he was particularly popular among the avant-garde and the young. His mysticism—based on a system of Hegelian opposites (thesis and antithesis, pagan and Christian, old and new)—attracted the attention of a public grown weary of the stagnation and oppression of the Russian Church. His aesthetics—a peculiar combination of modernism and symbolism—attracted the tastes of those fed up with generations of simplistic and idealistically colored positivism. Though to modern readers his symbolism seems rather artificial and shallow, lacking in those qualities that made the true symbolists' works more than mere patchworks composed of intersecting lines drawn between obvious dualities, Merezhkovsky's works were—for the time and place—both important and beneficial. They brought to the Russian reader a wealth of new ideas; they stirred up controversy and in many ways, notwithstanding their unidimensionality, served as an important catalyst for a religious revival in Russia.

Finally, Merezhkovsky's criticism had a lasting influence on the Russian mind, which has perhaps been ignored in the West. His interpretation of the lives, personalities, and works of Tolstoy and Dostoevski in *Tolstoi as Man and Artist, with an Essay on Dostoievski* dominated not only Russian but also German discussion of the subject for years, focusing in minute detail on the religions of the two great writers as the prime movers of their works. To Merezhkovsky, Tolstoy was the great pagan and pantheist, the "seer of the flesh," while Dostoevski was the opposite—the great Christian of Russian letters, the "seer of the spirit." *Tolstoi as Man and Artist, with an Essay on Dostoievski* marked Merezhkovsky's transition from the West to the East, from Europe back to Russia—from the Hellenic ideal of his classical studies back to the mystical, though primarily Christian, ideal of his Russian roots. The "great Christian" Dostoevski was consistently lauded at the expense of the "great Pagan" Tolstoy, and throughout the work, Russia's messianic destiny is stressed and supposedly revealed. After *Tolstoi as Man and Artist, with an Essay on Dostoievski*, Merezhkovsky would frequently return to this mystical and antithetical theme, but never quite so lucidly as he did in the original critical work.

BIOGRAPHY

Dmitry Sergeyevich Merezhkovsky was born in St. Petersburg, Russia, on August 14, 1865. His father, Serge Ivanovich Merezhkovsky, an inspector of buildings for the Imperial Court, was known to be stern and puritanical—he was even supposed to have thrown one of young Dmitry's older brothers out of the house for expressing sympathy for a woman nihilist who recently had been executed. The father was proud of his youngest son, however, and when, at the age of fifteen, Dmitry began his first efforts at writing verse, Serge dragged the youth to Dostoevski to read his work aloud. After the reading, Dostoevski's response was reportedly that "to write, one must suffer."

On entering the University of St. Petersburg, Merezhkovsky proved to be a brilliant student. He immersed himself in the Greek and Roman classics and completed his studies in two years. He grew fascinated by the works of Herbert Spencer, John Stuart Mill, Auguste Comte, and Charles Darwin, as well as that of Friedrich Nietzsche, but soon found that such readings left the religious urge fostered in him since childhood unsatisfied. Turning to literature instead, he joined a student-formed Molière club; so reactionary and suspicious was the czarist government at this time, however, that the club was suppressed, and if it had not been for the intervention of his aristocratic father, Merezhkovsky would have been exiled. This, in addition to his frail health, led to his spending the year after graduation in the Caucasus and Crimea.

While there, Merezhkovsky met Zinaida Hippius, at that time the best-known woman poet in Russia. They were married in 1889. Soon afterward, Zinaida fell gravely ill; before she recovered, Merezhkovsky's beloved mother died, and he found himself unwillingly following Dostoevski's dictum. His response to these trials was mysticism, and as he grew older his mysticism correspondingly deepened. He and his wife began traveling throughout Greece, Turkey, and the Near East, and this experience, linked to his newfound beliefs, eventually resulted in the trilogy of philosophical novels focusing on Julian the Apostate, Leonardo da Vinci, and Peter the Great, collectively titled *Christ and Antichrist*.

After his return to St. Petersburg, Merezhkovsky began pursuing his literary career in earnest. As early as 1883, he had published verse in the "civic" style (*Stikhotvoreniya, 1883-1887*) but had found no real success. Nearly a decade later, he published the first book of symbolist poetry written in Russian, *Simvoly*, followed immediately by his first collection of critical essays, *O prichinakh upadka i o novykh techeniyakh sovremennoy russkoy literatury*. Soon thereafter appeared his first work of classicism, *Vechnye sputniki* (1897; eternal companions), and Merezhkovsky's reputation as a modernist critic, classical scholar, and symbolist poet was fixed. It was not until the release of the *Christ and Antichrist* trilogy, however, that Merezhkovsky's reputation became international and he found himself a true celebrity in his own land.

Like many other artists cast suddenly into the limelight, Merezhkovsky began to take himself too seriously. His mysticism intensified and, as a result, his criticism became more virulent and dogmatic. His fiction developed into a pulpit from which he proselytized the heathen, and he subjugated plot and characterization to turgid philosophy. After 1900, he founded a religion known as the New Road, with which he tried to reconcile Nietzsche's egoism with Tolstoy's altruism and synthesize the pagan, Hellenic cult of the flesh with the Christian cult of the spirit—all into one new entity. For a time, Merezhkovsky and his wife conducted salons devoted to the spreading of this new religion, and shortly devotees of this Society of Religion and Philosophy began to appear. Merezhkovsky rejected in his teachings the "heresy" of historical Christianity and preached instead a personal, apocalyptic Christianity of the "Third Testament," in which Hellenism and Christ would be synthesized when history came to an end—which, he asserted, would be soon. Over time, his doctrine evolved into the worship of an Eternal Woman-Mother as the Holy Spirit, the third person of the Trinity and simultaneously an embodiment of Russia's destiny. He also exalted hermaphrodites as symbols of a Being who would eventually unite the sexes on Judgment Day. Thus, as his religion became more arcane, his fiction became more unreadable.

Merezhkovsky supported the abortive Revolution of 1905 in the hope that it would become a religious revolution overthrowing Russia's established church and state, leading in turn to the Kingdom of God on earth. The revolution, however, did not achieve this goal, and he and his wife fled to Paris. In 1910, they returned to Russia and subsequently opposed World War I. Merezhkovsky opposed the Bolsheviks even more zealously, and, in

1918, he was sent to Siberia. In 1920, he and Zinaida escaped, settling first in Poland and then in Paris, where they spent the remainder of their lives as émigrés. There he produced bitter tracts against the Soviets and books (which were generally ignored) attempting to explain the New Road. Merezhkovsky died in Paris on December 9, 1941, of a brain hemorrhage.

ANALYSIS

Once, in 1905, at the peak of his literary success, Dmitry Merezhkovsky complained that "in Russia they did not like me and upbraided me; abroad they like me and praised me; but equally here and there they failed to comprehend 'what is mine.'" Indeed, most writers, in their darkest moments, will bewail what they consider the low comprehension levels of critics and the general reading public; few, however, are caught doing this at the time of their triumph, and perhaps, in a circuitous manner, this very complaint provides an insight into the complex and often tumultuous art and life of Merezhkovsky. How does one finally interpret his phrase "what is mine"? In the final analysis, one must conclude that he does not mean his fiction, poetry, or criticism, but rather his religious beliefs and his messianic attempt to give the world what was in his opinion the true means for its salvation.

This discovery of the absolute religious truth was the motivating force behind all of Merezhkovsky's work. At the beginning of his career, he valued above all else the "liberation of life through Beauty" and dreamed of Hellenic perfection. Over time, however, this worship of the beautiful narrowed, away from the general sense intended by most idealists, toward a more limited definition—a more sensual and erotic one in which beauty came to mean the aesthetics of the leisured class. Merezhkovsky's other beliefs and theories also narrowed as his age increased, so that eventually he cut himself off from all but a very select group of initiates—and finally from them also.

What makes an understanding of Merezhkovsky's life and art even more difficult is that, though his search for truth was unswerving, his choice of vehicles for that search swung wildly from one end of the pendulum's arc to the other. He first sought truth through the populist ideal of service to the people; soon, however, he discovered that this would be an impossibility, because at heart he never could love individuals. Again and again this problem springs up in Merezhkovsky: He is more enamored of generalities, the "big ideas," than he is of "little truths" or individuals. In even his best works of fiction, his main characters are not characters at all, but rather embodiments of ideals.

After populism, Merezhkovsky swung to the opposite extreme. He extolled the classical virtues and posited a Nietzschean "superhumanity" as humankind's ultimate goal. Eventually, he would abandon even this, concluding that this system denied God. Merezhkovsky would always be torn by these swings in his philosophy and allegiance—his love for Russia and Europe, for God and humanity, for the old and new, for Christian spiritualism and Hellenic hedonism—and never reconciled the fundamental duality of his nature.

Up to a point, this duality informs and strengthens his work; after that point, when his religious beliefs finally gelled, this same duality tore his creations down. The dividing line seems to be the early 1990's, before the publication of *Peter and Alexis*, and indeed it is only his first two novels, *The Death of the Gods* and *The Romance of Leonardo da Vinci*, which are still read today. After that, his writing became too polemical, too mystical, and finally too hysterical and arcane to be enjoyed or even understood, increasingly bogged down in a gamesmanship of Hegelian dialectics in which he tried unsuccessfully to reconcile his dual truths—so much so, in fact, that one seems to be reading a new type of philosophical formula writing.

The *Death of the Gods* and *The Romance of Leonardo da Vinci* are masterpieces of historical romance, however, and the international renown that sprang from them was well deserved. Though sometimes clumsily constructed, the two novels do possess a kind of raw power in the depiction of the historical panorama, usually executed in mosaic form. Original documents, excerpts, quotes, and other historical tidbits are employed to re-create the life and spirit of fourth century Rome or fifteenth century Italy: Merezhkovsky was even dubbed by one critic as the "Napoleon of Quotes." Oddly enough, though his protagonists Julian and Leonardo seem little more than abstractions, his minor characters— Caesar Constantius, Gallus Flavius, Arsinoe, Cesare Borgia, Machiavelli, Pope Leo X, Mona Lisa (La Gioconda), and others—all live. Once again, this is indicative of the fact that when Merezhkovsky tries to prove a thesis, he stumbles, but when he simply writes, his narrative flies.

CHRIST AND ANTICHRIST TRILOGY

Merezhkovsky's trilogy *Christ and Antichrist*, which includes the novels *The Death of the Gods*, *The Romance of Leonardo da Vinci*, and *Peter and Alexis*, presents in partly Nietzschean, partly mystical terms the advance of European history as an ongoing battle between the forces of paganism and Christianity. Julian is presented as torn between Christ and Apollo: He is a monk at first, but adores the nude, white beauty of a marble Aphrodite and seeks the divinity and understanding of Apollo. When Julian becomes Emperor of Rome, he returns Hellenic paganism to its lost splendor, but a mob of fanatic Christians destroys a new temple. The collapse of the temple's columns symbolizes the death of the old gods. Merezhkovsky presents this as a tragic event; however, his spirits rise once more when he shows the Renaissance's resurrection of these Olympians, who are now beyond good and evil. Leonardo, who never takes sides, is seen as half Christian, half pagan—and the highest embodiment of the two. He realizes that perfect knowledge leads to perfect love and yet, like Merezhkovsky, is unable to reconcile the two extremes. Finally, Christ and Antichrist wage war in Russia at the turn of the eighteenth century: Peter the Great, shown as a Leonardo of action, clashes with his superstitious and doctrinaire son, Alexis. In the end, Merezhkovsky's message is that the struggle to achieve a balance between the flesh and the spirit is a terrible, never-ending one.

LATER NOVELS

The later novels—*December the Fourteenth*, *The Birth of the Gods*, and *Akhnaton, King of Egypt*—explore the same themes but are never as well realized. *December the Fourteenth* is the story of the unsuccessful Decembrist Revolution against the newly crowned Nicholas I, and the harsh treatment meted out by the czar against those implicated. That this book was published in 1918 gives it some historical interest: The Bolshevik Revolution had already taken place by then, but at the end of this book, Merezhkovsky seems to hint that a more pervasive revolt of the spirit based on a belief in Russia as the "Holy Mother" will sweep the nation and eventually the world.

Merezhkovsky's last two works of fiction, *The Birth of the Gods* and *Akhnaton, King of Egypt*, are a pair of connected stories, the first taking place in Crete, the second in Egypt. In *The Birth of the Gods*, Tutankhamon, son-in-law and envoy of the Egyptian pharaoh, arrives in Minoan Crete, where he meets the virginal Dio, priestess of the sacred bull. Through Tutankhamon, Dio comes to realize that her native religion is evil, and so kills the sacred bull. In the second book, Dio is now associated with King Akhnaton and his mystical plans to reform the world and establish universal peace. Both characters die in the end, but Akhnaton is revealed as one who will somehow rise again and save the world.

The Death of the Gods and its sequel, *The Romance of Leonardo da Vinci*, cannot, like Merezhkovsky's other works of fiction, be called second-rate. In many ways, *The Death of the Gods* is similar to another famous work of historical fiction—Robert Graves's *I, Claudius* (1934)—in that all the intricate plots, counterplots, and court intrigues of Imperial Rome are related in superb detail. Julian Flavius, the protagonist and cousin to Caesar Constantius, the Emperor of Rome, survives to become Caesar himself simply by staying out of his cousin's reach. In fact, he does lose a brother, Gallus Flavius, to the Emperor and wonders how much longer he himself has to live.

After Julian's ascension to power, the book spends less time with temporal affairs and begins instead to establish the mystical blueprint on which the rest of the trilogy is based. The goal of the trilogy *Christ and Antichrist*, as stated earlier, was to establish a synthesis between flesh and spirit, life and faith. To Merezhkovsky, life, as represented by the Olympian gods (Dionysius in particular), and faith, as symbolized by Christ, were inseparable: One without the other was incomplete. Recorded history was to be interpreted as a dialectic of these two opposing yet complementary forces.

In *The Death of the Gods*, this synthesis is not yet explicitly presented—it is still too early in the scheme of the trilogy. Instead, the reader is meant to glean hints of it. Near the beginning of the novel, one notices such a hint in the representation of Christ as the Good Shepherd, hidden away in a dark corner of the church where Julian goes to pray as a child. Later, it is revealed in the dying words of a secondary character when she states that everyone—the righteous and the sinners—will be redeemed by Christ's love and that everything, even Bacchic celebrations, is sacred. This idea of the holiness of Bacchus is a recurring one in Merezhkovsky's work; in many ways he seems to believe that Christ's return to earth will be as a combination of the Bacchic and the divine. Finally, Merezhkovsky's theme can be seen near the novel's end when a hymn to Pan and a monkish chant to God are symbolically merged. As the curtain falls on the death of Julian and the triumph of historical Christianity, one is left with the feeling that something irreplaceable has been lost.

All is not completely lost, however, for in the beginning of *The Romance of Leonardo da Vinci* the resurrection of the Olympians is signified by the discovery of a marble Venus that had been hidden away for centuries. The time is the late fifteenth century, during the Italian Renaissance; the Middle Ages—a period of ignorance and superstition in which the Church reigned supreme—has passed. With the Olympians' resurrection comes a resurrection of knowledge, and presiding over it all is that Nietzschean patron saint of knowledge, Leonardo da Vinci.

To Merezhkovsky, Leonardo is beyond good and evil: He is willing to serve any master, simply because he exists on a plane above earthly concerns. Merezhkovsky wants his reader to believe that Leonardo embodies the hoped-for synthesis of paganism and Christianity, though it is also posited that he is too advanced for his time. Thus, Leonardo is drawn to prove a thesis and, as is often the case in Merezhkovsky's work, ends up a pale shadow compared to those fleshed-out others who do not straddle such philosophical fences. The purely Christian characters (Savonarola, the Grand High Inquisitor), purely pagan ones (Cesare Borgia, Duke Moro), or even those who aspire to Leonardo's greatness yet remain caught in the old webs of belief, all seem more real than Leonardo himself—which in itself is perhaps revealing of the conflict between Merezhkovsky's stated beliefs and his true ones. In any case, Leonardo seems an abstraction until the point when he falls in love with his model Mona Lisa (La Gioconda); even then, however, he hesitates and loses her to an early death.

Perhaps it is because Merezhkovsky fails to portray convincingly Leonardo as this prophesied synthesis that the character gains stature as an artist instead, for it is during Leonardo's search for truth, rather than during his supposedly otherworldly contemplation of it, that Leonardo becomes real. That everything in nature reveals God is the ultimate answer lying at the bottom of the abyss for both Leonardo and Merezhkovsky; furthermore, both are convinced that perfect knowledge leads to God. Instead of detracting from faith and love, knowledge increases their power. In the end, this seems to be Merezhkovsky's final conclusion—a conclusion that leaves considerable room for artistic elaboration. It is unfortunate that he failed to recognize this and became bogged down in mysticism instead.

Joe W. Jackson, Jr.

Other major works

 Plays: *Makov tsvet*, pb. 1908; *Pavel I*, pb. 1908; *Budet radost'*, pb. 1916; *Romantiki*, pb. 1917; *Tsarevich Aleksey*, pb. 1920.

 Poetry: *Stikhotvoreniya, 1883-1887*, 1888; *Simvoly*, 1892.

NONFICTION: *Flober v svolkh pis' makh*, 1888 (*The Life Work of Flaubert*, 1908); *Kal'deron*, 1891 (*The Life Work of Calderon*, 1908); *Mark Avreliy*, 1891 (*The Life Work of Marcus Aurelius*, 1909); *Montan*, 1893 (*The Life Work of Montaigne*, 1907); *O prichinakh upadka i o novykh techeniyakh sovremennoy russkoy literatury*, 1893; *Vechnye sputniki*, 1897; *L. Tolstoy i Dostoyevsky*, 1901-1902 (*Tolstoi as Man and Artist, with an Essay on Dostoievski*, 1902); *Akropol'*, 1897 (*The Acropolis*, 1909); *Joseph Pilsudski*, 1920 (English translation, 1921); *Tsarstvo Antikhrista*, 1921 (with Z. N. Gippius, D. V. Filosofov, and N. V. Zlobin); *Napoleon*, 1929 (2 volumes; includes *Napoleon, cheloviek* [*Napoleon, the Man*, 1928; also known as *Napoleon: A Study*, 1929] and *Zhizn' Napoleona* [*The Life of Napoleon*, 1929]); *Atlantida-Yevropa*, 1930 (*The Secret of the West*, 1933); *Michael Angelo, and Other Sketches*, 1930.

TRANSLATION: *Dafnis i Khloya*, 1897 (of Longus).

BIBLIOGRAPHY

Bedford, C. Harold. *The Seeker: D. S. Merezhkovsky*. Lawrence: University Press of Kansas, 1975. Bedford provides a detailed analysis of Merezhkovsky's religious beliefs. Includes a bibliography, an index, and a list of Merezhkovsky's works.

Frajlich, Anna. "The Contradictions of the Northern Pilgrim: Dmitry Merezhkovsky." In *The Legacy of Ancient Rome in the Russian Silver Age*. Amsterdam: Rodopi, 2007. Frajlich discusses how the renewal of classical scholarship in nineteenth century Russia led Merezhkovsky and other Russian symbolists to find inspiration in ancient Rome. Includes examinations of some of Merezhkovsky's novels and poems.

Hellman, Ben. *Poets of Hope and Despair: The Russian Symbolists in War and Revolution, 1914-1918*. Helsinki, Finland: Institute for Russian and East European Studies, 1995. This study of Russian symbolism includes a chapter on Merezhkovsky. Analyzes how he and other symbolists interpreted the deeper meaning of the events of World War I and the Russian Revolution.

Pachmuss, Temira. *D. S. Merezhkovsky in Exile: The Master of the Genre of Biographie Romancée*. New York: Peter Lang, 1990. Pachmuss focuses on 1919 through 1941, the years Merezhkovsky spent in exile. She analyzes the unpublished fictionalized biographies and the other works he wrote during this period.

Rosenthal, Bernice Glatzer. *Dmitri Sergeevich Merezhkovsky and the Silver Age: The Development of a Revolutionary Mentality*. The Hague, the Netherlands: Martinus Nijhoff, 1975. Rosenthal examines Merezhkovsky's role in the Russian cultural renaissance at the turn of the twentieth century and discusses the political implications of the renaissance's aesthetics.

VLADIMIR NABOKOV

Born: St. Petersburg, Russia; April 23, 1899
Died: Montreux, Switzerland; July 2, 1977
Also known as: Vladimir Vladimirovich Nabokov; V. Sirin

PRINCIPAL LONG FICTION

Mashenka, 1926 (*Mary*, 1970)
Korol', dama, valet, 1928 (*King, Queen, Knave*, 1968)
Zashchita Luzhina, 1929 (serial), 1930 (book; *The Defense*, 1964)
Kamera obskura, 1932 (*Camera Obscura*, 1936; revised as *Laughter in the Dark*, 1938)
Podvig, 1932 (*Glory*, 1971)
Otchayanie, 1934 (serial), 1936 (book; *Despair*, 1937; revised 1966)
Priglashenie na kazn', 1935-1936 (serial), 1938 (book; *Invitation to a Beheading*, 1959)
Dar, 1937-1938 (serial), 1952 (book; *The Gift*, 1963)
The Real Life of Sebastian Knight, 1941
Bend Sinister, 1947
Lolita, 1955
Pnin, 1957
Pale Fire, 1962
Ada or Ardor: A Family Chronicle, 1969
Transparent Things, 1972
Look at the Harlequins!, 1974

OTHER LITERARY FORMS

Vladimir Nabokov (nah-BO-kof) began, as many novelists do, as a poet. As a youth, he published privately what now would be called a chapbook and a full book of poetry before emigrating from Russia. Throughout his life, he continued to publish poetry in periodicals and several book-length collections, including *Stikhotvorenia, 1929-1951* (1952), *Poems* (1959), and *Poems and Problems* (1970). Some critics even consider the long poem "Pale Fire" (an integral part of the novel *Pale Fire*) a worthy neo-Romantic poem in itself. Nabokov also published a good deal of short fiction, first in a variety of short-lived émigré publications such as *Rul'*, *Sovremennye Zapiski*, and *Russkoe ekho*, and later in such prominent magazines as *The New Yorker*, *The Atlantic Monthly*, *Playboy*, *Harper's Bazaar*, and *Tri-Quarterly*. His stories were collected in *Vozrashchenie Chorba* (1930; the return of Chorb), which also included twenty-four poems, *Soglyadatay* (1938; the eye), *Nine Stories* (1947), and *Nabokov's Dozen* (1958), among others. His plays include *Smert'* (pb. 1923; death), *Tragediya gospodina Morna* (pb. 1924; the tragedy of Mister

Vladimir Nabokov
(Library of Congress0

Morn), *Chelovek iz SSSR* (pb. 1927; the man from the USSR), *Sobytiye* (pr., pb. 1938; the event), and *Izobretenie Val'sa* (pb. 1938; *The Waltz Invention*, 1966). He also worked on a screenplay for the film version of *Lolita* (1962). In addition to translating his own works from Russian to English (and vice versa, as well as occasionally from French to Russian to English), he often translated the works of other writers, including Lewis Carroll's *Alice's Adventures in Wonderland* (1865) and poetry of Rupert Brooke, Alexander Pushkin, Arthur Rimbaud, William Shakespeare, and Alfred de Musset. In nonfiction prose, Nabokov's fascinating life is recalled in three volumes of memoirs, *Conclusive Evidence* (1951), *Drugie Berega* (1954; other shores), and *Speak, Memory: An Autobiography Revisited* (1966, a revision and expansion of the earlier works). Throughout his life, his often idiosyncratic criticism was widely published, and the publication after his death of several volumes of his lectures on world literature provoked much discussion among literary scholars. As a lepidopterist, Nabokov published a number of scholarly articles in such journals as *The Entomologist*, *Journal of the New York Entomological Society*, *Psyche*, and *The Lepidopterists' News*.

ACHIEVEMENTS

Vladimir Nabokov's strength as a writer lay in his control and mastery of style. Writers are sometimes successful in a language other than their native language, but only a select few are capable of writing equally well in two languages, and Nabokov may be alone in his ability to master the insinuations of two such extraordinarily different and subtle languages as Russian and English. Under the pen name "V. Sirin," Nabokov was recognized as a noteworthy émigré novelist and poet in Berlin and Paris. After fleeing the rise of Nazism and settling in the United States, he became recognized as a major English-language author with the publication of *Lolita* in 1955. As was the case with Gustave Flaubert, James Joyce, and D. H. Lawrence, all of whose international sales were aided by the controversies surrounding their works, Nabokov received worldwide attention as critics debated the morality of *Lolita*, prompting the republication and translation of many of his earlier works. Few writers with such an uncompromising style achieve such popularity. Nabokov was often in financial difficulty before *Lolita*, yet he always remained the consummate craftsman. He has come to be regarded as one of the literary giants of his generation.

BIOGRAPHY

Vladimir Vladimirovich Nabokov was born to Vladimir Dmitrievich and Elena Rukavishnikov Nabokov in St. Petersburg, Russia, the eldest of five children. He grew up in comfortable circumstances, tracing his ancestry back to a Tartar prince of the 1380's and through a number of military men, statesmen, Siberian merchants, and the first president of the Russian Imperial Academy of Medicine. His father was a noted liberal who had helped found the Constitutional Democratic Party, was elected to the first Duma, and coedited the sole liberal newspaper in St. Petersburg. In his childhood, the young Nabokov was taken on trips to France, Italy, and Spain, and he summered on the country estate of Vyra, accumulating memories that would become woven into his later writings. His father, an Anglophile, provided governesses who taught the boy English at a very early age. He once remarked that he had learned to read English even before he had learned Russian. He was also taught French.

Entering puberty, Nabokov attended the liberal Prince Tenishev School, where he first developed a hatred of coercion but played soccer and chess, started collecting butterflies, and showed some artistic talent. He began writing poetry, and a now lost brochure of a single poem "in a violet paper cover" was privately published in 1914. In 1916, he privately published a recollection that provoked his cousin to beg him to "never, never be a writer," and in 1918, he collaborated on a collection with Andrei Balashov. Nabokov inherited an estate and the equivalent of two million dollars when his Uncle Ruka died and seemed to be on his way to the comfortable life of a Russian bourgeois when history intervened. His father became part of the Provisional Government in the March Revolution of 1917, but in October, when the Bolsheviks displaced the Alexander Kerensky government, the

Nabokov family fled, first to the Crimea and then, in 1919, into permanent exile in the West on an old Greek ship ironically named *Nadezhda* ("Hope").

Nabokov studied at Trinity College, Cambridge University, paying little attention to anything but soccer, tennis, and girls. He did, however, do many translations (of Rupert Brooke, Seumas O'Sullivan, William Butler Yeats, Lord Byron, and others) and came under the influence of English poetry. He also read and was influenced by James Joyce. Despite his claim that he never once visited the library, he graduated with honors in French and Russian literature in 1923. This was shortly following his father's assassination in Berlin in March, 1922, as two reactionaries shot the elder Nabokov in error as he was introducing their intended victim. After Cambridge, the twenty-five-year-old Nabokov moved to Berlin, where, in 1925, he married Vera Evseevna Slonim, and a year later he published his first novel, *Mary*, under a pseudonym. He felt that his father had prior claim to the name "Vladimir Nabokov," and he wrote all of his early Russian works as "V. Sirin."

With very little money, Nabokov published poems, stories, and essays in Berlin's émigré newspapers, and later, as the Nazis grew in power (his wife was Jewish), in similar Parisian publications. He survived by teaching tennis, devising crossword puzzles in Russian, making up chess problems, teaching Russian, and translating. He sold the Russian translation of *Alice's Adventures in Wonderland* (*Anya v strane chudes*, 1923), for example, for the equivalent of five dollars. In 1934, his only son, Dmitri, was born, and four years later, Nabokov fled to Paris. As early as 1935, he decided to immigrate to the United States, probably recognizing that Europe was no longer safe. He was invited by the Soviet government during the 1930's to return to Russia several times, but he refused.

Nabokov's novels published in Berlin and Paris had been relatively successful, and several had been translated into English with and without his assistance. He made the remarkable and difficult decision to abandon the language in which he had written so well. "My private tragedy," he later wrote, "which cannot, indeed should not, be anybody's concern, is that I had to abandon my natural idiom, my untrammeled, rich, and infinitely docile Russian tongue for a second-rate brand of English." Stanford University invited him to teach in the summer of 1940, and he set sail for the United States on the liner *Champlain* in May, just ahead of the German invasion. He had already begun writing his first English novel, *The Real Life of Sebastian Knight*, while in Paris, and, in 1941, it was published in the United States after several friends helped him edit it. He taught Russian grammar and literature at Wellesley College from 1941 to 1948, also serving as a research fellow at the Museum of Comparative Zoology at Harvard University. He became a prominent lepidopterist, publishing many monographs, articles, and reviews. He spent summers roaming the United States searching for butterflies and discovered several species and subspecies, including one that came to be called Nabokov's wood nymph. After seeing praise for his work on the *Lycaeides* genus in a field guide, Nabokov is said to have remarked, "That's real fame. That means more than anything a literary critic could say."

In 1944, Nabokov published a critical book on Nikolai Gogol, and in 1947, his first novel written in the United States, *Bend Sinister,* appeared. From 1948 to 1959, he taught at Cornell University, carefully writing out his lectures, combining his attacks on such intellectual touchstones as Karl Marx, Charles Darwin, and especially Sigmund Freud with dramatic classroom readings. Well before the publication of *Lolita,* he was recognized as a remarkable talent in certain quarters, as is indicated by his receipt of grants from the Guggenheim Foundation in 1943 and 1953 and by an award from the American Academy of Arts and Letters in 1953; students in his classes at Cornell, however, were often unaware that their teacher was also a writer, although he published stories and articles in *The New Yorker, The Atlantic Monthly, Hudson Review,* and other periodicals. *Lolita* changed all that. Rejected by several American publishers, it was brought out by publisher Maurice Girodias's Olympia Press in Paris in 1955. As one of the most controversial books ever published—banned for a while in France, debated in Parliament in England, and forbidden in many American libraries—it swept the best-seller lists and freed Nabokov from teaching. In addition to the royalties, he received $150,000 and a percentage from the sale of the film rights. He also wrote a screenplay (which was later substantially changed) for the film version to be directed by Stanley Kubrick, which was released in 1962. (A second film version of *Lolita,* directed by Adrian Lyne, was released in 1997.)

In 1960, Nabokov moved to Montreux, Switzerland, where he and his wife lived in a sixth-floor apartment in the Palace Hotel overlooking Lake Geneva, in order to be near their son Dmitri, who was having some success as an opera singer. In the wake of *Lolita,* Nabokov and his son translated many of his earlier novels into English and introduced several collections of his short stories to American readers. His novels *Pale Fire, Ada or Ardor, Transparent Things,* and *Look at the Harlequins!* were all published during this period. He was regularly discussed as a possible recipient of the Nobel Prize until his death of a viral infection in 1977.

ANALYSIS

In 1937, Vladeslav Khodasevich, an émigré poet and champion of "V. Sirin's" work, wrote, "Sirin [Nabokov] proves for the most part to be an artist of form, of the writer's device, and not only in that . . . sense of which . . . his writing is distinguished by exceptional diversity, complexity, brilliance, and novelty." Khodasevich went on to say that the key to all Sirin's work was his ability to put all his literary devices on display, with little or no attempt to conceal them, thus entertaining his readers more with the revelation of how the magician performs his tricks, than with the trick itself. "The life of the artist and the life of a device in the consciousness of an artist—this is Sirin's theme." Khodasevich, although he had not yet read *The Gift*—purported to be Vladimir Nabokov's greatest Russian novel—had discovered the most important element of Nabokov's fiction.

Throughout his entire life, although Nabokov underwent great changes in his circumstances, he was consistent, whether writing in Russian or English, in his unflagging delight in literary devices of all sorts, art for its own sake, and a contempt for mimetic conventions, simplistic psychological motivation, ordinary plot structure, and anything that inhibits the literary imagination. He can, in many respects, be called an aesthete, but his rejection of most schools of thought makes him difficult to classify. He strove for and achieved a uniqueness that runs as a thread throughout his oeuvre. Clarence Brown once commented in a critical essay that "for well over a quarter of a century now . . . [Nabokov] has been writing in book after book about the same thing," and Nabokov is said to have admitted that Brown was probably correct.

MARY *and* KING, QUEEN, KNAVE

Nabokov's first novel, *Mary*, is rather sentimental and probably based on Nabokov's regret for a lost love, but it already contains two elements he would use repeatedly—the love triangle and uncertain identity. *King, Queen, Knave*, however, is an even more obvious reflection of the Nabokov canon. In it, a character named Franz Bubendorf, a country bumpkin on his way to the city, apparently to be corrupted by the bourgeois life, is, in fact, already corrupted by his distaste for his own class, which distorts his perception. As if to emphasize this distortion of perception, Franz steps on his glasses and Berlin becomes a blur. Again, there is a love triangle, and each of the participants is, in his or her own way, unable to perceive reality. The melodrama of a love triangle and a planned murder is handled with the authorial detachment that is one of Nabokov's hallmarks. The novel becomes a parody of traditional forms, and the characters become obvious contrivances of the author. Derived from a Hans Christian Andersen work of the same title, the novel consists of thirteen chapters, as there are thirteen cards in each suit in a deck of cards. The card metaphor is carried throughout the work, even in the description of clothes.

LAUGHTER IN THE DARK

Laughter in the Dark opens with a parody of the fairy tale revealing the entire plot, here a relatively conventional bourgeois love story that Nabokov typically manipulates. The main character, blinded by love, becomes literally blinded and trapped in a love triangle, which results in his murder (accomplished in a scene that is a parody of motion-picture melodrama). This type of parody, which partially represents Nabokov's delight in mocking inferior art, can also be seen as a parody of the reader's expectations. Nabokov constantly thwarts the reader who wants a nice, comfortable, conventional novel. The writer is always in control, always tugging the reader this way and that, never allowing a moment of certainty. Perceptions are distorted on all levels. The characters have distorted perceptions of one another. The reader's perception of events is teasingly distorted by the author. Nabokov operates a house of mirrors. If a reader expects realism, there will be no pleasure in the warped mirrors Nabokov presents. One must delight instead in the odd shapes and obvious deformities in the mirrors he has shaped.

NABOKOV'S CHARACTERS

Character types in the Russian novels also recur throughout Nabokov's career, so much so that some critics have attempted to pair earlier Russian novels with later English ones. Usually, the central figure is an outsider, an unusual person in his milieu. Bubendorf of *King, Queen, Knave* is a country boy in the city. In *The Defense*, the chess master Luzhin does not fit in with his family or his school, and is sent into exile after the Revolution. Martin Edelweiss of *Glory* is in exile in London.

What is more important, however, is that these and many more of Nabokov's characters are isolated as much by their mental states as by their physical surroundings. Their fantasies, dreams, ambitions, and obsessions set them utterly apart from the ordinary world. Luzhin, for example, is so obsessed with chess that he cannot deal with the disorder of life. Cincinnatus in *Invitation to a Beheading* is thought peculiar by his fellow workers in the doll factory. In later English novels, immigrant Timofey Pnin is thought mad by his academic colleagues, Humbert Humbert and Adam Krug are seen as dangers to society, and Charles Kinbote intrudes and imposes on people. Generally, the main characters of Nabokov's novels are perceived as talented men, in some sense more valuable than the soulless people and society that persecute them. They are outsiders because they are extraordinary. They are free, imaginative, and capable of a kind of heroism that ordinary people lack: the ability to remake the world according to their own obsessions.

THE GIFT

The Gift is generally thought of as Nabokov's best Russian novel. It was originally published serially in *Sovremennye Zapiski*, an émigré periodical, and the fourth section was not included (for political reasons) in a complete edition until 1952. In *The Gift*, the central figure is Fyodor Godunov-Cherdyntsev, a brilliant émigré poet. As the book opens, he has just published a collection of poems, and much of the early part concerns his literary career. Later, his obsession with the memory of his father begins to dominate his everyday life, and he becomes caught in the typical confusions of the biographer: What is the truth and how can one see it? He feels an obligation to write a biography of his father but becomes trapped in assessing the various versions of his father's life. Later, he does succeed in writing a biography of Nikolai Gavrilovich Chernyshevski, a so-called poetic history based on the idea that reconstructing the past is essentially a creative act—history exists only in the historian's imagination—and that the best biographies are literary creations.

The Gift has been seen as the summing up of Nabokov's experiences as an émigré writer, and similarities have been seen between the author's biography and the events and people in the novel. The book is heavy with allusions to Russian literature and has been called the Russian counterpart to *Ada or Ardor*, an extremely allusive and complex book that also focuses on the nature of the writer. In *The Gift*, many of Nabokov's favorite devices are employed: the love triangle, the ironic suicide, and the heightened perception of the hero, in which he imagines conversations with the dead.

THE REAL LIFE OF SEBASTIAN KNIGHT

After his decision to begin writing in English, Nabokov produced two novels before the *succès de scandale* of *Lolita*. *The Real Life of Sebastian Knight* was begun in Paris and is ostensibly the biography of a fiction writer, Sebastian, narrated by his brother, "V." V. is shocked to discover upon his brother's death in 1936 that there was more to learn of Sebastian from his novels than he had learned in person. Once again, Nabokov introduces the theme that art surpasses reality. V. fights the various distortions of Sebastian's life yet, at the end of his biography, confesses that "Sebastian's mask clings to my face." V. created Sebastian, so Sebastian is V. (as both characters were created by Nabokov). Again, the novel is characterized by the use of parodistic techniques and distorted characters. One can easily recognize this novel as a Nabokov work, yet because of Nabokov's uncertainty at writing in the English language at this stage, the work is not completely satisfying. Nabokov admitted, for example, to having had native speakers help him with the editing, something he would never permit later.

BEND SINISTER

Many resemblances have been noted between Nabokov and his brother Sergei, and V. and his brother Sebastian. Sergei, unlike Vladimir, stayed in Europe during the Nazi period and died of starvation in a concentration camp near Hamburg on January 10, 1945. These events perhaps explain the harsh allegorical tone of *Bend Sinister*, a novel that is, in some ways, better than its predecessor and perhaps one of the most accessible of Nabokov's novels. The hero, Adam Krug, is an intellectual whose ideas are largely responsible for the new regime in an Eastern European country. Krug, however, refuses to swear allegiance to the ruler of the regime, a fellow student from childhood named Paduk. "I am not interested in politics," he says. Inexorably, the ring of tyranny tightens around Krug, resulting in the arrest of friends, the death of his son, and Krug's death as he attempts to attack Paduk in a mad vision of schoolyard life.

The artist, the literary craftsman in Nabokov, was incapable, however, of writing a straightforward novel of outrage against Fascists or Communists. The country is not specified; numerous vague descriptions of setting give the work a Kafkaesque flavor. The regime is tyrannical—it wants the souls of its people as well as their cooperation (not unlike Big Brother in George Orwell's *Nineteen Eighty-Four*, 1949)—yet it is not a specific ideology that is being attacked. Any form of coercion that limits the imagination of the artist or the intellectual is the target. Although some critics have argued that Krug's flaw is that he refuses to become involved in politics, it is difficult to imagine *Bend Sinister*, in the light of other works, as being a call to commitment. Krug has made a commitment to his own intellectual life. He, like many Nabokov heroes, does not "fit in" and, like many Nabokov heroes, comes to a tragic end. The supremacy of the individual imagination is Nabokov's "message"; art is his morality. There is an abundant helping of satire and parody directed against the intellectual community and the "great" political leaders of the world. Paduk is shown as a sniveling, ugly weakling who craves Krug's approval, but the alternatives to his tyranny are shown to be equally preposterous. Even in reacting to the horrors of dictatorship, Nabokov remains the detached artist.

LOLITA

Lolita, the novel that would provide a comfortable living for the author for the rest of his life, has been called everything from pornography to one of the greatest novels of the twentieth century. Today, when virtually every sexual predilection has been the subject of motion pictures and television, it is hard to appreciate the whirlwind of controversy that was stirred up by *Lolita*'s publication. Humbert Humbert, the central character and narrator, has an obsession with young girls that he has hidden by unhappy affairs with older women. He comes to the United States after inheriting a business and separating from his childish wife Valeria. Eventually, he becomes the boarder of Charlotte Haze and becomes sexually obsessed with her twelve-year-old daughter, Lolita. He marries Mrs. Haze to be near Lolita, and when the mother is killed, he takes the girl on a trip across the United States. She is eventually stolen by Clare Quilty, who is, in many ways, Humbert's double, and Humbert goes on a two-year quest to rescue the girl. He finds the sad, pregnant Lolita married to a man named Richard Schiller and, in revenge, shoots Quilty. The novel is allegedly Humbert's manuscript, written as he awaits trial. According to the foreword, Humbert died in jail of a coronary thrombosis, and the manuscript was transmitted to one John Ray, Jr., Ph.D., who prepared it for publication.

As in all of Nabokov's works, however, a plot summary is absurdly inadequate in characterizing the book. *Lolita* is protean in its directions and effects. It has been seen as a satire on the United States (though Nabokov denied it), as a psychological study (although Nabokov called Freud a "medieval mind"), and as a parody of the Romantic novel. Lionel Trilling argued that, since adultery was such a commonplace in the modern world, only a perverse love could cause the adequate passion mixed with suffering characteristic of great Romantic loves: Tristan and Isolde, Abélard and Héloise, Dante and Beatrice, Petrarch and Laura. Humbert often justifies his pedophilia by references to the courtly love tradition. There is also much reference to the story of Edgar Allan Poe's love for Virginia Clemm (Humbert's first teenage love was a girl named Annabel Leigh).

Although many critics attempted to justify *Lolita* as having an important moral message, Nabokov rebuked the notion by saying, "I am no messenger boy." His aesthetic philosophy would never have permitted him to subordinate his art to a moral. He once said that Lolita was about his love for the English language, but even that is an oversimplification of an immensely complex book. Among the various elements critics have noted are the doppelgänger relation of Quilty to Humbert, chess metaphors, puns on names, the question of the masks of the narrator (the probably unreliable Humbert through the clinical Ray through the mischievous Nabokov), and the supposed immortality of Humbert's love, a love that becomes timeless through a work of art. It has even been argued that

Nabokov's description of Lolita very much resembles his description of a certain species of butterfly in his scientific studies. While *Lolita*'s place in the canon of world literature is still debated, there is little doubt that it may be the finest example of the author's "game-playing" method of artistic creation.

PALE FIRE

With the publication of *Pale Fire*, readers were once again amused, perplexed, or horrified by Nabokov's ironic wit. This experimental novel inspired extremes of praise—such as Mary McCarthy's judgment that "it is one of the great works of art of this century"—and mockery. The novel is presented in the form of a scholarly edition of a poem titled "Pale Fire" by John Shade, with commentary by Charles Kinbote. Both worked at Wordsmith University, where Kinbote seems to have believed that Shade was writing a poem about Kinbote's obsession with Charles Xavier Vseslav, "The Beloved," the king of Zembla who was forced to flee the revolution that replaced him.

Pale Fire can be described as a series of Russian dolls, one enclosed within another. John Shade's poem (as edited by Kinbote) is explained by Kinbote, who intends to give life to the extraordinary personality of Shade. He writes in the foreword, "Without my notes Shade's text simply has no human reality at all," but the reader soon recognizes that Kinbote is a madman who either is or imagines himself to be the displaced king of Zembla, and whatever human reality Shade may have exists only through his colleague's warped interpretation of events. On another level, the reader finds some of Shade's "reality" in the text of his poem and reads much into and between Kinbote's lines as the madman gradually exposes his own madness.

Nabokov never wants his reader to forget, however, that all this invention is entirely of his making. The author intends much more in *Pale Fire* than a mere parody of scholarly editions, scholars, and neo-Romantic poetry. Once more, Nabokov wittily develops his lifelong theme that reality exists only in the eyes of its interpreter.

J. Madison Davis

OTHER MAJOR WORKS

SHORT FICTION: *Vozrashchenie Chorba*, 1930; *Soglyadatay*, 1938 (title novella and short stories); *Nine Stories*, 1947; *Vesna v Fialte i drugie rasskazy*, 1956; *Nabokov's Dozen: A Collection of Thirteen Stories*, 1958; *Nabokov's Quartet*, 1966; *A Russian Beauty, and Other Stories*, 1973; *Tyrants Destroyed, and Other Stories*, 1975; *Details of a Sunset, and Other Stories*, 1976; *The Stories of Vladimir Nabokov*, 1995.

PLAYS: *Dedushka*, pb. 1923; *Smert'*, pb. 1923; *Polius*, pb. 1924; *Tragediya gospodina Morna*, pb. 1924; *Chelovek iz SSSR*, pb. 1927; *Izobretenie Val'sa*, pb. 1938 (*The Waltz Invention*, 1966); *Sobytiye*, pr., pb. 1938.

POETRY: *Stikhi*, 1916; *Dva puti*, 1918; *Gorny put*, 1923; *Grozd'*, 1923; *Stikhotvorenia, 1929-1951*, 1952; *Poems*, 1959; *Poems and Problems*, 1970.

SCREENPLAY: *Lolita*, 1962 (adaptation of his novel).

NONFICTION: *Nikolai Gogol*, 1944; *Conclusive Evidence: A Memoir*, 1951; *Drugie berega*, 1954; *Speak, Memory: An Autobiography Revisited*, 1966 (revision of *Conclusive Evidence* and *Drugie berega*); *Strong Opinions*, 1973; *The Nabokov-Wilson Letters: Correspondence Between Vladimir Nabokov and Edmund Wilson, 1940-1971*, 1979 (Simon Karlinsky, editor); *Lectures on Literature*, 1980; *Lectures on Russian Literature*, 1981; *Lectures on Don Quixote*, 1983; *Vladimir Nabokov: Selected Letters, 1940-1977*, 1989.

TRANSLATIONS: *Anya v strane chudes*, 1923 (of Lewis Carroll's novel *Alice's Adventures in Wonderland*); *Three Russian Poets: Translations of Pushkin, Lermontov, and Tiutchev*, 1944 (with Dmitri Nabokov); *A Hero of Our Time*, 1958 (with Dmitri Nabokov; of Mikhail Lermontov's novel); *The Song of Igor's Campaign*, 1960 (of the twelfth century epic); *Eugene Onegin*, 1964 (of Alexander Pushkin's novel).

BIBLIOGRAPHY

Alexandrov, Vladimir E. *Nabokov's Otherworld*. Princeton, N.J.: Princeton University Press, 1991. Argues that "the central fact of both Nabokov's life and his art was something that could be described as an intuition about a transcendent realm of being." Shows how an awareness of this "otherworld" informs Nabokov's works, focusing on the autobiography *Speak, Memory* and on six of Nabokov's novels. Seeks to correct the widely accepted view of Nabokov as an aloof gamesman preoccupied with verbal artifice for its own sake. Includes notes, a secondary bibliography, and an index.

Bloom, Harold, ed. *Vladimir Nabokov*. New York: Chelsea House, 1987. Collection of essays addresses such topics as Nabokov's handling of time, illusion and reality, and art. Includes an informative editor's introduction, essays on Nabokov's major novels, chronology, and bibliography.

Boyd, Brian. *Vladimir Nabokov: The Russian Years*. Princeton, N.J.: Princeton University Press, 1990.

_____. *Vladimir Nabokov: The American Years*. Princeton, N.J.: Princeton University Press, 1991. Prodigiously researched two-volume biography is based in part on material found in Nabokov's archives, to which Boyd gained unprecedented access. Recounts the events of Nabokov's life and charts his development as a writer. Each volume includes illustrations, extensive notes, and an exceptionally thorough index.

Connolly, Julian W., ed. *The Cambridge Companion to Nabokov*. New York: Cambridge University Press, 2005. Collection of essays offers a good introduction to Nabokov's life and writings. Topics addressed include Nabokov as a storyteller, a Russian writer, a modernist, and a poet; also covered are his transition to writing in English and the reception of *Lolita*.

De la Durantaye, Leland. *Style Is Matter: The Moral Art of Vladimir Nabokov*. Ithaca, N.Y.: Cornell University Press, 2007. Focuses on *Lolita* but also looks at some of Nabokov's other works to discuss the ethics of art in Nabokov's fiction. Asserts that although some readers find Nabokov to be cruel, his works contain a moral message—albeit one that is skillfully hidden.

Field, Andrew. *VN: The Life and Art of Vladimir Nabokov.* New York: Crown, 1986. Critical biography recounts the events of Nabokov's life and places his works within personal and historical context. Includes discussion of *Lolita, Pale Fire, The Gift,* and other works.

Foster, John Burt. *Nabokov's Art of Memory and European Modernism.* Princeton, N.J.: Princeton University Press, 1993. Scholarly work divides discussion of Nabokov's work into three parts: Nabokov's early years in Russia, his period in Europe, and his prolonged period in the United States. Intended for advanced students.

Glynn, Michael. *Vladimir Nabokov: Bergsonian and Russian Formalist Influences in His Novels.* New York: Palgrave Macmillan, 2007. Glynn disagrees with other critics who have called Nabokov a Symbolist writer, arguing that he was an anti-Symbolist who was influenced by the philosopher Henri Bergson and by Russian Formalism. Useful for advanced students of Russian literature and philosophy.

Grayson, Jane, Arnold B. McMillin, and Priscilla Meyer, eds. *Nabokov's World: Reading Nabokov.* New York: Palgrave Macmillan, 2002.

_____. *Nabokov's World: The Shape of Nabokov's World.* New York: Palgrave Macmillan, 2002. Two-volume collection of essays written by an international group of Nabokov scholars provides comprehensive discussion of his work. Presents analyses of individual novels as well as coverage of topics such as intertextuality in Nabokov's works and the literary reception of his writings.

Parker, Stephen Jan. *Understanding Vladimir Nabokov.* Columbia: University of South Carolina Press, 1987. Introductory guide to Nabokov for students and nonacademic readers focuses on individual analyses of five of his Russian novels and four of his American novels. Begins with a chapter on the self-reflexive aspects of Nabokov's narrative technique.

Pifer, Ellen, ed. *Vladimir Nabokov's "Lolita": A Casebook.* New York: Oxford University Press, 2002. An interview with Nabokov and a collection of essays provide a range of approaches to the reading of *Lolita,* including discussions of the novel and the art of persuasion, the Americanization of Humbert Humbert, and *Lolita* and the poetry of advertising.

Wood, Michael. *The Magician's Doubts: Nabokov and the Risks of Fiction.* Princeton, N.J.: Princeton University Press, 1995. Close readings of Nabokov's works show the power and beauty of his language and subtlety of his art. This examination also reveals the ethical and moral foundations of his work, which Nabokov denied existed.

BORIS PASTERNAK

Born: Moscow, Russia; February 10, 1890
Died: Peredelkino, near Moscow, Russia, Soviet Union (now in Russia); May 30, 1960
Also known as: Boris Leonidovich Pasternak

PRINCIPAL LONG FICTION

Doktor Zhivago, 1957 (*Doctor Zhivago*, 1958)

OTHER LITERARY FORMS

Boris Pasternak (PAS-tur-nak) wrote only one novel, *Doctor Zhivago*; this work was the final product of a creative life devoted largely to poetry. Pasternak was initially recognized as a lyric poet who synthesized Symbolist musicality and Futurist colloquialism, but after the 1917 Revolution, as he indicated in his address to the First Congress of the Union of Soviet Writers in 1934, he came to believe that poetry was in fact "pure prose in its pristine intensity." During the Stalinist purges of the 1930's and through World War II, Pasternak took refuge in the long and distinguished Russian tradition of poetic translation, and he produced outstanding versions of many classic Western dramas. Pasternak also wrote epic poems on revolutionary themes; two prose autobiographies, *Okhrannaya gramota* (1931; *Safe Conduct*, 1945) and *Avtobiograficheskiy ocherk* (1958; *I Remember: Sketch for an Autobiography*, 1959); short fiction, of which several sketches are early studies for his novel; and an unfinished play, *Slepaya krasavitsa* (pb. 1969; *The Blind Beauty*, 1969), which he intended as a nineteenth century prologue to *Doctor Zhivago*. By incorporating "The Poems of Yuri Zhivago" into the fabric of the novel *Doctor Zhivago*, Pasternak returned to the lyricism of his youth.

ACHIEVEMENTS

Doctor Zhivago was the first major Russian work not to be first published in the former Soviet Union. By 1959, it had already appeared in twenty-three other languages, but even though Boris Pasternak had been chosen to receive the Nobel Prize in Literature in 1958, Soviet governmental pressure forced him to refuse it. For the brief remainder of his life, as he observed in his pain-filled lyric "The Nobel Prize," he was "caught like a beast at bay" in his homeland, one of the most tragic figures of modern literature.

Literature, particularly poetry, plays in Russian life a role almost inconceivable to Westerners. To Russians, art, politics, and morality have always been inseparable. From their ancient oral folk epics, the *byliny*, to twentieth century verse recitals and the explosion of samizdat (self-published) works, poetry has helped shape the Russians' responses to social and political issues. In the vein of Russia's greatest poets, Alexander Pushkin and Mikhail Lermontov, Pasternak's famous public reading in 1948 intensified both his listen-

Boris Pasternak
(The Nobel Foundation)

ers' love of poetry and their desperate yearning to witness a Russian poet challenging unreasonable governmental oppression. Pasternak's early poetry, somewhat resembling T. S. Eliot's difficult allusive verse, did not achieve wide popularity, but after the government prevented his acceptance of the Nobel Prize, Pasternak's *Stikhotvoreniya i poemy* (1965, 1976; collected poems) sold 170,000 copies in the Soviet Union by 1972.

Pasternak's moral dilemma as a Russian artist in Soviet society should not be underrated. As *Doctor Zhivago* unequivocally demonstrates, Pasternak was incapable of adapting his artistic message to political expediency. At the same time, however, his integrity made him vulnerable to indirect threats not against himself but against his family and, still more grievous, against Olga Ivinskaya, his beloved "Lara."

Olga Ivinskaya recalled that in the late 1950's, "The easiest way of dealing with intellectuals like us was simply to starve us into submission." For Pasternak, starvation meant a deepening isolation from his fellow artists and the audience of his countrymen, the constant fear for his loved ones, and a continuing horror at the unwanted fame abroad that caused much of his torment, and he eventually bowed to pressure. He signed a letter drafted by Ivinskaya renouncing the Nobel Prize on October 31, 1958, asking only that she write "that I was born not in the Soviet Union, but in Russia." As a child of Russia's old intelligentsia, Pasternak lacked the furious stamina born of famine, war, and the camps, that stiffened the dissent of "men with their backs to the wall" like Aleksandr Solzhenitsyn or Vladimir Bukovsky. Pasternak's literary posture, no less intensely moral, sprang from his commitment to "live life to the end," as he wrote in Yuri Zhivago's poem "Hamlet," recited at Pasternak's burial.

BIOGRAPHY

Boris Leonidovich Pasternak's life was shaped by Russia's twentieth century agony. Pasternak's father, the artist Leonid Pasternak, and his mother, the pianist Rosa Kaufman, assured him easy familiarity with the artistry of the West in their warm and affluent home in Moscow, which remained Pasternak's "holy city" throughout his life. With Anna Akhmatova, Osip Mandelstam, Marina Tsvetayeva, Vladimir Mayakovsky, and Sergei Esenin, the constellation of Russian twentieth century poets, Pasternak grew up in the nervous splendor of prerevolutionary Russia. In his father's house, Pasternak, at the age of ten, first met the poet Rainer Maria Rilke, whose work profoundly affected Pasternak's concept of the spiritual value of individual destiny, and his early acquaintance with composer Aleksandr Scriabin reinforced his youthful decision in 1903 to study music.

Russia's discontent under Nicholas II had been smoldering, and it erupted in the "Bloody Sunday" massacre of January, 1905, adding internal strife to the external drain on Russia posed by the Russo-Japanese War. Pasternak's father staunchly supported the liberals, who succeeded in establishing a Russian duma, or legislative assembly, but after a harrowing year of illness, cold, and civil disorder, the family left for Germany, where young Pasternak was constantly exposed to experimental art forms.

A crucial audition with Scriabin in 1909 caused Pasternak to search his soul for a vocation, and he turned first to law and then to philosophy, which he studied at the universities of Moscow and Marburg. The idealistic Symbolism that had dominated Russian poetry at the turn of the century was being superseded by the more concrete school of Acmeism, founded in 1911 by Nikolai Gumilyov, Akhmatova's husband for eight years. Pasternak was then at work on his first collection of poetry, *Bliznets v tuchakh* (1914; a twin in the clouds), influenced heavily by the Futurist Mayakovsky.

The reforms reluctantly granted by the czar in 1905 had proved painfully transitory, and at the outbreak of war with Germany in August, 1914, Russia's badly led and even more poorly equipped army faced the enemy with disquieting unrest. Lame from a boyhood injury, Pasternak was exempted from military service, but he spent the war years in managerial positions for factories in the Ural Mountains, increasingly impressed by Mayakovsky's strident poetic calls to revolution in the name of the laboring masses. Pasternak's second verse collection, *Poverkh barierov* (1917; *Above the Barriers*, 1959), was a product of such revolutionary zeal.

The world forgets that there were two Russian revolutions in 1917, and for Pasternak, the February revolt installing the constitutional government of Prince Aleksandr F. Kerensky ushered in a perfect summer, "a moment that transformed everything and opened up hearts and minds." A hope for renewal swept the broad land of Russia, and in those shining weeks Pasternak wrote *Sestra moia zhizn': Leto 1917 goda* (1922; *My Sister, Life*, 1964; also known as *Sister My Life*), the poetry collection he considered his first, in which he identified the life of the artist with the life of the common man. Tsvetayeva, his sister in poetry, commented that during the summer of 1917, Pasternak was "listening attentively" to the atmosphere of the revolution.

Red revolution soon followed White in the Bolshevik rising of October, 1917. During the ruinous Civil War, Pasternak worked as a librarian in the Soviet Ministry of Education; his parents, increasingly dismayed at the political chaos around them, emigrated to Germany in 1921, where Pasternak joined them the following year, shortly before his first marriage. Through the New Economic Policy (NEP), a brief accommodation with capitalism forced on the Soviet regime by the postrevolutionary economic debacle, Pasternak experimented with impressionistic short fiction prior to 1929, concentrating on the relationship between the artist and his society. By 1931, after Mayakovsky's suicide and after his own separation from his first wife, Pasternak had completed *Safe Conduct*, his autobiographical response to the severe problems of conscience following Joseph Stalin's brutal collectivization of Russia's farmlands and its horrifying aftermath of famine and epidemic. *Safe Conduct*, dedicated to Rilke, records Pasternak's successive renunciations of music, philosophy, and the poetic style of Mayakovsky, whom he had once idolized. Pasternak now chose to strike out in an artistic direction wholly new to him, one that Henry Gifford has described as "the rarest kind of autobiographical writing, which . . . deals with living ideas and the mind's allegiance to them."

The title of Pasternak's volume of poems from that period, *Vtoroye rozhdeniye* (1932; *Second Birth*, 1964), aptly describes the violent inner struggle Pasternak endured through the 1930's, when more than six hundred writers, many of them his friends, perished in Stalin's "gulag archipelago." Early in the decade, Pasternak married again and made two trips to Soviet Georgia, commemorated in his translations of Georgian lyrics published in 1935. Translating verse was in fact to support him and his family—at the cost of his original poetry—for the rest of his life.

Throughout the history of Russian literature, poets have turned to translation to express thoughts impossible to convey to their countrymen more directly. Pasternak succeeded brilliantly, even working with literal translations from languages he did not know. He affixed his own creativity to what he called a "technical vow," a "commitment to immediacy" in which his Russian version transmitted its original in a burst of genuine emotion. Over the years, he translated voices as diverse as those of Lord Byron, John Keats, and Percy Bysshe Shelley, the Ukrainian Taras Shevchenko, the Hungarian Sándor Petofi, the Polish Juliusz Slowacki, the German Heinrich von Kleist, and the transcendent Rilke.

Pasternak's major translations, those that speak most clearly of tragic fate and the possibility of redemption, include the great dramas of William Shakespeare, Johann Wolfgang von Goethe, and Friedrich Schiller. These accompanied the protracted gestation of *Doctor Zhivago*, begun in 1941, when Pasternak achieved a new realization of his Christianity.

In the spring of 1941, Nazi Germany renounced its peace treaty with the Soviet Union and turned to ravage its former ally, grimly forcing Stalin's attention away from the cannibalization of his own people. The German invasion made it necessary for Pasternak to move his family to Chistopol in the Urals, close to the village where Tsvetayeva, destitute, committed suicide that August. By his translation contracts, Pasternak, who remained at Peredelkino, near Moscow, managed to support his family and provide what material and moral comfort he could to his friends. Pasternak's championship of Mandelstam had caused him to fall from official favor in the late 1930's, and when his translation of Shakespeare's *Hamlet, Prince of Denmark* (pr. c. 1600-1601) appeared in 1941, it revealed a personal and political tragedy much like that raging all around him. His translation of Shakespeare's *Romeo and Juliet* (pr. c. 1595-1596), published in 1943, and *Antony and Cleopatra* (pr. c. 1606-1607), published in 1944, were sympathetic renderings of dramas of doomed love that strangely foreshadowed events in Pasternak's own life. His translation in 1945 of Shakespeare's *Othello, the Moor of Venice* (pr. 1604), a parable of betrayal, paralleled the unfavorable reception the official critics gave Pasternak's war poetry volume, *Zemnoy prostor* (1945; *The Vastness of Earth*, 1964).

The figure of Lara, to become the heart of *Doctor Zhivago*, appeared almost casually to Pasternak at the offices of the literary journal *Novy mir* in 1946, the year Soviet authorities undertook a massive campaign, the *zhdanovshchina* (Zhdanov era), against "decadent cosmopolitanism" in art and literature. At a meeting that Pasternak did not attend, claiming illness, Anna Akhmatova and Mikhail Zoshchenko were condemned and expelled from the Writers' Union. After meeting Olga Ivinskaya in October, Pasternak began to see her daily, and the following spring they declared their love.

The joy Pasternak and Ivinskaya shared became paradoxically their worst torment. At first, Pasternak's financial burden was eased somewhat by a contract to translate Goethe's *Faust* (1808, 1833), that archetypal vision of human striving, and after Andrei Zhdanov's death, in 1948, Pasternak received wide popular support for his public poetry readings and his translation of Shakespeare's *Henry IV* (pr. c. 1597-1598), a denunciation of the political principle that "might makes right." In 1949, however, he suffered the first of a long series of heart attacks, and in a government ploy to force Pasternak's recantation of positions unfavorable to the regime, Ivinskaya was arrested, held for more than one year in the Lyubyanka Prison, and sent to a Siberian labor camp because she refused to incriminate him. Appropriately enough at this time of misery, Pasternak was translating Shakespeare's *King Lear* (pr. c. 1605-1606).

Upon the death of Stalin in 1953 and the ensuing general amnesty, Ivinskaya was released, and Pasternak took up residence with her in Moscow. Despite his worsening physical condition, he was supporting both of their families. In 1954, the periodical *Znamia* published ten poems from *Doctor Zhivago*, and Pasternak finished the novel in the fall of 1955. He then started on *I Remember*, which he hoped would be a preface for his collected work.

Pasternak also naïvely expected that *Doctor Zhivago* might appear in *Novy mir*, but after a complicated series of events during which the novel was rejected in the Soviet Union, it appeared in Italian in 1957. Pasternak began to translate again in 1959 after being forced to refuse the Nobel Prize, choosing Schiller's *Maria Stuart* (pr. 1800; *Mary Stuart*, 1801), a woman's tragedy of epic proportion. A combination of cancer, heart disease, and emotional prostration overcame him at last, and he died at Peredelkino on May 30, 1960. Less than three months later, Ivinskaya and her daughter were sentenced to a Siberian labor camp again. Even in the early twenty-first century, on the anniversary of Pasternak's death he is remembered as Hedrick Smith noted in *The Russians* (1976): "Scores of Muscovites . . . quietly . . . [lay] their unpretentious bouquets on his white tombstone . . . all the more meaningful an occasion because it [has] been forgotten by the state and remembered by private individuals."

ANALYSIS: DOCTOR ZHIVAGO

Boris Pasternak worked on *Doctor Zhivago* between 1938 and 1956, when the savage circumstances within the Soviet Union permitted, but the evidence of his short fiction indicates that all of his creative life went into *Doctor Zhivago*. Incidents, characterizations, and the style of his other stories strongly resemble elements of the novel, and Ivinskaya saw in Zhenia Luvers "the Lara of the future," a sensitive portrayal of the sad lot of women, one of Pasternak's recurring themes. Nadezhda Mandelstam, the wife of Osip Mandelstam, observed that Pasternak could not proceed with the novel until the war provided "a momentarily restored sense of community" impossible during the purges of the 1930's. Pasternak's fruitless defense of Osip Mandelstam, who died in a transit camp en route to the mines of Kalyma, may also have strengthened his resolve to produce a chronicle of Russia's intelligentsia, the "children of Russia's terrible years," as they are called in *Doctor Zhivago*. It became nothing less than his sacred duty.

By 1950, when he had survived physical and emotional blows that were only the beginning of his anguish, Pasternak observed to one of his many correspondents that "love of people and gratitude to the past for its brilliance . . . a concern for repaying it with the same kind of beauty and warmth" were for him "spiritual values . . . at the foundation of taste." He gladly accepted the heavy price for his artistic and humanistic convictions: "If there is suffering anywhere, why should not my art suffer and myself with it? I am speaking of the most artistic in the artist . . . of the sacrifice without which art becomes unnecessary."

Beyond the practical sacrifices of Pasternak's own restricted life, for which political compromise might have meant considerable but soulless comfort, and even beyond the emotional sacrifice of watching friends endure hardships he could not share, Pasternak, in creating *Doctor Zhivago*, had to be reborn into a new form of artistic expression entirely new to him and to Russian literature. The technical innovations of *Doctor Zhivago*, often ignored or misunderstood, are Pasternak's chief means of voicing his major themes, art as sacrifice and its resulting spiritual redemption. In his shift from the lyric to the epic mode, in his departure from the form of the great Russian nineteenth century novels, and in his impressionistic use of symbolic coincidence, Pasternak implemented an effective new medium of fictional expression.

POINT OF VIEW

For *Doctor Zhivago*, Pasternak deliberately abandoned the first-person narrative he had used in his earlier prose sketches for the less subjective third person, a vital transposition of emphasis by which he could develop the character of Yuri Zhivago in important directions hinted at in his laconic description of the hero, which appeared prefatory to the ten poems published in *Znamia:* "a physician, a thinking man in search [of truth], with a creative and artistic bent." Pasternak's main character, his evocation of the cultured Russian intellectual at the mercy of historical forces beyond human control, is first a physician, his title significantly used by Pasternak in the novel's name to emphasize the duty as healer and teacher that Zhivago fulfills through his personal sacrifice. "Zhivago" itself derives from the Russian verb "to live," lending irony to the opening scene of the novel, the funeral of Zhivago's mother: "'Who's being buried?'—'Zhivago' [the living one]." The name also has a wealth of religious connotations stemming from the risen Christ's question in the Orthodox Easter liturgy, "Why seek you the living [*zhivago*] among the dead?" In his search for truth, the thinking man Yuri Zhivago at first naïvely embraces revolution as the natural result of the czarist repression of the people, only gradually realizing that enforced collectivization under the Soviets means the spiritual slavery of the very souls it falsely purported to free. The truth at which Yuri Zhivago at last arrives, after his long journey through the revolutions of 1905 and 1917, the savagery of World War I and the Civil War, and the struggle for survival that faced his people during the 1920's, is the old truth of humanity's youth—that an individual can be fulfilled only by free choice in pursuing his own creativity, his own love, unhampered by political or social stricture. By viewing Zhivago through many different eyes in the major section of the novel, Pasternak can reflect with stunning accuracy the myriad beams and shadows cast by the flickering light that is a human soul.

STRUCTURE

At first glance, *Doctor Zhivago* appears to resemble the traditional Russian novel, spread over near-boundless time and space and probing uncannily into the recesses of human suffering. Its structure, however, is not panoramic but multigeneric, presenting the life of Yuri Zhivago in three discrete treatments like the movements of a great literary sonata: the discursive past, a personalized and omniscient narrative incorporating many motifs throughout the first fifteen chapters of the book, spanning the years from 1905 to 1929, and dominated by the great duet between the masculine theme of Zhivago and its feminine counterpart of Lara; the brief melodic and retrospective epilogue, chapter 16, hymning Zhivago's blessing on the future of his "holy city" and the world, his song of "the freedom of the soul" embodied in his illegitimate daughter Tania; and "The Poems of Yuri Zhivago," a lyric cycle of love and redemption in an eternal now gained by heroic self-sacrifice joined to the divine sacrifice of Christ. The musical metaphor for the novel is suggested by Pasternak's lifelong love of Frédéric Chopin, not only for his monumental music, in which Pasternak said Chopin "regarded his own life as a means of apprehending every life in the world," but also for Chopin's "wider significance," as seen in the *Études*, which teach "a theory of childhood," "an introduction to death," and "history, the *structure* [Pasternak's italics] of the universe and whatever is more remote and general than playing the piano." Pasternak especially acclaimed Chopin's ability to "utter his new statement in the old language, without examining whether it was old or new."

The gains Pasternak realized by this tripartite structure are more felt in *Doctor Zhivago* than understood, in part because of the spirit of shared suffering that Virginia Woolf claimed in "The Russian Point of View" to produce the "sense of brotherhood" that permeates all Russian literature. In *Doctor Zhivago*, however, Pasternak advanced materially beyond the nineteenth century, employing a strange and lovely novelistic structure to merge past and present and future into a timeless moment of sacrifice and renewal.

Pasternak willingly gave *Doctor Zhivago* priority over the poetry to which he had devoted so many years. Ivinskaya records his assertion, "All my life I have wanted to write prose . . . writing poetry is easier!" Pasternak's reliance in the novel on coincidence, often criticized as violating the bounds of literary verisimilitude, is an impressionistic poetic technique, assembling apparently contradictory elements into a system of symbolism so intricate that each human name, each smallest detail of nature, possesses an amazingly complex signification unfortunately closed to most English-speaking readers. The enigmatic Evgraf, for example, Zhivago's mysterious half brother, appears at crucial episodes in the novel's first section to save Yuri first from physical disaster and at last from spiritual sterility. Evgraf's name is taken from the Greek words for "well written"; he is a youth with slanted Kirghiz eyes and a Siberian reindeer garment, a shamanistic figure who may represent Zhivago's "twin in the clouds," his heaven-sent poetic creativity, not the least of whose talents enabled Zhivago to survive in spirit through his writing.

Balancing the supernatural role of Evgraf is the contrapuntal role of Lara, who has been described as "the most poeticized woman in Russian literature." Lara, brutalized in her adolescence by the pragmatic survival specialist Komarovsky, surely represents Russia at least in part, demeaned by materialism under the Romanov czars, forced into shamelessness by the revolutionaries, eventually perishing no one knows where in the Far North, yet through everything a genuinely human figure inspiring such a love in Zhivago that he can create the writings that "confirm and encourage" the feeling of "tenderness and peace" that sustains Zhivago's old friends as they read the novel's epilogue.

Lara's husband, Pasha Antipov, clearly represents the spirit of revolution, a slum boy who idealizes Marxism and becomes the killer Strelnikov, a Red commander who typifies all that is dangerously nonhuman in the new regime: "'He needs a heart in addition to his principles,' said Yuri later, 'if he is to do good.'" In one of the climactic coincidences of the novel, Zhivago "the living one" and Strelnikov "the shooter" pass a night at Varykino talking of the Lara they both love. In the morning, Zhivago finds Strelnikov's body in the snow, a suicide, with frozen drops of blood recalling the rowanberries that symbolize Lara, a folk image from ancient tradition: "I shall see you, my perfect beauty, my rowan princess, drop of my very blood." In the final symbolic meeting of Zhivago and Antipov/ Strelnikov, Evgraf conducts Yuri, ill and aging, to write and die in the Moscow room where Antipov began his life with Lara, as Zhivago, outside, glimpsed through a glass darkly the candle of love that he was never to forget.

FINAL MOVEMENT

Pasternak employed "the simple everyday words of sturdy unceremonious talk" that Lara praised in her lament over Yuri's body throughout the twenty-five poems that form the last chapter of his novel, recognizing with his mighty predecessor Lermontov that "there are words whose sense is obscure or trivial—yet one cannot listen to them without a tremor." This last movement of the sonata-novel that is *Doctor Zhivago* is a cycle praising the eternal rhythms of nature so closely bound to the Russian soul and echoing the religious cycle of the Savior's death and Resurrection presented in the liturgical year. Beginning with "Hamlet," which Pasternak's friend Aleksandr Gladkov recalled hearing him recite in an epiphany impossible to repeat, the poetic cycle opens, like the church year, with the agony of a Gethsemane: "For the present, release me from the cast," the poet begs. Through the Passion of Holy Week, over "Bad Roads in Spring" and after "Summer in Town," the poet bids farewell in "August" to "the image of the world through words made manifest/ And to creativity, and to working wonders" as Russia settles into a "Winter Night." "It snowed and snowed, the whole world over," and only "a candle burned," a small flame of hope that eventually blossoms for the poet into the "Star of the Nativity," "gazing on the Maid," for Pasternak, like Zhivago, believed that all conceptions were immaculate. The poems close upon another Holy Week, the "Evil Days" of a return to the "holy city" on Palm Sunday, in which the "dark forces of the Temple/ Gave Him up to be judged by the offscourings," and upon the vision of Mary Magdalene, perhaps modeled on Ivinskaya (in whose presence Pasternak rewrote many of these poems, originally composed in 1946), who learns "to embrace/ The squared beam of the cross." The last of Yuri Zhivago's poems, "Garden of Gethsemane," returns the cycle to its opening, with the agony of abandonment and betrayal that culminates in the vision of the third day, when

Even as rafts float down a river,
So shall the centuries drift, trailing like a caravan,
Coming for judgment, out of the dark, to me.

Although Pasternak insisted that *Doctor Zhivago* "must not be judged along theological lines," and his prime intention was always to depict the fate of the Russian intelligentsia in the first decades of the twentieth century, the mythic dimension of *Doctor Zhivago* exemplifies the endurance that the religious historian Mircea Eliade argued is humanity's only support through "the catastrophes and horrors of history." These cannot be tolerated, in Eliade's view, if they are at worst only the result of the liberties taken by a minority "on the stage of universal history," precisely the stage on which Pasternak played his vital role.

In reacting against the liberties imposed by the Communist minority on the helpless Russian people by writing *Doctor Zhivago*, Pasternak exercised what the Trappist monk and poet Thomas Merton called "the problematical quality" of his Christianity, "that it is reduced to the barest and most elementary essentials: intense awareness of all cosmic and human reality as 'life in Christ,' and the consequent plunge into love as the only dynamic and creative force which really honors this 'Life' by creating itself anew in Life's—Christ's—image." In the glorious healing lesson of *Doctor Zhivago*, that modern man's renewal lies in identification of his sufferings with those of his Savior, undistracted by selfish materialistic desire, the poet of *Doctor Zhivago* thus is "the living one" against whom godless history cannot prevail. In this remarkable novel, as Pasternak said of all art, "The man is silent, and the image speaks."

Mitzi M. Brunsdale

OTHER MAJOR WORKS

SHORT FICTION: "Pisma iz Tuly," 1922 ("Letters from Tula," 1945); "Detstvo Liuvers," 1923 ("The Childhood of Luvers," 1945); *Rasskazy*, 1925; *Sochineniya*, 1961 (*Collected Short Prose*, 1977).

PLAY: *Slepaya krasavitsa*, pb. 1969 (*The Blind Beauty*, 1969).

POETRY: *Bliznets v tuchakh*, 1914; *Poverkh barierov*, 1917 (*Above the Barriers*, 1959); *Sestra moia zhizn': Leto 1917 goda*, 1922 (*My Sister, Life*, 1964; also known as *Sister My Life*); *Temy i variatsii*, 1923 (*Themes and Variations*, 1964); *Vysokaya bolezn'*, 1924 (*High Malady*, 1958); *Carousel: Verse for Children*, 1925; *Devyatsot pyaty' god*, 1926 (*The Year 1905*, 1989); *Lyutenant Shmidt*, 1927 (*Lieutenant Schmidt*, 1992); *Spektorsky*, 1931; *Vtoroye rozhdeniye*, 1932 (*Second Birth*, 1964); *Na rannikh poezdakh*, 1943 (*On Early Trains*, 1964); *Zemnoy prostor*, 1945 (*The Vastness of Earth*, 1964); *Kogda razgulyayetsa*, 1959 (*When the Skies Clear*, 1964); *Poems*, 1959; *The Poetry of Boris Pasternak, 1917-1959*, 1959; *Poems, 1955-1959*, 1960; *In the Interlude: Poems, 1945-1960*, 1962; *Fifty Poems*, 1963; *The Poems of Doctor Zhivago*, 1965; *Stikhotvoreniya i poemy*, 1965, 1976; *The Poetry of Boris Pasternak*, 1969; *Selected Poems*, 1983.

NONFICTION: *Pis'ma k gruzinskim*, n.d. (*Letters to Georgian Friends by Boris Pasternak*, 1968); *Okhrannaya gramota*, 1931 (autobiography; *Safe Conduct*, 1945, in *The Collected Prose Works*); *Avtobiograficheskiy ocherk*, 1958 (*I Remember: Sketch for an Autobiography*, 1959); *An Essay in Autobiography*, 1959; *Essays*, 1976; *The Correspondence of Boris Pasternak and Olga Freidenberg, 1910-1954*, 1981; *Pasternak on Art and Creativity*, 1985.

TRANSLATIONS: *Hamlet*, 1941 (of William Shakespeare's play); *Romeo i Juliet*, 1943 (of Shakespeare's play); *Antony i Cleopatra*, 1944 (of Shakespeare's play); *Othello*, 1945 (of Shakespeare's play); *King Lear*, 1949 (of Shakespeare's play); *Faust*, 1953 (of Johann Wolfgang von Goethe's play); *Maria Stuart*, 1957 (of Friedrich Schiller's play).

MISCELLANEOUS: *The Collected Prose Works*, 1945; *Safe Conduct: An Early Autobiography, and Other Works by Boris Pasternak*, 1958 (also known as *Selected Writings*, 1949); *Sochinenii*, 1961; *Vozdushnye puti: Proza raznykh let*, 1982; *The Voice of Prose*, 1986.

BIBLIOGRAPHY

Barnes, Christopher. *Boris Pasternak: A Literary Biography*. 2 vols. New York: Cambridge University Press, 1989-1998. Comprehensive biography covers the events of Pasternak's life and his literary works. The second volume contains information about the controversy surrounding the publication of *Doctor Zhivago* and Pasternak's receipt of the Nobel Prize in Literature.

Ciepiela, Catherine. *The Same Solitude: Boris Pasternak and Marina Tsvetaeva*. Ithaca, N.Y.: Cornell University Press, 2006. Clearly written, accessible work examines the ten-year love affair between Pasternak and Tsvetaeva, whose relationship was limited primarily to long-distance letters. Reveals the similarities between Pasternak and Tsvetaeva by painting a portrait of their lives and personalities; scrutinizes their poetry and correspondence, much of which is reprinted here. In addition to the correspondence between Pasternak and Tsvetaeva are letters from Rainer Maria Rilke, who completed the couple's literary love triangle.

De Mallac, Guy. *Boris Pasternak: His Life and Art*. Norman: University of Oklahoma Press, 1981. Extensive biography also provides interpretation of the most important features of Pasternak's works. Includes a detailed chronology of Pasternak's life, illustrations, and an exhaustive bibliography.

Erlich, Victor, ed. *Pasternak: A Collection of Critical Essays*. Englewood Cliffs, N.J.: Prentice-Hall, 1978. Skillfully arranged collection of essays covers all important facets of Pasternak's work, with an emphasis on *Doctor Zhivago* and his poetry.

Fleishman, Lazar. *Boris Pasternak: The Poet and His Politics*. Cambridge, Mass.: Harvard University Press, 1990. Comprehensive study focuses on Pasternak's life and works written under the oppressive Soviet political system. Chapters on the *Doctor Zhivago* affair are especially poignant. An important resource for readers who are interested in the nonliterary influences on literary creations.

Gifford, Henry. *Boris Pasternak: A Critical Study.* New York: Cambridge University Press, 1977. Chronicles the stages in Pasternak's life and discusses the works he wrote during those stages in order to establish the author's achievements as a prose writer, poet, and translator. Supplemented by a chronological table and a select bibliography.

Rowland, Mary F., and Paul Rowland. *Pasternak's "Doctor Zhivago."* Carbondale: Southern Illinois University Press, 1967. Fascinating interpretation of *Doctor Zhivago* attempts to clarify the novel's allegorical, symbolic, and religious meanings, including the meanings of virtually all the characters' names.

Rudova, Larissa. *Understanding Boris Pasternak.* Columbia: University of South Carolina Press, 1997. Provides a general introduction to the full range of Pasternak's works. Includes an analysis of *Doctor Zhivago*, but seeks to correct the misconception that this novel was Pasternak's only contribution to world literature.

Sendich, Munir. *Boris Pasternak: A Reference Guide.* New York: Maxwell Macmillan International, 1994. Indispensable reference contains a bibliography of Pasternak editions with more than five hundred entries, a bibliography of criticism with more than one thousand entries, and essays on topics such as Pasternak's poetics, his relations with other artists, and his literary influences.

Weir, Justin. *The Author as Hero: Self and Tradition in Bulgakov, Pasternak, and Nabokov.* Evanston, Ill.: Northwestern University Press, 2002. Analyzes *Doctor Zhivago*, Mikhail Bulgakov's *The Master and Margarita*, and Vladimir Nabokov's *The Gift* to describe how character in these three Russian novels is defined as the act of writing itself.

ALEXANDER PUSHKIN

Born: Moscow, Russia; June 6, 1799
Died: St. Petersburg, Russia; February 10, 1837
Also known as: Alexander Sergeyevich Pushkin

PRINCIPAL LONG FICTION

Evgeny Onegin, 1825-1832, 1833 (*Eugene Onegin*, 1881)
Arap Petra velikogo, 1828-1841 (*Peter the Great's Negro*, 1896)
Kirdzhali, 1834 (English translation, 1896)
Kapitanskaya dochka, 1836 (*The Captain's Daughter*, 1846)
Dubrovsky, 1841 (English translation, 1892)
Yegipetskiye nochi, 1841 (*Egyptian Nights*, 1896)
Istoriya sela Goryukhina, 1857 (*History of the Village of Goryukhino*, 1966)

OTHER LITERARY FORMS

Although Alexander Pushkin (POOSH-kuhn) wrote in almost every genre a nineteenth century author could attempt, he was primarily a poet. In a literary career spanning twenty-four years, he published a rich and varied collection of verse. He wrote two important historical poems, three major comic poems, a half dozen verse narratives, four *skazki* (fairy tales in verse), and numerous lyric poems.

Pushkin's canon contains several dramatic works: *Boris Godunov* (pb. 1831; English translation, 1918) is a long play, written in the manner of William Shakespeare's historical plays, about a crucial period in Russian civilization, the "Time of Troubles." Four short plays make up Pushkin's "Little Tragedies": *Pir vo vryemya chumy* (pb. 1833; *The Feast in Time of the Plague*, 1925), *Motsart i Salyeri* (pr., pb. 1832; *Mozart and Salieri*, 1920), *Skupoy rytsar* (pr., pb. 1852; *The Covetous Knight*, 1925), and *Kamyenny gost* (pb. 1839; *The Stone Guest*, 1936); each of these plays concentrates on a crucial moment in an individual's life. Though cast as drama, all five works are more lyric than theatrical; they are more intent on presenting character than on keeping the stage busy.

In addition to his long fiction, Pushkin wrote several short stories. The most famous and skillful of these works is *Pikovaya dama* (1834; *The Queen of Spades*, 1858), a story of greed, murder, and revenge set among the gaming tables of the aristocracy. Nearly as good are five stories collected as *Povesti Belkina* (1831; *Russian Romance*, 1875; better known as *The Tales of Belkin*, 1947): They depict, both comically and seriously, the life of the rural gentry and townspeople. Pushkin's research for his novel *The Captain's Daughter* provided him with materials for the nonfictional work *Istoriya Pugacheva* (1834; *The Pugachev Rebellion*, 1966). Pushkin wrote hundreds of letters to personal friends and fellow officials. The almost seven hundred surviving letters vividly chronicle both Pushkin's personal life and his literary development.

Alexander Pushkin
(Library of Congress)

No complete, uniform, and authoritative English translation of Pushkin's work exists. Several volumes offer a selection of his verse, though translators agree that rendering Pushkin's lyricism is well nigh impossible. Translations that capture somewhat more of the original are readily available for Pushkin's plays and stories. *Alexander Pushkin: Complete Prose Fiction* (1983), translated and annotated by Paul Debreczeny, is a valuable edition for English-speaking readers. Pushkin's letters have been collected into a well-annotated edition by J. Thomas Shaw: *The Letters of Alexander Pushkin* (1963). The handiest compendium of Pushkin in all of his genres is still the Modern Library volume *The Poems, Prose, and Plays of Pushkin*, edited by Avram Yarmolinsky and first published in 1936.

ACHIEVEMENTS

Alexander Pushkin is Russia's poet as Homer is Greece's, Dante is Italy's, and John Milton is England's. The nation mourned when he died, and Nikolai Gogol, a writer of the next generation, called him a unique manifestation of the Russian spirit. Four decades later, Fyodor Dostoevski proclaimed Pushkin a prophetic phenomenon whose characters embodied the people Russians would become in the late 1800's. After the 1917 Revolution, Soviet scholars produced an extraordinary amount of research and criticism on Pushkin. Modern Russian readers still turn to Pushkin's poetry for a distillation of their hopes and fears and for its lyricism. Virtually every one of Pushkin's works is regarded as a classic by his admirers, and, for once, the idolaters are mostly correct.

Unlike Russian writers of the previous century who imitated Western classicism and produced mostly pale reflections, Pushkin used European literary models to discover—or even to create—a literary Russia. When he began to write in the first decade of the nineteenth century, Russian literature was at a turning point. For the previous sixty years, it had imitated the forms and themes of French classicism and English sentimentalism. A new sensibility was then sweeping Europe, the Romanticism of Johann Wolfgang von Goethe, Lord Byron, André-Marie Chénier, and Sir Walter Scott. Pushkin responded with amazing alacrity. Reading Pushkin's letters, one is struck by how aware he was of not only the literary currents of his own country but also those of the Continent.

Still, Pushkin brought into his country's literature places, characters, and themes unmistakably Russian. His reading of Byron inspired him to works as diverse as *Kavkazskiy plennik* (1822; *The Prisoner of the Caucasus*, 1895), which discovered primitive southern Russia as a backdrop, and *Eugene Onegin*, which delineated the upper-class soul in its sicknesses. His reading of Shakespeare and Scott led him to the presentation of Russian historical themes on a small scale of ordinary lives as well as on a grand scale of royal lives.

Pushkin's lyric verse, begun under the tutelage of Byron and Chénier, gradually grew freer as he experimented with the rhythms and rhymes of the Russian language as a tool for the recording of what it was like to live, love, and suffer as one who came of age in the 1820's. He gave folktales, proverbs, and native speech shelf space in literature's emporium. Whatever the genre or theme of the work, Pushkin's crowning achievement was his style. Though a contemporary of the great European Romantics, Pushkin owed more to their lean classical style than to their richness. His thoughts were always compressed, the scene or emotion always sketched with a few quick, apt words, the story told with pointed economy. The non-Russian reader, unfortunately, misses what the average Russian reader loves him for most: the interplay of sensuous sound and simple sense.

One of Pushkin's classical features is his authorial objectivity. Unlike other Romantics, whose works are often autobiographical, Pushkin was not a confessional writer. Neither was he the distanced, detached, and "official" observer that the neoclassical poet was. His works are, more specifically, objective renderings—parables almost—of the emotional, psychological, and social life of the sensitive and intelligent contemporary Russian.

In this regard, Pushkin's long narratives (one work in verse and two in prose) may be most valuable to the non-Russian reader. *Eugene Onegin, Dubrovsky,* and *The Captain's*

Daughter form a useful introduction to the second half of Pushkin's life and career. They record in straightforward narratives the writer's hopes and fears for his society, both about the personal integrity of individuals and about society's path toward freedom and justice. In Pushkin's Russia, the burning question for individuals was the priorities of virtue (did individual love and honor outweigh obedience and social conformity?) and the burning question for the body politic was social progress (could it be achieved on the back of serfdom and autocracy?). Pushkin felt as if the answers were sometimes yes, sometimes no. In the latter moments, he seemed unsure whether to react to that realization with tears, laughter, or anger.

BIOGRAPHY

Alexander Sergeyevich Pushkin was born into a Moscow family that boasted a six-hundred-year lineage of nobility. Each parent contributed something to his makeup. From his mother, descended from an Abyssinian princeling who had served Peter the Great, Pushkin received his fierce, dark looks and a passionate nature. From his well-educated father, who wrote poetry, Pushkin inherited a love of literature and gained early access to a family library well stocked with European classics.

In 1811, Pushkin was one of thirty boys chosen for the first class of the *lycée* at Tsarskoe Selo, a new school designed to train administrators for Czar Alexander's government. Flourishing in a liberal arts curriculum, Pushkin rapidly became the poet among his peers and, by 1814, published his first poem. His work soon became known to established poets and to the literary societies that looked to Europe for literary models to make Russian writing as good as any in the world. Having seen their nation defeat Napoleon I in 1815, young Russians were eager to match France culturally and to improve their country by importing European political ideals that would eliminate what liberal-thinking Russians thought were the twin cancers of their society: serfdom and autocracy.

Appointed to undemanding work in the Ministry of Foreign Affairs after graduation in 1817, Pushkin combined his literary and political fervors by writing poems like the ode "Vol'most': Oda" ("Ode to Freedom") with revolutionary themes. For three years, he pursued liberal ideals—and actresses of liberal virtue—until his poems attracted the attention of St. Petersburg's military governor, who decided that the young firebrand needed the cooling discipline of service in remoter regions.

In 1820, Pushkin was officially transferred and unofficially exiled to southern Russia and spent time in the Crimea and the Caucasus before settling in Kishinev. Here Pushkin met young army officers who dreamed of political change and primitive tribesmen who lived fiercely and independently. These experiences, combined with his reading of the English Romantic poet Byron, helped Pushkin create several Romantic verse narratives about men who lived on the frontier of civilization and lived passionately according to their own wills. Pushkin would repeat throughout his career the pattern established here: Forced by circumstances into isolation, he would combine his own passionate apprehension of European literary fashions with distinctive Russian settings, characters, and themes.

In 1823, Pushkin secured a transfer to the Black Sea port of Odessa, but his reluctance to perform official duties and a letter expressing his atheist sentiments again earned for him official disapproval. He was dismissed from the service and sent to the family estate at Mikhailovskoe (three hundred safe miles from the capital), where his father, a local abbot, and the secret police could keep his political and religious views under surveillance. Once again cut off from society, Pushkin turned to literature, writing more verse and composing a play, *Boris Godunov*, modeled on Shakespeare's histories.

The exile at Mikhailovskoe kept Pushkin safe while a group of army officers—a few of them his friends, most of them readers of his revolutionary verse—led the unsuccessful Decembrist Revolt to block the accession of Nicholas I, presumed unsympathetic to Western reforms. At liberty, Pushkin's temperament might have led him to join the coup and thus to share the officers' fate of death or Siberian exile. By May of 1826, Pushkin, eager to leave exile and hoping that Nicholas might prove progressive, petitioned for and received pardon. There was only one stipulation: Nicholas himself would censor Pushkin's writing.

For four years, Pushkin lived and worked in St. Petersburg but accomplished little, writing only one poem and continuing *Eugene Onegin*, his magnum opus begun in 1823. In 1830, he determined to wed and successfully wooed the beautiful and younger Natalia Goncharov. The marriage seemed to settle Pushkin's adherence to Nicholas's regime: His wife's beauty made the couple in demand at palace balls; Pushkin reentered government service as a historiographer. Later, Nicholas appointed Pushkin to a court post, but the poet's fiercely independent and proud spirit did not allow easy mingling with aristocrats whose main political virtue was subservience.

In 1830, Pushkin began a period of intense creativity. Isolated for three autumn months at Boldino (far from Moscow and St. Petersburg), Pushkin completed *Eugene Onegin*, wrote several short stories and plays, and composed verse. Returning to St. Petersburg, he used the position of historiographer to research the peasant rebellion led by Yemelyan Pugachov in the 1770's, an uprising so destructive and traumatic that it halted the enlightened ideals of Catherine the Great and convinced subsequent czars that only ironfisted rule prevented revolution from below. Another retreat to Boldino in the autumn of 1833 produced several works, including a history of the rebellion and the great poem *Medniy vsadnik* (1837; *The Bronze Horseman*, 1899). In 1836, Pushkin concluded six years of concentrated writing with a novel and a literary journal.

His uneasy relationship with Nicholas's court reached a critical point in late 1836 when an anonymous wit awarded Pushkin a diploma as a member in good standing of "The Order of Cuckolds," a reference to the flirtatious attentions by the young French officer Georges d'Anthès to Natalia. After two months of anger and hesitation, Pushkin issued the inevitable challenge to a duel that took place on January 29, 1837. Pushkin was shot first, was critically wounded, and died a week later.

ANALYSIS

Alexander Pushkin's three major works, *Eugene Onegin, Dubrovsky,* and *The Captain's Daughter,* reflect many dimensions of his literary achievement. They show his ability to adapt Western genres to a Russian context; they demonstrate his stylistic mastery that is simultaneously economical and rich. Finally, in their emotional variety, they chart Pushkin's attempts to reconcile himself to czarist society and politics.

Each of these three works owes a literary debt. *Eugene Onegin,* a novel in verse, takes its inspiration from Byron's *Childe Harold's Pilgrimage* (1812-1818) and *Don Juan* (1819-1824) but tempers their exuberance with characterization and scene setting from the eighteenth century novel of manners. *Dubrovsky* is kin to the robber tales of German Romanticism, which paint a heroic picture of an outlaw who is really more a self-willed outcast in opposition to social tyranny than an ordinary brigand. *The Captain's Daughter* is a historical novel in the manner of Sir Walter Scott, using the life of an ordinary participant to witness and to interpret some crucial national event. Pushkin's debt to foreign models is not surprising, because his letters show that he read practically everything, not only what was being produced in Russian but also what was being written in French, German, and English.

Like the greatest writers, Pushkin is a master of styles rather than a master of style. His long fictions are as varied as his whole corpus with its poems, plays, and folktales. *Eugene Onegin* is a complexly organized poem: There are eight chapters, each composed of at least 40 fourteen-line stanzas (389 stanzas all told), and each stanza follows a rigorous and formal rhyme scheme that disciplines a wealth of characterization, authorial commentary, and social observation into a coherent narrative. *Dubrovsky* is a quick-paced, dark-spirited, third-person narrative built around a stark contrast of justice and tyranny. *The Captain's Daughter* is a more leisured, romantic, first-person story in which youth and honor triumph over various obstacles.

The most interesting thing about Pushkin's three major long fictional works is the thematic course they chart. They all seek to depict life as led by members of the gentry, that social class that lives with one foot in the urban corridors of power and one in the rural paths of peasant-filled estates. No two of these works offer exactly the same perspective. *Eugene Onegin,* almost ten years in the writing during a crucial period of Pushkin's life, is the most complex and ambiguous work. No one emotion sums it up; by turns it is comic, satiric, pathetic, and tragic. *Dubrovsky* is an angry book, ruthless in its depiction of the petty tyrannies that infect the gentry with devastating effects. *The Captain's Daughter* shows murderous rebellion and government blindness but offers some small hope for the individual to steer between these twin disasters. Taking these works in order, the reader can trace Pushkin's diagnosis of the sickness of Russian society and his prescription for its remedy.

EUGENE ONEGIN

Eugene Onegin is a unique work. It is a product of the Romantic imagination that delighted in experimenting with literary conventions; it is a novel in verse, an attempt to mix the lyric insight of poetry with narrative's opportunity for social observation. Most other nineteenth century novels in verse failed, but Pushkin succeeded in writing both a powerful poem and an important work of fiction. To the Russian reader, sensitive to the nuances of tone and the play of imagery, *Eugene Onegin* is primarily a narrative poem. To the non-Russian reader who must rely on translation, *Eugene Onegin* is more accessible as a lyric novel. Once past the first chapter (the least novel-like), in which Pushkin sketches the subtle strains of Negin's soul as molded by society, the reader of the translation begins an intriguing love story. Novel-like, this love story traces the evolution of a romance from a country estate to a city drawing room: It depicts both the private reveries of the lovers and their passionate, hurtful encounters, and evaluates their relationship as they understand it and as it mirrors the society at large.

Eugene Onegin is a fashionable young man of contemporary St. Petersburg. His wealth and social status allow him to play the game he knows best: the seduction of beautiful women amid the endless round of teas, tête-à-têtes, and palace balls. An unbroken string of romantic conquests, however, makes him bored with life in general. At his uncle's death, Eugene inherits a country estate and retires to it. Here, he meets Vladimir Lensky, an eighteen-year-old who has all of Onegin's passionate nature but who has not yet had the chance to indulge it. All of Lensky's attention is directed toward Olga Larin, whom he loves romantically and for whom he writes poems. Through Lensky, Onegin meets Olga's sister Tatyana, an introspective and withdrawn girl who is convinced at first sight that Onegin is her destined lover. After several days of self-inflicted torment, knowing love only through novels, Tatyana writes Onegin a letter proclaiming her devotion. Two days later, he responds by lecturing her about the impossibility of anyone impressing his heart. Tatyana's spirit is crushed, but her love lives on.

Afterward, at Tatyana's name-day party, Onegin flirts outrageously with Olga, who unthinkingly enjoys his attentions. Vladimir does not enjoy them, suspecting his friend of trying to steal Olga's affection. He challenges Onegin to a duel that neither especially wants but that both know society demands when there is a woman in dispute. Onegin kills Vladimir and quickly departs on a foreign tour; Olga remains grief-stricken until another suitor replaces Vladimir; Tatyana haunts the house Onegin recently vacated, searching for a clue to his character, until her mother takes her to Moscow for the winter social season and a prospective husband.

When the story continues two years later, Tatyana is the wife of an army general. Onegin, returning to the social round, meets her and immediately falls in love. Making himself an intimate of the general's circle, Onegin dotes on Tatyana: helping with her cloak, opening doors for her, making constant small talk. Thoroughly infatuated but unsure of her feelings, Onegin writes her several letters professing his love. She grants him an interview at which she confesses that, although she still loves him, she rejects his love because she now has a wife's duty. She did not marry for love; she married the general only because he was the least unattractive of bad choices, but she is determined to remain faithful to her role. The novel ends as the husband enters to reclaim Tatyana from a thunderstruck Onegin.

The story is told through a series of parallels and contrasts. The quick-paced, dissolute, and spiritually enervating life at St. Petersburg contrasts with the tedious, controlled, and unimaginative life of the country. Tatyana's letter to Onegin and his reply (chapters 3 and 4) are ironically reversed in his letters to her and the subsequent interview (chapter 8). Tatyana's notions of sentimental love derive from her reading of eighteenth century novelists in the same degree that Onegin's spiritual lethargy is an imitation of nineteenth century Romantic angst. Lensky and Olga are more fulsome lovers than Tatyana and Onegin, yet their affection dies more quickly. Eugene dispatches the troublesome jealousy of Lensky with as little conscience as he dispatches the jejune affection of Tatyana.

Complicating the story is the presence of an obtrusive narrator. He has known Onegin, in fact, has shared many of his attitudes. Like Onegin, he has missed the possibility for real passion by playing at too many imitations of it. Like Onegin, the narrator has a sharp eye for the absurdities of those people who live the social pattern without sensing its limitations.

Eugene Onegin is the novel's protagonist, but he is not a hero. If anything, he is an early version of the traditional Russian antihero, the "superfluous man." A superfluous man is one who possesses the creature comforts his society can offer but who does not have any reason to possess them. The ultimate superfluous man is Ivan Goncharov's Oblomov, who thinks long and hard at trying to discover a reason that would get him up from the couch. Pushkin's Onegin is less extreme, but the times and his temperament have combined to drain him of real sensation and passion. Only when Tatyana is out of reach (is it because she is out of reach?) does Onegin think to discover some motivation for participating actively in life, once again taking charge of his existence and seeking to connect with another human soul. Too often Onegin is content to follow the code of his social class: live as lord of the estate but take more notice of neighbors than of management; maintain honor over a trifle even at the expense of a friend's life; if one's emotions run too high or too seriously, become a poet as an outlet.

Tatyana is better than Onegin: She lives an imaginative life that is at least honest, although she succumbs in the end to the same social code that grips Onegin. Though superstitious about omens that signal a true love, she is at least anxious to know something about Onegin. Though her visits to his unoccupied house originate in simplistic devotion, they do lead to insights about his character. Though she partakes of St. Petersburg's fashionable whirl, she keeps aloof enough to remember her domestic commitment. On the outside, Tatyana is a lovely hoyden while Onegin is a work of fashion's art, but on the inside Tatyana draws two breaths and two heartbeats to every one of Eugene's.

The ending of the novel, in which Tatyana leaves the interview on her husband's arm while Onegin stands perplexed, is not a resolution. Though encouraged by friends to complete the story, Pushkin did not. Perhaps the tale ends appropriately as it stands, with the major characters etched in postures that represent their moral choices. Tatyana chooses sacrifice over happiness, and Eugene is doomed to pursue the unpursuable woman. The dramatic ending offers readers none of the traditional comforts by which characters are parceled out some share of contentment.

DUBROVSKY

Dubrovsky is, like *Eugene Onegin*, an unfinished work. Unlike *Eugene Onegin*, it depicts oppression, violence, and death with only a few mitigating moments in which young love and honorable conduct win a momentary triumph. The story recounts the conversion of a young man, Vladimir Dubrovsky, from landowner to outlaw. Like Onegin, Dubrovsky is a member of the generation born around the end of the nineteenth century, but his family's relative poverty leaves little of the leisure allowed a young gallant of St. Petersburg. The novel's theme is political rather than social: the tyranny of the landowning class.

The elderly Andrey Dubrovsky owns a few serfs and the village of Kistenyovka; he is a mild and appreciative master. The neighboring landowner Kirila Troyekurov owns a much larger estate and is known to tyrannize his serfs. Though Dubrovsky and Troyekurov served together in the army and had become friends, two minor disputes over hunting dogs and hunting rights blossom into a full-scale animosity. Unaccustomed to having his will challenged in anything, Troyekurov plots to take over Dubrovsky's estate by filing a highly technical lawsuit under the guidance of a cunning lawyer. When Troyekurov's claim prevails, Dubrovsky goes mad at this outrage against justice. Invalided at home, Dubrovsky summons his son Vladimir from army service back to the estate. Vladimir sets to work to regain the estate legally, but before he can accomplish it, Troyekurov drives the elder Dubrovsky into a fatal seizure by riding insolently into the courtyard of the mansion he will soon occupy. On the day of the funeral, Troyekurov sends officers to seize control of the estate and the village before young Vladimir can claim his inheritance.

Galled by this triumph of tyranny, young Vladimir Dubrovsky and his peasants lock the officials in the occupied mansion and set the building afire. Disappearing into the forest, Vladimir's band begins to terrorize the neighborhood: robbing travelers, seizing the mail, torching manor houses. The only estate to escape attack belongs, oddly enough, to Kirila Troyekurov.

Meanwhile, Troyekurov has hired a French tutor, Deforges, for his daughter Masha. He decides to have fun with the handsome young foreigner by locking him in a room with a hungry bear. Much to the sadistic landlord's surprise, the tutor pulls a gun from his pocket and shoots the bear. Deforges proves as charming as he does forearmed, and soon Masha is in love with him.

On a festival day, all the neighboring gentry gather for a party at Troyekurov's estate.

One of them arrives late: Anton Pafnutyich, the lawyer who directed the suit against Vladimir and who was recently robbed by him. His story sets the guests to comparing tales about the notorious robber who steals with pomp and grace from only the richest of the local ruling class. Pafnutyich refuses to leave the safety of the estate and stays for the night in Deforges's room, only to discover that the tutor is actually Vladimir in disguise.

His identity now dangerously compromised, Vladimir plans to leave the estate after confessing his love to Masha, revealing his identity, and securing her promise that she will call for him if she ever needs assistance.

The promise seems superfluous until the next summer, when Troyekurov makes plans to marry Masha to his neighbor, Prince Vereysky. Twice Masha's age and driven to ennui and dissipation by unrestricted indulgence, Vereysky is a repugnant suitor in Masha's eyes, but her father insists on the marriage. Masha secures Vladimir's assistance in case she cannot talk her father out of his determination. She even writes a letter to Vereysky frankly avowing her repugnance, but it simply whets both his appetite and her father's to exert their authority. Forced to attend the wedding ceremony, Masha expects any minute to be rescued by Vladimir Dubrovsky, but he fails to appear before the priest pronounces the vows over bride and groom. Not until Vereysky's carriage is homeward bound does Dubrovsky appear; he seizes the Prince and pronounces Masha free, but she insists that like it or not, she is now a wife. Though wounded in the shoulder by a bullet and to the heart by her reply, Dubrovsky withdraws without hurting anyone or stealing a thing. In revenge, the authorities send soldiers to track Dubrovsky down. As they besiege his forest fortress, Dubrovsky escapes into the woods. The robberies and attacks on the local gentry cease, and Dubrovsky is rumored to have gone abroad.

Dubrovsky has all the plot conventions of late eighteenth, early nineteenth century robber fiction. Its hero is young, dashing, handsome, and no ordinary criminal. There is a maiden in distress who is, of course, his beloved. Her distress arises from the tyranny of a cruel parent and a lustful suitor. There is adventure, violence, and death in dark and unexpected places. Characters are little more than cardboard figures, for the emphasis is on a fast moving plot filled with dramatic confrontations of innocence and guile, good and evil.

What is sensational about *Dubrovsky* is its theme. Pushkin creates a rebellious hero who wins the reader's sympathy; Vladimir Dubrovsky is after all, like Robin Hood, on the side of justice and true love. In the Russia of Nicholas I, where even verbal dissent quickly caught official notice, such an ennobling of a man in opposition to the political system was an act of heresy. In painting such a stark contrast between the tyranny of Troyekurov and the nobility of Dubrovsky, however, Pushkin seems to have written the story into a corner from which there is no escape. Commonly regarded as unfinished, *Dubrovsky* may have been abandoned where it stood because the author could think of no satisfactory conclusion. The heroine is cruelly married, the system has asserted an overwhelming power in defense of the local tyrant, and the pillaging by Dubrovsky's band is but an annoying hangnail on the strong fist of autocracy. Dubrovsky himself, as the manuscript ends, is in a hopeless situation. Like Eugene Onegin at the end of his novel, Vladimir Dubrovsky has lost his beloved to an older military man and has no means to extract any satisfying revenge to compensate for that loss. Pushkin wisely took leave of Onegin at that incomprehensible moment that Tatyana walks away with her husband. Similarly, Pushkin seems instinctively to have left Dubrovsky at that point because he has literally no future worth recounting; he is beaten. *Dubrovsky* may not be unfinished as much as it is unfinishable.

THE CAPTAIN'S DAUGHTER

Pushkin's final fictional work, *The Captain's Daughter*, offers thematic resolutions that *Dubrovsky* could not achieve. *The Captain's Daughter* is another tale of a young man of a gentry family who must oppose the system, but the hero of this novel is able to both fight for personal justice and remain (although with difficulty) in harmony with the political and social system. Perhaps by setting his story sixty years in the past, Pushkin was better able to see how an individual could control his own life and yet remain a part of society. The person who maintains his honor may in fact contribute to the betterment of the whole society.

The Captain's Daughter is set in the days of a peasant uprising, the Pugachov rebellion, which broke out in eastern Russia in the mid-1770's and was subdued in a few years after great difficulty by the armies of Catherine the Great. This uprising tempered Catherine's enthusiasm for bringing Western ways and ideas to Russia by showing precisely how fragile was the monarch's grip on the sprawling Russian landscape. Afterward, the Pugachov rebellion symbolized the autocracy's nightmare about the dangers that seethed under the surface of Russian civilization, that demanded constant vigilance; it was perhaps the one thing that made the ruling class reluctant to follow Europe's lead toward parliamentarian and constitutional government. In Nicholas I's Russia, where memories of the Decembrist coup were always fresh, to write about the Pugachov rebellion was practically to write about contemporary politics.

The Captain's Daughter tells how Peter Grinyov enters military service. Instead of sending his son Peter to elegant service with a St. Petersburg battalion, the elder Grinyov, who is a believer in the old-fashioned values of sacrifice and hard work, has Peter assigned to a regiment on the eastern frontier of the empire at Orenburg. In disgust, Peter sets off with his faithful serf Savelyich and meets with two adventures along the way: An army veteran gets him drunk and cheats him at pool; a peasant saves Peter and Savelyich when they become lost in a snowstorm, and Peter repays the man with an expensive coat.

At Orenburg, Peter is assigned to a small outlying fort; he is only one of three regular army officers overseeing a ragtag battalion of local men. The second of the three is Shvabrin, a young dandy who has been exiled from St. Petersburg for dueling. The third is the commandant of the fort, Captain Mironov, a somewhat comic figure who occasionally drills his troops in the distinctly unmilitary garb of nightshirt and nightcap. The only society for the three officers is provided by Mironov's wife, Vasilisa, and his maiden daughter Masha.

Rather quickly, Peter and Shvabrin become rivals for Masha and, in St. Petersburg-like manner, engage in a duel. Peter is seriously wounded, but the injury turns out favorably because his convalescence requires the constant attention of Masha. This intimacy quickly leads the young people to confess their love for each other. Peter writes home for permission to wed Masha but receives a stinging and firm letter of refusal from his father.

As the unhappy lovers ponder their next move, the peasant rebellion led by Yemelyan Pugachov begins, and its main army approaches the mud-and-wood fort. The defenders are quickly overwhelmed. The captain is killed, Shvabrin goes over to the enemy, Masha goes into hiding, and Peter is spared execution because the rebel leader Pugachov is the same peasant to whom Peter generously gave his coat.

Returning to his own fortress at Orenberg, Peter eagerly counsels an attack in order to free Masha, but the commander is reluctant to stir from the city's safety. When Peter learns that Masha has been discovered and given to Shvabrin, he sets out alone to rescue her. Captured by rebel sentries, Peter is brought before Pugachov. Impressed by Peter's bravery and honesty, Pugachov decides to let the young man take Masha away. Escaping from the rebel camp, the lovers meet with a Russian detachment. Peter sends Masha to his family estate while he continues to serve against the rebels.

By the uprising's end, Masha has won the hearts of Peter's parents so that they no longer object to the marriage. Peter, however, is arrested on the charge of having helped the enemy. Unwilling to explain his movements back and forth between enemy camp and duty post in order to protect Masha, Peter risks court trial. Masha travels to Moscow to beg for mercy from the empress herself. Telling her story to a woman she meets in the palace garden, Masha surprisingly discovers the next day that she had unknowingly spoken to Catherine herself. Catherine grants Peter pardon, and the lovers are free to wed.

In the character of Peter, Pushkin draws a composite of the young Russian of gentry class. Like others, Peter has to reconcile the conflicting claims of his European and Slavic heritages. It is not easy, because both heritages are mixtures of good and bad. The European inheritance has taught him to be an individual and to pursue Masha's love as a high good, but Europe is also the source of the dandyism and false honor represented by Shvabrin. The Slavic inheritance brings a high demand for loyalty to family and state, but its class structure hinges on oppression and cruelty. Peter tries to bring together the best of each heritage. He is a loyal subject of the empress, but he is sensitive enough to the humanity of the rebel peasants to wish that reform would do away with those conditions that breed revolution.

Pushkin makes in political terms a daring parallel. Peter and Masha each undertake a solitary journey to save the other: Peter goes to Pugachov and Masha goes to Catherine. The monarchs behave remarkably alike: They detect the honesty and honor within the petitioner, which justifies granting mercy to an apparent enemy. For Pushkin to suggest that Pugachov was anything less than a madman or a devil's henchman or the epitome of betrayal was political heresy. While Peter never condones Pugachov's taking up arms, he is impressed by the leader's sincerity and—amid the expected horrors of the war—comparative humaneness.

Masha herself emerges an emblem of Russia. Like her country in the eighteenth century, poised between a Slavic past and a European future, the maidenly Masha is about to determine her future. Wisely, she rejects the superficial Western ways of Shvabrin in favor of the cultured but natural impulses of Peter. Endangered by rebellion, Masha's future hangs in the balance until she is rescued by the bravery, even foolhardiness, of one who loves her. In turn, she repays love with love, risking public embarrassment to support the proposition that a man can talk to his country's enemy, even cooperate with him, and still be a patriot.

Peter's fate offers, then, a hope for autocratic, unchanging Russia. Horrified by the rapine and destruction, Peter is convinced that rebellion is no cure for what ails his country. He is living proof, however, that ideals and manners can change for the better. Peter is less class-conscious than his father; he rejects the cronyism and immoral ways of the aristocratic soldier; he learns to see the humanity of the peasant beneath the rough exterior. Peter escapes the consequences of his new attitudes only because of Catherine's intervention. Still she does intervene, and she sees what a progressive monarch ought to see: Firm rule is not incompatible with individual integrity and public morality.

Set in the reign of one ironfisted monarch, *The Captain's Daughter* speaks to another. It seeks to reassure Nicholas I that certain Western ideals (of love and personal honor) are not incompatible with traditional Russian virtues of obedience and loyalty. It suggests that a ruler can hasten national improvement by recognizing and cooperating with the heartfelt desire of others to improve the country. It reminds the monarch that statecraft is more than minding the jail so the prisoners do not escape. *The Captain's Daughter* is Pushkin's most positive fictional work because it suggests that although love will not overcome or solve all, love—personal and social—has a better chance than whatever is in second place to ameliorate the lot of the individual and consequently the nation.

Robert M. Otten

OTHER MAJOR WORKS

SHORT FICTION: *Povesti Belkina*, 1831 (*Russian Romance*, 1875; better known as *The Tales of Belkin*, 1947); *Pikovaya dama*, 1834 (*The Queen of Spades*, 1858).

PLAYS: *Boris Godunov*, pb. 1831 (wr. 1824-1825; English translation, 1918); *Motsart i Salyeri*, pr., pb. 1832 (*Mozart and Salieri*, 1920); *Pir vo vryemya chumy*, pb. 1833 (*The Feast in Time of the Plague*, 1925); *Rusalka*, pb. 1837 (*The Water Nymph*, 1924); *Kamyenny gost*, pb. 1839 (wr. 1830; *The Stone Guest*, 1936); *Skupoy rytsar*, pr., pb. 1852 (wr. 1830; *The Covetous Knight*, 1925); *Stseny iz rytsarskikh vryemen*, pr., pb. 1937 (wr. 1835); *Little Tragedies*, 1946 (includes *The Covetous Knight*, *The Stone Guest*, *Mozart and Salieri*, and *The Feast in Time of the Plague*).

POETRY: *Ruslan i Lyudmila*, 1820 (*Ruslan and Liudmila*, 1936); *Gavriiliada*, 1822

(*Gabriel: A Poem*, 1926); *Kavkazskiy plennik*, 1822 (*The Prisoner of the Caucasus*, 1895); *Bratya razboyniki*, 1824; *Bakhchisaraiskiy fontan*, 1827 (*The Fountain of Bakhchisarai*, 1849); *Graf Nulin*, 1827 (*Count Nulin*, 1972); *Tsygany*, 1827 (*The Gypsies*, 1957); *Poltava*, 1829 (English translation, 1936); *Domik v Kolomne*, 1833 (*The Little House at Kolomna*, 1977); *Skazka o mertvoy tsarevne*, 1833 (*The Tale of the Dead Princess*, 1924); *Skazka o rybake ir rybke*, 1833 (*The Tale of the Fisherman and the Fish*, 1926); *Skazka o tsare Saltane*, 1833 (*The Tale of Tsar Saltan*, 1950); *Skazka o zolotom petushke*, 1834 (*The Tale of the Golden Cockerel*, 1918); *Medniy vsadnik*, 1837 (*The Bronze Horseman*, 1899); *Collected Narrative and Lyrical Poetry*, 1984; *Epigrams and Satirical Verse*, 1984.

NONFICTION: *Istoriya Pugacheva*, 1834 (*The Pugachev Rebellion*, 1966); *Puteshestviye v Arzrum*, 1836 (*A Journey to Arzrum*, 1974); *Dnevnik, 1833-1835*, 1923; *Pisma*, 1926-1935 (3 volumes); *The Letters of Alexander Pushkin*, 1963 (3 volumes); *Pisma poslednikh let 1834-1837*, 1969.

MISCELLANEOUS: *The Captain's Daughter, and Other Tales*, 1933; *The Poems, Prose, and Plays of Pushkin*, 1936; *The Works of Alexander Pushkin*, 1936; *Polnoye sobraniye sochineniy*, 1937-1959 (17 volumes); *The Complete Prose Tales of Alexander Pushkin*, 1966; *A. S. Pushkin bez tsenzury*, 1972; *Pushkin Threefold*, 1972; *Polnoye sobraniye sochineniy*, 1977-1979 (10 volumes); *Alexander Pushkin: Complete Prose Fiction*, 1983.

BIBLIOGRAPHY

Bethea, David M. *Realizing Metaphors: Alexander Pushkin and the Life of the Poet*. Madison: University of Wisconsin Press, 1998. Describes the relationship between Pushkin's life and his art and discusses why, more than two hundred years after the author's birth, his work remains relevant. Includes illustrations and index.

Binyon, T. J. *Pushkin: A Biography*. New York: Alfred A. Knopf, 2004. Winner of the Samuel Johnson Prize for British nonfiction, this biography chronicles Pushkin's literary success alongside his personal failures. Describes how the writer included small pieces of his life in *Eugene Onegin* and other works.

Debreczeny, Paul. *The Other Pushkin: A Study of Alexander Pushkin's Prose Fiction*. Berkeley: University of California Press, 1983. Encompassing study examines all of Pushkin's prose works, including a lengthy discussion of his short stories, drawing on the extensive scholarship on the subject.

_____. *Social Functions of Literature: Alexander Pushkin and Russian Culture*. Stanford, Calif.: Stanford University Press, 1997. Discussion of Pushkin is divided into three parts: the first is devoted to selected readers' responses to Pushkin, the second explores the extent to which individual aesthetic responses are conditioned by environment, and the third concerns the mythic aura that developed around Pushkin's public persona.

Evdokimova, Svetlana. *Pushkin's Historical Imagination*. New Haven, Conn.: Yale University Press, 1999. Focuses on Pushkin's fictional and nonfictional works on the subject of history, including the novels *The Captain's Daughter* and *Peter the Great's Negro*. Considers Pushkin's ideas on the relationship between chance and necessity, the significance of great individuals, and historical truth.

Feinstein, Elaine. *Pushkin: A Biography.* London: Weidenfeld & Nicolson, 1998. Biography draws on previously undiscovered documents to recount the events of Pushkin's life, describe his paradoxical personality, and provide new information about his death.

Kahn, Andrew, ed. *The Cambridge Companion to Pushkin.* New York: Cambridge University Press, 2006. Collection of essays by Pushkin scholars discusses a wide range of topics, including *Eugene Onegin* and Pushkin's other prose fiction; Pushkin and politics, history, and literary criticism; and Pushkin's position in Soviet and post-Soviet culture.

Lezhnev, Abram. *Pushkin's Prose.* Ann Arbor, Mich.: Ardis, 1974. In one of the rare examples of Russian scholarship translated into English, Lezhnev presents views of a native scholar on Pushkin's prose as seen in the thought and criticism of Pushkin's contemporaries.

Ryfa, Juras T., ed. *Collected Essays in Honor of the Bicentennial of Alexander Pushkin's Birth.* Lewiston, N.Y.: Edwin Mellen Press, 2000. Selection of scholarly essays examines various works by Pushkin and his influence on his literary descendants. Some of the essays discuss *Eugene Onegin* and *The Captain's Daughter* and compare Pushkin to Russian writers Leo Tolstoy and Anton Chekhov.

Terras, Victor. "Pushkin's Prose Fiction in an Historical Context." In *Pushkin Today*, edited by David M. Bethea. Bloomington: Indiana University Press, 1993. Discusses Pushkin's importance in the ascendancy of prose fiction in Russia in the nineteenth century and comments on the basic characteristics of Pushkin's prose style.

Tertz, Abram. *Strolls with Pushkin.* New Haven, Conn.: Yale University Press, 1994. Free-flowing and sometimes irreverent analysis critically contests the major works, artistic habits, and persisting cultural legacy of the prominent Russian poet and novelist.

Vitale, Serena. *Pushkin's Button.* Translated by Ann Goldstein and Jon Rothschild. New York: Farrar, Straus and Giroux, 1999. Presents a cultural history and narrative of the last months of Pushkin's life before his fatal duel. Draws on new research and on information gleaned from secondary literature and the memoirs and letters of Pushkin's contemporaries to bring to life the world of St. Petersburg in the 1830's.

AYN RAND

Born: St. Petersburg, Russia; February 2, 1905
Died: New York, New York; March 6, 1982
Also known as: Alisa (Alice) Zinovievna Rosenbaum

PRINCIPAL LONG FICTION

We the Living, 1936
Anthem, 1938 (revised 1946)
The Fountainhead, 1943
Atlas Shrugged, 1957
The Early Ayn Rand: A Selection from Her Unpublished Fiction, 1984 (Leonard Peikoff, editor)

OTHER LITERARY FORMS

In addition to her three novels and one novelette, Ayn Rand published a play and several philosophical disquisitions. An early critique, *Hollywood: American Movie City,* was published in the Soviet Union in 1926 without Rand's permission.

ACHIEVEMENTS

Ayn Rand won the Volpe Cup at the Venice Film Festival in 1942 for the Italian motion-picture dramatization of *We the Living,* a novel about the failures of the Soviet system. She was awarded an honorary degree, a doctor of humane letters, by Lewis and Clark College in Portland, Oregon, in 1963, but this sole award does not reflect the significance of her influence on America's philosophical and political economic thought.

BIOGRAPHY

Ayn Rand was born Alisa (Alice) Zinovievna Rosenbaum, the eldest of three children, into a Russian Jewish middle-class family in Czarist Russia. When her father's pharmacy was nationalized following the Bolshevik Revolution of 1917, Rand, who had been writing stories since she was nine, found a calling: She turned against collectivism, and she elevated individualism—personal, economic, political, and moral—into a philosophy that eventually attracted a large, occasionally distinguished, following. Early in her career she declared herself to be an atheist.

At the University of Petrograd (now St. Petersburg), Rand studied philosophy, English, and history, graduating with highest honors in history in 1924. By then the works of French writers Victor Hugo and Edmond Rostand, and of Polish writer Henryk Sienkiewicz, had inspired her passion for the heroic and the ideal. Fyodor Dostoevski and Friedrich Nietzsche also left their mark.

Unhappy because the Soviet system was not moving in the direction of her republican

Ayn Rand
(Library of Congress)

ideals and because she had a dead-end job, Rand accepted an invitation from relatives and went to Chicago in 1926. It was while in the United States that she restyled herself Ayn Rand, and within a few months moved to Hollywood, California.

Working as a film extra, a file clerk, and a waiter and doing other odd jobs from 1926 to 1934, Rand perfected her language skills and became a screenwriter at various motion-picture studios. In 1937, she worked as an unpaid typist for Eli Jacques Kahn, a well-known New York architect, in preparation for her first major novel, *The Fountainhead*. Given her early experience in totalitarian Russia, Rand soon became known as the most driven of American anticommunists. She had acquired U.S. citizenship in 1931. In 1947, she appeared as a "friendly witness" before the House Committee on Un-American Activities (HUAC) during the period of the communist witch-hunts—an action she later admitted regretting. Along the way, in 1929, Rand married Charles Francis (Frank) O'Connor, a minor actor and amateur painter. He died in 1979.

After her major literary successes, Rand devoted herself exclusively to philosophizing, writing, and lecturing. She spoke on numerous Ivy League university campuses. She became a regular at the Ford Hall Forum and a columnist for the *Los Angeles Times*. She was coeditor or contributor to several philosophical publications. She was active in the

Nathaniel Branden Institute, created to spread her philosophy of objectivism, until her personal and professional break with Nathaniel and Barbara Branden in 1968. This triangular relationship had played an important part in Rand's life, because the Brandens formed the nucleus of a close group of followers, ironically known as the collective.

Rand, a chain smoker whose loaded cigarette holder had become a symbol of her persona, was diagnosed with lung cancer in her seventies. She died in March, 1982, in the New York City apartment in which she had lived since 1951. Her wake was attended by hundreds of people, including Alan Greenspan, an early Rand devotee and later chair of the Federal Reserve Board Bank. Philosopher Leonard Peikoff, Rand's intellectual and legal heir, also was present.

Rand's publications have sold well over twenty million copies in English and in translation even as literary critics generally dismissed her ideas as reactionary propaganda or pop philosophy. Rand was a paradox. She was a writer of romantic fiction whose ideas were often taken seriously, but she was also a controversial individualist and a contrarian who defied the moral, political, social, and aesthetic norms of her times.

ANALYSIS

In her two major works of fiction, Ayn Rand explicated her philosophy of objectivism in dramatic form. Thus, in *The Fountainhead* and especially in *Atlas Shrugged*, Rand argues that reality exists independent of human thought (objectively), that reason is the only viable method for understanding reality, that individuals should seek personal happiness and exist for their own sake and that of no other, and that individuals should not sacrifice themselves or be sacrificed by others. Furthermore, unrestricted laissez-faire capitalism is the political economic system in which these principles can best flourish. Underlying this essence is the philosophy of unadulterated individualism, personal responsibility, the power of unsullied reason, and the importance of Rand's special kind of morality.

In her long fiction, the philosopher-novelist spells out her concept of the exceptional individual as a heroic being and an "ideal man," with "his" happiness as the highest moral purpose in life, with productive achievement the noblest activity, and reason the only absolute. Rand advocates minimal government intrusion and no initiation of physical force in human interactions. She represents such a system as enshrining the highest degree of morality and justice.

Because Rand also focuses on the denial of self-sacrifice and altruism, a staple of conventional morality and welfarism, she opposes both Christianity and communism. She finds it irrational to place the good of others ahead of one's own rational self-interest. Likewise, she denies mysticism and promotes the Aristotelian view that the world that individuals perceive is reality, and there is no other. Both her major novels can be considered elitist and antidemocratic in that they extol the virtues of a few innovative, far-thinking individuals over the mediocre majority, which is either ignorant and uncaring or, even worse, actively striving to destroy the brilliant individuals of great ability. Besides disparaging mediocrity, Rand also decried the power of connections, conformity with what has been done before, a trend she found far too evident in the American welfare state, and the intellectual bankruptcy she deemed it to have fostered.

Rand considered herself a practitioner of Romanticism, who was concerned with representing individuals "in whom certain human attributes are focused more sharply and consistently than in average human beings." Accordingly, in both these novels the characters of the heroes, sharply drawn, are idealized creations—not depictions of real individuals—who are in control of their own destinies despite major odds.

THE FOUNTAINHEAD

The Fountainhead is the story of Howard Roark, Rand's ideal man, an architect who has a vision of how buildings should really be designed. He is innovative and efficient; he also has a strong aesthetic sense and has integrity—in short, he is a man of principle and artistic individuality. Roark is contrasted with Peter Keating, a former classmate and fellow architect but a "secondhander," constantly replicating conventional styles because he has no originality of his own. He achieves a seeming success by manipulating others. Unlike Roark, whom he envies, Keating does not know who he really is.

Another of Roark's adversaries is Ellsworth Toohey. He writes a column for the *Banner*, arguing that architecture should reflect the art of the people. Gail Wynand is the *Banner*'s owner and newspaper magnate; he appreciates Roark's creativity but buckles under societal pressures, disregards his vision, and thereby engineers his own downfall as a worthy human being. The love interest is embodied in Dominique Francon, the daughter of Guy Francon, the principal owner of the architectural firm that employs Peter Keating. She is a typical Rand heroine, a self-reliant idealist alienated by the shallow conventions of her day in interwar America and convinced that a life of principle is impossible in a world ruled by mediocrity. Her affair with Roark is motivated not by physical or emotional passion but by the recognition that he is a man of great worth. Along the way, in between and sometimes during other affairs, she marries Keating and then Wynand before finally marrying Roark. Dominique seems inconsistent in her ideals, attitudes, and critiques of architectural designs, but the inconsistencies are all part of her effort to spare Roark from ultimate destruction.

Roark, long professionally unsuccessful because he is unwilling to compromise the integrity of his creations, preferring not to work at all or to do menial tasks, eventually overcomes not only financial difficulties but also numerous intrigues by the likes of Keating. For instance, through the mean-spirited Toohey, Roark is assigned to build an interdenominational temple for a patron, Hopton Stoddard, a traditionalist who is abroad at the time. Toohey knows that Stoddard will hate Roark's radically innovative design. Roark makes the building's centerpiece Dominique's nude figure. Toohey incites public condemnation and persuades the patron to sue Roark for breach of contract. Stoddard wins the case, as Roark fails to defend himself in court.

Paradoxically, a friendship develops between Roark and Wynand, attracted to each other for different reasons. Wynand helps Roark in his defense at a second trial, which follows Roark's dynamiting a low-income housing project that Keating had commissioned. The latter had agreed not to alter Roark's design in any way in exchange for Roark's allowing Keating to claim credit for the former's innovative and cost-effective blueprint. When Keating fails to keep his promise and adulterates the design, Roark, with Dominique Francon's assistance, destroys the structure. The trial gives Roark the opportunity to spell out his—that is, Rand's—defense of ethical egoism and opposition to a world perishing from an "orgy of self-sacrifice" and conventional morality. After Roark's exoneration, Wynand commissions him to build the tallest skyscraper in New York City despite Wynand's losing Dominique to Roark.

Ultimately, *The Fountainhead* is a novel of ideas, of heroic characters who are the fountainhead of human progress and of their opposites, who live secondhand, second-rate lives and constantly seek social approval for their beliefs. The philosophy in the novel alternates with the action, and neither can be understood without the other.

ATLAS SHRUGGED

Rand's philosophy extolling the myth of absolute, rugged individualism and its relationship to society is most fully explicated in what proved to be her last work of fiction, several years in the making: the twelve-hundred-page *Atlas Shrugged*. In this novel, Rand tries to answer the question raised by one of her earlier heroes: "What would happen to the world without those who do, think, work, produce?" In this apocalyptic parable, it is John Galt of Twentieth Century Motors, a physicist, engineer, inventor, and philosopher, who is Rand's ideal man and leads the other "men of the mind" on a strike against the exploitation of the genuine creators of wealth by all the leeches and parasites—the nonproducers— whom they had been sustaining.

Rand's philosophy is played out through the stories of the four heroes, the authentic moneymakers. They are the Argentine Francisco d'Anconia, heir to the world's leading copper enterprise; the Scandinavian Ragnar Danneskjold, a onetime philosopher who turns pirate in order to steal wealth back from the looters and return it to the producers of legitimate values; Henry (Hank) Rearden, an American steel magnate and inventor of a metal better than steel; and finally, the other American, John Galt, who, with the others, stops the ideological motor of the world in a strike before rebuilding society. The heroine, rail heir Dagny Taggart, wonders where the individuals of ability have gone.

Confronting them is an array of villains, manipulative appropriators, enemies of individualism and free enterprise, scabs, and moochers profiting from the achievements of the producers and united by their greed for unearned gains. Especially, there is Dr. Robert Stadler, the counterpart of Gail Wynand in *The Fountainhead*. Stadler, once the greatest physicist of his time, fully cognizant of the value of the human mind, fails to stand up for his principles. The progressive decay of James Taggart, Dagny's brother and the titular president of Taggart Transcontinental Railroad, parallels that of the society in which he lives.

In the novel, set some time in the vaguely defined future, the United States is following Europe down the long, hopeless path of socialism, government regulation, and a predatory state into a new Dark Age. The heroes join forces with other intelligent, freedom-loving leaders of commerce, industry, science, and philosophy to reverse the slide. They do this as Atlas may have done had he grown tired of holding the world on his shoulders without reward.

Eventually, the heroes repair to a secret Colorado mountain citadel, where they wait for their time to rebuild the decaying collectivist society whose end their "strike of the mind" against productive work is hastening. Galt, arrested and tortured by the looters but finally freed by the other heroes, delivers a thirty-five-thousand-word oration via a commandeered radio, epitomizing Rand's objectivism and views of the ideal man. Galt's (Rand's) philosophy then becomes that of the new society: "I swear by my life and my love of it that I will never live for the sake of another man, nor ask another man to live for mine." By the end of the novel, socialism has produced a bankrupt world pleading for the return of the men of the mind, who, after a confrontation with the parasites, start to rebuild society. *Atlas Shrugged* is Rand's most thorough exploration of the social ramifications of politics, economics, psychology, metaphysics, epistemology, aesthetics, religion, and ethics.

Peter B. Heller

OTHER MAJOR WORKS

PLAYS: *Night of January 16th*, pr. 1934 (also known as *Woman on Trial* and *Penthouse Legend*); *The Unconquered*, pr. 1940 (adaptation of her novel *We the Living*).

SCREENPLAY: *The Fountainhead*, 1949.

NONFICTION: *For the New Intellectual: The Philosophy of Ayn Rand*, 1961; *The Virtue of Selfishness: A New Concept of Egoism*, 1964; *Capitalism: The Unknown Ideal*, 1966; *Introduction to Objectivist Epistemology*, 1967, second enlarged edition, 1990 (Harry Binswanger and Leonard Peikoff, editors); *The Romantic Manifesto*, 1969; *The New Left: The Anti-Industrial Revolution*, 1971; *Philosophy: Who Needs It?*, 1982; *The Ayn Rand Lexicon: Objectivism from A to Z*, 1984 (Peikoff, editor); *The Voice of Reason: Essays in Objectivist Thought*, 1988 (Peikoff, editor); *The Ayn Rand Column*, 1991; *Letters of Ayn Rand*, 1995 (Michael S. Berliner, editor); *Journals of Ayn Rand*, 1997 (David Harriman, editor); *The Art of Fiction: A Guide for Writers and Readers*, 2000 (Tore Boeckmann, editor); *The Art of Nonfiction: A Guide for Writers and Readers*, 2001 (Robert Mayhew, editor); *Ayn Rand Answers: The Best of Her Q and A*, 2005 (Mayhew, editor).

MISCELLANEOUS: *The Objectivist Newsletter*, 1962-1965 (later known as *The Objectivist*, 1966-1971, edited by Rand); *The Ayn Rand Letter*, 1971-1976 (published by Rand).

BIBLIOGRAPHY
Baker, James T. *Ayn Rand*. Boston: Twayne, 1987. A brief introductory overview of Rand's life and work, written in an objective and highly readable style. Includes a chronology, references, a bibliography, and an index.

Branden, Nathaniel. *My Years with Ayn Rand*. Reprint. San Francisco, Calif.: Jossey-Bass, 1999. A personal account by Rand's disciple, organizer, spokesman, lover, and, ultimately, enemy. Includes photographs and an index. Originally published in 1989 as *Judgment Day: My Years with Ayn Rand*.

Branden, Nathaniel, and Barbara Branden. *Who Is Ayn Rand?* New York: Random House, 1962. This book contains three essays on objectivism's moral philosophy, its connection to psychological theory, and a literary study of Rand's methods in her fiction. It contains an additional biographical essay, tracing Rand's life from birth to her mid-fifties.

Britting, Jeff. *Ayn Rand*. Woodstock, N.Y.: Overlook Press, 2005. A readable biography of Rand's literary and personal life but lacking in scholarly analysis.

Gladstein, Mimi Reisel. *The New Ayn Rand Companion*. Rev. and expanded ed. Westport, Conn.: Greenwood Press, 1999. Provides biographical information, a summary of Rand's fiction and nonfiction, information about her characters, criticism of her writing, and a comprehensive bibliography. This revised edition contains newly discovered information about Rand's posthumous publications, updated biographical data, and summaries of books and articles published since her death.

Gladstein, Mimi Reisel, and Chris Matthew Sciabarra, eds. *Feminist Interpretations of Ayn Rand*. University Park: Pennsylvania State University Press, 1999. Collection of essays examining Rand's life and work from a feminist perspective. Includes pieces by cultural critics Susan Brownmiller and Camile Paglia and analysis of *Atlas Shrugged*.

Peikoff, Leonard. *Objectivism: The Philosophy of Ayn Rand*. New York: Dutton, 1991. A comprehensive overview of objectivist philosophy, written by the philosopher who was closest to Rand during her lifetime. Includes a discussion of Rand's ideas about reason, the good, virtue, happiness, government, art, and capitalism.

Pierpont, Claudia Roth. *Passionate Minds: Women Rewriting the World*. New York: Alfred A. Knopf, 2000. Evocative, interpretive essays on the life paths and works of twelve women, including Rand, connecting the circumstances of their lives with the shapes, styles, subjects, and situations of their art.

Sciabarra, Chris M. *Ayn Rand: The Russian Radical*. University Park: Pennsylvania State University Press, 1995. Sciabarra charts the evolution of the author as a philosopher, of her dialectics, and of her philosophy, beginning with her early years. Includes a bibliography and photographs.

Younkins, Edward W., ed. *Ayn Rand's "Atlas Shrugged": A Philosophical and Literary Companion*. Burlington, Vt.: Ashgate, 2007. Includes discussions of the novel's ideas about aesthetics, economics, and human relationships, the novel as a work of science fiction, and its characterization.

MIKHAIL SHOLOKHOV

Born: Kruzhilino, Russia; May 24, 1905
Died: Kruzhilino, Russia, Soviet Union (now in Russia); February 21, 1984
Also known as: Mikhail Aleksandrovich Sholokhov

<small>PRINCIPAL LONG FICTION</small>

Tikhii Don, 1928-1940 (partial translation *And Quiet Flows the Don*, 1934, also known as *The Don Flows Home to the Sea*, 1940; complete translation *The Silent Don*, 1942, also known as *And Quiet Flows the Don*, 1967)

Podnyataya tselina, 1932, 1960 (translation of volume 1 *Virgin Soil Upturned*, 1935, also known as *Seeds of Tomorrow*, 1935; translation of volume 2, *Harvest on the Don*, 1960; complete translation *Virgin Soil Upturned*, 1979)

Oni srazhalis za rodinu, 1943-1944 (serial), 1971 (book; *They Fought for Their Country*, 1959)

Sud'ba cheloveka, 1956-1957 (novella; *The Fate of a Man*, 1958)

<small>OTHER LITERARY FORMS</small>

Mikhail Sholokhov (SHAWL-eh-kawf) published collections of short stories, *Donskiye rasskazy* and *Lazorevaya Step*, in 1926. In 1931, *Lazorevaya Step* was expanded to include *Donskiye rasskazy* and was translated in 1961 as *Tales from the Don*. His short stories form volume 1 of his complete works, *Sobranie sochinenii* (1956-1960; *Collected Works in Eight Volumes*, 1984), which were first published in Moscow in eight volumes; war stories and essays form volume 8. They also are available in English as *One Man's Destiny, and Other Stories, Articles, and Sketches, 1923-1963* (1967) and *At the Bidding of the Heart: Essays, Sketches, Speeches, Papers* (1973).

<small>ACHIEVEMENTS</small>

Mikhail Sholokhov occupies a unique place in Soviet literature as the author of *The Silent Don*, the greatest novel to be published in the Soviet Union. He has been compared to Leo Tolstoy in his creation of a national epic, to Fyodor Dostoevski in his portrayal of Grigorii Melekhov, and to Nikolai Gogol and Anton Chekhov in his evocations of the steppe. In 1965, he was permitted by Soviet authorities to receive the Nobel Prize in Literature, a privilege denied to Boris Pasternak, who wrote a more profoundly philosophical novel. In addition, Sholokhov held numerous positions of honor in the Communist Party and the Union of Soviet Writers. He won the Stalin and Lenin prizes for literature (1941, 1960) and received honorary degrees from Western and Soviet universities.

In his two major works, *The Silent Don* and *Virgin Soil Upturned*, Sholokhov succeeds in bringing to life the Cossack world that he knew so well. Shrouded in legends, scorned for their barbarity, the Cossacks were little known to the Russians and totally unknown to

Mikhail Sholokhov
(Library of Congress)

Western readers. Sholokhov speaks in their dialect, clothes his characters in colorful Cossack traditions, and arms the soldiers with a spirit of courage and adventure. Part 1 of *The Silent Don* in particular and much of *Virgin Soil Upturned* shows them in their daily occupations, their celebrations and their interaction, much in their colorful and often crude language. Through his fictitious characters, all modeled on his own friends and acquaintances, the image of a people emerges.

Particularly in *The Silent Don*, Sholokhov skillfully combined Socialist Realism and art. Officially promulgated in 1934, Socialist Realism required that literature served the ideals of the Communist Party and portrayed a positive Soviet citizen. Early Soviet critics—with the exception of Aleksandr Serafimovich and Maxim Gorky—could not understand that *The Silent Don*, with its vacillating hero and its objective portrayal of both Reds and Whites, was a true proletarian novel, and they tried desperately to block its publication. Eventually, however, the critics accepted it because it showed the triumph of the Revolution through suffering and violence on both sides. Yet it was the artistic qualities of the novel, already evident in Sholokhov's early short stories, and to be continued in *Virgin Soil Upturned*, that won millions of readers in the Soviet Union and abroad. The humanness of suffering, the tenderness of love, and the uncertainty of truth touched them.

It was not without difficulty that Sholokhov acquired this reputation. Particularly in *The Silent Don*, the censors mercilessly changed and deleted some of his most brilliant passages. Joseph Stalin asked that the hero of *The Silent Don*, Grigorii Melekhov, accept Communism, but Sholokhov refused, saying that this was against the artistic conception of the work. Although *Virgin Soil Upturned* received less criticism, the death of Davydov was a concession to Stalin's wishes, since Sholokhov had planned a suicide. Yet the changes imposed on Sholokhov or accepted by him did not dim the original ideas that he had researched and reflected on painstakingly from 1925 to 1940 for *The Silent Don*, and from 1930 to 1960 for *Virgin Soil Upturned*. Outspoken like his Cossack hero Grigorii, Sholokhov says that an artist must follow his heart. He did not hesitate to criticize the inefficiency of the Soviet system and to express the depth of human suffering that accompanied the Revolution. On the other hand, as a dutiful Communist, he said that one's heart must follow the party. This was a difficult reconciliation, yet Sholokhov seems to have effected it more successfully than any other writer in the Soviet Union.

It should be noted, however, that ever since the publication of the first part of *The Silent Don*, Sholokhov's authorship of this masterwork, which clearly stands above the rest of his production, has been questioned. Among those to raise this charge was Aleksandr Solzhenitsyn, who believed that the actual author was a Cossack officer named Fyodor Kryukov, who had written several books about the Don region before his death in the Civil War. This charge against Sholokhov has yet to be conclusively proved or disproved.

Biography

Born on May 24, 1905, in the Cossack village of Kruzhilino near Veshenskaya, Mikhail Aleksandrovich Sholokhov was himself not a true Cossack. His father, Aleksandr Mikhailovich, did not marry his mother, Anastasiya Danilovna Chernikova, until 1912, when Sholokhov's birth was legitimated and the Cossack status he had held from his mother's first husband was abrogated. Nevertheless, he grew up in the customs and traditions of the Cossack world that he was later to convey with such realism to his readers. His early education in his native village was minimal when he left for a year in Moscow in 1914. Financial reasons precluded his continuing, but he was subsequently enrolled in an eight-year *Gymnasium* (college-preparatory secondary school) in Boguchar. The German invasion of 1918 marked the end of his formal education but did not interrupt his love of reading and writing. In the years between 1918 and 1922, Sholokhov worked for the new Soviet regime in many capacities, especially grain-requisitioning, and wrote plays for young people. His home was in an area controlled by the Whites. He saw much violence, participated in it himself, and was twice at the point of being killed. This experience is reflected especially in the violence and objectivity of *The Silent Don*, where Grigorii broods confusedly on the injustices committed by both sides.

In 1922, Sholokhov married Maria Petrovna Gromoslavskaya, the daughter of a well-to-do and long-established Cossack family. She was to prove an ideal "comrade" for him.

The couple, who would have four children, moved to Moscow, where Sholokhov began his first serious commitment to literature. He published a number of short stories, uneven in literary value but extremely popular. In their vividness of language, diversity of speech, and lively dialogue, they anticipate the achievements of his mature fiction. Never at home in the capital, or in any city, Sholokhov returned to Kruzhilino in 1924.

Sholokhov began working on his masterpiece, *The Silent Don*, in 1925, amid innumerable difficulties with the censors. It was only the intercession of Aleksandr Serafimovich, editor of the monthly *Oktyabr'*, that permitted publication of the initial segment of the novel. Serafimovich's support, however, did not prevent the many attacks on the novel and on Sholokhov himself, who was first accused of plagiarism in 1929-1930. Later, Gorky's intervention, and ultimately Stalin's, permitted him to complete publication of the novel. Sholokhov worked on *The Silent Don* almost constantly from 1925 to 1930, the most productive years of his career. He interrupted *The Silent Don* in 1930 to begin *Virgin Soil Upturned*. In 1932, he gained admission into the Communist Party, and in 1934 he was elected to the presidium of the Union of Soviet Writers. He visited Sweden, Denmark, Great Britain, and France as a representative of the Writers' Union. His success did not prevent him from speaking out fearlessly against the bureaucracy, which ultimately placed him in a dangerous position, especially in 1938, when he narrowly escaped liquidation. His personal friendship with Stalin saved him, and he always remained loyal to his friend, even after Stalin's death.

During World War II, in which he experienced much personal suffering, including the loss of his manuscripts, Sholokhov became a war correspondent. His writings as a reporter are not his best; nevertheless, after the war he devoted himself mainly to journalism, with the exception of volume 2 of *Virgin Soil Upturned*; *They Fought for Their Country*, an unfinished novel in a war setting; and a very successful novella, *The Fate of a Man*. In the postwar era, he enjoyed unparalleled success in the Soviet Union, receiving many prizes, the most notable of which was the Nobel Prize in Literature in 1965. He became a staunch defender of party policies, attacking such dissidents as Pasternak, Solzhenitsyn, Yuli Daniel, and Andrei Sinyavsky, all of whom are superior to him as writers. Typical of his attacks on the West was an invective against Harry S. Truman, then-president of the United States.

Until his death in 1984, Sholokhov lived in the village where he was born. He hunted and fished, traveled widely in Europe, the United States, and Japan, and enjoyed his substantial wealth and international reputation.

ANALYSIS

The critic Herman Ermolaev has observed that Mikhail Sholokhov's art embraces the epic, the dramatic, the comic, and the lyric; to this one might justly add the tragic, at least in *The Silent Don*. Helen Muchnic, for example, sees in the character of Grigorii the fatal flaw that marks the heroes of Greek tragedy: Grigorii is doomed by his failure to recognize the greatness of Bolshevism. His error lies in his independence. Like Oedipus, Grigorii cannot *not* know the truth, but unlike Sophocles' hero, Sholokhov's is destined never to know clearly. Even Soviet critics noted the tragic element in *The Silent Don*, and in 1940, Boris Emelyanov compared *The Silent Don* to Aeschylus's *The Persians* (472 B.C.E.), since both were written from the viewpoint of the vanquished. *The Silent Don* is of epic proportions because of its length and its scope in time (1912-1922) at a crucial period in Western history, World War I and the Soviet Revolution. It was serialized in *Oktyabr'* and *Novy mir* from 1928 to 1940. Volume 1 was published by Moskovskii Rabochii in 1928, volume 2 in 1929; Khudozhestvennaya Literatura published volumes 3 and 4 in 1933 and 1940 respectively.

THE SILENT DON

The novel is the story of the fall of a people seen through some of its most representative families: Melekhov, Korshunov, and Koshevoi in particular. Often compared to Tolstoy's *War and Peace* (1865-1869), *The Silent Don* unfolds a vast panorama of people and world-shaking events, and 1917 is to Sholokhov what 1812 was to Tolstoy. Yet Sholokhov is no Tolstoy. He lacks Tolstoy's depth of vision, moral intensity, and psychological analysis. Sholokhov's choice of a secluded and anachronistic prerevolutionary society places *The Silent Don* in the category of the primitive and popular epics, as David Stewart demonstrates through his analysis of action, character, language, and meaning in the novel.

Early in his career, Sholokhov was attracted to the theater, and thus it is not surprising that in both of his novels dialogue and action are of extreme importance. Sholokhov uses lively and spirited conversation, filled with dialectical and sometimes crude Cossack expressions, and often incorrect Russian. In fact, the major part of the novels is dialogue rather than narrative, and important events come to light through the characters rather than through the author. Sholokhov does not write reflective philosophical works. Grigorii Melekhov's search for truth is less evident in his thoughts than in his actions, as he vacillates constantly between Red and White, and between his wife, Natalia, and his mistress, Aksinia. Collectivization is not a well-thought-out plan in *Virgin Soil Upturned* but rather a process that occurs because each farmer moves in that direction.

Both people and nature are actors in Sholokhov's works, and he moves effortlessly and harmoniously from one to the other. The poetic evocations of nature that make up at least one-fourth of *The Silent Don* and a good part, though less, of *Virgin Soil Upturned* show Sholokhov's lyric mastery at its height. Most are placed at strategic positions, such as the beginning and end of chapters, and convey the union of people with nature. In somewhat pantheistic exultation, Sholokhov rejoices with nature in its cycle of birth, death, and resurrection. As one might expect from the titles of his novels, the Don mirrors human hopes and sorrows. Sholokhov's books convey the feel of the earth—the Russian soil—and evoke the rhythm of nature.

Nature is frequently associated with love in Sholokhov's fiction. Ermolaev, who has studied the role of nature in Sholokhov, identifies floral blooming with Aksinia; Easter, the spring, and rain, with Natalia. In Grigorii and Aksinia, one finds perhaps the tenderest love story in Soviet literature. Their passionate and fatal love recalls Anna Karenina or Dmitri Karamazov. As with Sholokhov's poetic lyricism, his love stories are close to the earth and show the deep bond of human beings with nature. The tenderness of maternal love also plays an important role in Sholokhov's works, as seen in the tender farewell of Ilinichna for her dead son, Piotra, and contrasts sharply with the brutality and violence of war.

Sholokhov's humorous vein is more evident in *Virgin Soil Upturned* but is not absent from *The Silent Don*, where one might cite Panteleimon Melekhov's wit. *Virgin Soil Upturned* abounds in comic characters and scenes: Shchukar's endless stories, the exuberance of the induction into the party, the initial reactions to collectivization at the village meetings. Sholokhov's dialogue is brisk and witty; his colloquial and dialectical language, always appropriate to the speaker, lightens the heavy subject and makes both novels highly readable.

Indeed, Sholokhov's style is brisk and light; the chapters, composed of short vignettes, leave the reader momentarily in suspense, for Sholokhov knows where to break his tale. His rapid transitions from humor to violence, from love to war, from nature to humanity, show the all-encompassing unity of life and the complexity of the Revolution and its effects. He shows the stark reality of war, the atrocities of both Reds and Whites, and humankind's inhumanity to others. On the other hand, he portrays the tenderness of love and the exultation of nature, as in his beautiful apostrophe to the steppe that rivals Gogol. He works in a linear manner, without flashbacks or foreshadowing, much in the tradition of the nineteenth century or indeed the ancient and medieval epic. He portrays life and love, the endless rhythm of birth and death, as seen in one great epoch, the Soviet Revolution.

The Silent Don was first conceived as an epic of the Don and of the role of the Don Cossacks in the Revolution, and Sholokhov projected the title *Donshchina*, later abandoning it because of its archaic allusions. The story begins in 1912 and ends in 1922. It shows the peaceful agrarian life of the Don Cossacks in the small village of Tatarsk. The domineering patriarch Panteleimon Melekhov and his independent and passionate son, Grigorii, clash often, especially in regard to Grigorii's liaison with the bewitching Aksinia. Neither the father's wrath and the arranged marriage with the beautiful and virtuous Natalia Korshunova, daughter of the prosperous Miron, nor the abuse by Aksinia's husband, Stepan Ashtakov, can break the liaison. The two lovers, defying all convention, finally choose to live together as hired help on the estate of Listnitsky.

The calm of the Cossack existence, broken only by such outbursts of passion, is shattered by mobilization in Tatarsk in 1914. Grigorii is called into battle, where his attraction and repulsion toward killing and violence are first evident. The war provides Grigorii's first contact with Bolshevism, for which he also feels both an attraction and repulsion. On leave in Tatarsk because of a wound, he learns of Aksinia's unfaithfulness and returns to his wife, who later gives birth to twins.

Like World War I, the Revolution is portrayed through the eyes of the soldiers and villagers and evoked through images of nature: "Above blood-soaked White Russia, the stars wept mournfully." The desertion of the troops, Kornilov's arrest, and the fall of Kerensky are moments of confusion to the Don Cossack soldiers. Grigorii embraces Bolshevism and becomes an officer but is incapable of the cold dedication exemplified by Bunchuk, whose brief idyll with the Jew Anna Pogudko softens the drama, and by Mishka Koshevoi, Grigorii's former friend and henceforth implacable enemy.

When Grigorii joins the Whites, his position becomes more dangerous. The violence grows more senseless and immediate, with victims such as Miron Korshunov and Piotra Melekhov, the latter killed by Mishka Koshevoi. Family tragedies also cloud Grigorii's existence and confuse his values. His sister-in-law, Daria, commits suicide; his wife, Natalia, dies as the result of an abortion after learning of Grigorii's return to Aksinia; his father dies of typhus. Parallel to Grigorii's uncertainty is Mishka's advance in the Soviet ranks and in coldheartedness. Even his marriage to Grigorii's sister, Dunia, does not dull his determination to kill Grigorii, which the reader surmises will occur when Grigorii returns home, having lost Aksinia to a stray bullet. Only his son, Mishatka, remains, and the implacable march of history will destroy the unwilling Grigorii, born to greatness at a point in history when only conformity can save him.

In 1930, Sholokhov interrupted his work on *The Silent Don* to address a contemporary problem: collectivization. He published part 1 of *Virgin Soil Upturned* in 1932, practically without any censorship difficulties. Part 2 was not completed until 1960 and is radically different in spirit. This novel is much more concentrated in scope, since it covers only the period between 1930 and 1932, has fewer characters, and is confined to the small Cossack village of Gremyachy Log. Although it does not have the epic sweep of *The Silent Don*, it is an on-the-spot documentary of a crucial phase in Soviet history.

VIRGIN SOIL UPTURNED

Also unlike *The Silent Don*, *Virgin Soil Upturned* has no main tragic character. Stewart observes that the heroes are dissolved by the party, so that the real hero is perhaps the collective people at Gremyachy Log. The logical hero is Siemion Davydov, a former factory worker and sailor, who was mobilized in 1930 to organize collective farms. He becomes chair at Gremyachy Log and manifests the zeal and inefficiency typical of early Soviet leaders. He is a colorless but not unlikable character. His death at the end of part 2 is far less tragic than Grigorii's return to Tatarsk. Although he shows his human side in his love affairs with Nagulnov's former wife, Lukeria, and with a gentle, shy seventeen-year-old, Varia Kharlamova, he is not convincing as a lover.

Siemion's associate, the passionate and impulsive Makar Nagulnov, secretary of the Gremyachy Log Party nucleus and still secretly in love with his former wife, is more attractive. Even better portrayed is Andrei Razmiotov, chair of the village Soviet. His one passion is his deceased wife, Yevdokia, and the novel ends as he visits her grave and wistfully mourns her absence. Stewart, however, regards Kondrat Maidannikov as the novel's most convincing character: A "middling Cossack," Kondrat joins the collective farm because he believes in it, yet his instincts draw him to his own property. He does not join the party until he has reflected carefully. In his simplicity, he is the most philosophical and intellectually convinced Communist in the novel.

The plot of the story is simple: the gradual conversion of the village to the collective farm. The beginning reflects Sholokhov's portrayal of violence and brutality, as entire kulak families are deported. Although collectivization is presented as voluntary, those who withdraw after reading Stalin's pronouncement are left with no animals and inferior land. The end of part 1 is indecisive though promising. In part 2, collectivization is complete, and a revolt is suppressed. Thus, this volume becomes mainly a series of sketches and stories, mostly in a humorous vein. It seems to be the work of a writer who has totally accepted party policies, writing about an accomplished fact no longer questioned.

Actually Sholokhov's best creative period ended before World War II, and part 2, written in 1960, weakens what promised to be a powerful, though limited, novel. Nevertheless, Sholokhov's treatment of collectivization has not been surpassed, and his wit and lyricism make *Virgin Soil Upturned* a valuable contribution to literature.

Irma M. Kashuba

OTHER MAJOR WORKS

SHORT FICTION: *Donskiye rasskazy*, 1926; *Lazorevaya Step*, 1926, 1931 (1931 edition includes *Donskiye rasskazy; Tales from the Don*, 1961); *Early Stories*, 1966.

NONFICTION: *Pisatel i vozhd*, 1997; *Pisma*, 2003.

MISCELLANEOUS: *Sobranie sochinenii*, 1956-1960 (8 volumes; *Collected Works in Eight Volumes*, 1984); *One Man's Destiny, and Other Stories, Articles, and Sketches, 1923-1963*, 1967; *At the Bidding of the Heart: Essays, Sketches, Speeches, Papers*, 1973.

BIBLIOGRAPHY

Clark, Katerina. "Socialist Realism in Soviet Literature." In *The Routledge Companion to Russian Literature*, edited by Neil Cornwell. New York: Routledge, 2001. Clark's essay includes discussion of *The Silent Don* and *Virgin Soil Upturned*, placing these novels within the broader context of Soviet Social Realism.

Ermolaev, Herman. *Mikhail Sholokhov and His Art*. Princeton, N.J.: Princeton University Press, 1982. A study of Sholokhov's life and art, philosophy of life, and handling of style and structure, with a separate chapter on the historical sources of *The Silent Don* and another on the question of plagiarism. Includes maps, tables of similes, notes, and a bibliography.

Klimenko, Michael. *The World of Young Sholokhov: Vision of Violence*. North Quincy,

Mass.: Christopher, 1972. The introduction discusses the Sholokhov canon as well as his life and his critics. Other chapters explore the genesis of Sholokhov's novels, vision of life, heroes, and treatment of revolution. Includes a bibliography.

Medvedev, Roy. *Problems in the Literary Biography of Mikhail Sholokhov.* New York: Cambridge University Press, 1977. A piercing examination of *The Silent Don*, exploring the issue of Sholokhov's authorship of the novel and how it poses problems for his literary biography.

Mukherjee, G. *Mikhail Sholokhov: A Critical Introduction.* New Delhi: Northern Book Centre, 1992. A bilingual study, in both English and Russian. Mukherjee analyzes the major novels and other writings of Sholokhov, considering them in relation to Soviet literature and ideology, and he discusses Sholokhov's critical reception.

Scammell, Michael. "The Don Flows Again." *The New York Times Book Review,* January 25, 1998. Scammell's review of a new translation of Sholokhov's best-known novel provides a useful overview of the writer's life and literary reputation, including an update on new evidence supporting Sholokov's claim to be the author of the book.

Stewart, David Hugh. *Mikhail Sholokhov: A Critical Introduction.* Ann Arbor: University of Michigan Press, 1967. Found in most university libraries, this is an accessible overview of Sholokhov and his works. Includes a bibliography.

FRANS EEMIL SILLANPÄÄ

Born: Hämeenkyrö, Finland, Russian Empire (now in Finland); September 16, 1888
Died: Helsinki, Finland; June 3, 1964

PRINCIPAL LONG FICTION

Elämä ja aurinko, 1916
Hurskas kurjuus, 1919 (*Meek Heritage,* 1938)
Nuorena nukkunut, 1931 (*The Maid Silja,* 1933; also known as *Fallen Asleep While Young,* 1939)
Miehen tie, 1932
Ihmiset suviyössä, 1934 (*People in the Summer Night,* 1966)
Elokuu, 1941
Ihmiselon ihanuus ja kurjuus, 1945

OTHER LITERARY FORMS

In addition to his novels, Frans Eemil Sillanpää (SIHL-ahn-pah) published several volumes of short stories dealing with the topics that preoccupied him throughout his career. These topics include the Finnish Civil War of 1918 and the role of humans as integral parts of nature. He also wrote a number of causeries, which might best be characterized as autobiographical self-examinations. The collections from the 1920's are considered among the finest in twentieth century Finnish literature, while the short stories from the following decades are less significant. In 1953, Sillanpää produced a series of radio programs devoted to his memoirs, which were expanded and published in three volumes later in the 1950's, forming the last of his published works.

ACHIEVEMENTS

Frans Eemil Sillanpää belongs primarily to the great epic tradition in Finnish literature that began with Aleksis Kivi (1834-1872), combining a realistic depiction of rural life with a mystical awareness of nature. While Sillanpää's fiction reflects the influence of the nineteenth century realistic novel, largely unaffected by the currents of modernism, his blend of lyricism with an almost naturalistic emphasis on the power of instinct (prompting comparisons with the British novelist D. H. Lawrence) introduced a new and distinctive voice in Finnish literature. Several of Sillanpää's novels became international best sellers, and in 1939 he became the first Finnish writer to receive the Nobel Prize in Literature.

BIOGRAPHY

The son of a crofter and farmhand, Frans Eemil Sillanpää spent only a few years in grade school before he entered the *Gymnasium* (college-preparatory secondary school) of Tampere, from which he graduated in 1908. During his last years at the *Gymnasium,* while supporting himself through private tutoring, he read at the public library the works of Knut Hamsun, Selma Lagerlöf, and the great Russian writers Leo Tolstoy and Fyodor Dostoevski. At the University of Helsinki, Sillanpää studied natural sciences, particularly biology, for four years, and he was influenced by the philosophical theories of Ernst Haeckel and Friedrich Wilhelm Ostwald. Financial problems and failing health, however, forced him to give up his studies and return to his family home. During these years, August Strindberg and Maurice Maeterlinck became his favorite writers; later, Swedish neo-Romanticist Erik Axel Karlfeldt had the greatest artistic influence on him.

During the summer of 1914, Sillanpää visited the Baltic Exhibition in the Swedish city of Malmö, and from there he went to Copenhagen, Denmark. From both cities he sent travel letters home to the Finnish newspaper *Uusi Suometar,* together with some short stories written while he had attended the *Gymnasium* of Tampere, his first published works. After marrying Sigrid Maria Salomäki in 1916, Sillanpää moved to Helsinki. Gradually he came to be regarded as the grand old man of Finnish literature, but his life was disrupted by the death of his wife in 1939. A short and unhappy second marriage was one of the causes of his mental collapse in 1940, which forced him to spend three years in a hospital. In 1939, Sillanpää was awarded the Nobel Prize in Literature.

ANALYSIS

Frans Eemil Sillanpää's writings are rooted in his home region, the area around Tampere. Its people—crofters and farmhands—its animals, its changing seasons, and its natural surroundings constitute his fictional world. Only seldom did Sillanpää depart from this milieu to depict city life and the higher social classes, and then frequently with satire. His characters are for the most part passive beings governed by their instincts who, without intellectual insight, yield to blind fate. These characters are analyzed either undramatically and with cool objectivity or with concern and compassion, framed by descriptions of nature showing superb poetic inspiration.

Together with this duality in narrative attitude, readers find, on the stylistic level, a fluctuation between harsh, realistic expression and suggestive, lyric sequences of the highest sophistication, almost imperceptibly following the rhythms of nature. Sillanpää did not regard life from a psychological or metaphysical standpoint; rather, he treated it as a totality that includes all living things—humans, animals, and nature. This biological monism elevates his humble and tragic characters above their sufferings, breaks the pattern of decay and catastrophe, and lends them a heroic stature either through resignation or through a realization of their affinity with an ever-revitalizing nature.

ELÄMÄ JA AURINKO

Sillanpää's first novel, *Elämä ja aurinko* (life and the sun), turned out to be very different from all previous Finnish fiction. Animated nature was described with a hitherto unseen precision, counterbalanced by evocative sensitivity, together reflecting the undercurrents of the human mind: The internal and the external, the self and surrounding nature, merged in a unique and refined pattern. Into the magic world of a few summer months—and of rather secondary importance—is placed a love story describing the short-lived affairs of a peasant student who has returned to his village, with both a young girl of his own social background and, at the same time, a mature, upperclass woman.

MEEK HERITAGE

In Sillanpää's next novel, *Meek Heritage*, the narrative structure has been tightened and the characters have been given firm and precise contours. *Meek Heritage* was written immediately after the Finnish Civil War and reflects the author's discouraging experiences with both the communist and the anticommunist factions. It concentrates entirely on the destiny of the main character, containing few lyric descriptions of nature or philosophical reflections.

The novel is mainly about the life of Juha Toivola before the war. It tells of his childhood during the famine of the 1860's as a penniless orphan and the abuses to which he is subjected by relatives and other people for whom he works. He marries almost unthinkingly, leases a small piece of land, drifts because of his poverty into the Socialist movement, joins the Red Guard, and is shot by mistake at the end of the war. The book, however, is no novel of indignation and social accusation. Everything goes wrong for Juha because he is unable to take care of himself. He never commits any dishonest act; he simply falls prey to the whims of fate in a world in which dreariness and evil can be found everywhere. He remains, in spite of his spinelessness and filthiness, a pitiful yet valuable representative of humanity, worthy of protection.

Meek Heritage is considered the classic description of the Finnish Civil War and one of the literary catalysts in the process of national reconciliation. Twelve years went by—a period in which Sillanpää established his profile as a short-story writer—before he published his second masterpiece, *The Maid Silja*, his longest and most widely read novel.

THE MAID SILJA

In *The Maid Silja*, the narrative, too, is disrupted by exquisite descriptions of the Finnish summer. Sillanpää tells of the extinction of an old peasant family, the last years in the lives of an old man and his daughter. Like Juha in *Meek Heritage*, they, too, are unable to protect themselves, but unlike him, they are intellectually and emotionally mature. Somewhat idealized—and not without sentimentality—is the portrait of the girl Silja, who is placed in an everyday reality in which she does not belong and who finds escape from this reality mainly in her romantic fantasies. Her first and only erotic experience, with a student, becomes both the climax and the turning point in her life. He abandons her, her latent tuberculosis surfaces, and after hardship and suffering, she dies the following spring. The dramatic events are, however, presented not as tragic but rather as the entry into blissful peace. The story is enveloped in a chiaroscuro atmosphere, a manifestation of the inner strength of humankind when facing death—the author's demonstration of the spirit's victory over matter.

MIEHEN TIE

Greater epic breadth distinguishes the novel *Miehen tie* (the way of man), which, in contrast to Sillanpää's previous works, focuses on determined and hardworking human beings. The weak farmer, Paavo, must make many mistakes, including an unsuccessful marriage, before he is united with the strong-willed Alma, his youthful love and a direct contrast to the vulnerable Silja. Alma, who defies all conventional moral concepts, is from the outset aware that she and Paavo, by nature, are destined for each other—the influence of Lawrence has been suggested—and here we find Sillanpää's moral message: The peasant family is able to survive because of its acceptance of this fate. The otherwise somewhat robust character delineation and narrow realism of this novel alternates with poetic passages in which humans and nature fuse.

PEOPLE IN THE SUMMER NIGHT

In *People in the Summer Night*, the description and the mystique of nature again dominate. The action takes place during a few days and nights of summer and offers a cross section of human destinies from birth to death, either peaceful or violent. Here, Sillanpää allows a number of separate events and characters to appear as apparently insignificant and transitional elements of what proves to be an invisible and timeless totality.

ELOKUU *and* IHMISELON IHANUUS JA KURJUUS

In part as a result of his severe illness, Sillanpää's bright and optimistic mood in his early works yielded to a dark pessimism in his late novels. *Elokuu* (August), through its portrayal of a failing writer who succumbs to daydreams and alcoholism, presents a relentless study of human destruction. Related in topic and atmosphere is Sillanpää's last novel, *Ihmiselon ihanuus ja kurjuus* (life's beauty and mystery), the protagonist of which is a successful poet who is haunted by the tragic realization of having reached his peak artistically—perhaps a reflection of Sillanpää's own doubts.

In his last works, Sillanpää does not, with the same ease as earlier, offer an escape from disillusionment and decay through resignation, heroism, or consolation in nature. This skepticism adds a new dimension to his oeuvre and indicates that his pantheistic harmony is only tentative. The late works exhibit a tension between idealized Romanticism and brutal naturalism, with greater psychological nuances, a more complex narrative technique, and frequent changes in point of view; Sillanpää increasingly enhances the action with his own comments.

Sillanpää is a master in Finnish literature. His works are living classics, accessible in translation to a wide audience and still highly readable despite their period flavor.

Sven H. Rossel

OTHER MAJOR WORKS

SHORT FICTION: *Ihmislapsia elämän saatossa*, 1917; *Rakas isänmaani*, 1919; *Enkelten suojatit*, 1923; *Hiltu ja Ragnar*, 1923 (novelette); *Maan tasalta*, 1924; *Töllinmäki*, 1925; *Rippi*, 1928; *Kiitos hetkistä, Herra*, 1930; *Virran pohjalta*, 1933; *Viidestoista*, 1936; *Erään elämän satoa*, 1948.

NONFICTION: *Poika eli elämäänsä*, 1953; *Kerron ja kuvailen*, 1955; *Päivä korkeimmillaan*, 1956.

BIBLIOGRAPHY

Ahokas, Jaakko. *A History of Finnish Literature*. 1973. Reprint. London: Routledge/ Curzon, 1997. There are many references to Sillanpää in this overview of Finnish literature, but the majority of them are in chapter 8, "Literature in Finnish Between the Two World Wars."

Alho, Olli, et al., eds. *Finland: A Cultural Encyclopedia*. Helsinki: Finnish Literature Society, 1997. An encyclopedic introduction to the culture of Finland, including its literature. Essays by close to eighty scholars and other contributors. Includes maps and an index.

Crouse, Timothy. "Past Present." *The Nation*, October 1, 1990. A portrait of Sillanpää, containing biographical information and a discussion of some of his works, including the novels *People in the Summer Night* and *Meek Heritage*.

Envall, Markku. "Earlier Authors Continue: Koskenniemi and Sillanpää." In *A History of Finland's Literature*, edited by George C. Schoolfield. Lincoln: University of Nebraska Press, in cooperation with the American-Scandinavian Foundation, 1998. One of the few English-language books that contains information about Sillanpää. This history of Finnish literature includes a chapter discussing Sillanpää's work, placing it within the broader context of Finnish fiction.

Laitinen, Kai. "F. E. Sillanpää, Life and Sun: The Writer and His Time." *Books from Finland* 22, no. 2 (1988). An overview of Sillanpää's life and writings.

Stark, Tuula. "Frans Eemil Sillanpää." In *The Nobel Prize Winners: Literature*, edited by Frank N. Magill. Vol. 2. Pasadena, Calif.: Salem Press, 1987. Provides a brief but thorough study and analysis of Sillanpää's works.

ANDREI SINYAVSKY

Born: Moscow, Russia, Soviet Union (now in Russia); October 8, 1925
Died: Fontenay-aux-Roses, France; February 25, 1997
Also known as: Andrei Donatovich Sinyavsky; Abram Tertz

PRINCIPAL LONG FICTION

Sad idzie, 1959 (in Polish; in Russian as *Sud idyot*, 1960; as Abram Tertz; *The Trial Begins*, 1960)
Lyubimov, 1963 (in Polish; Russian translation, 1964; as Tertz; *The Makepeace Experiment*, 1965)
Kroshka Tsores, 1980 (novella; *Little Jinx*, 1992)
Spokoynoy nochi, 1984 (*Goodnight!*, 1989)

OTHER LITERARY FORMS

Andrei Sinyavsky (sihn-YAHV-skee) is the author of an important book-length essay, *Chto takoe sotsialisticheskii realizm* (1959; *On Socialist Realism*, 1960), published under the pseudonym Abram Tertz, in which he maintains with some humor that realism is not the proper medium for the mythmaking inherent in a communist society. Because he believed that the grandiose neoclassicism inherited from eighteenth century Russian literature had also become inadequate, Sinyavsky proposed that the more appropriate genre would be fantasy, and he himself became a writer of fantasy. His collection *Fantasticheskie povesti* (1961; *Fantastic Stories*, 1963; also known as *The Icicle, and Other Stories*, 1963), including a novella and several short stories, is surrealistic, an excursion into the literature of the absurd. *Mysli vrasplokh* (1966; as Tertz; *Unguarded Thoughts*, 1972), a collection of aphorisms, came as a revelation to Sinyavsky's Western readers, disclosing for the first time his profound faith as a Russian Orthodox believer.

In addition to these works, all of which were signed with the pen name Abram Tertz and published abroad before his arrest, Sinyavsky has published a number of important critical studies, including an introductory essay to Boris Pasternak's *Stikhotvoreniya i poemy* (1965, 1976; verses and poems); an analysis of the nineteenth century writer Nikolai Gogol, *V teni Gogolya* (1975; in the shadow of Gogol); and a book on the poet Alexander Pushkin, *Progulki s Pushkinym* (1975; walks with Pushkin). Sinyavsky's *Golos iz khora* (1973; *A Voice from the Chorus*, 1976), largely composed of letters that he wrote to his wife during his six years in a labor camp, is in the tradition initiated by Fyodor Dostoevski and continued by such twentieth century writers as Aleksandr Solzhenitsyn. The essay "Literaturnii protess v Rossii" (literary process in Russia), published in the dissident journal *Kontinent* in 1976, is both a savage analysis of the Soviet mind and an extraordinary literary manifesto that transcends its occasion. Finally, Sinyavsky's *Little Jinx*, with the Yiddish word *tsores* in the original title, serves as a reminder that he identifies with Jews as alienated people outside the normal parameters of Soviet existence.

The true identity of the elusive writer Abram Tertz (a pen name taken from the hero of an underworld ballad) became known to readers in the Soviet Union and the West only after his arrest in 1965 and subsequent imprisonment. Tertz turned out to be the gifted and sophisticated critic Andrei Sinyavsky. Prior to this catastrophe, Sinyavsky had mastered the extremely difficult task of keeping his two voices, that of the writer Tertz and the critic Sinyavsky, separate. Writing as Tertz, Sinyavsky produced fantastic stories and short novels, as well as the famous essay *On Socialist Realism*, a devastating critique of officially tolerated literary practice.

So accomplished a writer was Sinyavsky that his achievements were considered far superior to those of his contemporaries, and it was even thought for a time that Tertz might be the brilliant prose writer Yury Olesha, from the 1920's. Writing during a period when Russian prose had only just begun to emerge from the stultifying limitations of Socialist Realism, Sinyavsky managed to continue the earlier ornamentalist prose tradition of Andrey Bely, Alexey Remizov, and, ultimately, Gogol.

The sophistication of Sinyavsky's worldview is equal to that of his style, for he presents society with all of its inherent contradictions, limitations, and absurdities, a far cry from the narrow vision peculiar to Socialist Realism and official Soviet ideology. With his stylistic brilliance and metaphysical depth, Sinyavsky has rightly come to be considered one of the finest Russian authors of the post-Stalin period.

BIOGRAPHY

Andrei Donatovich Sinyavsky was born in Moscow in 1925 and grew up there. He served in the Russian army during World War II. After the war, he was a student at the philological faculty of Moscow State University, one of the nation's most prestigious institutions of higher learning. He eventually became a candidate of philological sciences, a degree equivalent to a doctorate in the United States, and he obtained a position as a senior staff member with the Gorky Institute of World Literature in Moscow. Sinyavsky immediately came to be regarded as a gifted critic; his book on postrevolutionary Russian poetry, *Poeziya pervykh let revolyutsii, 1917-1920* (1964), coauthored with A. Menshutin, was considered one of the best studies of its time. His interests extended beyond literature to the plastic arts, and he collaborated with I. N. Golomshtok on a work about Pablo Picasso, *Pikasso* (1960).

Simultaneously with his activities as a critic, Sinyavsky pursued a secret career as a fantasy writer, using the name Abram Tertz; it was the revelations of de-Stalinization in 1956 that converted him from establishment critic to dissident author. Madame Hélène Peltier-Zamoyska, daughter of the French naval attaché in Moscow, had become close friends with Sinyavsky when they were students together at Moscow State University, and it was she who arranged for the publication of the works of "Tertz" in the West. In spite of Sinyavsky's discretion, he was unmasked in 1965. He was tried in February, 1966, with fellow dissident writer Yuli Daniel, who had achieved fame in the West and notoriety in the Soviet Union as Nikolay Arzhak. Sinyavsky was sentenced to six years in prison, spending the time in a labor camp in Mordovia. He left the Soviet Union for France in 1973, thereafter teaching at the Sorbonne. The fine works that he has published since his departure attest Sinyavsky's continued development as a writer.

Analysis

Any attempt to analyze Andrei Sinyavsky's fiction must take the essay *On Socialist Realism* into account, for the ideas developed in that essay provide the basis for his fictional works. Socialist Realism has been defined in the Soviet Union as a depiction of "reality in its revolutionary development," the favored official medium being an anemic descendant of the so-called critical realism of the nineteenth century. This realism, Sinyavsky believes, is inadequate for expressing the heroic purpose, a purpose essential to the ideology forming the basis for the Soviet state. The neoclassicism of the eighteenth century, normally the ideal vehicle for the purpose of the autocratic state, could not be used for contemporary Soviet literature; the debunking of the Stalinist myth and absence of a figure of similar stature robbed the Russians of anyone or anything to glorify. The only remaining method possible is one based on hypothesis instead of purpose, and that method has to be fantasy. It is with this premise in mind that Sinyavsky has approached the novel.

The Trial Begins

Sinyavsky's first novel, *The Trial Begins*, is set in Moscow during the last days of Joseph Stalin. It is ostensibly a realistic novel dealing with such well-known phenomena of the time as the "doctors' plot," which resulted in the stepped-up persecution of the Jews, the terrifying inner workings of the secret police, and the mass panic immediately following the death of Stalin. Sinyavsky's principal characters include the public prosecutor Vladimir Petrovich Globov, his idealistic son, Seryozha, and Seryozha's friend, Katya. Globov's second wife, Marina, and Yuri Karlinsky, a defending attorney, eventually manage to become lovers behind Globov's back. Globov's former mother-in-law, Yekaterina Petrovna, is an old Bolshevik idealist.

Globov is scheduled to prosecute the gynecologist S. Y. Rabinovich, who performed an illegal abortion, but the woman in question is Globov's beautiful and sexy but soulless wife, Marina. Rabinovich is Jewish, and his predicament is a transparent reference to Stalin's anti-Semitic campaign in the 1950's. Globov's life is complicated further by the fact that his adolescent son, Seryozha, has written a notebook calling for a new Communist society that will be free of the corruption that has stained the old one, a society in which those in the highest offices would earn the lowest wages, money would be abolished, and everyone would receive "according to his needs." Seryozha shares his ideas with Katya and gives her the notebook. She takes it to Karlinsky for advice, protesting against Seryozha's orthodoxy that a noble end should be served by noble means; Karlinsky counters that power corrupts, with the noble means soon forgotten. After she leaves, he gives vent to his jealous rage against Marina's husband, deciding to strike at him by blowing the whistle on his son, Seryozha. Seryozha is eventually tried and sent to a labor camp, where he is joined by Rabinovich. Finally given the opportunity to consummate his affair with Marina, Karlinsky proves to be impotent. Katya is trampled to death in the mass stampede following Stalin's funeral.

At first glance, *The Trial Begins* appears to be a realistic work that reveals corruption and evil in the Soviet Union, a critique of the system in the tradition of Vladimir Dudintsev's *Ne khlebom yedinym* (1956; *Not by Bread Alone*, 1957) or Ilya Ehrenburg's *Ottepel* (1954; *The Thaw*, 1955). Appearances, however, are deceiving, and *The Trial Begins* stands apart from its fellows by virtue of Sinyavsky's use of fantasy.

The Trial Begins is introduced by a narrator, one of a series of Sinyavsky's quirky, neurotic narrators. He bears a close resemblance to Yury Olesha's hero Kavalerov in the novel *Zavist* (1927; *Envy*, 1936), and it is easy to see why a number of Western critics initially assumed that the novelist and critic known as Tertz was actually Olesha. Tertz's narrator, similar to but not identical with Tertz himself, is the author of the manuscript that constitutes the major portion of the novel. He is a writer, the generic, nonconformist Soviet writer. The narrator is victimized in the middle of the night by two secret police agents, Vitya and Tolya, who work as a team and bear a strong resemblance to Thompson and Thomson from Hergé's series of children's books on the young French reporter Tintin. Vitya and Tolya, like Thompson and Thomson, are the enemies of freedom and originality, and their purpose is to destroy art. One of them scoops all the letters and punctuation marks off the page and crushes one caught trying to escape. The manuscript they have confiscated is *The Trial Begins*, but the characters and events in the work come to life as if they had been written by an omniscient, not a first-person, narrator. The narrator himself disappears from the story, not to surface again until the end, when he is shown in prison camp with his invented characters Rabinovich and Seryozha. Thus, the body of the novel is sandwiched between the reader's introduction to the narrator at the beginning and the reader's final, sad view of him at the end.

The most fantastic element of the frame technique used by Sinyavsky is that two characters who are part of the body of the novel—that is, part of the manuscript written by the convict author—actually appear with him in prison at the conclusion of the story. The reader is then left with the uneasy sensation that the manuscript has taken over and somehow become actuality, that the omniscient and first-person narrators might possibly be the same individual. The implications of this confusing situation are enormous.

Beneath the surface of an apparent protest novel, a novel peppered with such peculiar events as the appearance of the hand of God to the narrator at the beginning or Marina's gift of liqueur-filled chocolates to Seryozha at the end, other factors are at work.

Sinyavsky's novel is only superficially about political events and the illicit love affair between Karlinsky and Marina. It is actually about art, specifically about literature and the intricacies involved in the writing of fiction. As such, it follows in the tradition of Russian works that are consciously but obliquely about literature or art, works such as Olesha's *Envy*—a tradition that ultimately extends back to the subtle plays and short stories of Pushkin.

Sinyavsky is, of course, concerned with political abuses and is clearly against the overwhelming domination of all aspects of Soviet life by Stalin's dictatorship, but he is primarily preoccupied with artistic freedom. The arrest, to which any citizen was subject at any time, without warning, was a commonplace of Soviet life during the Terror of the 1930's and then again after World War II. Sinyavsky's account of the narrator's arrest uncannily anticipates his own later arrest and imprisonment; it is the fictional arrest that sets in motion the events of the novel, for only through the narrator's arrest do the police (and the readers) learn of the existence of the formerly secret manuscript. The apparent fragility of the narrator's creation is touchingly depicted in the opening scene, when an escaping letter is destroyed like a bug. The author of the manuscript is himself fragile, easily trapped by the state and sent to prison.

This leads to the realization that there is yet another layer of fantasy operative here, for the entire novel—including both the frame story and the manuscript—actually resurfaces and is subsequently published; the manuscript of the story is only a larger portion of the real manuscript that exists in the form of Sinyavsky's novel. The captured letters have escaped after all, coming to new life in print. The captured narrator, an unfortunate prisoner who is the product of Sinyavsky's imagination, achieves new life within his larger, real novel. If straightforward art cannot appear, Sinyavsky suggests, then the writer must resort to the art of circumlocution. If a literary work is helpless in a police state, then an entire manuscript can be incorporated into another work, and that novel can somehow escape the predatory actions of official limitation. It is through the cunning of fantasy that art survives at all. This is fitting, because fantasy itself is the product of the artistic imagination, an answer to the superficial strictures enforced by politics. The survival of art is the answer to the state, because the actual reality envisioned by art is of a different order from that of the apparent reality of a political system; the boundary between the visible and the hidden is nowhere better demonstrated than in the encounter between the awesome hand of God and the tiny fist of Stalin in Sinyavsky's initial frame segment. The relative disparity between them is but a symbol of the enormous gulf separating apparent and absolute values, be they religious or aesthetic.

THE MAKEPEACE EXPERIMENT

Fantastic elements are more easily discernible in *The Makepeace Experiment* than in *The Trial Begins*. The Russian title of Sinyavsky's second novel is *Lyubimov*, the name of the town that provides the setting for the incredible events of the novel. *The Makepeace*

Experiment was published three years after *The Trial Begins*, and Sinyavsky's greater expertise as a novelist is reflected in the more intricate characterization, fantastic plot, and convoluted narration.

Like his nineteenth century predecessors, Sinyavsky abandons the setting of Moscow in favor of the small, remote town of Lyubimov. It has the flavor of the innumerable squalid hamlets peppering Gogol's prose masterpieces, but it is especially reminiscent of the town in Mikhail Saltykov's novel *Istoriya odnogo goroda* (1869-1870; *The History of a Town*, 1981). *The Makepeace Experiment*, however, is only ostensibly a story of rural life. As circumstances of the plot make amply clear, the events taking place there are actually a microcosm of the larger politico-historical world. Lyonya Tikhomirov's dictatorship (his name means "peaceful world"), the fruitful result of his ability to apply mass hypnosis to the populace of an entire town, bears a certain resemblance to the larger one bedeviling Russians in hundreds of small towns all across the Soviet Union. Lyonya, however, has heeded the idealism of Seryozha in *The Trial Begins*, for this dictatorship is devoid of corruption, greed, and coercion. Through the magic wand of Lyonya's hypnotic powers, the locals believe that toothpaste has changed into fish paste, the local river runs with champagne for thirty minutes, and ordinary bottled water, the sort normally avoided by most of the residents, seems to have turned into grain alcohol and in fact causes the death of one drinker.

Lyonya's aristocratic ancestor, Samson Samsonovich Proferantsov, owned a leather-bound book from India titled *The Magnet of the Soul*. Having accidentally acquired the book, Lyonya masters the contents and sets out to acquire the two things he desires: mind control over the citizens of Lyubimov and the love of the previously indifferent beauty Serafima Petrovna Kozlova. He celebrates his wedding to Serafima simultaneously with his formal installment as official leader of the town of Lyubimov; for a while, events run smoothly, and Serafima is his willing slave. Lyonya has audiences directly with his citizens, attempting to please all of those under his jurisdiction, and they turn Stakhanovite for the dubious reward of ersatz luxuries. He has an elaborate alarm system installed to foil incursions from the outside, using his magnetic powers to baffle would-be enemies, but he becomes increasingly bored with the obedient Serafima and is exhausted by the heavy demands of his office.

Unwilling to be left out of the action, the original owner of the book asserts himself. He scrambles Lyonya's magnetic powers, and our hero's every thought turns into a command subconsciously transmitted to the residents of Lyubimov. A young man silently commanded to "drop dead" collapses and dies of a heart attack; an old woman rides her broom, having become a witch in accordance with Lyonya's desires. The entire utopian society falls apart, and Lyonya escapes in the end, enabling his town to return to normal.

It is in *The Makepeace Experiment* that Sinyavsky introduces a Jewish character for the first time—Serafima Petrovna. The narrator gossips to Lyonya about her ethnic origins and, in the end, the reader learns that she really is part Jewish and that Kozlov was only the name of her first husband. She had kept the existence of her husband and small daughter secret from Lyonya, and there is a hint that these scandalous facts are all related to her Jewishness. Having warned Lyonya that his intended is not really "Russian," the narrator allows himself a digression about Jews. He admires them; they are survivors. They are scattered in society like indissoluble specks, like "raisins" or "black pepper" but never salt. They have Jewish eyes, sad eyes with *tsores* (trouble); Proferantsov calls them "desert eyes."

Sinyavsky's intense interest in Jews extends even to his selection of a Jewish pseudonym, Abram Tertz, a choice that must be regarded as highly unusual for a Russian writer. There are various reasons for his singular interest. In the first place, Sinyavsky resembles Olesha in regarding the writer as a foreign element in society, particularly Soviet society. The writer is like the Jew in his cosmopolitanism, his resultant separation from the mainstream, and his awareness of "trouble." Sinyavsky even flavors his writing with a Jewish accent when describing the Jewish woman who had once been part of his life, a stylistic touch that does not come across in the English translation.

Sinyavsky, however, has yet another complex reason for his apparent obsession: his sense of history. The Jews encountered in Russian society are a reminder that "history did not begin today and it is still not known how it will end." Those desert eyes are sad because of "historical memories." The Jews—and, by extension, the writer—are somehow outside the deterministic orthodoxy that history has evolved along certain lines from the beginning of time. Official Soviet history centers on the concept that the October Revolution was the great break from the capitalism dominating nineteenth century Europe, an economic and political structure giving way to the socialism and eventual communism that will someday grace the Soviet Union. Sinyavsky counters this supposition through his narrator Proferantsov, stating that no one knows how history will end. This incredible statement flies in the face of Marxist orthodoxy, for the presumed final result is the withering away of the state with the triumph of communism. Reality, says Sinyavsky, is unpredictable and cannot be controlled, and he underlines this firmly by his use of fantasy and multiple narrators.

The seeming ordinariness of life gives way at the conclusion of the novel to the ramblings of the narrator Proferantsov, for *The Makepeace Experiment* is a frame story introduced and ended by a chatty writer, in a genre ultimately going back to Pushkin's stories. The narrative here is complicated by the presence of a second narrator, Samson Samsonovich Proferantsov himself, who intrudes into Proferantsov's story in the form of corrective footnotes; it is an irritating practice that does not endear him to his descendant.

By such devices, Sinyavsky makes it impossible for his readers to maintain that "willing suspension of disbelief" so crucial to the flow of most fictional works. He constantly reminds us that we are reading a work of fiction and have entered an artificial world. He underscores this unreality with his pterodactyl, a creature rumored by Dr. Linde, one of the novel's several eccentrics, to inhabit the swampy woods outside town. The pterodactyl indeed exists; it appears to Colonel Almazov, commander of the forces sent to storm the town, during his final drugged moments and seems to speak perfect French. What better witness to this impossible horror than the supporter of state power, a man who would never allow for the oddities of events outside the orthodox conception of reality. The scene between the two is the high point of the novel, the sort of confrontation for which Sinyavsky himself pushed in creating a fantastic world as rival to the rigidity of the real one.

Sinyavsky's fiction provides an excellent illustration of the sort of fantasy he advocated in his theoretical writing. Serving as an antidote to the rigidity of Socialist Realism, it is a reminder that Russian literature still has room for the incredible and unorthodox. Fantasy for Sinyavsky is a vehicle for addressing crucial questions, for it is by circumventing the real world that he is able to deal with such issues as the role and methods of the writer, the meaning of history, and the problems and inequities of the dictatorship that provided the setting for his works. As both artist and thinker, he must be accounted one of the most interesting and significant of contemporary Russian authors.

Janet G. Tucker

OTHER MAJOR WORKS

SHORT FICTION: *Fantasticheskie povesti*, 1961 (*Fantastic Stories*, 1963; also known as *The Icicle, and Other Stories*, 1963).

NONFICTION: *Istoriya russkoy sovetsky literatury*, 1958, 1961; *Chto takoe sotsialisticheskii realizm*, 1959 (as Abram Tertz; *On Socialist Realism*, 1960); *Pikasso*, 1960 (with I. N. Golomshtok); *Poeziya pervykh let revolyutsii, 1917-1920*, 1964 (with A. Menshutin); *Mysli vrasplokh*, 1966 (as Tertz; *Unguarded Thoughts*, 1972); *For Freedom of Imagination*, 1971 (essays); *Golos iz khora*, 1973 (*A Voice from the Chorus*, 1976); *Progulki s Pushkinym*, 1975 (*Strolls with Pushkin*, 1993); *V teni Gogolya*, 1975; *"Opavshie list'ya" V. V. Rozanova*, 1982; *Soviet Civilization: A Cultural History*, 1990; *Ivandurak: Ocherk russkoi narodnoi very*, 1991 (*Ivan the Fool: Russian Folk Belief—A Cultural History*, 2007); *The Russian Intelligensia*, 1997.

BIBLIOGRAPHY

Fenander, Sara. "Author and Autocrat: Tertz's Stalin and the Ruse of Charisma." *Russian Review* 58 (April, 1999): 286-297. Examines Sinyavsky in his role as both cultural critic and the provocateur Abram Tertz; claims that by turning the discredited Joseph Stalin into a double for himself, Sinyavsky/Tertz reveals both the artistry of Stalinism and the mythical privileged place of the writer in Russian culture.

Frank, Joseph. "The Triumph of Abram Tertz." *The New York Review of Books*, June 27, 1991. A brief biographical and critical discussion of the events of Sinyavsky's life and the nature of his fiction. Notes the importance of his trial for having his works published outside the Soviet Union.

Genis, Alexander. "Archaic Postmodernism: The Aesthetics of Andrei Sinyavsky" and "Postmodernism and Sots-Realism: From Andrei Sinyavsky to Vladimir Sorokin." In

Russian Postmodernism: New Perspectives on Post-Soviet Culture, by Mikhail Epstein, Alexander Genis, and Slobodanka Vladiv-Glover. Translated and edited by Vladiv-Glover. New York: Berghahn Books, 1999. These two essays about Sinyavsky's postmodernist writings are included in this examination of Russian fiction, poetry, art, and spirituality after the demise of the Soviet Union.

Grayson, Jane. "Back to the Future: Andrei Siniavskii and Kapitanskaia Dochka." In *Reconstructing the Canon: Russian Writing in the 1980's,* edited by Arnold B. McMillin. Amsterdam: Harwood Academic, 2000. This discussion of Sinyavsky's work is included in a collection of essays examining Soviet writers whose work appeared during the 1980's, a decade in which artists were allowed greater freedom of expression.

_____. "Picture Windows: The Art of Andrei Siniavskii." In *Russian Literature, Modernism, and the Visual Arts,* edited by Catriona Kelly and Stephen Lovell. New York: Cambridge University Press, 2000. Grayson's examination of Sinyavsky's work is included in a collection of essays about the influence of the visual arts on Russian modernist literature, focusing on collaborations between writers and artists, designers, and theater and film directors.

Kolonosky, Walter F. *Literary Insinuations: Sorting Out Sinyavsky's Irreverence.* Lanham, Md.: Lexington Books, 2003. Kolonosky's examination of Sinyavsky's writing focuses on the satire in his work, exploring how the writer uses allegory, parody, and irony to criticize abuses and foolishness.

Lourie, Richard. *Letters to the Future: An Approach to Sinyavsky-Tertz.* Ithaca, N.Y.: Cornell University Press, 1975. Lourie analyzes Sinyavsky's novels, short stories, and other work, placing them within the context of Soviet history and Slavic literature. Compares Sinyavsky's "philosophical satire" to the work of Nikolai Gogol. Includes notes, a bibliography, and an index.

Mathewson, Rufus W., Jr. *The Positive Hero in Russian Literature.* 1975. Reprint. Evanston, Ill.: Northwestern University Press, 1999. Mathewson includes an analysis of Sinyavsky's writing in this examination of the "positive hero," a character who sets an example for readers' behavior. Describes how this model character was a long-standing source of controversy in Russian literature.

Sandler, Stephanie. "Ending/Beginning with Andrei Sinyavsky/Abram Tertz." In *Commemorating Pushkin: Russia's Myth of a National Poet.* Stanford, Calif.: Stanford University Press, 2004. Sandler analyzes Russia's complex relationship with Alexander Pushkin, describing how his work has influenced Sinyavsky and other Russian writers and how his legacy is reflected in museums and other Russian cultural institutions.

Theimer Nepomnyashchy, Catherine. "Sinyavsky/Tertz: The Evolution of the Writer in Exile." *Humanities in Society* 7, no. 314 (1984): 123-142. After providing a brief overview of Sinyavsky's career during his first decade in the West, the author goes on to detail Sinyavsky's concerns with the role of the writer in relationship to reality and society at large. Concludes with a discussion of *Little Jinx.*

ALEKSANDR SOLZHENITSYN

Born: Kislovodsk, Russia, Soviet Union (now in Russia); December 11, 1918
Died: Moscow, Russia; August 3, 2008
Also known as: Aleksandr Isayevich Solzhenitsyn

PRINCIPAL LONG FICTION

Odin den' Ivana Denisovicha, 1962 (novella; *One Day in the Life of Ivan Denisovich*, 1963)
Rakovy korpus, 1968 (*Cancer Ward*, 1968)
V kruge pervom, 1968 (*The First Circle*, 1968)
Avgust chetyrnadtsatogo, 1971, expanded version 1983 (*August 1914*, 1972; expanded version 1989, as *The Red Wheel*)
Lenin v Tsyurikhe, 1975 (*Lenin in Zurich*, 1976)
Krasnoe koleso, 1983-1991 (includes *Avgust chetyrnadtsatogo*, expanded version 1983 [*The Red Wheel*, 1989]; *Oktiabr' shestnadtsatogo*, 1984 [*November 1916*, 1999]; *Mart semnadtsatogo*, 1986-1988; *Aprel' semnadtsatogo*, 1991)

OTHER LITERARY FORMS

Although the literary reputation of Aleksandr Solzhenitsyn (sohl-zheh-NEET-seen) rests largely on his long prose works, this prolific writer experimented in numerous genres. The short story "Matryona's House" is an excellent example of Solzhenitsyn's attention to detail as well as his reverence for old Russian values as exemplified by the peasant woman Matryona and her home. In addition to his short stories, in 1964 Solzhenitsyn published *Etyudy i krokhotnye rasskazy*, a collection of prose poems (translated in *Stories and Prose Poems by Alexander Solzhenitsyn*, 1971), each of which generally conveys a single message by focusing on a solitary image. Solzhenitsyn also composed the long poem *Prusskie nochi* (1974; *Prussian Nights*, 1977), which he committed to paper only after his release from prison. Drama, as well, interested Solzhenitsyn from his early years as a writer. His dramatic trilogy was written between 1951 and 1954, but the plays were never published or staged in the Soviet Union. Solzhenitsyn's eagerness to experiment with different genres and to mesh them makes him an unusually interesting writer. Fairy tales, film scenarios, drama, poetry, and prose are continually found interwoven in Solzhenitsyn's works. A particularly striking example of his desire to mix genres is his history of the Stalinist labor camps, *Arkhipelag GULag, 1918-1956: Opyt khudozhestvennogo issledovaniya* (1973-1975; *The Gulag Archipelago, 1918-1956: An Experiment in Literary Investigation*, 1974-1978).

Aleksandr Solzhenitsyn
(The Nobel Foundation)

ACHIEVEMENTS

 The publication of Aleksandr Solzhenitsyn's first work, *One Day in the Life of Ivan Denisovich*—in Russian in 1962 and in English in 1963—sent shock waves throughout both the East and the West. Suddenly a new voice was heard in the Soviet Union, shattering the long, oppressive decades of silence and revealing forbidden truths of Stalinist society. In his preface to *One Day in the Life of Ivan Denisovich*, Aleksandr Tvardovsky, an established Soviet poet and editor of the journal *Novy mir,* notes that the talent of the young writer is as extraordinary as his subject matter. Tvardovsky states that *One Day in the Life of Ivan Denisovich* is a work of art. The decision to make this comment is revealing, for, from the outset, it has been difficult, if not impossible, for readers both in the East and in the West to evaluate Solzhenitsyn as an artist apart from his political views. Solzhenitsyn became a symbol of hope. Born after the Russian Revolution, educated in the Soviet system, and tempered by war and the Stalinist camps, he was in every sense a Soviet man.

With the publication of *One Day in the Life of Ivan Denisovich*, he also became a Soviet writer published in the Soviet Union—a writer who, through the actions and words of a simple peasant, unmasked decades of terror and tyranny.

Solzhenitsyn's focus on the peasant in *One Day in the Life of Ivan Denisovich* and in the short story "Matryona's House" contributed to the tremendous upsurge and success of the village theme in contemporary Soviet literature. "Village prose," as the movement has been called, treating the concerns of the Soviet Union's vast rural population, represents one of the dominant and interesting trends in the 1960's and 1970's. Solzhenitsyn's initial success undoubtedly encouraged other writers to turn to such subjects as a means of speaking the truth, a means of "acceptable" protest.

The nomination of Solzhenitsyn for the Lenin Prize in 1964 demonstrates the height of popularity and prestige that the author attained in his own country. Although he was not to receive his country's highest literary honor, six years later, in 1970, he was accorded worldwide recognition when he received the Nobel Prize in Literature. In his Nobel lecture, Solzhenitsyn stressed the writer's responsibility to the truth, a responsibility that he took seriously throughout his career. Solzhenitsyn took it upon himself to record—in both his fiction and his nonfiction works—events that would otherwise be lost to the world. His history of the Stalinist camps (*The Gulag Archipelago*) as well as his writings on the prerevolutionary politics of Russia (such as *August 1914*, *Lenin in Zurich*, and *November 1916*) and on the workings of the Soviet literary machine in *Bodalsya telyonok s dubom* (1975; *The Oak and the Calf*, 1980) will serve as historical sources for future generations. Solzhenitsyn's works had been translated into more than forty languages only ten years after his first publication. Popularity and politics aside, Solzhenitsyn will be remembered as a master of Russian prose whose works are among the finest of the twentieth century. His preoccupation with the profound issues confronting humankind and his search for a literary means to express these themes mark him as a great writer.

BIOGRAPHY

Aleksandr Isayevich Solzhenitsyn was born in Kislovodsk, a city in the north Caucasus, on December 11, 1918, one year after the Russian Revolution. His father, whose studies at the university were interrupted by World War I, died in a hunting accident six months before his son was born. Solzhenitsyn's mother, Taisiya Zakharovna Shcherbak, worked as an office clerk throughout Solzhenitsyn's childhood, earning very little money. In 1924, Solzhenitsyn and his mother moved to Rostov-on-Don, a city at that time of nearly a quarter million people. Because of financial considerations and the poor health of his mother, Solzhenitsyn was to continue his education there until he graduated in 1941 from the University of Rostov-on-Don, specializing in mathematics and physics. From an early age, Solzhenitsyn dreamed of being a writer. Having displayed a natural talent for math and finding no adequate literary institution in Rostov-on-Don, however, Solzhenitsyn studied mathematics and physics. Nevertheless, in 1939, Solzhenitsyn decided to pursue his literary interests and began a two-year correspondence course in literature at the Moscow Institute of History, Philosophy, and Literature while continuing his studies in mathematics and physics. He finished this course of study in 1940, the same year that he married Natal'ya Alekseyevna Reshetovskaya (the apparent prototype of Nadya in *The First Circle*). Reshetovskaya, a specialist in physical chemistry and biochemistry, taught at the Agriculture Institute in Rostov-on-Don. On October 18, 1941, Solzhenitsyn was drafted into the Soviet army; he hardly saw his wife for the next fifteen years.

Solzhenitsyn served in the army in various capacities, working his way up to battery commander. He was a decorated and inspiring leader, but his army duty was cut short in February, 1945, when he was summoned to his commanding officer's quarters and arrested. The charges, as was typical throughout the Stalinist era, were not made clear to Solzhenitsyn at that time. Later, he determined that he had been arrested for oblique, derogatory remarks concerning Joseph Stalin and his mismanagement of the war that he had made in a personal journal and in a letter to a friend. Upon his arrest, he was taken to the Lubyanka, the notorious prison in Moscow. On July 7, 1945, after four months of interrogation, he was sentenced to eight years of hard labor. Solzhenitsyn's novella *One Day in the Life of Ivan Denisovich*, his novel *The First Circle*, and his multivolume work *The Gulag Archipelago* are all based on his firsthand experience of the Stalinist labor camps. He, like countless other Soviet citizens, was sentenced, under section 58 of the Soviet penal code, for counterrevolutionary crimes. Solzhenitsyn spent the beginning of his term at Butyrka, a Moscow prison, laying parquet floors, as does Nerzhin, the protagonist of *The First Circle*. Later in 1946, because of his training in mathematics and physics, he was transferred to a *sharashka* (a prison where scientists work on special projects for the state) very similar to the one depicted in *The First Circle*. After one year in the *sharashka*, Solzhenitsyn was sent to a labor camp in northern Kazakhstan. During his stay there, he had a tumor removed; the prisoner was not told that it was malignant.

In February, 1953, Solzhenitsyn was released from prison only to enter perpetual exile (a common Stalinist practice) in Kok-Terek, Kazakhstan. There, Solzhenitsyn taught mathematics until his health deteriorated so severely that, in 1954, he was permitted to travel to Tashkent for treatment. In Tashkent, he was admitted to a clinic where he was treated for cancer and where he gathered material for his novel *Cancer Ward*. After his treatment, he returned to Kok-Terek to teach and began working on the play *Olen'i shalashovka* (pb. 1968; also known as *Respublika truda*; *The Love Girl and the Innocent*, 1969) as well as *The First Circle*. In June, 1956, as a result of the "thaw" that followed Stalin's death in 1953, Solzhenitsyn was released from exile, and he moved to Ryazan, where he taught physics and mathematics until the end of 1962. In Ryazan, he saw his wife for the first time in many years. She had remarried and had two children from her second marriage. In that same year, Reshetovskaya left her second husband and reunited with Solzhenitsyn.

Solzhenitsyn and his wife stayed in Ryazan, where they both taught and where

Solzhenitsyn continued to write in secret. In 1961, upon hearing Aleksandr Tvardovsky's speech to the Twenty-second Party Congress, in which he called for writers to tell the whole truth, Solzhenitsyn, in a bold move, sent his novella *One Day in the Life of Ivan Denisovich* to Tvardovsky's then-liberal journal *Novy mir* (new world). The literary battles waged for the publication of this work and subsequent works by Solzhenitsyn are documented by the author in *The Oak and the Calf* and by Vladimir Lakshin in *Solzhenitsyn, Tvardovsky, and "Novy Mir"* (1980). The response to the novel made Solzhenitsyn an immediate celebrity, and he was nominated for the Lenin Prize in 1964. The political tide was beginning to turn, however, and with it the possibilities for the future publication of Solzhenitsyn's works.

At this time, Solzhenitsyn's unpublished works were already being circulated in samizdat (a self-publishing underground network for literary, philosophical, and political works) and were being smuggled abroad. In 1964, his prose poems appeared in the West German journal *Grani* (facets). By 1966, when Solzhenitsyn's "Zakhar-the-Pouch" appeared in the Soviet press, the political and artistic tensions were further intensified by the highly publicized trials of Andrei Sinyavsky and Yuli Daniel. That same year, permission to publish *Cancer Ward* in the Soviet Union was denied. Finally, in 1968, both *The First Circle* and *Cancer Ward* were published in the West without authorization from Solzhenitsyn.

The following year, Solzhenitsyn was expelled from the Union of Soviet Writers, a fatal blow to his career in the Soviet Union, for without membership, publication there was impossible. The situation was quite serious in 1970, when Solzhenitsyn was awarded the Nobel Prize in Literature. The author did not travel to Sweden to accept the prize at that time for fear that he would not be allowed to return to his country. From that point on, Solzhenitsyn, recognizing the impossibility of publication within his own country, authorized the publication of some of his works abroad. Personal attacks as well as attacks from the Soviet press continued to mount, and, in 1974, after ignoring two summons from the State Prosecutor's Office, Solzhenitsyn was arrested and taken to Lefortovo prison. There he was interrogated, charged with treason, and placed on a plane. Only upon landing was he informed that he had been exiled. Six weeks later, Solzhenitsyn was joined in Zurich by his second wife, Natal'ya Svetlova (he had divorced Reshetovskaya in 1973), their three sons, and his stepson.

In October of 1974, the U.S. Senate conferred honorary citizenship on Solzhenitsyn (an honor bestowed only twice before—on the Marquis de Lafayette and Sir Winston Churchill). He soon settled in Vermont, where he continued to write, deliver occasional lectures, and promote the publication of materials dealing with the Soviet Union.

Living by choice in his Vermont isolation, Solzhenitsyn turned his attention to the past, writing historical works centered on the early twentieth century. His antipathy toward his adopted country was matched only by his lack of contact with his native land and his failure to stay in touch with the evolution of that complex country. He eventually returned to

Russia in 1994, a few years after the collapse of the Soviet Union. Somewhat to his surprise, instead of revisiting the land of the evil gulags and oppressed but saintly people, Solzhenitsyn arrived in a consumerized, highly commercial country striving to compete in European and global contexts. The gulags were remembered only by the oldest and were largely dismissed as uninteresting by the young. Irony had dealt Russian history a new blow by reinstating Russian Orthodoxy and removing secular saintliness—including the monastic, agrarian ideals propounded by Solzhenitsyn, Russia's self-conscious prophet.

Undaunted by his lack of popularity, Solzhenitsyn continued to pursue his platform with the support of many respectable nationalist factions. He tried to reach out to Russians of the post-Soviet era through a television talk show on which he propounded his ideals of a special Slavic nationality and its mission in the world. The program lasted only a few months, however, as objections to his verbosity and unwillingness to listen prevailed. On August 3, 2008, Solzhenitsyn died in Moscow after suffering heart failure.

ANALYSIS

Aleksandr Solzhenitsyn and his novels are better appreciated and understood when the author's vision of himself as a writer is taken into consideration; he believed that a great writer must also be a prophet of his or her country. In this tradition of the great Russian novelists Leo Tolstoy and Fyodor Dostoevski, Solzhenitsyn sought to discover a place for the individual in history and in art. Solzhenitsyn viewed art, history, life, and people as continually interacting, forming a single pulsing wave that creates a new, vibrant, and oftentimes disturbing vision of reality and the future. From his first publication, *One Day in the Life of Ivan Denisovich*, to his cycle of historical novels, *Krasnoe koleso*, Solzhenitsyn concentrated on people's ability to survive with dignity in environments that are fundamentally inhumane. Whatever the situation of his protagonist—whether in a Stalinist prison camp, a hospital, the army, or exile—Solzhenitsyn demands from that character a certain moral integrity, a code of behavior that separates him or her from those who have forsaken their humanity. It is the ability or inability to adhere to this code that renders the protagonist triumphant or tragic.

Given the importance of the interrelationship of history, art, and life in Solzhenitsyn's works, it is not surprising that the works are often preoccupied with the larger issues confronting humanity. For the most part, Solzhenitsyn's novels are concerned less with action and plot than with ideas and ethical motivation. Radically different characters are thrown together into artificial environments, usually state institutions, which are separated from society as a whole and are governed by laws and codes of behavior that are equally estranged from society. Such institutions serve as a means of bringing together and equalizing people who would normally not have contact with one another; previous status and education become meaningless. Physical survival itself is usually at issue—prisoners and soldiers struggle for food, patients for treatment, and "free" people for continued freedom and integrity. For Solzhenitsyn, however, physical survival is not the only issue, or even the primary one. Several of his characters, including Alyosha in *One Day in the Life of Ivan Denisovich* and Nerzhin in *The First Circle*, actually welcome the prison camp experience, for they find their time in camp to be conducive to reflection on fundamental questions.

Nerzhin, like many of the other *zeks* (prisoners in the Stalinist camps), is also aware that, in contrast to the "free" members of Stalinist society, prisoners are allowed greater opportunity to speak their minds, to debate issues freely and openly, and to come to terms with the society and state that have imprisoned them. The freedom that some of the prisoners enjoy, the freedom that the ill-fated patients experience in the *Cancer Ward*, is the freedom encountered by those who have nothing left to lose. As the author indicates through one of the prisoners in *The First Circle*, society has no hold over a person once it has taken everything from him or her. Solzhenitsyn repeatedly returns to the theme of materialism as a source of manipulation and a potential evil in people's lives. According to Solzhenitsyn, those who maintain material ties can never be entirely free, and therefore their integrity can always be questioned and tested. Worldly possessions per se are not evil, nor is the desire to possess them, nor does Solzhenitsyn condemn those who do have or desire them. He is skeptical of their value, however, and ultimately holds the conscience to be humankind's single treasured possession.

Solzhenitsyn's insistence on integrity extends beyond the life of the individual. Solzhenitsyn asserts that because a person has only one conscience, he or she must not allow that conscience to be compromised on a personal level by justifying personal actions or the actions of the state by insisting that the end, no matter how noble, justifies the means. This single observation is the foundation of Solzhenitsyn's attack on the Soviet state. A brilliant, perfect Communist future is not motivation or justification enough for a secretive, censor-ridden socialist state, not in Stalin's time or in the author's lifetime. In Solzhenitsyn's view, corrupt means cannot produce a pure end.

Detractors of Solzhenitsyn in both the East and the West have claimed that his writings are too political and generally unconcerned with stylistic matters. Given the life and the times of the man, these objections fail to be particularly persuasive. Solzhenitsyn's language is rich and textured, and both a glossary (Vera Carpovich, *Solzhenitsyn's Peculiar Vocabulary*, 1976) and a dictionary (Meyer Galler, *Soviet Prison Camp Speech*, 1972) of his language have been produced. Prison slang, camp jargon, political slogans, colloquialisms, and neologisms all mesh in Solzhenitsyn's texts. His attention to language is often voiced by his characters, such as Ignatich in "Matryona's House" or Sologdin in *The First Circle*, and his prose is sprinkled with Russian proverbs and folk sayings that often summarize or counteract lengthy philosophical debates. A further indication of his concern for language can be seen in his insistence on commissioning new translations of many of his works, which were originally issued in hurried translations to meet the worldwide demand for them.

On another stylistic level, Solzhenitsyn employs two narrative techniques that enhance his focus on the exchange of ideas and debate as a means of attaining truth: *erlebte rede*, or quasi-direct discourse, and polyphony. Quasi-direct discourse involves the merging of two or more voices, one of these voices usually being that of a third-person narrator and the other the voice of the character depicted. Through this device, Solzhenitsyn draws the reader as close as possible to the thoughts, perceptions, and emotions of the character without interrupting the narrative with either direct or indirect speech. Similarly, polyphony, a term introduced by the Soviet critic Mikhail Bakhtin in regard to Dostoevski's narrative and structural technique and a term that Solzhenitsyn himself applied to his own novels, is employed in order to present more empathetically a character's point of view. Polyphony allows each character in turn to take center stage and present his or her views either directly or through quasi-direct discourse; thus, throughout a novel, the narrative focus continually shifts from character to character. The third-person omniscient narrator serves as a linking device, seemingly allowing the debates to continue among the characters alone.

In addition to these literary techniques, Solzhenitsyn's prose, particularly in *The First Circle*, is permeated with irony and satire. A master of hyperbole and understatement, Solzhenitsyn is at his best when caricaturing historical figures, such as Vladimir Ilich Lenin and Joseph Stalin, to name but two. Solzhenitsyn further deepens the irony by underscoring small physical and verbal gestures of his targets. The target need not be as powerful as Lenin or Stalin to draw the author's fire, and there are touches of self-irony that provide a corrective to Solzhenitsyn's occasionally sanctimonious tone.

ONE DAY IN THE LIFE OF IVAN DENISOVICH

Not all of Solzhenitsyn's works are dependent on irony and satire. *One Day in the Life of Ivan Denisovich* is striking for its restraint, verbal economy, and controlled tone. This *povest'*, or novella, was originally conceived by the author in 1950-1951 while he was in the Ekibastuz prison. The original draft, written in 1959 and titled "One Day in the Life of a Zek," was significantly revised, politically muffled, and submitted to *Novy mir.*

Set in a labor camp in Siberia, *One Day in the Life of Ivan Denisovich* traces an ordinary day in the life of a prisoner. The author reveals through a third-person narrator the stark, grim world of the *zek* in meticulous detail, including the daily rituals—the searches, the bed checks, the meals—as well as the general rules and regulations that govern his daily existence: little clothing, little contact with the outside world, little time to himself. Every detail of Ivan Denisovich's day resounds in the vast, cold emptiness of this remote camp. As György Lukács noted of the novel, "Camp life is represented as a permanent condition"; into this permanent condition is thrust a common person who quietly and simply reveals the essence of retaining one's dignity in a hopeless, inhumane environment.

Uncharacteristic of Solzhenitsyn's works, the tone of *One Day in the Life of Ivan Denisovich* is reserved, solemn, and dignified; irony surfaces only occasionally. The tone is probably somewhat attributable to the editing of Tvardovsky, whose language is felt here. Throughout the work, which is uninterrupted by chapter breaks, the focus remains on Ivan Denisovich and the passage of this one day. Secondary characters are introduced only insofar as they touch his day, and flashbacks and background information are provided only to deepen the reader's understanding of Ivan Denisovich's present situation. Unlike Solzhenitsyn's later novels, which focus largely on an institution's impact on many different individuals, *One Day in the Life of Ivan Denisovich* focuses on one man. Criticism of the camps is perceived by the reader, who slowly observes and absorbs the daily steps of this man. Only after Solzhenitsyn has revealed the drudgery of that one day, one almost happy day, does he place it in its context, simply stating that "there were three thousand six hundred and fifty-three days like this in his sentence, from reveille to lights out. The three extra ones were because of leap year."

CANCER WARD

Unlike its predecessor, *Cancer Ward* directly reveals the constant intense emotional pressure of its characters and its themes. Solzhenitsyn fixed upon the idea of writing this novel at his discharge from the Tashkent clinic in 1955. He did not begin writing the novel until 1963, and only after a two-year hiatus did he return to serious work on *Cancer Ward*. In 1966, having finished the first part of the work, Solzhenitsyn submitted it to the journal *Novy mir*; it was rejected by the censor. Meanwhile, Solzhenitsyn completed the novel, which soon began to circulate in samizdat. Eventually, *Cancer Ward* was smuggled to the West and published, first in excerpts and later in its entirety. It was never published in the Soviet Union.

On the surface, *Cancer Ward* depicts the lives of the doctors, patients, and staff of a cancer clinic. The two protagonists of the novel, Pavel Rusanov and Oleg Kostoglotov, are socially and politically polar opposites: Rusanov is a member of the Communist Party, well established, living a comfortable life with a wife and a family; Kostoglotov is a former prisoner who arrives at the hospital with no one and nothing. Because of the cancer that has afflicted them both, they find themselves in the same ward with an equally diverse group of patients. The novel is largely plotless and focuses on the contrasting attitudes of the patients in regard to the institution, their treatment, and life and death, as well as other philosophical and political issues.

The one plot line that runs through the novel centers on Kostoglotov, who, having been imprisoned and consequently deprived of female companionship for years, becomes an avid "skirt chaser," pursuing both his doctor, Vera Gangart, who ironically falls victim to the very cancer in which she specializes, and a young medical student, Zoya. Kostoglotov throughout the novel continually objects to the secrecy that surrounds his treatment and demands that he has a right to know. In a twist characteristic of Solzhenitsyn, Zoya informs Kostoglotov that the X-ray treatment that he is receiving will temporarily render him impotent. This serves as another reminder to Kostoglotov that, as in prison, his fate, his manhood, and in fact his life are beyond his control and in the hands of yet another institution. Throughout *Cancer Ward*, the abuses, idiocies, and tragedies of Soviet medical care are revealed, as terminally ill patients are released believing they are cured, patients are misdiagnosed, and hospitals prove to be poorly staffed and supplied.

Unfortunately, *Cancer Ward* suffers from its near absence of plot, its heavy-handed dialogues and debates, and its lack of focus, either on a genuine protagonist or on an all-encompassing theme. The reader feels little sympathy for Rusanov, a Communist Party member, or for Kostoglotov, despite the fact that he has been unjustly imprisoned and is a victim of cancer. Kostoglotov is generally impatient, intolerant, and at times completely insensitive to others. Nevertheless, he does grow in the course of the novel. In a discussion with Shulubin, another patient in the ward, Kostoglotov dismisses Shulubin's warning that happiness is elusive and only a mirage, but when he is finally dismissed from the clinic, Kostoglotov, wandering the streets free from prison and free from cancer, realizes that an appetite can be more easily stimulated than satisfied. By the conclusion of the work, Kostoglotov understands Shulubin's warning and abandons his dreams of love with Vera and Zoya.

Despite the work's significant shortcomings, there are scenes in *Cancer Ward* that remain unforgettable for their sensitivity and poetry. One such scene involves the two adolescents Dyomka and Asya. Dyomka is to lose his leg; Asya, a breast. Asya, a seventeen-year-old, worries about her appearance in a swimsuit and her future with men, lamenting that no man will ever touch her breast. In an act of both hope and despair, Asya asks Dyomka to kiss her breast before, as the narrator observes, it is removed and thrown into the trash. Throughout the novel, compassion, sensitivity, poetry, and philosophy are shamelessly interrupted by the reality of the cancer ward. The sharp contrast between the human spirit of hope and the ominous presence of death and destruction in the form of cancer simultaneously underscores the fragility of human existence and the immortality of the human spirit. It is this spirit that is admired and celebrated in this novel and that is also a feature of Solzhenitsyn's finest work, *The First Circle*.

THE FIRST CIRCLE

The First Circle, like *Cancer Ward*, is largely autobiographical, based in this case on Solzhenitsyn's experiences in the *sharashka*. The author began writing the novel while in exile in Kok-Terek in 1955. Between 1955 and 1958, Solzhenitsyn wrote three redactions of the novel, none of which has survived. After 1962, he wrote four additional redactions of the novel, the last of which appeared in 1978. The novel was first published abroad in 1968 and, like *Cancer Ward*, was never published in the Soviet Union. The 1978 redaction differs from the sixth redaction (the edition used for all foreign translations) largely in the addition of nine chapters. The discussion below is based on the sixth redaction.

The First Circle masterfully combines all of Solzhenitsyn's finest assets as a writer. It is by far the most artistic of his novels, drawing heavily on literary allusions and abounding with literary devices. The title itself is a reference to Dante's *La divina commedia* (c.

1320; *The Divine Comedy*, 1802), alluding to the first circle of Hell, the circle designated for pagan scholars, philosophers, and enlightened people, where the pain and the suffering of Hell are greatly diminished. The *sharashka*, as Lev Rubin indicates in the chapter "Dante's Idea" (chapter headings are particularly revealing in this novel), is the first circle of the Stalinist camps. Unlike Ivan Denisovich, who is in a hard-labor camp, the *zeks* in the *sharashka* have adequate food and livable working conditions. The *zeks* inhabiting the *sharashka* thus have a great deal to lose, for if they do not conform to the rules governing the *sharashka*, they may fall from the first circle into the lower depths of the Stalinist camps.

Three of the four protagonists of the novel, Gleb Nerzhin, Lev Rubin, and Dmitri Sologdin, face a decision that may endanger their continued stay at the *sharashka*. Each must decide whether he is willing to work on a scientific project that may result in the imprisonment of other citizens or whether he will retain his integrity by refusing to work on the project, consequently endangering his own life. The debates and discussions that permeate this novel are thus well motivated, playing a significant role in revealing the character and philosophies of these prisoners while drawing the reader deeply into their lives and minds. The tension of the novel arises as the reader attempts to determine whether each prisoner will act in accordance with his conscience. Placed in a similar situation, Innokenty Volodin, a free man and the fourth protagonist of the novel, decides to risk imprisonment by warning a fellow citizen that he may be in danger. Volodin decides to follow his conscience in the first chapter of the novel; in his case, suspense depends on the questions of whether he will be caught and punished for his actions and whether he will continue to endorse the decision that he has made.

The First Circle is a novel of characters and choices; the choices that must be made by nearly all the characters, primary and secondary, are of compelling interest to the reader, for each choice functions as an echo of another person's choice. The overall impact of nearly every character (free and imprisoned) being faced with a life-threatening decision based on moral issues vividly demonstrates the inescapable terror of the time. Furthermore, the multidimensional aspects of this novel—the wide range of characters from virtually every social stratum, the numerous plots, the use of polyphony, the shifting to and from radically different settings, the views of peasant and philosopher, the plethora of literary allusions, the incredible richness of the language—show the sophistication and remarkable depth of the author.

AUGUST 1914

Solzhenitsyn's historical works were first seen with the publication of *August 1914* in the West in Russian in 1971 and its English translation in 1972. This book was a greatly shortened variant of the intended whole book, and it was met with general perplexity. Paralleling the "literary experimentation" style of his nonfiction work *The Gulag Archipelago* (published in English 1974-1978), Solzhenitsyn casts his figures as embodiments of historical situations and ethical issues. Whereas in *The Gulag Archipelago* he wrote from personal experience, in *August 1914* he tries to reconstruct a past of which he was not a part, with varying results. The book's chapter on Lenin, deliberately withheld from publication in the first edition, was published separately in Paris in 1975 as *Lenin v Tsyurikhe* and translated in 1976 as *Lenin in Zurich*. Solzhenitsyn had expanded and reworked it after his 1974 exile. Many other chapters were written and added in 1976 and 1977.

KRASNOE KOLESO

August 1914 was republished in English in 1989, this time in its entirety. It was identified as a section, or "knot," of Solzhenitsyn's historical series *Krasnoe koleso* (words that translate into English as "the red wheel"). Confusingly, this version was published under the title *The Red Wheel* rather than *August 1914*. By the time of the 1989 translation, Solzhenitsyn had published two more knots of *Krasnoe koleso* in Russian, *Oktiabr' shestnadtsatogo* (1984; translated as *November 1916* in 1999) and *Mart semnadtsatogo* (1986-1988). A fourth knot, *Aprel' semnadtsatogo*, appeared in 1991. That same year the Soviet Union collapsed. The "evil empire" that had formed the fulcrum for the critical leverage of Solzhenitsyn's prose was gone, and Solzhenitsyn became a prophet without a cause. The work, while historical in nature and presumably impervious to the vagaries of political change, settled into Russian literary history almost like an anachronism. It had a very limited readership.

The structure of the work was intended to reveal the nature of Russia's history as Solzhenitsyn believed it to be. Unlike the first publication (*August 1914*), *The Red Wheel* and *Krasnoe koleso* as a whole used a framework composed of "knots," nodes at which historical events are compressed. Solzhenitsyn's philosophy, responding to Tolstoy's from *Voyna i mir* (1865-1869; *War and Peace*, 1886), conforms to the proposition that history is shaped not so much by great people as by all people striving to make the proper ethical choices when forced to take part in significant events. Tolstoy's ideas, however, are revealed in the narration; Solzhenitsyn uses narrative structure instead of describing the idea, leaving the narration in large measure beyond the ordinary means of artistic forms. His intention was to reveal the "full column" of historical actors, yet such a structure tends to obscure history at the same time that it loses literary form through diffusion of the plot.

Solzhenitsyn created an enormous role for himself as a prophet of Russian history with his first novella, *One Day in the Life of Ivan Denisovich*. In his later life, history granted him only a piece of the past. *Krasnoe koleso* fell outside the interest of the Russian readership it was intended to instruct. Moreover, Solzhenitsyn's ambitions and personal interests came under hostile scrutiny by the Russian literati, who questioned his motivation for returning to Russia in 1994. Solzhenitsyn remained unmoved by the criticism, however, and continued to work as before, motivated from within, defiant of the exterior world.

Suzan K. Burks
Updated by Christine D. Tomei

OTHER MAJOR WORKS

SHORT FICTION: *Dlya pol'zy dela*, 1963 (*For the Good of the Cause*, 1964); *Dva rasskaza: Sluchay na stantsii Krechetovka i Matryonin dvor*, 1963 (*We Never Make Mistakes*, 1963); *Krokhotnye rasskazy*, 1970; *Rasskazy*, 1990.

PLAYS: *Olen'i shalashovka*, pb. 1968 (also known as *Respublika truda*; *The Love Girl and the Innocent*, 1969); *Svecha na vetru*, pb. 1968 (*Candle in the Wind*, 1973); *Dramaticheskaya trilogiya-1945: Pir Pobediteley*, pb. 1981 (*Victory Celebrations*, 1983); *Plenniki*, pb. 1981 (*Prisoners*, 1983).

POETRY: *Etyudy i krokhotnye rasskazy*, 1964 (translated in *Stories and Prose Poems by Alexander Solzhenitsyn*, 1971); *Prusskie nochi*, 1974 (*Prussian Nights*, 1977).

SCREENPLAYS: *Tuneyadets*, 1981; *Znayut istinu tanki*, 1981.

NONFICTION: *Les Droits de l'écrivain*, 1969; *A Lenten Letter to Pimen, Patriarch of All Russia*, 1972; *Nobelevskaya lektsiya po literature 1970 goda*, 1972 (*The Nobel Lecture*, 1973); *Solzhenitsyn: A Pictorial Autobiography*, 1972; *Arkhipelag GULag, 1918-1956: Opyt khudozhestvennogo issledovaniya*, 1973-1975 (*The Gulag Archipelago, 1918-1956: An Experiment in Literary Investigation*, 1974-1978); *Iz-pod glyb*, 1974 (*From Under the Rubble*, 1975); *Pis'mo vozhdyam Sovetskogo Soyuza*, 1974 (*Letter to Soviet Leaders*, 1974); *Amerikanskiye rechi*, 1975; *Bodalsya telyonok s dubom*, 1975 (*The Oak and the Calf*, 1980); *Warning to the West*, 1976; *East and West*, 1980; *The Mortal Danger: How Misconceptions About Russia Imperil America*, 1980; *Kak nam obustroit' Rossiiu? Posil'nye soobrazheniia*, 1990 (*Rebuilding Russia: Reflections and Tentative Proposals*, 1991); *Russkii vopros*, 1994 (*The Russian Question: At the End of the Twentieth Century*, 1994); *Invisible Allies*, 1995; *Dvesti let vmeste, 1795-1995*, 2001.

MISCELLANEOUS: *Sochineniya*, 1966; *Six Etudes by Aleksandr Solzhenitsyn*, 1971; *Stories and Prose Poems by Alexander Solzhenitsyn*, 1971; *Mir i nasiliye*, 1974; *Sobranie sochinenii*, 1978-1983 (10 volumes); *Izbrannoe*, 1991.

BIBLIOGRAPHY

Bloom, Harold, ed. *Aleksandr Solzhenitsyn*. Philadelphia: Chelsea House, 2001. Collection of critical essays includes analyses of *One Day in the Life of Ivan Denisovich*, the representation of detention in works by Solzhenitsyn and Fyodor Dostoevski, and Solzhenitsyn's experiences as a creative artist in a totalitarian state.

Ericson, Edward E. *Solzhenitsyn and the Modern World*. Washington, D.C.: Regnery Gateway, 1993. Argues that Solzhenitsyn was never antidemocratic and that his criticisms of the West were made in the spirit of love, not animosity.

_____. *Solzhenitsyn: The Moral Vision*. Grand Rapids, Mich.: Wm. B. Eerdmans, 1980. Presents an analysis of Solzhenitsyn's work from the perspective of the author's Christian vision. Begins with discussion of Solzhenitsyn's theory of art, as enunciated in his Nobel Prize lecture, and then devotes chapters to his major novels as well as to his short stories and prose poems.

Ericson, Edward E., and Alexis Klimoff. *The Soul and Barbed Wire: An Introduction to Solzhenitsyn.* Wilmington, Del.: ISI Books, 2008. Two major Solzhenitsyn scholars provide a detailed biography of the writer and analyses of all of his major fiction.

Feuer, Kathryn, ed. *Solzhenitsyn.* Englewood Cliffs, N.J.: Prentice-Hall, 1976. Collection of thirteen essays includes discussions of Solzhenitsyn's uses of structure and symbolism, the theme of war in his works, and epic and dramatic elements in the works. Also provides an evaluation of the English-language translations of his writings.

Klimoff, Alexis. *"One Day in the Life of Ivan Denisovich": A Critical Companion.* Evanston, Ill.: Northwestern University Press, 1997. Useful guide for readers encountering Solzhenitsyn's novel for the first time. Provides primary source materials, a discussion of the novel within the context of Solzhenitsyn's body of work and of Russian literary tradition, and an annotated bibliography.

Lakshin, Vladislav. *Solzhenitsyn, Tvardovsky, and "Novy Mir."* New York: Oxford University Press, 1980. Presents an insider's view of the publication history of *A Day in the Life of Ivan Denisovich*, involving Aleksandr Tvardovsky, a poet and the editor of the journal *Novy mir.*

Mahoney, Daniel J. *Aleksandr Solzhenitsyn: The Ascent from Ideology.* Lanham, Md.: Rowman and Littlefield, 2001. Focuses on Solzhenitsyn's political philosophy and its impact on twentieth century thinking.

Medina, Loreta, ed. *Readings on "One Day in the Life of Ivan Denisovich."* San Diego, Calif.: Greenhaven Press, 2001. Collection of critical essays is designed to assist students and other readers of the novel. Contributors interpret the novel from a variety of perspectives and provide biographical information about Solzhenitsyn.

Moody, Christopher. *Solzhenitsyn.* 2d rev. ed. New York: Barnes & Noble Books, 1976. Discussion of Solzhenitsyn's literary works to 1975 takes an essentially negative view, in contrast to the generally favorable reception of his early work.

Pearce, Joseph. *Solzhenitsyn: A Soul in Exile.* New York: HarperCollins, 1999. Generally uncritical biography chronicles Solzhenitsyn's evolution from pro-Marxist youth to anti-Soviet writer and, finally, to literary anachronism after the demise of the Soviet Union. Features exclusive personal interviews with Solzhenitsyn, previously unpublished poetry, and rare photographs.

Scammell, Michael. *Solzhenitsyn.* New York: W. W. Norton, 1984. Exhaustive and lively biography deals with practically all important aspects of Solzhenitsyn's life, but does not discuss his writings in detail.

Thomas, D. M. *Alexander Solzhenitsyn: A Century in His Life.* New York: St. Martin's Press, 1998. Personal portrait of the writer provides insights into Solzhenitsyn's struggle with Joseph Stalin and his successors as well as the author's relationships with the two women who provided strong support for his efforts to expose the evils of the Communist regime. Imaginative, well-documented, and at times combative biography includes a discussion of Solzhenitsyn's return to Russia in 1994.

LEO TOLSTOY

Born: Yasnaya Polyana, Russia; September 9, 1828
Died: Astapovo, Russia; November 20, 1910
Also known as: Leo Nikolayevich Tolstoy; Lev Tolstoy

PRINCIPAL LONG FICTION

Detstvo, 1852 (*Childhood*, 1862)
Otrochestvo, 1854 (*Boyhood*, 1886)
Yunost', 1857 (*Youth*, 1886)
Semeynoye schast'ye, 1859 (*Family Happiness*, 1888)
Kazaki, 1863 (*The Cossacks*, 1878)
Voyna i mir, 1865-1869 (*War and Peace*, 1886)
Anna Karenina, 1875-1877 (English translation, 1886)
Smert' Ivana Il'icha, 1886 (novella; *The Death of Ivan Ilyich*, 1887)
Kreytserova sonata, 1889 (*The Kreutzer Sonata*, 1890)
Voskreseniye, 1899 (*Resurrection*, 1899)
Khadzi-Murat, 1911 (wr. 1904; *Hadji Murad*, 1911)

OTHER LITERARY FORMS

The works of Leo Tolstoy (TAWL-stoy), like those of many Russian writers, cannot be divided neatly into long fiction and short fiction. Tolstoy wrote only three full-length novels: *War and Peace, Anna Karenina,* and *Resurrection. Family Happiness, The Cossacks, The Kreutzer Sonata, Hadji Murad,* and the trilogy comprising *Childhood, Boyhood,* and *Youth* could be termed novellas or short novels; the distinction between the two is often not well defined, but most readers would classify *The Cossacks*—the longest of this group—as a short novel. More problematic are the works that exceed the length of the traditional short story (as defined by English-language criticism) but not by a large margin. One such work is *The Death of Ivan Ilyich,* which may be regarded either as a novella (although it is about half the length of *Hadji Murad,* for example) or as a long short story. In turn, such well-known stories as "Khozyain i rabotnik" ("Master and Man"), "Dyavol" ("The Devil"), and "Otets Sergy" ("Father Sergius") are only slightly shorter than *The Death of Ivan Ilyich.*

The point of the foregoing is not to split terminological hairs but rather to emphasize the fact that the term "story," often loosely applied to Tolstoy's fiction, can be misleading. Tolstoy wrote relatively few "short stories" in the classic sense of the term; among those, some of the best known are "Nabeg" ("The Raid"), "Mnogo li cheloveku zemli nuzhno?" ("How Much Land Does a Man Require?"), and the stories collected in *Sevastopolskiye rasskazy* (1855-1856; *Sebastopol,* 1887). Finally, Tolstoy published a number of very short, moralistic tales, largely inspired by the religious reorientation that he experienced in the 1870's.

In addition to his fiction, Leo Tolstoy published a substantial body of nonfiction, par-

Leo Tolstoy
(Library of Congress)

ticularly after his "conversion" to a new—and, in Orthodox terms, heretical—type of Christianity based on his idiosyncratic interpretation of the Gospels. In *Ispoved'* (1884; *A Confession*, 1885), he undertook a penetrating and negative self-evaluation, continued in *V chom moya vera* (1884; *What I Believe*, 1885), while detailing the tenets of this new-found faith. He began to dissect all around him, and specifically the world of art, which led to his two most famous literary essays: *Chto takoye iskusstvo?* (1898; *What Is Art?*, 1898) and *O Shekspire i o drame* (1906; *Shakespeare and the Drama*, 1906), in which Tolstoy attacked the world of Western art. Tolstoy is also the author of a voluminous correspondence stretching from his early adolescence to his death. His collected works appeared in Russia over a thirty-year period (1928-1958), in ninety volumes.

ACHIEVEMENTS

Leo Tolstoy's literary career spanned sixty years of the most productive period in Russian literary history. Tolstoy was a "realist," in the sense that he focused chiefly on the outward physical aspects of human life. He was a master of the psychophysical—that is, the depiction of the inner selves of his characters through carefully honed descriptions of their physical beings. From the first words of his diary to the very last, he perfected a style extraordinary for its logical precision and prosaic, unpoetic tone. His was a world of gray tones and pale colors rather than the black and white of his equally famous contemporary Fyodor Dostoevski. Tolstoy's fiction oscillates between the poles of memoir and invention, war and peace, moralism and neutrality. He is never lighthearted. His moralism, moreover, has frequently been misunderstood. He did not—as his great contemporary Ivan Turgenev thought—abandon fiction for moralism and moralistic essays. Rather, after 1880, he simply changed the emphasis in his fiction. He remained throughout his life a great artistic creator.

Tolstoy's influence has been enormous: By destroying Romantic conventions, he depoeticized the literary universe and gave it a sharpness, even a coarseness, that it theretofore had not known. One sees Tolstoy's influence in the stories of his contemporaries Nikolai Leskov and the great Anton Chekhov, and even in lesser figures such as Maxim Gorky. Tolstoy's impact, however, has been worldwide—in the Thomas Mann of *Buddenbrooks: Verfall einer Familie* (1901; English translation, 1924), in Marcel Proust, in James Joyce, in the ugliness of Stephen Crane's war, in the Saul Bellow of *The Adventures of Augie March* (1953), in the architectonic fiction of Mario Vargas Llosa. More than 180 years after his birth, Tolstoy remains a vital force in world literature.

BIOGRAPHY

Leo Nikolayevich Tolstoy's life was long and eventful, at times even overwhelming his work. Born the fourth child of a noble family, at its estate of Yasnaya Polyana in 1828, he was reared by a nanny, an aunt, a grandmother, and a succession of tutors. Tolstoy's mother—who, before her marriage, was Princess Marya Nikolayevna Volkonsky—died before his second birthday, leaving him only with idealized memories; his father, who died in 1837, left a much more distinct impression. Tolstoy's father, Nikolay Ilyich, a retired lieutenant-colonel, was very much the country gentleman, with a passion for hunting and little interest in literature. From his youth, Tolstoy himself had an extraordinary appetite for physical exercise, especially hunting. He was a gifted linguist, and when he went to Kazan University, he entered as a student of Far Eastern languages but left without a degree. A voracious reader, he inclined toward moral dissatisfaction and self-analysis even as a young man; his diary, which he began on March 17, 1847 (he was then eighteen years old), reveals a constant battle between his reason and his soul.

Once he inherited the family estate, Tolstoy attempted in vain to help the peasants through social reform: He was always at war with the conventions of the world around him. Frustrated by his failure as a reformer, he went to St. Petersburg, then to Moscow, leading the dissipated life of the young noble he was. Despite his considerable social exploits, he managed to earn a degree in literature and philosophy from the University of St.

Petersburg. His first work, written in 1851 but not published until many years after its completion, was "A History of Yesterday," an attempt to re-create in verbal detail a simple day in his life. It illustrates the central preoccupation of his literary existence: How can one transform the reality of events and the fantasy of dreams into words? This initial effort began an outpouring of fiction and nonfiction that dwarfs in volume the writing of any other Russian to this day.

In 1851, Tolstoy entered the army and traveled in the Caucasus—for him, as for many other Russian writers, a paradise on earth. Having become an officer, he became preoccupied with war and the behavior of the soldier during battle; he is said to have looked into the eyes of a soldier firing a gun to attempt a reading of his soul. After the siege of Sebastopol and the fall of the city late in 1855, Tolstoy's active military career was effectively at an end, although he did not officially resign his commission until September, 1856.

By the time of his marriage in 1862, Tolstoy had already achieved a substantial reputation in Russian literary circles. His wife was Sophia Andreyevna Behrs, the daughter of a court physician; at the time of their marriage, Tolstoy was thirty-four, Sophia only eighteen. Their first son was born in 1863; they were to have thirteen children in all. Happy and inspired, Tolstoy began thinking of a great cyclic novel, which was to become *War and Peace*. No sooner was it finished, however, than Tolstoy suffered a letdown: He plunged into a reading of the pessimistic German philosopher Arthur Schopenhauer, and he began to moralize on the great issues of life and death. This produced his second great novel, *Anna Karenina*, clearly a much more pessimistic work than *War and Peace*. Both books were immensely successful and made him world-famous.

As early as 1870, Tolstoy had begun to study Greek. In the years that followed, he read the Gospels as if for the first time. He began to believe that the Orthodox Church—and Christendom in general—had misinterpreted and distorted the teachings of Christ, and he advanced a revolutionary interpretation of Christianity based on his reading of Christ's own words. *A Confession* made him more than a literary figure; he became a prophet of sorts, preaching a religion the kernel of which is nonviolent resistance to evil. His passion for reform led him to visit slums, provide food for starving peasants, and appeal to the czar for mercy for condemned terrorists. He openly associated with social outcasts; his family and relatives came to feel that he had betrayed them, and he was placed under police surveillance.

Concluding that the impulse to do good is killed by civilization and modern culture, Tolstoy asserted the sanctity of the Russian peasant. His outspoken views attracted a following of disciples, among the most prominent of whom was Vladimir Grigoryevich Chertkov, who was soon managing Tolstoy's literary affairs. This led to bitter and prolonged conflict between Chertkov and Tolstoy's wife over the copyrights to Tolstoy's books. Sophia Andreyevna wanted them for the children, while Tolstoy wished to give them up entirely. Meanwhile, Tolstoy sought to practice what he was preaching: He dressed as a peasant, worked in the fields, and gave up wine, meat, and tobacco, although not sex—despite his assault on sexual love in *The Kreutzer Sonata*.

Tolstoy's last full-length novel, *Resurrection*, was written to raise money to send a pacifist sect, the Dukhobors, to Canada. In the novel, Tolstoy continued his criticism of the Orthodox Church, which finally excommunicated him in 1901. His greatest artistic work of his final years, *Hadji Murad*, took Tolstoy back to the Caucasus he so loved. When the Revolution of 1905 shook Russia, he publicly condemned both sides. Angry at his wife, he willed control of his literary estate, without his wife's knowledge, to his daughter Alexandra. His last years were troubled: He had become a sort of world-conscience, and he was tortured by the fact that his life did not live up to his ideals; the almost constant hysteria of his wife added to his misery. Still, he retained a surprising vigor; he was planning a new novel shortly before his death. The manner of his death was indeed characteristic: Sick with pneumonia and confined to bed, he escaped, ostensibly to reach his beloved Caucasus, only to die in the Astapovo railroad station on November 20, 1910.

ANALYSIS

Leo Tolstoy's literary works may be viewed as repeated assaults on Romantic conventions. His view, expressed numerous times throughout his diary, was that such conventions blind both writer and reader to reality. Thus, his goal was to construct a new style, prosaic, matter-of-fact, but sharp and full of contrasts, like life itself. To depict all in motion, the inner world of people and the life surrounding them, is the basic creative method of Tolstoy. He sought to reveal the reality underneath by removing the veneer of custom. Precisely for that reason, Tolstoy was able to write *War and Peace*, a work depicting the ordinary life of an entire period of history in all of its movements, contradictions, and complexity.

Tolstoy, ever the moralist, sought to attain truth through art. In his conception, art is the great unmasker; as he wrote in his diary on May 17, 1896, "Art is a microscope which the artist aims at the mysteries of his soul and which reveals these mysteries common to all." The microscope focuses attention on the telling detail, the apparently meaningless gesture, the simplest expression. To Tolstoy, every inner thought, sense, and emotion was reflected in some physical detail; the resulting psychophysical method was to have a profound influence on later writers. Throughout Tolstoy's fiction, characters are reduced to one or two physical features; the palpable, the perceptible, the visible—this is the universe of Tolstoy.

Tolstoy believed that the literary patterns inherited from the Romantics did not get to the essence of meaning and were thus obsolete. His task: to destroy them. In his diary, he began a series of literary experiments: He made lists, he drew up columns, he numbered propositions in sequence. He was seeking a rational creative method—he wanted to construct narratives that were both factual, that is, true to experience, and aesthetically right.

Tolstoy's first artistic work, "A History of Yesterday," is telling in this respect. It is simply an account of uninteresting things that happen in the course of a day. Tolstoy's problem was to write down an accurate account of a full day: He verges on stream of consciousness as he follows his mental associations and perceives how one thing leads to another. To explain something, one must go back in time to explain its causes; this is Tolstoy the rational analyst. Moreover, there is the problem of what verbal expression does to what it describes. Thus, Tolstoy becomes a dual creator: He is not only the writer writing but also the analyst observing the writer writing. He continually makes remarks, interrupts them, questions himself. Tolstoy the analyst is also a creator, one who is attempting to impose rational order on a series that is nothing more than a random succession of human acts. He pushes analysis to extremes, and because he realizes that there is no limit in time to causation and that he could theoretically go back all the way to the beginning of history, he arbitrarily stops himself and leaves the fragment unfinished.

Thus, even at the beginning of his career, Tolstoy was experimenting with point of view and the literary re-creation of consciousness. This acute self-awareness runs through his oeuvre. As he said in his diary on February 29, 1897, a life that goes by without awareness is a life that has not been lived: "The basis of life is freedom and awareness—the freedom to be aware." To promote such awareness, Tolstoy sought to present things in a new way. To do so, he was obliged to distort, to make the familiar strange. It is no accident that when the Russian Formalist critic Viktor Shklovsky wanted to illustrate the technique he called *ostranenie* ("making strange," or "defamiliarization"), he turned first to the works of Tolstoy, perhaps the supreme practitioner of this device—as in the famous opera scene in *War and Peace* or the church service in *Resurrection*. In such passages, the reader sees familiar experiences as if for the first time. Art has become a path to truth: Tolstoy dissects reality and reconstructs it verbally in a new, more palpable form.

Tolstoy never abandoned this way of looking at reality: He portrayed cause and effect, in sequence. First he selected the facts to be described; then he arranged them. Before him, and even in a novelist such as Dostoevski, the artist's method was to show the result and then explain how it came to be—that is, to go back into the past after depicting the present. Tolstoy's method was the reverse: to show the cause and then the result. Show the wickedness of Napoleon and the strength of Mikhail Kutuzov, for example, and the reader can understand why Russia triumphed against the French.

Of Tolstoy's three full-length novels, only the last, *Resurrection*, is not representative of his distinctive method. This novel, which tells the tale of a repentant noble who seeks to resurrect the life of a young girl whom he once seduced, is full of moral strictures. Precisely because Tolstoy frequently forgot his psychophysical method, the novel fails as a work of art, in contrast to his two earlier and greater novels, which are examples of his method at its best.

WAR AND PEACE

If a conventional novel is a novel with a linear plot focused on one or two central characters, then *War and Peace* is a very unconventional novel. It has no single plot, and it includes more than 550 characters, some fifty of whom play important roles. *War and Peace* is like a gigantic epic, and while it may be called a historical novel, it is not a historical novel in the vein of Sir Walter Scott: There is no great historical distance between the time of composition of the book and the period depicted. It is a book of enormous contrasts, as suggested by the title: war and peace, hate and love, death and life, hero and ordinary person, city and country. For Tolstoy, the world of peace, love, life, and country was the ideal world, but the world of war is the world of *War and Peace.*

The novel began as a story of the ill-fated Decembrist revolt, which took place after the death of Czar Alexander I, in 1825, and before the accession to power of his successor, Czar Nicholas I. Tolstoy seeks to explain the events of 1825. Ever the rationalist, he realizes that to explain 1825, one must examine 1824; to explain 1824, one must examine 1823; and so on. This reasoning (as in "A History of Yesterday") would have carried Tolstoy back to the beginning of time. Arbitrarily, he stopped in 1805 and began his novel there. He never reached 1825: The book covers the period from 1805 to 1812, followed by a twelve-year hiatus, after which the epilogue continues through 1824 to the eve of the 1825 Decembrist revolt. Tolstoy's original plan was to write a family novel rather than a historical novel, with history the scenic decor in which families lived. He completed five versions of the novel: The first, titled "1805," does not resemble the fifth at all.

The book, rather than focusing on individual characters, concentrates on family blocks: Tolstoy used the same contrast technique in portraying the families that he used in treating ideas and events. The main backdrop of the action is the Napoleonic invasion of Russia. From the opening pages in the Moscow salon where Tolstoy first gives a glimpse of his major noble figures, the echoes of the coming Napoleonic invasion can be heard. The reader will watch it develop throughout the novel and will see it ultimately crumble as the great French army is conquered by the Russian climate and expanse.

The book poses two major questions, to both of which it gives answers. First, under what circumstances do people kill one another and expose themselves to death? Tolstoy answers that they do so out of self-preservation and duty. Second, in the battle between life and death, who wins? Life wins, Tolstoy answers, despite the ravages of time. Underlying the whole narrative is a gigantic theory of history based on the idea that the world spins not on the movements of single individuals (heroes) but rather on the movements of masses of people. Thus, the Russian mass will overwhelm the French army and its "hero," Napoleon. It will do this because its commanding officer, Kutuzov, understands that it is the movement of the people that determines the course of history; he is wisely passive. Tolstoy is uncompromisingly a fatalist: Events occur as they do because they are fated to do so; nothing that any single individual does can alter the course of fate. Thus, it is the fate of Russia to undergo the great trials and tribulations of the Napoleonic horror, as it is the fate of Napoleon to lose the crucial battle on Russian soil. Indeed, to underline the importance of this theory, Tolstoy includes, at the end of his novel, a famous epilogue in which he discusses the movements of masses. (Much has been made of this epilogue, but it should be borne in mind that Tolstoy himself omitted it from the 1873 edition of the novel and that the evidence for it is in any case given in the book itself.) *War and Peace* is thus a book with a thesis.

The novel, completely static, in which scenes replace one another but do not flow in a continuous stream, unfolds on two planes: the historical and the familial. Tolstoy writes as if he were composing a massive history of the period. There is an omniscient narrator with a severe national bent. Instead of descriptions of personalities, the reader is given, as in Homer's *Iliad* (c. 750 B.C.E.; English translation, 1611), the everyday facts of human life: birth, marriage, family life, death, and so on. There are no heroes; there is, rather, a sweeping vision of human life, moving one critic to call the book an "encyclopedia of human existence." The novel is characterized by sheer bulk: It presents so much material in such large blocks that the material itself seems to go on after the story has ended. Because of the nontemporal scheme, the reader secures less a feel of artistic framework imposed on all material than a sense of the vivid disconnectedness of real life. Memorable and important as some of the characters may be, no single character dominates the book. Only one is involved from beginning to end: Pierre Bezukhov, the fat, awkward, and bespectacled illegitimate son of a very rich nobleman. His personal quest, to find the meaning of his life, unfolds with the book's events, but in no sense is the novel his story.

The reader looking for great "heroic" characters had best look elsewhere. Heroic characters are a dishonest Romantic convention. The novel contains no great sympathetic or unpleasant figures, none who is extraordinarily beautiful and extraordinarily appealing at the same time. Indeed, the two main contrasting families are combinations of good and bad. The Bolkonskys are a tense mixture of sensibility, intelligence, and narrow-mindedness. Andrey is a hero without a battle who claims to seek peace even though he is at home only at war. Maria—unattractive, mystical, totally devoted—exemplifies almost unjustifiable self-sacrifice. Both characters are dominated by an outwardly detestable father whose peace comes only through his own inner rage. The Rostovs, considerably steadier of mind and background, are a mixture of openness, altruism, and ignorant fear. Natasha is not beautiful, exceptionally intelligent, or extraordinarily adept, but she has unending charm and great possibilities of love. Her parents are wonderful, warm, loving, and foolish. Her brother Nicholas is handsome, intelligent, and dangerously narrow-minded. That Andrey and Natasha eventually come together and almost marry makes no sense, but then history does not have to make sense. That Pierre and Natasha do come together at the end of the novel does, however, make sense, for they share an openness common to virtually no one else in the book. Even the Kuragin family, so attractive and so given to extremes of behavior, is unheroic: The handsome Anatole, who almost marries Natasha, is last seen dying, his leg amputated; his sister Helen, the most beautiful woman in Russia, who marries Pierre and who seems so self-centeredly evil, is redeemed by her apparent willingness to realize that she is restless and can cause only misery to others.

Tolstoy does not write in black and white: All of his characters come in shades of gray, and all wind up fighting Tolstoy's own inner duel, the duel between reason and emotion. Tolstoy was convinced that a natural existence is the best; thus, Pierre and Natasha survive because they are natural, while Andrey perishes because he is not. Kutuzov triumphs over Napoleon because he is more natural.

Tolstoy exploits to the utmost his famous psychophysical technique of showing people through various gestures and traits. Numerous characters come equipped with single pre-dominant features that forever identify them: the upper lip of Lise, the beautiful wife of Andrey, who dies in childbirth; the beautiful white shoulders of Helen; Pierre's habit of looking out over his glasses; the thick, little white hands of Napoleon; the dimpled chin of the French prisoner; the pimple on the nose of the man who leads the merchant delegation that meets Napoleon as he invades Moscow; the round face and composure of Platon Karatayev, the peasant whom Pierre meets in prison, whose roundness is a symbol of his moral completeness and of his ability to accept the world as it is.

Tolstoy rips away conventions: He redraws the world by changing the point of view of the observer. Just as he identifies characters by physical traits and cuts them down to size by knocking the hero out of them, so he destroys conventional perceptions of other elements of life. The battle of Austerlitz, in Tolstoy's description, consists only of a strange little sun, smoke, two soldiers in flight, one wounded officer, and finally Napoleon's little white hand. To Tolstoy, this was the real battle as seen by the soldier. In Tolstoy's view, battle as depicted by the likes of Scott had nothing to do with the real world: It was a result of conventions, and so Tolstoy deconventionalized it, as he did with opera. In placing Natasha, who has never before seen an opera, in an opera house, Tolstoy destroys the essence of opera by refusing to accept its conventions: Thus, a piece of cardboard on which a tree is painted is exactly that.

Tolstoy has rewritten the novel. It is not the form that existed before him; rather, it is a brand-new one that combines philosophy, ordinary people, and large masses and blocks of time. Curiously, *War and Peace* is frequently read to be an affirmation of life, but in fact it is all about death. It is death at the end, leaving the reader on the eve of the brutish Decembrist revolt, where death awaits those, like Pierre, who will be involved. Moreover, the life that will be led as married couples by Pierre and Natasha, and Maria and Nicholas, is not a happy life: It is a life of conventions in which the wives will bear children, the husbands will supply the finances, and so on.

As Tolstoy was completing *War and Peace*, he began to read more and more philosophy and more and more of the Bible. The cycle of pessimism that began in *War and Peace* and turned darker as the book wound toward its end culminated in the gloomy and tragic *Anna Karenina*.

ANNA KARENINA

Written between 1873 and 1877, *Anna Karenina* at first appears to be a completely different novel. The title immediately suggests that the book is centered on one dominant personality around which the book spins its plot. Anna's is the story of the fallen woman. Her fall is intertwined with moral and social questions of behavior, and like an expanding pool, the novel becomes all-encompassing of the Russian society of its day. What the book achieves is no less original than what *War and Peace* achieved: It is the classic story of the fallen woman, but it is combined as never before with the burning moral and social questions of the author's day.

The book begins with the pessimistic note with which *War and Peace* ended. It is a book about disorder. There are no happy couples and there are no happy events. Everything is discordant, as if fate had intended the world not to harmonize. Thus, Anna, who is married to a man whom she does not love, falls in love with a man, Vronsky, who cannot satisfy her. Because the story is contemporaneous with Tolstoy's time, he is able to introduce character types of his day that would not have appeared in *War and Peace*. Chief among them is Stiva Oblonsky, Anna's brother, a shameless opportunist and careerist; he exemplifies much of the evil in the Russian bureaucracy. It is he and his suffering family whom the reader sees first: The Oblonsky family introduces the themes of adultery (Stiva is a philanderer) and contemporary society.

From its opening lines, *Anna Karenina* is a serious and critical book. It develops many of the same contrasts that animate *War and Peace*—city and country, good and evil—but it also adds new conflicts: between sex and love, between guilt and truth. Sex, Tolstoy explains, as did Gustave Flaubert in *Madame Bovary* (1857; English translation, 1886), is a path to trouble. Anna follows her sexual instincts, and as those instincts are produced by modern society, they lead her to her doom. In *War and Peace*, everything seemed logical and sequential, as Tolstoy the rationalist led us from one event to another; in *Anna Karenina*, everything is irrational. The world has become a system of irrational correspondences. Consider the scene in which Anna first meets Vronsky: Fate operates through signs. Vronsky and Anna look at each other and sense a curious bond. The reader is never told why, as would have been the case in *War and Peace*. The stationman is accidentally crushed to death: This is an omen that will culminate many pages later in the famous and gruesome suicide of Anna, when she throws herself beneath a train. Almost unconscious on her way to the station, she reviews her life and her affair with Vronsky in a long passage of stream of consciousness in which readers sense doom, in the form of the dead stationman, pulling her on. Tolstoy, always given over to interior monologues, now goes one step further and gives the free associations of a character bent on self-destruction. Unlike *War and Peace*, this book is unconscious mystery.

Anna Karenina is a long series of emotional collisions. Various pairs of people line up and contrast with one another: Anna-Vronsky, Stiva-Dolly (Stiva's suffering wife), Kitty-Levin. The latter pair is curious. Kitty, Dolly's younger sister, who is originally engaged to Vronsky, is a superficial version of Natasha, with all the playfulness and none of the true openness. Levin, long considered a mouthpiece for the author, is a continuation of a long line of such Tolstoyan moral spokesmen. At the end of the novel, however, one is left with a Levin who senses but a yawning gap in his existence. Nothing is resolved. Everything will go on as before—but in the absence of Anna, now dead.

Every one of the characters is seriously blemished. Anna has a capacity for genuine love, but she also uses people and ultimately cannot bear what fate has in store for her. Vronsky is honest and honorable but lacks real spirit and is not truly perceptive. Stiva is a foolish, fat bureaucrat, content to live in a class structure he does not understand. Anna's husband, Aleksei (note that both he and Vronsky have the same first name, another mysterious correspondence), is shallow and cold but at the death of Anna shows a magnanimity of spirit foreign to Vronsky. Kitty is romantic and playful but in the end conventional; she accepts what fate has done to her. Levin is well meaning and open, but he is a dead generalization, put in the book to make the case for living close to nature (which, in any case, bores him).

The book's tension is extreme. By contrasting the Anna-Vronsky story with that of Kitty-Levin, Tolstoy plays with the reader's perception, as he does in the opera scene in *War and Peace*. In the famous scene in which Anna's husband discusses divorce with a lawyer who keeps trying (unsuccessfully) to catch a moth, the tension becomes almost unbearable. Humans are alive in a world that simply does not care. Thus, the details that in *War and Peace* make up the tapestry of history appear here to form a set of incomprehensible correspondences. Since *Anna Karenina* is focused so clearly on one intrigue, however, it is considerably more conventional in form than *War and Peace:* Its aura of moral gloom is thus directly communicated. The world, Tolstoy is saying, is not worth preserving.

It is no wonder, then, that Tolstoy's next burst of creative energy was given over to nonfiction. In *Anna Karenina*, Tolstoy had blasted not only the Russian bureaucracy but also the school system, the Orthodox Church, and even the peasantry; in his later work, he fully assumed the role of a social critic. Immediately following the completion of *Anna Karenina*, he burst forth in a fit of moral fervor with *A Confession*. As one critic put it, Tolstoy came under the power of his own method, and art retreated before the pressure of self-observation and analysis; his own soul became material for exposition and clarification. Tolstoy changed the proportions in his creative work and became more the moralist than ever before, but he never ceased being an artist, as any reader of *The Death of Ivan Ilyich* or even *Resurrection* well knows.

Philippe Radley

OTHER MAJOR WORKS

SHORT FICTION: *Sevastopolskiye rasskazy*, 1855-1856 (*Sebastopol*, 1887); *The Kreutzer Sonata, The Devil, and Other Tales*, 1940; *Notes of a Madman, and Other Stories*, 1943; *Tolstoy Tales*, 1947; *Tolstoy's Short Fiction*, 1991; *Divine and Human, and Other Stories*, 2000.

PLAYS: *Vlast tmy: Ili, "Kogotok uvyaz, vsey ptichke propast,"* pb. 1887 (*The Dominion of Darkness*, 1888; better known as *The Power of Darkness*, 1899); *Plody prosvesheniya*, pr. 1889 (*The Fruits of Enlightenment*, 1891); *I svet vo tme svetit*, pb. 1911 (*The*

Light Shines in Darkness, 1923); *Zhivoy trup*, pr., pb. 1911 (*The Live Corpse*, 1919); *The Dramatic Works*, 1923.

NONFICTION: *Ispoved'*, 1884 (*A Confession*, 1885); *V chom moya vera*, 1884 (*What I Believe*, 1885); *O zhizni*, 1888 (*Life*, 1888); *Kritika dogmaticheskogo bogosloviya*, 1891 (*A Critique of Dogmatic Theology*, 1904); *Soedinenie i perevod chetyrekh evangeliy*, 1892-1894 (*The Four Gospels Harmonized and Translated*, 1895-1896); *Tsarstvo Bozhie vnutri vas*, 1893 (*The Kingdom of God Is Within You*, 1894); *Chto takoye iskusstvo?*, 1898 (*What Is Art?*, 1898); *Tak chto zhe nam delat?*, 1902 (*What to Do?*, 1887); *O Shekspire i o drame*, 1906 (*Shakespeare and the Drama*, 1906); *The Diaries of Leo Tolstoy, 1847-1852*, 1917; *The Journal of Leo Tolstoy, 1895-1899*, 1917; *Tolstoi's Love Letters*, 1923; *The Private Diary of Leo Tolstoy, 1853-1857*, 1927; *"What Is Art?" and Essays on Art*, 1929; *L. N. Tolstoy o literature: Stati, pisma, dnevniki*, 1955; *Lev Tolstoy ob iskusstve i literature*, 1958; *Last Diaries*, 1960.

CHILDREN'S LITERATURE: *Azbuka*, 1872; *Novaya azbuka*, 1875 (*Stories for My Children*, 1988); *Russkie knigi dlya chteniya*, 1875; *Classic Tales and Fables for Children*, 2002 (includes selections from *Azbuka* and *Novaya azbuka*).

MISCELLANEOUS: *The Complete Works of Count Tolstoy*, 1904-1905 (24 volumes); *Tolstoy Centenary Edition*, 1928-1937 (21 volumes); *Polnoye sobraniye sochinenii*, 1928-1958 (90 volumes).

BIBLIOGRAPHY

Bayley, John. *Tolstoy and the Novel*. London: Chatto & Windus, 1966. Influenced by Henry James's organic conception of the novel, Bayley concentrates on trenchant analyses of *War and Peace* and *Anna Karenina*. He also perceptively examines *Family Happiness*, *The Kreutzer Sonata*, and *The Devil*.

Benson, Ruth Crego. *Women in Tolstoy: The Ideal and the Erotic*. Urbana: University of Illinois Press, 1973. Interesting and provocative piece of feminist criticism concentrates on Tolstoy's changing vision of the role and importance of family life. Suggests that Tolstoy struggled most of his life with a dichotomous view of women, regarding them in strictly black-and-white terms, as saints or sinners, and analyzes the female characters in the major and several minor works in terms of such a double view.

Christian, R. F. *Tolstoy: A Critical Introduction*. New York: Cambridge University Press, 1969. Clearly written work by a leading Tolstoyan who is knowledgeable about his subject's sources and influences. Provides particularly helpful interpretations of *Family Happiness* and *The Kreutzer Sonata*.

Gustafson, Richard F. *Leo Tolstoy, Resident and Stranger: A Study in Fiction and Theology*. Princeton, N.J.: Princeton Univ. Press, 1986. Gustafson seeks to rescue Tolstoy from those who would classify him solely as a realist. By focusing on what he sees as the inherently and uniquely Russian attributes of Tolstoy's writing, Gustafson reunites the preconversion artist and the postconversion religious thinker and prophet. Includes a bibliography divided into two sections: books devoted to Tolstoy and books focusing on Eastern Christian thought.

McLean, Hugh. *In Quest of Tolstoy*. Boston: Academic Studies Press, 2008. Essays by a longtime Tolstoy scholar examine Tolstoy's writings and ideas and assess his influence on other writers and thinkers.

Orwin, Donna Tussig. *Tolstoy's Art and Thought, 1847-1880*. Princeton, N.J.: Princeton University Press, 1993. Attempts to trace the origins and growth of the Russian master's ideas. Focuses on the first three decades of Tolstoy's literary career, first examining his initial creative vision and then analyzing, in depth, his principal works.

_____, ed. *The Cambridge Companion to Tolstoy*. New York: Cambridge University Press, 2002. Collection of essays includes analyses of *War and Peace*, *Anna Karenina*, and *Resurrection* as well as discussions on topics such as Tolstoy as a writer of popular literature, the development of his style and theme, his aesthetics, and Tolstoy in the twentieth century.

Rowe, William W. *Leo Tolstoy*. Boston: Twayne, 1986. Offers a concise introduction to Tolstoy's life and work, with special emphasis on the major novels and later didactic writings. Discusses, briefly, most of Tolstoy's major concerns, and presents excellent treatment of individual characters in the major novels. Includes bibliography.

Shklovsky, Viktor. *Energy of Delusion: A Book on Plot*. Translated by Shushan Avagyan. Champaign, Ill.: Dalkey Archive Press, 2007. English-language translation of the book that some scholars have called the greatest critical work on *War and Peace*. Shklovsky, a prominent Soviet literary critic who died in 1984, examines the form of the novel, what it was like to read the book in the 1980's, and many other aspects of the epic work.

Tolstaia, Sophia Andreevna. *The Diaries of Sophia Tolstoy*. Translated by Cathy Porter, edited by O. A. Golinenko et al. New York: Random House, 1985. This massive personal record of Tolstoy's wife, detailing their life together, spans the years 1862-1910. Sophia Tolstoy kept an almost daily account of her husband's opinions, doubts, and plans concerning his literary activity and social ventures as well as of his relationships with other writers and thinkers. Her notes give a fascinating and intimate view of the Tolstoy family and of the extent to which it served as background for many of her husband's literary episodes. Illustrated.

Wasiolek, Edward. *Tolstoy's Major Fiction*. Chicago: University of Chicago Press, 1978. Superb study concentrates on thorough analyses of ten of Tolstoy's works, including *Family Happiness*, *The Death of Ivan Ilyich*, and "Master and Man." Provides a close and acute reading that is influenced by Russian Formalists and by Roland Barthes. Includes an illuminating brief chronicle of Tolstoy's life and work.

Wilson, A. N. *Tolstoy*. New York: W. W. Norton, 1988. A long but immensely readable biography, breezy, insightful, and opinionated, by a highly regarded British novelist. Includes illustrations and a useful chronology of Tolstoy's life and times as well as notes, bibliography, and index.

IVAN TURGENEV

Born: Orel, Russia; November 9, 1818
Died: Bougival, France; September 3, 1883
Also known as: Ivan Sergeyevich Turgenev

PRINCIPAL LONG FICTION

Rudin, 1856 (*Dimitri Roudine*, 1873; better known as *Rudin*, 1947)
Asya, 1858 (English translation, 1877)
Dvoryanskoye gnezdo, 1859 (*Liza*, 1869; also known as *A Nobleman's Nest*, 1903; better known as *A House of Gentlefolk*, 1894)
Nakanune, 1860 (*On the Eve*, 1871)
Pervaya lyubov, 1860 (*First Love*, 1884)
Ottsy i deti, 1862 (*Fathers and Sons*, 1867)
Dym, 1867 (*Smoke*, 1868)
Veshniye vody, 1872 (*Spring Floods*, 1874; better known as *The Torrents of Spring*, 1897)
Nov, 1877 (*Virgin Soil*, 1877)
The Novels of Ivan Turgenev, 1894-1899 (15 volumes)

OTHER LITERARY FORMS

The literary reputation of Ivan Turgenev (tewr-GYAYN-yuhf) rests primarily on his narrative prose works, which, aside from his novels, include novelettes, novellas, and short stories, the latter a genre in which he excelled and became prolific. In 1847, he began putting together a collection of stories that was published in 1852 bearing the title *Zapiski okhotnika* (*Russian Life in the Interior*, 1855; better known as *A Sportsman's Sketches*, 1932), highly admired by Leo Tolstoy, which includes many of Turgenev's well-known pieces. Turgenev's naturalism was well adapted to the portrayal of the life of poor countryfolk—enough to evoke compassion while inciting indignation at their lot.

Turgenev tried his hand at drama, too, achieving reasonable success with *Gde tonko, tam i rvyotsya* (pr. 1912; *Where It Is Thin, There It Breaks*, 1924), *Kholostyak* (pr. 1849; *The Bachelor*, 1924), *Provintsialka* (pr. 1851; *A Provincial Lady*, 1934), and especially *Mesyats v derevne* (pb. 1855; *A Month in the Country*, 1924), a play whose innovations in many ways adumbrate those of Anton Chekhov.

Turgenev began writing poetry as a student and had some verses published in 1838. Toward the end of his life, he assembled a collection of his poetic works titled *Senilia* (1882, 1930; better known as *Stikhotvoreniya v proze; Poems in Prose*, 1883, 1945). The total profile of Turgenev's literary activities encompasses other forms as well, including opera libretti, essays, articles, autobiographical pieces and memoirs, and even a semi-scientific study on nightingales.

Ivan Turgenev
(Library of Congress)

ACHIEVEMENTS

In the world of letters, Ivan Turgenev stands out as a naturalist, although not in the hammering manner of Émile Zola, the depressing manner of Thomas Hardy, or the milder, veristic manner of Giovanni Verga. Even if the words "idealization" and "sentimentality" are often used in connection with Turgenev, his "Nature school" tonality has neither the idealizing tendency of Sergei Aksakov nor the sentimental tendency of Dmitrii Vasil'evich Grigorovich, both of whom were his compatriots and contemporaries. On the surface, these qualities are there; when one digs further, they are not. If, on one hand, the reader luxuriates in Turgenev's intensely felt descriptions of nature, he or she is, on the other hand, struck by Turgenev's devastating irony (especially as applied to the upper classes) and by the uncompromising realism of his portrayals (of all classes, including the peasantry). Turgenev's worldview—more exactly, the view of his Russia, whose social history his novels chronicle for two decades—is not optimistic. His most famous hero, the controversial Bazarov in *Fathers and Sons*, is a nihilist; otherwise, his "heroes" are nonheroes, that is, "superfluous men." His heroines appear affirmative only in the perhaps important but not exhilarating sense of loyalty and self-sacrifice. Turgenev's sentimental hue coats a tragic substance, and his instinctive idealism is pared by a naturalistic objectivity.

One reason for the initial positive flavor is the constant appearance of the love motif and the delicate treatment of that special aspect of it, its awakening. Another is the sensual way in which nature fits Turgenev's creative scheme, particularly landscapes, which may or may not shape a background to events but reflect, along with his compassion for the serfs, what may well be the author's most genuine inspiration of all. Finally, there is the softening effect produced by a manicured style; a sense of language and its need for immediate communication at the proper level; the use of several adjectives to enhance descriptiveness, individualizing it through incorrectness or strange words or French phrases; and the author's care not to allow an idea to become so involved that it mars the basic tenet: clarity (Turgenev liked the short sentence as much as he disliked the metaphor). He was a craftsman.

Turgenev profited from his many and admired Western friends and writers, Alphonse Daudet, George Sand, Gustave Flaubert, Prosper Mérimée, and Henry James among them. Despite his preoccupation with things Russian, he is the most "Western" of Russian authors and among the most tempered, the least given to extremes, even when he presents the peasants as far more human than their masters. To speak of his friends' influence, however, would be to stretch the point, for, in his homeland, there were also Alexander Pushkin, Mikhail Lermontov, Tolstoy, Aleksandr Herzen, and Fyodor Dostoevski (who hated Turgenev, as shown by the character Karmazinof in Dostoevski's *Besy*, 1871-1872; *The Possessed*, 1913)—to mention but a few Russian writers. Turgenev unquestionably felt an aesthetic and cultural affinity with the West, and he surely believed in the Europeanization of Russia, but he was his own artist, and he wrote his own way as a creator who could see and say more through his personal optic than through varied imitation.

Turgenev's irony notwithstanding, moderation shaped this optic, a moderation that could come down hard on both sides of an issue (why else were both conservatives and radicals outraged at the portrayal of Bazarov?). It was a moderation that implied that, whatever the desirability of Romantic idealism and the rationality of what is reasonable, there are no answers to life's problems. The important thing is to maintain a balanced, liberal altruism. In his speech titled "Gamlet i Don Kikhot" (1860; "Hamlet and Don Quixote," 1930), Turgenev showed that Don Quixote's accomplishments are secondary to the way he feels about people, to his sense of ideal and of sacrifice, his ability to act on indignation, although his fantasy makes him appear a madman. Hamlet, on the other hand, is the total egocentric, doubting, hesitating, and calculating, more concerned with his situation than with his duty. Only the Fates "can show us whether we struggled against visions, or against real enemies." The Knight of the Woeful Countenance made more of an impact on society than did the Prince of Denmark. Turgenev tended to emphasize the social over the human side of things, though one must be cautious in accepting this observation without qualification.

BIOGRAPHY

Ivan Sergeyevich Turgenev was born in Orel, Russia, and spent his early childhood on his mother's estate in Spasskoye. His father, Sergey Turgenev, a former cavalry officer, belonged to the nobility—the fallen nobility—and had acquired solvency with his marriage to a rich heiress, Varvara Petrovna Lutovinova. Unfortunately, this lady was unhappy, matching energy with despotism, loveless toward her husband and harsh toward her servants and three sons. Ivan's passion for reading sometimes managed to keep him out of the reach of her capricious cruelty. German and French tutors taught him their languages, and he listened eagerly when an old servant read to him from Gavriil Derzhavin, Lermontov, Pushkin, and others.

He began the study of philosophy at the University of Moscow, but after his father's death, when the family moved to St. Petersburg and he transferred to the university there, his literary inclinations began to take hold. He met P. A. Pletnev, the new editor (after Pushkin's death) of the journal *Sovremennik*, and published some poetry. Even after he made poetry secondary to prose, he never discarded its sense, either in his lyric view of life (not merely in his descriptions of nature) or in his refinement of style.

In 1838, Turgenev headed westward, first to Berlin, where his attendance at the university (in the faculty of philosophy) was incidental to the various friendships he made with "Westernizers" such as Nikolai Stankevich, Herzen, Timofei Nikolaevich Granovsky, Mikhail Bakunin, and other "progressives," who believed, as opposed to the more orthodox "Slavophiles," that Russia's cultural future lay in emulating the best of Western civilization. Turgenev became one of them ideologically, especially after wider travels in Europe that took him as far south as Rome and Naples. Indeed, after returning to his homeland in 1841, trying his hand at civil service and deciding on a career in writing, he returned to the West in 1847.

Despite the encouragement of Vissarion Belinsky, Turgenev had known more failures than successes in composing verse (much in the Romantic tradition) and came to see realistic narrative prose as his likely avenue as a creative writer. His mother expressed her dissatisfaction with his expressed vocation, as she did in response to his infatuation with the widowed French singer Pauline Viardot (with whom, and with whose family, he formed a strange but close lifetime relationship), by withdrawing financial support, but in 1847 Turgenev proved his point with his first literary success, the short story "Khor and Kalinych." As his short stories continued to appear with consistent success, he became confirmed in his decision and in his Western thrust.

In 1850, Turgenev inherited a large fortune. By his mother's seamstress, he had an illegitimate daughter, who was reared by Pauline and named Paulinette and about whom he was very sensitive (he challenged Tolstoy to a duel—unfought—over an uncomplimentary remark about her). With Pauline providing the music, he also wrote some libretti for light opera. He never married the French diva, but clearly she meant much to him: "Oh, thou, my only friend, oh thou whom I love so deeply and so tenderly," he wrote of her in a poem.

A Sportsman's Sketches was published in 1852. Turgenev, while following in the footsteps of Nikolai Gogol, Lermontov, and the early Dostoevski, aimed at accurate portrayal of the serfs, without idealizing them and without highlighting the negative side; this was well in the tradition of Honoré de Balzac, Sand, and especially Berthold Auerbach, whose *Schwarzwälder Dorfgeschichten* (1843-1860; *Black Forest Village Stories*, 1869), complete with local language, explored the lives and traditions of the German peasants. It is believed that Czar Alexander II was influenced by Turgenev's stories on the occasion of the emancipation of the serfs in 1861. The stories, however, had also displeased the censors under Alexander II's predecessor, Nicholas I, and as a result of an article on Gogol's death, Turgenev was arrested, detained in St. Petersburg, and then forced to reside for eighteen months on his Spasskoye property. He left it in 1853, and a few years later also left Russia—almost for good.

It was then that Turgenev the novelist emerged; his first novel, *Rudin*, appeared in 1856. He was already well known in Russia, France, and Germany, as well as England and Italy. The novels that followed, like the first, all written abroad but all concerned with the social and political problems of Russia, were awaited and discussed—and polemically debated, because, rather than engage in philosophical flights and metaphysical views of the human condition, Turgenev engaged immediate, recognizable issues realistically. In addition, the usual controversy between Westernizers (including Nikolay Dobrolyubov and Nikolay Chernyshevsky) and Slavophiles (including Aleksey Khomyakov, Ivan Vasil'evich Kireevsky, Yuri Samarin, the Aksakovs, and even, though with greater circumspection, Dostoevski) continued to rage, to the point that *Fathers and Sons* was deemed by some a criticism of the new generation. The fact was that at that time, because of the rapid interactions of shifting events and cultural conditions, opinions could change monthly. Hence, the intellectual points of reference in Turgenev's earlier novels are different from those in later novels.

When critics overstress the social importance of Turgenev's novels, they siphon off a good part of his vitality as an artist, for it is not only the social commentary that makes Balzac, Alessandro Manzoni, or Jane Austen great writers. Turgenev's handling of nature and character development alone—without elevating his works' psychological attributes to the level of Dostoevski or James—together with his sense of style and structure, are enough to welcome him to the writers' pantheon. His ability in character portrayal is evident in his comedies, so well interpreted by the young actor Maria G. Savina, with whom he fell madly in love in his twilight years. In his novels, short stories, and plays, however, he remained ultimately the poet rather than the social critic, as his deep and private interest in collecting his prose poems near the end of his life, with no intention of publishing them, suggests—indeed, symbolizes. It is fitting that he returned briefly to Russia in 1880 to deliver a telling lecture in honor of the poet Pushkin, whose monument was being unveiled. Turgenev died of cancer at the home of Pauline Viardot, to whom he had dictated his last story, "An End," in 1883.

ANALYSIS

The idealistic generation of the 1830's and 1840's, the so-called superfluous men and victims of the Russia of Nicholas I, comes to the fore in Ivan Turgenev's first novel, *Rudin*. It is a philosophically articulate generation, little given to action.

RUDIN

Dmitri Rudin fascinates and charms the household of Daria Mikhailovna Lasunskaia with his poetic linguistic abilities and his brilliant capacity for discussion drawing on keen aphorisms and on German Transcendentalists (including Georg Wilhelm Friedrich Hegel), so that instead of staying overnight, he remains for several months. In time, he declares his love for the young Natasha, yet, as the vainglorious human figure he is (something her "lioness" mother and patroness of the arts comes to discern), he withdraws spinelessly, though aware that his love is returned, when he learns of Lasunskaia's opposition. He departs, leaving Natasha hurt.

The story is told by his friend Leznev, not always sympathetically, and it is probable that Turgenev originally wanted to satirize the budding anarchist Bakunin (the novel's original, satiric title was "The Genius"). As such, Rudin would have emerged not as a superfluous man but simply as an unsavory boaster. Events in Russia changed quickly, however: Bakunin's arrest, the death of the admired historian Granovsky, who liked the rebel, and other circumstances invited an "Epilogue" (1855-1856) and finally a last paragraph (1860). Here Rudin dies in the Paris barricades of 1848 in a kind of hero's apologia, in which, from a vain failure, he becomes a tragic failure, a true superfluous man, full of remorse over his treatment of Natasha and conscious that he is "sacrificing [himself] for some nonsense in which [he does not] believe." Now the Russian radicals protested (again the events were changing) against what they believed was an ideological acquiescence to older values. This was a typical Turgenevian situation: the incarnation of a problem in a hero by the writer and the argumentative reaction to it by society.

A HOUSE OF GENTLEFOLK

One answer to the plight of the superfluous man is the return to the soil, to the Russian homeland, "tilling it the best way one can," a task that can be accomplished with a deep sense of religion. *A House of Gentlefolk*, published in 1859—a Slavophile novel that was enormously well received and stirred no polemics—provides this answer. The European-educated nobleman Fedor Ivanovich Lavretsky has remained spiritually Russian and returns to his homeland from Paris when his frivolous wife, Varvara Pavlovna Korobine, beguiled by the delights of the French capital, is unfaithful to him. His goal is to organize his lands with humility, seeing to the well-being of the serfs. He comes across a distant cousin, the serious, religious, and dutiful Liza Kalitina, one of Turgenev's most idealized portrayals—recalling Pushkin's Tatyana in *Evgeny Onegin* (1825-1832, 1833; *Eugene Onegin*, 1881)—of Russian womanhood. Although the shadow of Varvara cannot be dispelled, they fall in love. The impossible union appears briefly possible when a newspaper account reports Lavretsky's wife's death; the story is incorrect, however, and Varvara appears at his home in Russia, only to leave the country estate and move on to the social pleasures of St. Petersburg, where she acquires a new lover. Lavretsky becomes a model landlord, and Liza retires to a convent.

While the plot is typically sparse, the characterization is typically rich: Vladimir Nikolaevich Panshin, the deceptively charming and egotistical young careerist (a pro-Western foil to Lavretsky), who courts Liza before Lavretsky's appearance; her wealthy and widowed provincial mother, Maria Dmitrievna Kalitina; her old German music teacher, Christopher Lemm, a man of unrecognized talent reluctantly living in Russia; Lavretsky's despotic and narrow-minded father; his harsh and fierce Aunt Glafira; his idealistic and poor university friend, Mikhyalevich, who speaks nobly about the duties of landed gentry toward the country and the peasants—these figures and others are to be added to the characters of Lavretsky, Varvara, and above all Liza herself, an array of portraits that pleased the artistic reader and an espousing of ideas that pleased the social forces of the time (the model landlord for the radicals, the Russian consciousness for the Slavophiles, the profound faith and devotion, rectitude, and determination of Liza for those seeking a sociomoral message, like Turgenev's good, religious friend Countess Elizabeth Lambert).

ON THE EVE

On the Eve is also relatively plotless yet sensitive in its drawing of characters; it turns one's eyes back to the West, though the heart of the story throbs in Bulgaria through the most ideal pair of lovers Turgenev ever conceived. There is a contrast between the trifling pedantry of young Russians and the vital commitment of youth elsewhere: The elegant and superficial Pavel Yakovlich Schubin, a fine-arts student, represents the French leaning, while the awkward but good and learned Andrei Petrovich Bersenyev represents the German. Both pursue the superior and beautiful Elena Nikolaevna Strahof, an ardent and noble-minded daughter of a dissipated aristocrat and a faded society belle. Her willpower is no match for her wooers, and it is not surprising that when the Bulgarian patriot Dmitri Insarov passes through (his cause is the liberation of Bulgaria from the Turks), she falls in love with him. Both of his parents having been victims of the Turks, Insarov, though not of sound health, is regarded as the leader of the coming revolt. (The "eve" of the revolt could be the approaching Crimean War and the forthcoming reforms of Alexander II that followed that war.)

Because he returns her love, Insarov fears on the eve of the conflict that Elena is distracting him from his mission and leaves her, but she seeks him out and tells him that her idealism will make her forsake everything for him and his cause. They marry and leave for Bulgaria but get only as far as Venice before he dies. Elena follows the coffin to Bulgaria, where, having no country now, she joins the Sisters of Mercy, who act as army nurses.

Turgenev said that he derived the plot outline from a manuscript handed to him by one V. V. Karataev, who left for Crimea at the outbreak of the war in 1853. It would be reading something into the novel that is not there to see in the Bulgarian Insarov a forerunner of the Russian revolutionary hero, as it would be incorrect to see in the self-sacrificing and idealistic Elena, who is reminiscent of Anita, the wife of the famous Italian patriot Giuseppe Garibaldi, whom Turgenev much admired, a prototype of the revolutionary heroine. In their own way, one religious and one secular, Liza and Elena are the same. At first, the novel disappointed the public, which expected to see the willful Russian man dedicated to a noble cause; the protagonists pointed Westward, as it were, the way Ivan Goncharov's active Stolz, a German, pointed away from the dreamy Russian Oblomov. Here again, however, the value of the work is better sought less in the ideological orientation than in the series of types it presented—in other words, in the characterization (for example, of Uvar Ivanovich).

FATHERS AND SONS

Time and again, discussion of Turgenev's novels focused on his social concerns, relegating the artistic side of his endeavors, characterization (which, to be sure, is central to the communication of these concerns), to a secondary plane. Hence, his most famous novel, *Fathers and Sons*, completed in 1861, around the time of the emancipation of the serfs, and published with some modifications supposedly prompted by publisher M. N. Katkov in 1862, aroused widespread polemics about the ideological facets of the characters, particularly Bazarov, rather than about the balanced objectivity of the characterizations themselves. There is no doubt that Turgenev liked what his "nihilist" (a term that, while not coined by the author, gained currency through this novel) protagonist stood for, but there is equally no doubt that he did not like the way that he stood for it.

Evgeni Bazarov, a medical student, and his friend, Arkadi Kirsanov, stop at the latter's provincial home after a three-year absence. The widowed father, who has taken up with a peasant girl and is a mismanaging member of the landed gentry, especially after the emancipation, lives with Arkadi's uncle, a frustrated and intolerant ex-officer of the guard. In this sedentary, conservative atmosphere, the ineffectualness of which represented everything that the younger generation—the materialistic and utilitarian "new men and women" that Chernyshevsky (in his novel *Chto delat'?*, 1863; *What Is to Be Done?*, c. 1863) and Dobrolyubov (in his essay "Chto takoye Oblomovshchine," 1859-1860; "What Is Oblomovism?," 1903) praised with such ingenuous dullness—could not stand, the insolently cynical and aggressive libertarian views of Bazarov, let alone his uninhibited manner, are hardly received with smiles. In the words of his less militant friend Arkadi, Bazarov "bows before no authority and accepts no principle without examination."

His intellectually cold and antiromantic attitude toward women shocks the old Kirsanov brothers. When the students leave the estate, however, Bazarov meets a widow at a ball, Ana Odintsova, and falls in love withher, despite much self-struggle, in the sentimental, unmaterialistic way he most despised. She eludes him; Arkadi's admiration for his friend cools as he, too, leaves him, preferring to shape his life according to more traditional values. Now Bazarov goes to his own provincial parents (a former army doctor and an uneducated daughter of the lower nobility), lovable if rather naïve, who both love him and fear him. Through an infection sustained in a finger while performing an autopsy on a tubercular body, left unattended because of a lack of cauterizing medication as well as his own apathy, young Bazarov dies.

In the contrast between two generations, the novel divided Russia between "fathers" and "sons." Neither group liked what it read, and both forgot about the fine lines of character, the accurate descriptions of milieus, and the impressive landscapes. The two generations looked at rebellion or not, authority or not, tradition or not, the need to live (to Live) or not, the necessity for change (progress) or not, and in so doing betrayed their desire to have things stated in black-and-white terms: The revolutionaries were scum or could do no wrong; the conservatives were dangerous regressives or the sole pillars of moral strength. Turgenev made Bazarov not sufficiently satanic for the "sons" and not sufficiently godly for the "fathers."

Turgenev appreciated the social-minded impetus of Bazarov's ideas, and at times he gave his protagonist moving, human touches, but he also gave the character offensive, elitist attitudes toward the "oafs" he would use to do the dirty work. Bazarov's quixotic integrity and relentless single-mindedness under the banner of a social cause are not enough to offset his brash intemperance and lack of rational circumspection. Turgenev, like all true creators of types, drew from life synthetically, making his characters composites of what they represented. Bazarov's brutal cynicism and his anticlimactic end, almost making him a pointless victim of his "new realism" founded on science, encouraged the interpretation that Turgenev had parodied Chernyshevsky and Dobrolyubov by caricaturing the revolutionary—an act of faithlessness in the "new men and women." Such had not been his intent, however. Rather, his purpose had been to demonstrate the gap between generations, but more than that, on a more universal level that his immediate reading public by and large missed, to suggest the transience of all ideology—social, political, economic, even moral—in the light of the eternal and fundamental realities of love and death.

SMOKE

This same stress on milieu and characterization examined at arm's length (except for the author's mouthpiece Potúgin), but now with an even more intensified appreciation of the natural setting, obtains in *Smoke*, and the same displeasure on the parts of both radicals and conservatives ensued. Turgenev's idea of putting together a simple love story outside the homeland, in Baden-Baden, Germany, the meeting spot of the European international set, merged with a desire to follow up his observations on postreform Russia, on the biases interfering with the reform itself, the lack of depth of both revolutionaries and aristocracy, and the continuing controversy between Slavophiles and Westernizers. Too many things to say, perhaps, between the covers of one book, but Turgenev, whose career had already peaked, tried it anyway.

The love story involves the protagonist Grigóry Mikhailovich Litvinov and his former fiancé, Irína Pavlovna. Shortly before their wedding was to take place, Irína, embarrassed by her impoverished situation, and after a successful appearance at a high-society ball, jilted Litvinov and married for rank a fatuous and unattractive young general, Ratmírov. Now in Baden-Baden, Litvinov awaits the arrival of his new betrothed, his cousin Tátiana Petrovna Shestova, whose mother will accompany her. Irína is there, too, and the old love is rekindled; she and Litvinov plan to run away together—a plan that Litvinov divulges to the saddened Tátiana—but at the last moment, the general's wife changes her mind, thus disrupting Litvinov's life for a second time. Disconsolate, the latter returns to Russia, where his dedication to work succeeds in bringing about a reconciliation with Tátiana—unconvincing as this happy ending (unusual for Turgenev) sounds.

Innocent and naïve enough as a story, and whatever its autobiographical innuendos (the author had almost married his cousin Olga Turgeneva after a parting from Pauline Viardot in 1850), the novel hits hard at two groups of people: the hypocritical, mercenary, rabble-rousing intellectuals who call themselves radicals, and the vapid, narrow-minded bosses—the "planters"—who do not mend their ways after the emancipation as far as the serfs are concerned. In addition, a good part of the book deals with arguments quite extraneous to the story line: the long discourses by Potúgin, who upholds intransigently the Westernizing ideology as opposed to the cultural distinctiveness of Russia in which the Slavophiles believed. Aleksandr Herzen, with whom Turgenev had crossed swords and who could not embrace the Potúgin-Turgenev philosophy, ultimately seemed sympathetic to the novel (unlike publisher Katkov, who found this occasion to break away from the outspoken author), but the spiritualistically and nationalistically irritable Dostoevski found reason to be thoroughly vexed by it. The point, however, had been made: Matters Russian were enveloped in a symbolic smoke, whether in the cultural ineffectiveness inside the homeland or in its citizens' flavorless lives in Germany. Superfluous men abounded. Turgenev had lived too long away from this homeland to understand what was going on there—this became the facile charge, obviously a weak one, since what he had to say aroused such furor and such partisan passions.

VIRGIN SOIL

Without relinquishing his interest in portraying types, Turgenev turned to depicting the new (post-Alexander II) Russia in his longest and most complex novel, *Virgin Soil*, about the "going to the people" period of the mid-1870's. At the University of St. Petersburg, there is a student, the revolutionary Nezhdánov, the illegitimate son of a nobleman. Nezhdánov earns his living as preceptor at the home of a high dignitary and self-fancying though cautious liberal, Sipyágin. There Nezhdánov meets Sipyágin's crafty and attractive wife and a pair that shares his political persuasion: Sipyágin's poor niece Marianna and his fanatical brother-in-law Markélov, who loves the niece, though his love is unrequited. In fact, Marianna, who dislikes the Sipyágin couple, is drawn in her quest for freedom to Nezhdánov and his revolutionary goals. He, however, is too introspective for action and unsure of those goals, even of loving Marianna. A manager of a paper factory, Solómin, an active, progressive, but practical man, shields Nezhdánov and Marianna (they have fled the Sipyágin household) from the authorities. While Markélov tries to incite insurgency, Nezhdánov distributes pamphlets and attempts ineffectually to stir up revolution, and Marianna does her share by teaching the peasants' children. Attempts are aborted, the intellectuals are suspected by the peasants themselves, Markélov is arrested, and Nezhdánov, dramatically facing his besetting weakness—his inability to decide and to act, whether in a political or a personal context (as Leonard Schapiro has aptly said, "the tragedy of a Hamlet who longs to be a Don Quixote"—escapes arrest through suicide. Solómin and Marianna go into hiding and marry.

Turgenev's message was not revolution, as some of his contemporaries sought to demonstrate, but rather the Solómin brand of compassionate and sober evolution, constantly, efficiently, and practically working toward a diminishing of inequality. Only the educated class, not the well-intentioned and liberal gentry, will bring about reform, unless the gentry develop a true capacity for action and self-sacrifice. Around Solómin, the novel's hero, and the other frontline characters drift a host of secondaries—as usual, as important in the Turgenevian scheme as the primaries, for the message would lack both formation and relief without them: the homely and poor student revolutionary Mashurina, the lively but spineless Páklin (who speaks the author's mind), the wealthy and illiberal landlord Kollomietsev, the old aristocrats Fimushka and Fomushka, Sipyágin's beautiful man-eating wife, and many more. Again, Turgenev drew from reality, and his fundamental greatness continues today to lie in his naturalistic characterizations (alongside his stylistic and descriptive powers), without which he could not feel any confidence in his own ideas. He himself once wrote,

> When I do not have concrete figures before my eyes I am immediately disoriented and don't know where to go. I always feel that an idea opposite to my own could be affirmed with equal reason. But if I speak of a red nose or of a white hair, then the hair is white and the nose is red. No dialectics will be able to alter this state of things.

Jean-Pierre Barricelli

OTHER MAJOR WORKS

SHORT FICTION: *Zapiski okhotnika*, 1852 (*Russian Life in the Interior,* 1855; better known as *A Sportsman's Sketches*, 1932); *Povesti i rasskazy*, 1856; *First Love, and Other Stories*, 1989.

PLAYS: *Neostorozhnost*, pb. 1843 (*Carelessness,* 1924); *Bezdenezhe,* pb. 1846 (*A Poor Gentleman,* 1924); *Kholostyak,* pr. 1849 (*The Bachelor,* 1924); *Zavtrak u predvoditelya,* pr. 1849 (*An Amicable Settlement*, 1924); *Razgovor na bolshoy doroge*, pr. 1850 (*A Conversation on the Highway*, 1924); *Provintsialka*, pr. 1851 (*A Provincial Lady*, 1934); *Mesyats v derevne*, pb. 1855 (wr. 1850; *A Month in the Country*, 1924); *Nakhlebnik*, pb. 1857 (wr. 1849; *The Family Charge*, 1924); *Vecher v Sorrente*, pr. 1884 (wr. 1852; *An Evening in Sorrento*, 1924); *Gde tonko, tam i rvyotsya*, pr. 1912 (wr. 1851; *Where It Is Thin, There It Breaks*, 1924); *The Plays of Ivan Turgenev*, 1924; *Three Plays*, 1934.

POETRY: *Parasha*, 1843; *Senilia*, 1882, 1930 (better known as *Stikhotvoreniya v proze*; *Poems in Prose*, 1883, 1945).

NONFICTION: "Gamlet i Don Kikhot," 1860 ("Hamlet and Don Quixote," 1930); *Literaturnya i zhiteyskiya vospominaniya*, 1880 (*Literary Reminiscences and Autobiographical Fragments*, 1958); *Letters*, 1983 (David Lowe, editor); *Turgenev's Letters*, 1983 (A. V. Knowles, editor).

MISCELLANEOUS: *The Works of Iván Turgenieff*, 1903-1904 (6 volumes); *The Essential Turgenev*, 1994.

BIBLIOGRAPHY

Allen, Elizabeth Cheresh. *Beyond Realism: Turgenev's Poetics of Secular Salvation*. Stanford, Calif.: Stanford University Press, 1992. Attempts to expose the unique imaginative vision and literary patterns in Turgenev's work and argues that readers should not turn to Turgenev merely for transparent narratives of nineteenth century Russian life.

Bloom, Harold, ed. *Ivan Turgenev*. Philadelphia: Chelsea House, 2003. Collection of critical essays about Turgenev's work includes discussion of *Fathers and Sons*. Other essays compare Turgenev's works to those of Ernest Hemingway, Willa Cather, and Sherwood Anderson.

Costlow, Jane T. *Worlds Within Worlds: The Novels of Ivan Turgenev*. Princeton, N.J.: Princeton University Press, 1990. Focuses on four of Turgenev's early novels: *Rudin*, *A House of Gentlefolk*, *On the Eve*, and *Fathers and Sons*. Includes bibliographical references and index.

Dessaix, Robert. *Twilight of Love: Travels with Turgenev*. Washington, D.C.: Shoemaker & Hoard, 2005. Provides insights into Turgenev's life, particularly concerning the writer's experience of love. Dessaix, an Australian writer and scholar of Russian literature, traveled to Turgenev's homes and conducted research at the Moscow Library to locate the "soul" of the Russian writer.

Knowles, A. V. *Ivan Turgenev*. Boston: Twayne, 1988. Excellent introductory study offers a brief biographical sketch and chapters on the start of Turgenev's literary career, the establishment of his reputation, his individual novels, his letters, his final years, and his place in literature. Includes chronology, notes, and annotated bibliography.

Lowe, David A., ed. *Critical Essays on Ivan Turgenev*. Boston: G. K. Hall, 1989. Collection of essays on Turgenev's literary works presents many analyses of his novels, including discussions of *Fathers and Sons*, *On the Eve*, and *First Love*. Includes bibliography and index.

Magarshack, David. *Turgenev: A Life*. London: Faber & Faber, 1954. Illustrated biography by Turgenev's translator concentrates on the events that shaped the author's life, his relationships with Russian and foreign writers, and the factual circumstances surrounding his works. A useful introduction to Turgenev and his opus.

Seeley, Frank Friedeberg. *Turgenev: A Reading of His Fiction*. New York: Cambridge University Press, 1991. Thorough study of Turgenev's fiction is prefaced with an outline of Turgenev's life and a survey of his poetry and plays. This volume incorporates later findings and challenges some established views, especially the traditional notion of the "simplicity" of Turgenev's works. Seeley stresses the psychological treatment that Turgenev allotted to his characters.

Waddington, Patrick, ed. *Ivan Turgenev and Britain*. Providence, R.I.: Berg, 1995. Essays on Turgenev's reputation in England and the United States include reviews by distinguished critics such as Frank Harris, Virginia Woolf, and Edmund Gosse. Waddington provides a comprehensive introduction, explaining the historical context in which these reviews appeared. Includes extensive notes and bibliography.

Yarmolinsky, Avrahm. *Turgenev: The Man, His Art, and His Age*. 1959. Reprint. New York: Collier, 1962. Reliable short biography is useful as an introduction to Turgenev. Addresses all the important stages in his life and discusses the origins of his works, their salient features, and their overall significance for Turgenev and for Russian and world literature. Concludes with a useful chronology and a good bibliography.

YEVGENY ZAMYATIN

Born: Lebedyan, Russia; January 20, 1884
Died: Paris, France; March 10, 1937
Also known as: Yevgeny Ivanovich Zamyatin; Evgenii Ivanovich Zamiatin

PRINCIPAL LONG FICTION

Uyezdnoye, 1913 (novella; *A Provincial Tale*, 1966)
Na kulichkakh, 1914 (novella; *A Godforsaken Hole*, 1988)
Ostrovityane, 1918 (novella; *The Islanders*, 1972)
My, 1927 (wr. 1920-1921; corrupt text), 1952 (*We*, 1924)
Bich bozhy, 1939

OTHER LITERARY FORMS

The Russian literary lexicon includes a number of terms relating to prose fiction that have no exact equivalents in English. Among these is the term *povest'*, defined by Alex M. Shane in his study of Yevgeny Zamyatin (zuhm-YAWT-yihn) as "a fictional narrative of intermediate length"; as Shane notes, this term "frequently has been translated into English by the somewhat nebulous terms 'long short story,' 'short novel,' or the pejorative 'novelette.'" Shane himself prefers "tale" as a translation of *povest'*, but many readers will find "novella" the most useful equivalent.

Zamyatin published roughly a half dozen *povesti*, or novellas, in addition to several dozen short stories, including fables and other forms of short fiction. The dividing line between his short fiction and his long fiction is not always clear-cut, however, and to trace the development of his distinctive narrative techniques, one must consider his fiction as a whole.

Zamyatin was an influential critic and literary theorist as well as a writer of fiction, publishing articles on such writers as H. G. Wells, O. Henry, Anatole France, Andrey Bely, Anton Chekhov, and Maxim Gorky and devoting several broad essays to the evolution of art in general. In these essays, Zamyatin developed an interesting theory of artistic change based on a Hegelian dialectic.

Writing on Russian literature, Zamyatin perceived a "thesis" in the realism of the 1890's and early twentieth century, represented by writers such as Chekhov and Gorky. The "antithesis" came in the form of the Symbolist movement: The Symbolist writers delved into aspects of reality lying beneath the surface of everyday life; their literary techniques became more complex than those of the realists as they tried to capture the inner essence of things. Finally, a synthesis appeared in the form of neorealism, the representatives of which depicted everyday life with the knowledge that there is more to life than appears on the surface. While focusing on everyday reality, they utilized the complex techniques developed by the Symbolists to convey their visions with more power and verisimilitude. Zamyatin considered himself a neorealist along with Bely, Anna Akhmatova, Osip Mandelstam, and others. Zamyatin's observations on Russian art and literature help to illuminate a complicated period in the history of Russian culture.

In addition to his essays and prose fiction, Zamyatin also wrote several original plays, adaptations, and film scenarios. His first two plays, *Ogni svyatogo Dominika* (pb. 1922; *The Fires of Saint Dominic*, 1971) and *Attila* (pb. 1950, wr. 1925-1927; English translation, 1971), depict historical subjects: The former exposes the repressiveness of the Spanish Inquisition, while the latter deals with the epoch of the struggle between ancient Rome and its barbarian invaders. Later works include *Afrikanskiy gost* (pb. 1963; wr. 1929-1930; *The African Guest*, 1971), an original farce on accommodation to the Soviet system, and several adaptations of other writers' work for the screen. His most successful adaptation was of Gorky's *Na dne* (pr., pb. 1902; *The Lower Depths*, 1912) for Jean Renoir's film *Les Bas-fonds* (1936).

ACHIEVEMENTS

Yevgeny Zamyatin's most impressive contribution to world literature is his satiric antiutopian novel *We*, which he wrote from 1920 to 1921. A biting portrayal of a society in which the human spirit is curbed by a totalitarian state, *We* had an important influence on George Orwell's *1984* (1949). In his own country, however, Zamyatin's shorter prose works made a greater impact than his novel, which was not published in the Soviet Union until 1988. His innovative approach to narrative technique helped to shape the writing style of a number of contemporaries, and this impact was doubly enhanced by Zamyatin's role as literary critic and teacher in the post-Revolutionary period. Among those who attended Zamyatin's lectures on art and literature were writers Lev Lunts, Nikolay Nikitin, Veniamin Kaverin, and Mikhail Zoshchenko. Zamyatin's unique prose style and his unrelenting criticism of philistinism and human injustice have lost none of their power over the years, and his work continues to retain its vitality and relevance today.

BIOGRAPHY

The son of a rural schoolteacher, Yevgeny Ivanovich Zamyatin was born in the small town of Lebedyan on January 20, 1884. Located on the Don River, the town lies in the heart of old Russia, and Zamyatin notes that it was famed "for its cardsharpers, gypsies, horse fairs, and the most vivid Russian speech." Provincial Russia would figure prominently in Zamyatin's later fiction, but in his youth, he took little interest in it. Instead, his childhood was marked by a keenly felt isolation. Having few playmates, he regarded books as his real companions. Learning to read at the age of four, he called Fyodor Dostoevski and Ivan Turgenev his "elders" and Nikolai Gogol his "friend."

In 1896, after four years at the local school, Zamyatin enrolled in the *Gymnasium* (college-preparatory secondary school) in Voronezh. Six years later, he finished school with a gold medal, which he immediately pawned when he went to St. Petersburg to study naval engineering. During the next few years, he took classes at the Petersburg Polytechnic Institute, spending his summers working in shipyards and factories throughout Russia. He developed an interest in politics, and he soon joined the Bolshevik Party. During the frenetic political turmoil of St. Petersburg at the end of 1905, Zamyatin was picked up in a mass arrest and was forced to spend several months in solitary confinement; he spent his time in jail writing poetry and studying English. In the spring of 1906, he was released and exiled to Lebedyan, but he could not bear the torpor of the provincial town, and he returned to St. Petersburg illegally. It was not until 1911 that his true status was discovered, and he thus escaped renewed exile for several years.

In the interim, Zamyatin had graduated from the institute and had become a practicing naval engineer; in 1911, he was appointed lecturer at the institute. Moreover, he had just published his first stories: "Odin" (alone), which appeared in 1908, records the saga of an imprisoned student revolutionary who commits suicide because of frustrated love, and "Devushka" (1909; the girl) contains a similarly tragic theme of unfulfilled love. Neither story is the work of a mature artist, but both show that Zamyatin was already experimenting with prose technique. His first successful work was the novella *A Provincial Tale*, which he wrote from 1911 to 1912 during the weeks of seclusion in the country following his exile from the capital. This exposé of stagnation and cruelty in rural Russia sparked a glowing critical response upon its publication in 1913, while his next major novella, *A Godforsaken Hole*, so offended the authorities by its portrayal of inhumanity in a provincial military garrison that they confiscated the magazine in which it appeared.

In 1916, Zamyatin went abroad to work on icebreakers in England, where he wrote and gathered material for two satiric works, *The Islanders* and "Lovets chelovekov" (1922; the fisher of men), which depict the constrained reserve of the British with exceptional skill. After the abdication of Czar Nicholas II in 1917, Zamyatin returned to St. Petersburg and immersed himself in literary activities. During the years from 1917 to 1921, he completed fourteen stories, a dozen fables, a play, and the novel *We*. Zamyatin's works from this period exhibit a wide variety of styles and interests. They include stories that examine the undiluted passions still found in Russia's backwaters, such as "Sever" ("The North," 1966); stories that depict the struggle to preserve humanistic impulses in the difficult conditions of urban life after the Revolution, such as "Peshchera" ("The Cave"), "Mamay," and "Drakon" ("The Dragon"); and ribald parodies of saints' lives, such as "O tom, kak istzelen byl inok Erazm" ("The Healing of the Novice Erasmus").

In addition to writing fiction, Zamyatin gave lectures on writing to young authors in the House of Arts in Petrograd, held significant positions in literary organizations such as the All-Russian Union of Writers, and served as an editor for several journals and publishing ventures, including the World Literature publishing house. The immediate post-Revolutionary period was a time of intellectual ferment. In literature, all topics came under debate—the goals of literature, the proper style and technique for the age, and the relationship of literature to the Revolution itself. On one side of the debate were those groups that called for the creation of proletarian and socially useful literature; on the other were those who believed that literature should be free from any ideological direction. During this period, Zamyatin had considerable influence as a critic and literary mentor. His superbly written articles and speeches attracted a large audience and provoked a wide response.

Throughout his work, Zamyatin adopted the position of a perpetual opponent to the status quo. He attacked every kind of conformity and all attempts to channel a writer's output into an ideologically uniform direction. In his essay "Ya boyus" (1921; "I Am Afraid," 1970), he wrote that "true literature can exist only where it is created, not by diligent and trustworthy officials, but by madmen, hermits, heretics, dreamers, rebels and sceptics." Behind this stand lay a deep, humanistic concern for the individual's spiritual freedom in an era of growing absolutism. The spirit of defiance that had marked his student days in St. Petersburg had not faded, and in fact Zamyatin was in the process of developing a romantic philosophy of revolution that colored many of his articles, speeches, and fictional works.

In essence, Zamyatin believed in perpetual revolution, the ultimate effect of which is to combat what he termed "entropy"—stagnation, philistinism, static and vegetable life. All truths are relative; there is no final truth. It is the obligation of the heretic, the visionary, the imaginative writer to work for the revolution and the distant future. Attainment of one's goal paradoxically becomes defeat, not victory, because the result would be stagnation, not continuation of the struggle. Zamyatin never called for bloody revolution in the streets; on the contrary, he would protest at every manifestation of humankind's inhumanity to humans. His ideal seemed to be a balance of the rational and irrational in people, but his fear of stagnation and regimentation fired his imagination and resulted in his romantic concept of infinite revolution.

Yet, even if one dismisses these ideas as rhetoric, Zamyatin's earnest campaign for the rights of the individual was dangerous enough in a state that condemned individuality and glorified the collective. In 1922, Zamyatin was arrested along with 160 other intellectuals whose activities were considered undesirable. An order for his deportation was signed by the notorious head of the secret police, G. G. Yagoda. Unknown to Zamyatin, however, and very likely against his will, a group of writers and friends succeeded in having the order rescinded. When Zamyatin was released in 1923, he applied for permission to leave the country but was refused.

Zamyatin's production of prose fiction declined sharply after this incident, in part as a result of deepening involvement in his editorial and administrative duties, his growing interest in the theater, and the increasing influence of politics on the realm of literature. The political situation in the Soviet Union became more rigid during the mid-1920's. Joseph Stalin was then in the process of consolidating his dictatorial powers; he introduced the first Five-Year Plan into the economy late in 1928, and with it came a kind of Five-Year Plan in literature, too. A writers' organization named the Russian Association of Proletarian Writers (RAPP), headed by the strident critic Leopold Averbakh, began to dominate the literary arena and with the tacit approval of the party sought to discredit and harass all of those writers who deviated from their ideal of "artisans" producing ideologically sound works about the social benefits of the Five-Year Plan and collectivization.

Zamyatin, who had for some time been known as an "inner émigré," became one of the chief targets of this campaign of vilification. Productions of his plays were canceled, publishing houses were closed to him, and various writers' groups took turns criticizing him. In particular, he was reproached for "extreme individualism" and hostile attitudes toward the principles of Marxism-Leninism and class warfare. Yet Zamyatin, who had written in 1926, "a stubborn, unyielding enemy is far more deserving of respect than a sudden convert to communism," did not break down and confess his "errors" as others did.

Finally, in 1931, Zamyatin wrote a letter to Stalin asking permission to go abroad with the right to return "as soon as it becomes possible in our country to serve great ideas in literature without cringing before little men." Through the intercession of Gorky, Zamyatin's request was granted, and he left in November of that year with his wife. In Paris, he worked on translations, screenplays, and the first part of a novel, *Bich bozhy* (the scourge of God). He hoped to travel to the United States, where he could continue his work in drama and film, but his plans never reached fruition. He died on March 10, 1937.

ANALYSIS

In his essay "Sovremennaya russkaya literatura" (1956; "Contemporary Russian Literature," 1970), Yevgeny Zamyatin contrasts the narrative style of the realists to that of his own generation. He writes,

> By the time the Neorealists appeared, life had become more complex, faster, more feverish. . . . In response to this new way of life, the Neorealists have learned to write more compactly, briefly, tersely than the Realists. They have learned to say in ten lines what used to be said in a whole page.

His own work demonstrates how consistent he was in his search for a concise yet vivid narrative manner. Throughout his career, he experimented with language, imagery, colors, and sounds to craft his own personal narrative voice.

A PROVINCIAL TALE

The outlines of Zamyatin's mature narrative manner are evident in his first major prose work, the novella *A Provincial Tale*, written in 1911-1912. Zamyatin traces the life of a loutish brute named Anfim Baryba, from the moment he is thrown out of his house by his father, through an oppressive affair with a fat widow, a career of theft and dishonesty, and the attainment of a job as a police officer as a reward for betraying a close friend through perjury in a criminal court case. Zamyatin's treatment of Baryba's life highlights the callousness and ignorance that prevail in the primitive backwaters of Russia, and reflects his personal antipathy for stagnant, prejudice-ridden life. Heightening the verisimilitude of this dark vision is the colloquial narrative tone Zamyatin adopts in the story. This distinctive tone, in which the neutral language of an objective narrator is replaced by language drawing heavily on the vernacular of spoken Russian, is termed *skaz*, and Zamyatin's use of *skaz* reflects the influence of such writers as Nikolay Leskov and Alexey Remizov.

On the other hand, the devices that Zamyatin utilizes in character description already bear the hallmarks that later distinguish his mature work. A favorite method of characterization is the identification of a character with an object, animal, or distinctive physical attribute. With this device, Zamyatin can stress a character's personality traits and signal the presence of that character merely by mentioning the established association. When Chebotarikha, the widow with whom Baryba has an affair, first enters the story, Zamyatin notes that she was "spread out like dough." Later, when Baryba begins his liaison with her, Zamyatin writes, "Baryba turned around and . . . sunk his hands deep into something soft as dough." The scene concludes, "Baryba drowned in the sweet, hot dough." Finally, when the woman discovers Baryba's infidelity, she "shook like dough that's risen to the edge of the bucket." It is interesting to note that Zamyatin's penchant for concise yet striking forms of expression does not create a feeling of lightness in *A Provincial Tale*. His tone is somber, and images of stasis and grime prevail, as when the narrator sums up the life of his village: "And so they live in peace, sweating like manure in the heat."

By the end of the 1910's, Zamyatin had developed the vibrant, expressionistic style of *A Provincial Tale* to its fullest extent. His depiction in "The Cave" of Petrograd's urban landscape during the arduous winters following the Russian Revolution remains one of the most impressive representations of that city in Russian literature, which has a long tradition of exposing the unreal or fantastic aspects of the city. For this work, Zamyatin isolates the elements of darkness and cold on a winter night in Petrograd and weaves from them a broad "mother metaphor," to apply a term used by the critic D. S. Mirsky in his book *Contemporary Russian Literature, 1881-1925* (1926). Zamyatin once described his predilection for creating extended metaphoric images: "If I firmly believe in the image . . . it will inevitably give rise to an entire system of related images, it will spread its roots through paragraphs and pages."

The central image here casts Petrograd as a prehistoric, Ice Age setting and the city's inhabitants as cave dwellers who have regressed into a primitive lifestyle that includes worshiping the "greedy cave god: the castiron stove." Isolating one couple, Martin Martinych and his wife, Masha, Zamyatin records how the customs of civilization give way to the more primal instincts for survival. Needing fuel for the stove, Martin struggles with his urge to steal his neighbor's wood. As Zamyatin describes it, there were two Martins "locked in mortal combat: the old one, who loved Scriabin and who knew he must not, and the new one, the cave dweller, who knew—he must." In the frozen wasteland of this city, all choices are bad, and Zamyatin's taut narrative manner heightens the aura of entrapment and despair.

WE

Zamyatin's other memorable urban setting—the futuristic city of the novel *We*—transcends the boundaries of contemporary Russia and attains dimensions of universality. Influenced by his readings of H. G. Wells's utopian writings and repelled by the inflamed rhetoric of the new Soviet state, Zamyatin constructed an anti-utopian novel that both amuses the reader with its ironic humor and unsettles the reader with its startling prediction of totalitarian repression.

Written in the form of a journal by D-503, an engineer building a rocket ship to carry the ideals of the United State to less advanced worlds where people may still languish "in the primitive state of freedom," *We* describes a world in which nearly every action of its citizens is carried out according to strict schedules set by the government and its ruler, the Well-Doer. Even sexual activity is regulated by a rigid system of registration and appointments. Beneath the comic aspects of this society, however, lie such troubling phenomena as rigged elections, denunciations of one's fellow citizens, and the torture and execution of political dissidents.

The plot of the work centers on D-503's discovery of elements within himself that do not harmonize with his belief in order and control—the irrational emotions of love and passion. The object of his arousal is a female number, I-330, a member of a revolutionary group seeking to overthrow the government and to revitalize the world by reintroducing into society the energies of a primitive people who live beyond the Green Wall encircling the United State. I-330's conversations with D-503 contain the ideological message of the novel. An advocate of perpetual revolution, she articulates the fundamental concept that two forces exist in the world—entropy and energy: "One leads into blessed quietude, to happy equilibrium, the other to the destruction of equilibrium, to torturingly perpetual motion." She, of course, prefers the latter, but her revolutionary plans are uncovered by the secret police, the Guardians, and at the end of the novel, the forces of the United State seem to be winning the battle: I-330 has been arrested, and D-503 has undergone an operation to remove the source of his pain—his "fancy."

We unfolds at a rapid pace. D-503's journal entries are laconic, often breaking off in midthought; as in his other works, Zamyatin relies on bold imagery in characterization and description. Thus D-503 notes with shame that he has hairy, apelike hands—an indication of atavistic tendencies within him—while I-330 is distinguished by her black, slanting eyebrows, which form an X on her face—a kind of mathematical variable or unknown that troubles D-503. Zamyatin also makes use of vivid sounds and colors. At times, his manipulation of sounds recalls the prose of Andrey Bely, and his use of color creates an intense network of symbolic associations. Red, for example, is the color of blood and fire, and it is associated with the revolution and surging passion, while pink, a diluted version of red, is the color of the official forms through which the state regulates sexual contact. Zamyatin's handling of color and sound reflects his conviction that "a word has color and sound. From now on, painting and music go side by side."

Mathematics provides another major source of imagery in *We*. D-503 loves the precision of the multiplication tables and abhors imaginary and irrational numbers. Zamyatin's own support for the concept of the irrational in human affairs filters through D-503's opposition to it, and the reader recognizes that the writer owes a substantial debt to the works of Fyodor Dostoevski, particularly his *Zapiski iz podpolya* (1864; *Notes from the Underground*, 1913) and *Bratya Karamazovy* (1879-1880; *The Brothers Karamazov*, 1911). Reminiscent of the former work is the glass-enclosed world of the United State, in which human happiness is calculated according to exact mathematical formulas. This recalls the diatribe of Dostoevski's underground man against a world in which all human facts will be listed in something like logarithmic tables and people will be urged to live in an indestructible crystal palace. Zamyatin even invokes specific imagery used by Dostoevski. The underground man's animosity toward the "stone wall" of mathematics, symbolized in the simple equation $2 \times 2 = 4$, is echoed by D-503's ardent love for this same formula.

From *The Brothers Karamazov*, Zamyatin draws on the parable of the Grand Inquisitor to underscore his distaste for a self-serving ruling order that boasts of having eliminated individual freedom of choice for the sake of human happiness. *We* is a remarkably resonant piece of writing. Fusing dark dimensions of human oppression with light notes of affectionate satire, Zamyatin's novel remains an impressive model of the anti-utopian genre. After several years of working in the charged narrative mode of the early 1920's, Zamyatin gradually began to simplify his narrative techniques, and the tight austerity of his late fiction endows that body of work with understated power. The writer himself commented on the conscious effort he made to achieve this kind of effective simplicity: "It turned out that all the complexities I had passed through had been only a road to simplicity. . . . Simplicity of form is legitimate for our epoch, but the right to simplicity must be earned."

Zamyatin's evolution as a writer reflects the conscious striving of a dedicated artist, and the work he produced as a result consistently exhibits high quality. His innovative approach to narrative and descriptive techniques lends his fiction a special vibrancy and life, while his sensitivity to the demands of the human spirit and his aversion to all forms of repression add moral depth to his art. Although Zamyatin's work appeared as a draft of fresh air in the 1910's and 1920's, its appeal far transcends that time, and he has earned a place of lasting significance in the history of modern Russian literature.

Julian W. Connolly

OTHER MAJOR WORKS

SHORT FICTION: *Bol'shim detyam skazki*, 1922; *Nechestivye rasskazy*, 1927; *Povesti i rasskazy*, 1963; *The Dragon: Fifteen Stories*, 1966.

PLAYS: *Ogni Svyatogo Dominika*, pb. 1922 (*The Fires of Saint Dominic*, 1971); *Blokha*, pr. 1925 (*The Flea*, 1971); *Obshchestvo pochetnikh zvonarei*, pr. 1925 (*The Society of Honorary Bell Ringers*, 1971); *Attila*, pb. 1950 (wr. 1925-1927; English translation,

1971); *Afrikanskiy gost*, pb. 1963 (wr. 1929-1930; *The African Guest*, 1971); *Five Plays*, 1971.

SCREENPLAY: *Les Bas-fonds*, 1936 (*The Lower Depths*, 1937; adaptation of Maxim Gorky's novel *Na dne*).

NONFICTION: *Gerbert Uells*, 1922 (*H. G. Wells*, 1970); *Kak my pishem: Teoria literatury*, 1930; *Litsa*, 1955 (*A Soviet Heretic*, 1970).

MISCELLANEOUS: *Sobranie sochinenii*, 1929 (collected works); *Sochineniia*, 1970-1972.

BIBLIOGRAPHY

Brown, Edward J. "Zamjatin and English Literature." In *American Contributions to the Fifth International Congress of Slavists*. Vol. 2. The Hague, the Netherlands: Mouton, 1965. Discusses Zamyatin's interest in, and debt to, English literature stemming from his two-year stay in England before and during World War I.

Cavendish, Philip. *Mining the Jewels: Evgenii Zamiatin and the Literary Stylization of Rus'*. London: Maney, 2000. A thorough study of the folk-religious background of Zamyatin's sources of inspiration. It traces his attempts to reconcile the folkloric tradition and the vernacular through his artistic expression. In the process, drawing from the past and from the language of the people, he creates literature that is basically modernistic.

Collins, Christopher. *Evgenij Zamjatin: An Interpretive Study*. The Hague, the Netherlands: Mouton, 1973. In this ambitious study, Collins advances a rather complex interpretation of Zamyatin, mostly of *We*, based on Carl Jung's ideas about the conscious, the unconscious, and individualism.

Cooke, Brett. *Human Nature in Utopia: Zamyatin's "We."* Evanston, Ill.: Northwestern University Press, 2002. Cooke interprets the novel from the perspective of evolutionary psychology, analyzing its creation, style, content, and fascination for readers; he places the novel within the context of other works of utopian and dystopian fiction. Includes an index and a bibliography.

Kern, Gary, ed. *Zamyatin's "We": A Collection of Critical Essays*. Ann Arbor, Mich.: Ardis, 1988. A collection of essays on Zamyatin's magnum opus, covering the Soviet view of the novel, mythic criticism, aesthetics, and influences and comparisons. Edward J. Brown's essay *"Brave New World, 1984, and We: An Essay on Anti-Utopia"* offers a particularly incisive comparison of dystopian novels by Zamyatin, Aldous Huxley, and George Orwell.

Richards, D. J. *Zamyatin, a Soviet Heretic*. New York: Hillary House, 1962. An overview of the major incidents and issues in Zamyatin's life and work; an excellent, brief presentation of all facets of a very complex writer.

Russell, Robert. *Zamiatin's "We."* London: Bristol Classical Press, 2000. In the first part of the book, Russell discusses the novel within the context of the Russian civil war, when readers interpreted it as a satire on Soviet life; he also surveys major trends in modern criticism of the novel. The second part provides his own detailed analysis, based on a close reading of the "entries" in the protagonist's diary.

Shane, Alex M. *The Life and Works of Evgenij Zamjatin.* Berkeley: University of California Press, 1968. An unusually comprehensive overall study of Zamyatin in English. Shane covers Zamyatin's life and the most important features of his works, chronologically, in a scholarly but not dry fashion, and reaches his own conclusions. Includes extensive bibliographies.

Slonim, Mark. "Evgeny Zamyatin: The Ironic Dissident." In *Soviet Russian Literature: Writers and Problems, 1917-1977.* 2d ed. New York: Oxford University Press, 1977. Slonim offers a good portrait of Zamyatin as a leading literary figure of his time.

BIBLIOGRAPHY

Every effort has been made to include studies published in 2000 and later. Most items in this bibliography contain a listing of secondary sources, making it easier to identify other critical commentary on novelists, movements, and themes.

THEORETICAL, THEMATIC, AND HISTORICAL STUDIES

Altman, Janet Gurkin. *Epistolarity: Approaches to a Form.* Columbus: Ohio State University Press, 1982. Examines the epistolary novel, explaining how novelists use the letter form to develop characterization, further their plots, and develop meaning.

Beaumont, Matthew, ed. *Adventures in Realism.* Malden, Mass.: Blackwell, 2007. Fifteen essays explore facets of realism, which was critical to the development of the novel. Provides a theoretical framework for understanding how novelists attempt to represent the real and the common in fiction.

Brink, André. *The Novel: Language and Narrative from Cervantes to Calvino.* New York: New York University Press, 1998. Uses contemporary theories of semiotics and narratology to establish a continuum between early novelists and those of the postmodern era in their conscious use of language to achieve certain effects. Ranges across national boundaries to illustrate the theory of the development of the novel since the seventeenth century.

Brownstein, Rachel. *Becoming a Heroine: Reading About Women in Novels.* New York: Viking Press, 1982. Feminist survey of novels from the eighteenth century through the latter half of the twentieth century. Examines how "becoming a heroine" defines for women a sense of value in their lives. Considers novels by both men and women, and discusses the importance of the traditional marriage plot.

Bruzelius, Margaret. *Romancing the Novel: Adventure from Scott to Sebald.* Lewisburg, Pa.: Bucknell University Press, 2007. Examines the development of the adventure novel, linking it with the medieval romance tradition and exploring readers' continuing fascination with the genre.

Cavallaro, Dani. *The Gothic Vision: Three Centuries of Horror, Terror, and Fear.* New York: Continuum, 2005. Study of the gothic novel from its earliest manifestations in the eighteenth century to the early twenty-first century. Through the lenses of contemporary cultural theories, examines readers' fascination with novels that invoke horror, terror, and fright.

Doody, Margaret Anne. *The True Story of the Novel.* New Brunswick, N.J.: Rutgers University Press, 1996. Traces the roots of the novel, traditionally thought to have been developed in the seventeenth century, to classical Greek and Latin texts that exhibit characteristics of modern fiction.

Hale, Dorothy J., ed. *The Novel: An Anthology of Criticism and Theory, 1900-2000.* Malden, Mass.: Blackwell, 2006. Collection of essays by theorists and novelists. Includes commentary on the novel form from the perspective of formalism, structuralism, poststructuralism, Marxism, and reader response theory. Essays also address the novel through the lenses of sociology, gender studies, and feminist theory.

_____. *Social Formalism: The Novel in Theory from Henry James to the Present*. Stanford, Calif.: Stanford University Press, 1998. Emphasizes the novel's special ability to define a social world for readers. Relies heavily on the works of contemporary literary and cultural theorists. Provides a summary of twentieth century efforts to identify a theory of fiction that encompasses novels of many kinds.

Hart, Stephen M., and Wen-chin Ouyang, eds. *A Companion to Magical Realism*. London: Tamesis, 2005. Essays outlining the development of Magical Realism, tracing its roots from Europe through Latin America to other regions of the world. Explores the political dimensions of the genre.

Hoffman, Michael J., and Patrick D. Murphy, eds. *Essentials of the Theory of Fiction*. 2d ed. Durham, N.C.: Duke University Press, 1996. Collection of essays by influential critics from the late nineteenth century through the twentieth century. Focuses on the essential elements of fiction and the novel's relationship to the world it depicts.

Lodge, David. *The Art of Fiction: Illustrated from Classic and Modern Texts*. New York: Viking Press, 1993. Short commentaries on the technical aspects of fiction. Examples from important and minor novelists illustrate literary principles and techniques such as point of view, suspense, character introduction, irony, motivation, and ending.

Lynch, Deirdre, and William B. Walker, eds. *Cultural Institutions of the Novel*. Durham, N.C.: Duke University Press, 1996. Fifteen essays examine aspects of long fiction produced around the world. Encourages a redefinition of the genre and argues for inclusion of texts not historically considered novels.

Moretti, Franco, ed. *The Novel*. 2 vols. Princeton, N.J.: Princeton University Press, 2006. Compendium exploring the novel from multiple perspectives, including as an anthropological, historical, and sociological document; a function of the national tradition from which it emerges; and a work of art subject to examination using various critical approaches.

Priestman, Martin, ed. *The Cambridge Companion to Crime Fiction*. New York: Cambridge University Press, 2003. Essays examine the nature and development of the genre, explore works by writers (including women and ethnic minorities) from several countries, and establish links between crime fiction and other literary genres. Includes a chronology.

Scaggs, John. *Crime Fiction*. New York: Routledge, 2005. Provides a history of crime fiction, explores key subgenres, and identifies recurring themes that suggest the wider social and historical context in which these works are written. Suggests critical approaches that open crime fiction to serious study.

Shiach, Morag, ed. *The Cambridge Companion to the Modernist Novel*. New York: Cambridge University Press, 2007. Essays explaining the concept of modernism and its influence on the novel. Detailed examination of works by writers from various countries, all influenced by the modernist movement. Includes a detailed chronology.

Vice, Sue. *Holocaust Fiction.* New York: Routledge, 2000. Examines controversies generated by novels about the Holocaust. Focuses on eight important works, but also offers observations on the polemics surrounding publication of books on this topic.

Zunshine, Lisa. *Why We Read Fiction: Theory of Mind and the Novel.* Columbus: Ohio State University Press, 2006. Applies theories of cognitive psychology to novel reading, explaining how experience and human nature lead readers to constrain their interpretations of a given text. Provides numerous examples from well-known novels to illustrate how and why readers find pleasure in fiction.

THE RUSSIAN NOVEL

Brown, Deming. *The Last Years of Soviet Russian Literature: Prose Fiction, 1975-1991.* New York: Cambridge University Press, 1993. Explores trends in Soviet Russian fiction during the final years of the Soviet Union. Also examines changes in publication practices that allowed for the rehabilitation of some dissident writers. Considers work by established writers and those who emerged on the literary scene during this period.

Clark, Katerina. *The Soviet Novel: History as Ritual.* 3d ed. Bloomington: Indiana University Press, 2000. Critical analysis of Soviet fiction by writers who followed the dictates of Socialist Realism, the only approved form of literature in the Soviet Union. Examines elements of this form of fiction and explains how the genre was intended to support larger political aims.

Freeborn, Richard. *The Russian Revolutionary Novel: Turgenev to Pasternak.* New York: Cambridge University Press, 1982. Describes the phenomenon of the revolutionary novel and examines elements of the genre in a number of representative works. Stresses the importance of these novels in documenting imperialist rule and the totalitarian Communist state.

Gasperetti, David. *The Rise of the Russian Novel: Carnival, Stylization, and Mockery of the West.* DeKalb: Northern Illinois University Press, 1998. Study of eighteenth century Russian novels often ignored by literary historians. Explains how issues addressed in these works, and techniques developed by their authors, were important in shaping the great Russian novels of the nineteenth century.

Gillespie, David. *The Twentieth-Century Russian Novel: An Introduction.* Washington, D.C.: Berg, 1996. Study of characteristics of selected novels that illustrate the political situation in the Soviet Union during the seven decades of Communist Party rule. Provides brief plot summaries and critical discussions of key texts; also focuses on the fate of writers during this period.

Ungurianu, Dan. *Plotting History: The Russian Historical Novel in the Imperial Age.* Madison: University of Wisconsin Press, 2007. Theoretically based analysis of a genre popular during the nineteenth century. Explains how novelists use history as the basis of their fiction, and why Russian readers were attracted to this form. Includes a chronology of historical novels published in Russia between 1829 and 1917.

Unwin, Timothy. *The Cambridge Companion to the French Novel from 1800 to the Present*. New York: Cambridge University Press, 1997. Examines the evolution of the French novel from the early nineteenth century to the late twentieth century. Emphasizes major changes introduced by modernism, World Wars I and II, and the postcolonial period.

Laurence W. Mazzeno

GLOSSARY OF LITERARY TERMS

absurdism: A philosophical attitude, pervading much of modern drama and fiction, that underlines the isolation and alienation that humans experience, having been thrown into what absurdists see as a godless universe devoid of religious, spiritual, or metaphysical meaning. Conspicuous in its lack of logic, consistency, coherence, intelligibility, and realism, the literature of the absurd depicts the anguish, forlornness, and despair inherent in the human condition. Counter to the rationalist assumptions of traditional humanism, absurdism denies the existence of universal truth or value.

allegory: A literary mode in which a second level of meaning, wherein characters, events, and settings represent abstractions, is encoded within the surface narrative. The allegorical mode may dominate an entire work, in which case the encoded message is the work's primary reason for being, or it may be an element in a work otherwise interesting and meaningful for its surface story alone. Elements of allegory may be found in Jonathan Swift's *Gulliver's Travels* (1726) and Thomas Mann's *Der Zauberberg* (1924; *The Magic Mountain,* 1927).

anatomy: Literally the term means the "cutting up" or "dissection" of a subject into its constituent parts for closer examination. Northrop Frye, in his *Anatomy of Criticism* (1957), uses the term to refer to a narrative that deals with mental attitudes rather than people. As opposed to the novel, the anatomy features stylized figures who are mouthpieces for the ideas they represent.

antagonist: The character in fiction who stands as a rival or opponent to the *protagonist.*

antihero: Defined by Seán O'Faoláin as a fictional figure who, deprived of social sanctions and definitions, is always trying to define himself and to establish his own codes. Ahab may be seen as the antihero of Herman Melville's *Moby Dick* (1851).

archetype: The term "archetype" entered literary criticism from the psychology of Carl Jung, who defined archetypes as "primordial images" from the "collective unconscious" of humankind. Jung believed that works of art derive much of their power from the unconscious appeal of these images to ancestral memories. In his extremely influential *Anatomy of Criticism* (1957), Northrop Frye gave another sense of the term wide currency, defining the archetype as "a symbol, usually an image, which recurs often enough in literature to be recognizable as an element of one's literary experience as a whole."

atmosphere: The general mood or tone of a work; atmosphere is often associated with setting but can also be established by action or dialogue. A classic example of atmosphere is the primitive, fatalistic tone created in the opening description of Egdon Heath in Thomas Hardy's *The Return of the Native* (1878).

bildungsroman: Sometimes called the "novel of education," the bildungsroman focuses on the growth of a young *protagonist* who is learning about the world and finding his or her place in life; typical examples are James Joyce's *A Portrait of the Artist as a*

Young Man (1914-1915, serial; 1916, book) and Thomas Wolfe's *Look Homeward, Angel* (1929).

biographical criticism: Criticism that attempts to determine how the events and experiences of an author's life influence his or her work.

bourgeois novel: A novel in which the values, preoccupations, and accoutrements of middle-class or bourgeois life are given particular prominence. The heyday of the bourgeois novel was the nineteenth century, when novelists as varied as Jane Austen, Honoré de Balzac, and Anthony Trollope both criticized and unreflectingly transmitted the assumptions of the rising middle class.

canon: An authorized or accepted list of books. In modern parlance, the literary canon comprehends the privileged texts, classics, or great books that are thought to belong permanently on university reading lists. Recent theory—especially feminist, Marxist, and poststructuralist—critically examines the process of canon formation and questions the hegemony of white male writers. Such theory sees canon formation as the ideological act of a dominant institution and seeks to undermine the notion of canonicity itself, thereby preventing the exclusion of works by women, minorities, and oppressed peoples.

character: Characters in fiction can be presented as if they were real people or as stylized functions of the plot. Usually characters are a combination of both factors.

classicism: A literary stance or value system consciously based on the example of classical Greek and Roman literature. While the term is applied to an enormous diversity of artists in many different periods and in many different national literatures, "classicism" generally denotes a cluster of values including formal discipline, restrained expression, reverence for tradition, and an objective rather than a subjective orientation. As a literary tendency, classicism is often opposed to *Romanticism*, although many writers combine classical and romantic elements.

climax/crisis: The term "climax" refers to the moment of the reader's highest emotional response, whereas "crisis" refers to a structural element of plot, a turning point at which a resolution must take place.

complication: The point in a novel when the *conflict* is developed or when the already existing conflict is further intensified.

conflict: The struggle that develops as a result of the opposition between the *protagonist* and another person, the natural world, society, or some force within the self.

contextualist criticism: A further extension of *formalist criticism*, which assumes that the language of art is constitutive. Rather than referring to preexistent values, the artwork creates values only inchoately realized before. The most important advocates of this position are Eliseo Vivas (*The Artistic Transaction*, 1963) and Murray Krieger (*The Play and Place of Criticism*, 1967).

conventions: All those devices of stylization, compression, and selection that constitute the necessary differences between art and life. According to the Russian Formalists, these conventions constitute the "literariness" of literature and are the only proper concern of the literary critic.

deconstruction: An extremely influential contemporary school of criticism based on the works of the French philosopher Jacques Derrida. Deconstruction treats literary works as unconscious reflections of the reigning myths of Western culture. The primary myth is that there is a meaningful world that language signifies or represents. The deconstructionist critic is most often concerned with showing how a literary text tacitly subverts the very assumptions or myths on which it ostensibly rests.

defamiliarization: Coined by Viktor Shklovsky in 1917, this term denotes a basic principle of Russian Formalism. Poetic language (by which the Formalists meant artful language, in prose as well as in poetry) defamiliarizes or "makes strange" familiar experiences. The technique of art, says Shklovsky, is to "make objects unfamiliar, to make forms difficult, to increase the difficulty and length of perception. . . . Art is a way of experiencing the artfulness of an object; the object is not important."

detective story: The so-called classic detective story (or mystery) is a highly formalized and logically structured mode of fiction in which the focus is on a crime solved by a detective through interpretation of evidence and ratiocination; the most famous detective in this mode is Arthur Conan Doyle's Sherlock Holmes. Many modern practitioners of the genre, however, such as Dashiell Hammett, Raymond Chandler, and Ross Macdonald, have de-emphasized the puzzlelike qualities of the detective story, stressing instead characterization, theme, and other elements of mainstream fiction.

determinism: The belief that an individual's actions are essentially determined by biological and environmental factors, with free will playing a negligible role. (See *naturalism.*)

dialogue: The similitude of conversation in fiction, dialogue serves to characterize, to further the *plot*, to establish *conflict*, and to express thematic ideas.

displacement: Popularized in criticism by Northrop Frye, this term refers to the author's attempt to make his or her story psychologically motivated and realistic, even as the latent structure of the mythical motivation moves relentlessly forward.

dominant: A term coined by Roman Jakobson to refer to that which "rules, determines, and transforms the remaining components in the work of a single artist, in a poetic canon, or in the work of an epoch." The shifting of the dominant in a *genre* accounts for the creation of new generic forms and new poetic epochs. For example, the rise of *realism* in the mid-nineteenth century indicates realistic conventions becoming dominant and *romance* or fantasy conventions becoming secondary.

doppelgänger: A double or counterpart of a person, sometimes endowed with ghostly qualities. A fictional character's doppelgänger often reflects a suppressed side of his or her personality. One of the classic examples of the doppelgänger motif is found in

Fyodor Dostoevski's novella *Dvoynik* (1846; *The Double*, 1917); Isaac Bashevis Singer and Jorge Luis Borges, among others, offer striking modern treatments of the doppelgänger.

epic: Although this term usually refers to a long narrative poem that presents the exploits of a central figure of high position, the term is also used to designate a long novel that has the style or structure usually associated with an epic. In this sense, for example, Herman Melville's *Moby Dick* (1851) and James Joyce's *Ulysses* (1922) may be called epics.

episodic narrative: A work that is held together primarily by a loose connection of self-sufficient episodes. *Picaresque novels* often have episodic structure.

epistolary novel: A novel made up of letters by one or more fictional characters. Samuel Richardson's *Pamela: Or, Virtue Rewarded* (1740-1741) is a well-known eighteenth century example. In the nineteenth century, Bram Stoker's *Dracula* (1897) is largely epistolary. The technique allows for several different points of view to be presented.

euphuism: A style of writing characterized by ornate language that is highly contrived, alliterative, and repetitious. Euphuism was developed by John Lyly in his *Euphues, the Anatomy of Wit* (1578) and was emulated frequently by writers of the Elizabethan Age.

existentialism: A philosophical, religious, and literary term, emerging from World War II, for a group of attitudes surrounding the pivotal notion that existence precedes essence. According to Jean-Paul Sartre, "Man is nothing else but what he makes himself." Forlornness arises from the death of God and the concomitant death of universal values, of any source of ultimate or a priori standards. Despair arises from the fact that an individual can reckon only with what depends on his or her will, and the sphere of that will is severely limited; the number of things on which he or she can have an impact is pathetically small. Existentialist literature is antideterministic in the extreme and rejects the idea that heredity and environment shape and determine human motivation and behavior.

exposition: The part or parts of a fiction that provide necessary background information. Exposition not only provides the time and place of the action but also introduces readers to the fictive world of the story, acquainting them with the ground rules of the work.

fantastic: In his study *The Fantastic* (1970), Tzvetan Todorov defines the fantastic as a *genre* that lies between the "uncanny" and the "marvelous." All three genres embody the familiar world but present an event that cannot be explained by the laws of the familiar world. Todorov says that the fantastic occupies a twilight zone between the uncanny (when the reader knows that the peculiar event is merely the result of an illusion) and the marvelous (when the reader understands that the event is supposed to take place in a realm controlled by laws unknown to humankind). The fantastic is thus essentially unsettling, provocative, even subversive.

feminist criticism: A criticism advocating equal rights for women in political, economic, social, psychological, personal, and aesthetic senses. On the thematic level, the feminist reader should identify with female characters and their concerns. The object is to provide a critique of phallocentric assumptions and an analysis of patriarchal ideologies inscribed in a literature that is male-centered and male-dominated. On the ideological level, feminist critics see gender, as well as the stereotypes that go along with it, as a cultural construct. They strive to define a particularly feminine content and to extend the *canon* so that it might include works by lesbians, feminists, and women writers in general.

flashback: A scene in a fiction that depicts an earlier event; it may be presented as a reminiscence by a character in the story or may simply be inserted into the narrative.

foreshadowing: A device to create suspense or dramatic irony in fiction by indicating through suggestion what will take place in the future.

formalist criticism: Two particularly influential formalist schools of criticism arose in the twentieth century: the Russian Formalists and the American New Critics. The Russian Formalists were concerned with the conventional devices used in literature to defamiliarize that which habit has made familiar. The New Critics believed that literary criticism is a description and evaluation of its object and that the primary concern of the critic is with the work's unity. Both schools of criticism, at their most extreme, treated literary works as artifacts or constructs divorced from their biographical and social contexts.

genre: In its most general sense, this term refers to a group of literary works defined by a common form, style, or purpose. In practice, the term is used in a wide variety of overlapping and, to a degree, contradictory senses. Tragedy and comedy are thus described as distinct genres; the novel (a form that includes both tragic and comic works) is a genre; and various subspecies of the novel, such as the *gothic* and the *picaresque*, are themselves frequently treated as distinct genres. Finally, the term "genre fiction" refers to forms of popular fiction in which the writer is bound by more or less rigid conventions. Indeed, all these diverse usages have in common an emphasis on the manner in which individual literary works are shaped by particular expectations and conventions; this is the subject of genre criticism.

genre fiction: Categories of popular fiction in which the writers are bound by more or less rigid conventions, such as in the *detective story*, the *romance*, and the *Western*. Although the term can be used in a neutral sense, it is often used dismissively.

gothic novel: A form of fiction developed in the eighteenth century that focuses on horror and the supernatural. In his preface to *The Castle of Otranto* (1765), the first gothic novel in English, Horace Walpole claimed that he was trying to combine two kinds of fiction, with events and story typical of the medieval romance and character delineation typical of the realistic novel. Other examples of the form are Matthew Gregory

Lewis's *The Monk: A Romance* (1796; also known as *Ambrosio: Or, The Monk*) and Mary Wollstonecraft Shelley's *Frankenstein: Or, The Modern Prometheus* (1818).

grotesque: According to Wolfgang Kayser (*The Grotesque in Art and Literature*, 1963), the grotesque is an embodiment in literature of the estranged world. Characterized by a breakup of the everyday world by mysterious forces, the form differs from fantasy in that the reader is not sure whether to react with humor or with horror and in that the exaggeration manifested exists in the familiar world rather than in a purely imaginative world.

Hebraic/Homeric styles: Terms coined by Erich Auerbach in *Mimesis: The Representation of Reality in Western Literature* (1953) to designate two basic fictional styles. The Hebraic style focuses only on the decisive points of narrative and leaves all else obscure, mysterious, and "fraught with background"; the Homeric style places the narrative in a definite time and place and externalizes everything in a perpetual foreground.

historical criticism: In contrast to *formalist criticism*, which treats literary works to a great extent as self-contained artifacts, historical criticism emphasizes the historical context of literature; the two approaches, however, need not be mutually exclusive. Ernst Robert Curtius's *European Literature and the Latin Middle Ages* (1940) is a prominent example of historical criticism.

historical novel: A novel that depicts past historical events, usually public in nature, and features real as well as fictional people. Sir Walter Scott's Waverley novels established the basic type, but the relationship between fiction and history in the form varies greatly depending on the practitioner.

implied author: According to Wayne Booth (*The Rhetoric of Fiction*, 1961), the novel often creates a kind of second self who tells the story—a self who is wiser, more sensitive, and more perceptive than any real person could be.

interior monologue: Defined by Édouard Dujardin as the speech of a character designed to introduce the reader directly to the character's internal life, the form differs from other kinds of monologue in that it attempts to reproduce thought before any logical organization is imposed on it. See, for example, Molly Bloom's long interior monologue at the conclusion of James Joyce's *Ulysses* (1922).

irrealism: A term often used to refer to modern or postmodern fiction that is presented self-consciously as a fiction or a fabulation rather than a mimesis of external reality. The best-known practitioners of irrealism are John Barth, Robert Coover, and Donald Barthelme.

local colorists: A loose movement of late nineteenth century American writers whose fiction emphasizes the distinctive folkways, landscapes, and dialects of various regions. Important local colorists include Bret Harte, Mark Twain, George Washington Cable, Kate Chopin, and Sarah Orne Jewett. (See *regional novel*.)

Marxist criticism: Based on the nineteenth century writings of Karl Marx and Friedrich Engels, Marxist criticism views literature as a product of ideological forces determined by the dominant class. However, many Marxists believe that literature operates according to its own autonomous standards of production and reception: It is both a product of ideology and able to determine ideology. As such, literature may overcome the dominant paradigms of its age and play a revolutionary role in society.

metafiction: This term refers to fiction that manifests a reflexive tendency, such as Vladimir Nabokov's *Pale Fire* (1962) and John Fowles's *The French Lieutenant's Woman* (1969). The emphasis is on the loosening of the work's illusion of reality to expose the reality of its illusion. Other terms used to refer to this type of fiction include "irrealism," "postmodernist fiction," "antifiction," and "surfiction."

modernism: An international movement in the arts that began in the early years of the twentieth century. Although the term is used to describe artists of widely varying persuasions, modernism in general was characterized by its international idiom, by its interest in cultures distant in space or time, by its emphasis on formal experimentation, and by its sense of dislocation and radical change.

motif: A conventional incident or situation in a fiction that may serve as the basis for the structure of the narrative itself. The Russian Formalist critic Boris Tomashevsky uses the term to refer to the smallest particle of thematic material in a work.

motivation: Although this term is usually used in reference to the convention of justifying the action of a character from his or her psychological makeup, the Russian Formalists use the term to refer to the network of devices that justify the introduction of individual *motifs* or groups of motifs in a work. For example, "compositional motivation" refers to the principle that every single property in a work contributes to its overall effect; "realistic motivation" refers to the realistic devices used to make a work plausible and lifelike.

multiculturalism: The tendency to recognize the perspectives of those traditionally excluded from the canon of Western art and literature. In order to promote multiculturalism, publishers and educators have revised textbooks and school curricula to incorporate material by and about women, members of minority groups, persons from non-Western cultures, and homosexuals.

myth: Anonymous traditional stories dealing with basic human concepts and antinomies. According to Claude Lévi-Strauss, myth is that part of language where the "formula *tradutore, traditore* reaches its lowest truth value. . . . Its substance does not lie in its style, its original music, or its syntax, but in the story which it tells."

myth criticism: Northrop Frye says that in myth "we see the structural principles of literature isolated." Myth criticism is concerned with these basic principles of literature; it is not to be confused with mythological criticism, which is primarily concerned with finding mythological parallels in the surface action of the *narrative*.

narrative: Robert Scholes and Robert Kellogg, in *The Nature of Narrative* (1966), say that by "narrative" they mean literary works that include both a story and a storyteller. The term "narrative" usually implies a contrast to "enacted" fiction such as drama.

narratology: The study of the form and functioning of *narratives*; it attempts to examine what all narratives have in common and what makes individual narratives different from one another.

narrator: The *character* who recounts the *narrative*, or story. Wayne Booth describes various dramatized narrators in *The Rhetoric of Fiction* (1961): unacknowledged centers of consciousness, observers, narrator-agents, and self-conscious narrators. Booth suggests that the important elements to consider in narration are the relationships among the narrator, the author, the characters, and the reader.

naturalism: As developed by Émile Zola in the late nineteenth century, naturalism is the application of the principles of scientific *determinism* to fiction. Although it usually refers more to the choice of subject matter than to technical conventions, those conventions associated with the movement center on the author's attempt to be precise and scientifically objective in description and detail, regardless of whether the events described are sordid or shocking.

New Criticism: See *formalist criticism*.

novel: Perhaps the most difficult of all fictional forms to define because of its multiplicity of modes. Edouard, in André Gide's *Les Faux-monnayeurs* (1925; *The Counterfeiters*, 1927), says the novel is the freest and most lawless of all *genres*; he wonders if fear of that liberty is the reason the novel has so timidly clung to reality. Most critics seem to agree that the novel's primary area of concern is the social world. Ian Watt (*The Rise of the Novel*, 2001) says that the novel can be distinguished from other fictional forms by the attention it pays to individual characterization and detailed presentation of the environment. Moreover, says Watt, the novel, more than any other fictional form, is interested in the "development of its characters in the course of time."

novel of manners: The classic examples of this form might be the novels of Jane Austen, wherein the customs and conventions of a social group of a particular time and place are realistically, and often satirically, portrayed.

novella, novelle, nouvelle, novelette, novela: Although these terms often refer to the short European tale, especially the Renaissance form employed by Giovanni Boccaccio, the terms often refer to that form of fiction that is said to be longer than a short story and shorter than a novel. "Novelette" is the term usually preferred by the British, whereas "novella" is the term usually used to refer to American works in this *genre*. Henry James claimed that the main merit of the form is the "effort to do the complicated thing with a strong brevity and lucidity."

phenomenological criticism: Although best known as a European school of criticism practiced by Georges Poulet and others, this so-called criticism of consciousness is also propounded in the United States by such critics as J. Hillis Miller. The focus is less on individual works and *genres* than it is on literature as an act; the work is not seen as an object but rather as part of a strand of latent impulses in the work of a single author or an epoch.

picaresque novel: A form of fiction that centers on a central rogue figure, or picaro, who usually tells his or her own story. The plot structure is normally *episodic*, and the episodes usually focus on how the picaro lives by his or her wits. Classic examples of the mode are Henry Fielding's *The History of Tom Jones, a Foundling* (1749; commonly known as *Tom Jones*) and Mark Twain's *Adventures of Huckleberry Finn* (1884).

plot/story: "Story" refers to the full *narrative* of *character* and action, whereas "plot" generally refers to action with little reference to character. A more precise and helpful distinction is made by the Russian Formalists, who suggest that "plot" refers to the events of a narrative as they have been artfully arranged in the literary work, subject to chronological displacement, ellipses, and other devices, while "story" refers to the sum of the same events arranged in simple, causal-chronological order. Thus story is the raw material for plot. By comparing the two in a given work, the reader is encouraged to see the narrative as an artifact.

point of view: The means by which the story is presented to the reader, or, as Percy Lubbock says in *The Craft of Fiction* (1921), "the relation in which the narrator stands to the story"—a relation that Lubbock claims governs the craft of fiction. Some of the questions the critical reader should ask concerning point of view are the following: Who talks to the reader? From what position does the narrator tell the story? At what distance does he or she place the reader from the story? What kind of person is he or she? How fully is he or she characterized? How reliable is he or she? For further discussion, see Wayne Booth, *The Rhetoric of Fiction* (1961).

postcolonialism: Postcolonial literature emerged in the mid-twentieth century when colonies in Asia, Africa, and the Caribbean began gaining their independence from the European nations that had long controlled them. Postcolonial authors, such as Salman Rushdie and V. S. Naipaul, tend to focus on both the freedom and the conflict inherent in living in a postcolonial state.

postmodernism: A ubiquitous but elusive term in contemporary criticism, "postmodernism" is loosely applied to the various artistic movements that followed the era of so-called high modernism, represented by such giants as James Joyce and Pablo Picasso. In critical discussions of contemporary fiction, the term "postmodernism" is frequently applied to the works of writers such as Thomas Pynchon, John Barth, and Donald Barthelme, who exhibit a self-conscious awareness of their modernist predecessors as well as a reflexive treatment of fictional form.

protagonist: The central *character* in a fiction, the character whose fortunes most concern the reader.

psychological criticism: While much modern literary criticism reflects to some degree the impacts of Sigmund Freud, Carl Jung, Jacques Lacan, and other psychological theorists, the term "psychological criticism" suggests a strong emphasis on a causal relation between the writer's psychological state, variously interpreted, and his or her works. A notable example of psychological criticism is Norman Fruman's *Coleridge, the Damaged Archangel* (1971).

psychological novel: A form of fiction in which *character*, especially the inner lives of characters, is the primary focus. This form, which has been of primary importance at least since Henry James, characterizes much of the work of James Joyce, Virginia Woolf, and William Faulkner. For a detailed discussion, see *The Modern Psychological Novel* (1955) by Leon Edel.

realism: A literary technique in which the primary convention is to render an illusion of fidelity to external reality. Realism is often identified as the primary method of the novel form: It focuses on surface details, maintains a fidelity to the everyday experiences of middle-class society, and strives for a one-to-one relationship between the fiction and the action imitated. The realist movement in the late nineteenth century coincides with the full development of the novel form.

reception aesthetics: The best-known American practitioner of reception aesthetics is Stanley Fish. For the reception critic, meaning is an event or process; rather than being embedded in the work, it is created through particular acts of reading. The best-known European practitioner of this criticism, Wolfgang Iser, argues that indeterminacy is the basic characteristic of literary texts; the reader must "normalize" the text either by projecting his or her standards into it or by revising his or her standards to "fit" the text.

regional novel: Any novel in which the character of a given geographical region plays a decisive role. Although regional differences persist across the United States, a considerable leveling in speech and customs has taken place, so that the sharp regional distinctions evident in nineteenth century American fiction have all but disappeared. Only in the South has a strong regional tradition persisted to the present. (See *local colorists.*)

rhetorical criticism: The rhetorical critic is concerned with the literary work as a means of communicating ideas and the means by which the work affects or controls the reader. Such criticism seems best suited to didactic works such as satire.

roman à clef: A fiction wherein actual people, often celebrities of some sort, are thinly disguised.

romance: The romance usually differs from the novel form in that the focus is on symbolic events and representational characters rather than on "as-if-real" characters and events. Richard Chase says that in the romance, character is depicted as highly stylized, a function of the plot rather than as someone complexly related to society. The romancer is more likely to be concerned with dreamworlds than with the familiar world, believing that reality cannot be grasped by the traditional novel.

Romanticism: A widespread cultural movement in the late eighteenth and early nineteenth centuries, the influence of which is still felt. As a general literary tendency, Romanticism is frequently contrasted with *classicism.* Although many varieties of Romanticism are indigenous to various national literatures, the term generally suggests an assertion of the preeminence of the imagination. Other values associated with various schools of Romanticism include primitivism, an interest in folklore, a reverence for nature, and a fascination with the demoniac and the macabre.

scene: The central element of *narration*; specific actions are narrated or depicted that make the reader feel he or she is participating directly in the action.

science fiction: Fiction in which certain givens (physical laws, psychological principles, social conditions—any one or all of these) form the basis of an imaginative projection into the future or, less commonly, an extrapolation in the present or even into the past.

semiotics: The science of signs and sign systems in communication. According to Roman Jakobson, semiotics deals with the principles that underlie the structure of signs, their use in language of all kinds, and the specific nature of various sign systems.

sentimental novel: A form of fiction popular in the eighteenth century in which emotionalism and optimism are the primary characteristics. The best-known examples are Samuel Richardson's *Pamela: Or, Virtue Rewarded* (1740-1741) and Oliver Goldsmith's *The Vicar of Wakefield* (1766).

setting: The circumstances and environment, both temporal and spatial, of a *narrative.*

spatial form: An author's attempt to make the reader apprehend a work spatially in a moment of time rather than sequentially. To achieve this effect, the author breaks up the *narrative* into interspersed fragments. Beginning with James Joyce, Marcel Proust, and Djuna Barnes, the movement toward spatial form is concomitant with the *modernist* effort to supplant historical time in fiction with mythic time. For the seminal discussion of this technique, see Joseph Frank, *The Widening Gyre* (1963).

stream of consciousness: The depiction of the thought processes of a *character,* insofar as this is possible, without any mediating structures. The metaphor of consciousness as a "stream" suggests a rush of thoughts and images governed by free association rather than by strictly rational development. The term "stream of consciousness" is often used loosely as a synonym for *interior monologue.* The most celebrated example of stream of consciousness in fiction is the monologue of Molly Bloom in James Joyce's *Ulysses* (1922); other notable practitioners of the stream-of-consciousness technique include Dorothy Richardson, Virginia Woolf, and William Faulkner.

structuralism: As a movement of thought, structuralism is based on the idea of intrinsic, self-sufficient structures that do not require reference to external elements. A structure is a system of transformations that involves the interplay of laws inherent in the system itself. The study of language is the primary model for contemporary structuralism. The structuralist literary critic attempts to define structural principles that operate intertextually throughout the whole of literature as well as principles that operate in *genres* and in individual works. One of the most accessible surveys of structuralism and literature available is Jonathan Culler's *Structuralist Poetics* (1975).

summary: Those parts of a fiction that do not need to be detailed. In *Tom Jones* (1749), Henry Fielding says, "If whole years should pass without producing anything worthy of . . . notice . . . we shall hasten on to matters of consequence."

thematics: According to Northrop Frye, when a work of fiction is written or interpreted thematically, it becomes an illustrative fable. Murray Krieger defines thematics as "the study of the experiential tensions which, dramatically entangled in the literary work, become an existential reflection of that work's aesthetic complexity."

tone: The dominant mood of a work of fiction. (See *atmosphere.*)

unreliable narrator: A narrator whose account of the events of the story cannot be trusted, obliging readers to reconstruct—if possible—the true state of affairs themselves. Once an innovative technique, the use of the unreliable narrator has become commonplace among contemporary writers who wish to suggest the impossibility of a truly "reliable" account of any event. Notable examples of the unreliable narrator can be found in Ford Madox Ford's *The Good Soldier* (1915) and Vladimir Nabokov's *Lolita* (1955).

Victorian novel: Although the Victorian period extended from 1837 to 1901, the term "Victorian novel" does not include the later decades of Queen Victoria's reign. The term loosely refers to the sprawling works of novelists such as Charles Dickens and William Makepeace Thackeray—works that frequently appeared first in serial form and are characterized by a broad social canvas.

vraisemblance/verisimilitude: Tzvetan Todorov defines vraisemblance as "the mask which conceals the text's own laws, but which we are supposed to take for a relation to reality." Verisimilitude refers to a work's attempts to make the reader believe that it conforms to reality rather than to its own laws.

Western novel: Like all varieties of *genre fiction*, the Western novel—generally known simply as the Western—is defined by a relatively predictable combination of *conventions, motifs,* and recurring themes. These predictable elements, familiar from many Western films and television series, differentiate the Western from *historical novels* and idiosyncratic works such as Thomas Berger's *Little Big Man* (1964) that are also set in the Old West. Conversely, some novels set in the contemporary West are regarded as Westerns because they deal with modern cowboys and with the land itself in the manner characteristic of the *genre.*

Charles E. May

GUIDE TO ONLINE RESOURCES

WEB SITES

The following sites were visited by the editors of Salem Press in 2009. Because URLs frequently change, the accuracy of these addresses cannot be guaranteed; however, long-standing sites, such as those of colleges and universities, national organizations, and government agencies, generally maintain links when sites are moved or updated.

American Literature on the Web
http://www.nagasaki-gaigo.ac.jp/ishikawa/amlit

Among this site's features are several pages providing links to Web sites about specific genres and literary movements, southern and southwestern American literature, minority literature, literary theory, and women writers, as well as an extensive index of links to electronic text collections and archives. Users also can access information for five specific time periods: 1620-1820, 1820-1865, 1865-1914, 1914-1945, and since 1945. A range of information is available for each period, including alphabetical lists of authors that link to more specific information about each writer, time lines of historical and literary events, and links to related additional Web sites.

Books and Writers
http://www.kirjasto.sci.fi/indeksi.htm

This broad, comprehensive, and easy-to-use resource provides access to information about hundreds of authors throughout the world, extending from 70 B.C.E to the twenty-first century. Links take users from an alphabetical list of authors to pages featuring biographical material, lists of works, and recommendations for further reading about individual authors; each writer's page also includes links to related pages on the site. Although brief, the biographical essays provide solid overviews of the authors' careers, their contributions to literature, and their literary influences.

The Canadian Literature Archive
http://www.umanitoba.ca/canlit

Created and maintained by the English Department at the University of Manitoba, this site is a comprehensive collection of materials for and about Canadian writers. It includes an alphabetical listing of authors with links to additional Web-based information. Users also can retrieve electronic texts, announcements of literary events, and videocasts of author interviews and readings.

A Celebration of Women Writers

http://digital.library.upenn.edu/women

This site presents an extensive compendium of information about the contributions of women writers throughout history. The "Local Editions by Authors" and "Local Editions by Category" pages include access to electronic texts of the works of numerous writers, including Louisa May Alcott, Djuna Barnes, Grazia Deledda, Edith Wharton, and Virginia Woolf. Users can also access biographical and bibliographical information by browsing lists arranged by writers' names, countries of origin, ethnicities, and the centuries in which they lived.

Contemporary Writers

http://www.contemporarywriters.com/authors

Created by the British Council, this site offers "up-to-date profiles of some of the U.K. and Commonwealth's most important living writers (plus writers from the Republic of Ireland that we've worked with)." The available information includes biographies, bibliographies, critical reviews, news about literary prizes, and photographs. Users can search the site by author, genre, nationality, gender, publisher, book title, date of publication, and prize name and date.

Internet Public Library: Native American Authors

http://www.ipl.org/div/natam

Internet Public Library, a Web-based collection of materials, includes this index to resources about writers of Native American heritage. An alphabetical list of authors enables users to link to biographies, lists of works, electronic texts, tribal Web sites, and other online resources. The majority of the writers covered are contemporary Indian authors, but some historical authors also are featured. Users also can retrieve information by browsing lists of titles and tribes. In addition, the site contains a bibliography of print and online materials about Native American literature.

LiteraryHistory.com

http://www.literaryhistory.com

This site is an excellent source of academic, scholarly, and critical literature about eighteenth, nineteenth, and twentieth century American and English writers. It provides numerous pages about specific eras and genres, including individual pages for eighteenth, nineteenth, and twentieth century literature and for African American and postcolonial literature. These pages contain alphabetical lists of authors that link to articles, reviews, overviews, excerpts of works, teaching guides, podcast interviews, and other materials. The eighteenth century literature page also provides access to information about the eighteenth century novel.

Literary Resources on the Net

http://andromeda.rutgers.edu/~jlynch/Lit

Jack Lynch of Rutgers University maintains this extensive collection of links to Internet sites that are useful to academics, including numerous Web sites about American and English literature. This collection is a good place to begin online research about the novel, as it links to hundreds of other sites with broad ranges of literary topics. The site is organized chronically, with separate pages for information about the Middle Ages, the Renaissance, the eighteenth century, the Romantic and Victorian eras, and twentieth century British and Irish literature. It also has separate pages providing links to Web sites about American literature and to women's literature and feminism.

LitWeb

http://litweb.net

LitWeb provides biographies of more than five hundred world authors throughout history that can be accessed through an alphabetical listing. The pages about each writer contain a list of his or her works, suggestions for further reading, and illustrations. The site also offers information about past and present winners of major literary prizes.

The Modern Word: Authors of the Libyrinth

http://www.themodernword.com/authors.html

The Modern Word site, although somewhat haphazard in its organization, provides a great deal of critical information about writers. The "Authors of the Libyrinth" page is very useful, linking author names to essays about them and other resources. The section of the page headed "The Scriptorium" presents "an index of pages featuring writers who have pushed the edges of their medium, combining literary talent with a sense of experimentation to produce some remarkable works of modern literature." The site also includes sections devoted to Samuel Beckett, Umberto Eco, Gabriel García Márquez, James Joyce, Franz Kafka, and Thomas Pynchon.

Novels

http://www.nvcc.edu/home/ataormina/novels/default.htm

This overview of American and English novels was prepared by Agatha Taormina, a professor at Northern Virginia Community College. It contains three sections: "History" provides a definition of the novel genre, a discussion of its origins in eighteenth century England, and separate pages with information about genres and authors of nineteenth century, twentieth century, and postmodern novels. "Approaches" suggests how to read a novel critically for greater appreciation, and "Resources" provides a list of books about the novel.

Outline of American Literature

http://www.america.gov/publications/books/outline-of-american-literature.html

This page of the America.gov site provides access to an electronic version of the ten-chapter volume *Outline of American Literature*, a historical overview of prose and poetry from colonial times to the present published by the U.S. Department of State. The work's author is Kathryn VanSpanckeren, professor of English at the University of Tampa. The site offers links to abbreviated versions of each chapter as well as access to the entire publication in PDF format.

Voice of the Shuttle

http://vos.ucsb.edu

One of the most complete and authoritative places for online information about literature, Voice of the Shuttle is maintained by professors and students in the English Department at the University of California, Santa Barbara. The site provides thousands of links to electronic books, academic journals, association Web sites, sites created by university professors, and many, many other resources about the humanities. Its "Literature in English" page provides links to separate pages about the literature of the Anglo-Saxon era, the Middle Ages, the Renaissance and seventeenth century, the Restoration and eighteenth century, the Romantic age, the Victorian age, and modern and contemporary periods in Britain and the United States, as well as a page focused on minority literature. Another page on the site, "Literatures Other than English," offers a gateway to information about the literature of numerous countries and world regions.

ELECTRONIC DATABASES

Electronic databases usually do not have their own URLs. Instead, public, college, and university libraries subscribe to these databases, provide links to them on their Web sites, and make them available to library card holders or other specified patrons. Readers can visit library Web sites or ask reference librarians to check on availability.

Canadian Literary Centre

Produced by EBSCO, the Canadian Literary Centre database contains full-text content from ECW Press, a Toronto-based publisher, including the titles in the publisher's Canadian fiction studies, Canadian biography, and Canadian writers and their works series, *ECW's Biographical Guide to Canadian Novelists*, and *George Woodcock's Introduction to Canadian Fiction*. Author biographies, essays and literary criticism, and book reviews are among the database's offerings.

Literary Reference Center

EBSCO's Literary Reference Center (LRC) is a comprehensive full-text database designed primarily to help high school and undergraduate students in English and the humanities with homework and research assignments about literature. The database contains massive amounts of information from reference works, books, literary journals, and other materials, including more than 31,000 plot summaries, synopses, and overviews of literary works; almost 100,000 essays and articles of literary criticism; about 140,000 author biographies; more than 605,000 book reviews; and more than 5,200 author interviews. It also contains the entire contents of Salem Press's MagillOnLiterature Plus. Users can retrieve information by browsing a list of authors' names or titles of literary works; they can also use an advanced search engine to access information by numerous categories, including author name, gender, cultural identity, national identity, and the years in which he or she lived, or by literary title, character, locale, genre, and publication date. The Literary Reference Center also features a literary-historical time line, an encyclopedia of literature, and a glossary of literary terms.

MagillOnLiterature Plus

MagillOnLiterature Plus is a comprehensive, integrated literature database produced by Salem Press and available on the EBSCO*host* platform. The database contains the full text of essays in Salem's many literature-related reference works, including *Masterplots*, *Cyclopedia of World Authors*, *Cyclopedia of Literary Characters*, *Cyclopedia of Literary Places*, *Critical Survey of Long Fiction*, *Critical Survey of Short Fiction*, *World Philosophers and Their Works*, *Magill's Literary Annual*, and *Magill's Book Reviews*. Among its contents are articles on more than 35,000 literary works and more than 8,500 writers, poets, dramatists, essays, and philosophers, more than 1,000 images, and a glossary of more than 1,300 literary terms. The biographical essays include lists of authors' works and secondary bibliographies, and almost four hundred overview essays offer information about literary genres, time periods, and national literatures.

NoveList

NoveList is a readers' advisory service produced by EBSCO. The database provides access to 155,000 titles of both adult and juvenile fiction as well information about literary awards, book discussion guides, feature articles about a range of literary genres, and "recommended reads." Users can search by author name, book title, or series title or can describe the plot to retrieve the name of a book, information about the author, and book reviews; another search engine enables users to find titles similar to books they have enjoyed reading.

Rebecca Kuzins

CATEGORY INDEX

SUBJECT INDEX